IN DEFENSE OF JULIAN ASSANGE

IN DEFENSE OF JULIAN ASSANGE

EDITED BY TARIQ ALI AND MARGARET KUNSTLER

OR Books
New York · London

Visit our website at www.orbooks.com

All rights information: rights@orbooks.com

First printing 2019

Cataloging-in-Publication data is available from the Library of Congress. A catalog record for this book is available from the British Library.

paperback ISBN 978-1-68219-221-4
e-book ISBN 978-1-68219-223-8

Typeset by Lapiz Digital Services. Printed in Canada.

If there is one takeaway from these shared experiences in truth-telling and courage, it is a note of extreme caution: never doubt the mendacity and cruelty of the state. It will make pariahs and outcasts out of those who will someday be recognized as heroes.

—Michael Ratner (1943-2016)

CONTENTS

INTRODUCTION

I am unbroken, albeit literally surrounded by murderers, but the days when I could read and speak and organize to defend myself, my ideals and my people are over until I am free! Everyone else must take my place.

I am defenceless and am counting on you and others of good character to save my life... Truth, ultimately, is all we have.

—Julian Assange, in a letter to Gordon Dimmack from highly restrictive confinement in Belmarsh Prison, London, 13 May 2019.

"History," Friedrich Engels once wrote, "is made in such a way that the final result always arises from conflicts between many individual wills, of which each in turn has been made what it is by a host of particular conditions of life. Thus there are innumerable intersecting forces, an infinite series of parallelograms of forces which give rise to one resultant—the historical event."[1]

Let's start at the beginning. The birth of WikiLeaks in 2006 came just three years after the Iraq War was unleashed by the American Empire using 9/11 as the pretext. This brutal assertion of US military power to overthrow

---

[1] Letter to J. Bloch, London, September 21, 1890.

disfavored regimes took place despite some of the largest protests in world history. Millions marched in North America and Western Europe to try and stop the war, but to no avail. Other wars followed and the liberal media beat the war drums for them too. Fake news was manufactured with ease and often one got the feeling that foreign coverage in Euro-America was little more than the reprinting (sometimes without editing) of the same State Department handouts. TV networks that occasionally offered space to critics of the empire were brought under firm control.

As the new wave of imperial wars became normal, the media, which in a flurry of misleading, half-baked news and images loyally provided justifications at the start of each war, quickly lost interest. "It is the way our sympathy flows and recoils," D. H. Lawrence once wrote, "that really determines our lives." Events in far-away countries no longer intrigued a majority of the public that, hurrying onward with the current, felt no concern in what was and is really going on in Iraq, Somalia, Afghanistan, Libya, Yemen, Palestine, or Syria. The top-down Islamophobia has been effective.

There is, however, a more fundamental shift taking place in the Western world. There is a growing disconnect between the political structure of the American imperial state, and its various satrapies and protectorates in Europe on the one hand, and the social, economic, and political realities of the twenty-first-century world on the other. The fact is that the financial oligarchic system that typifies the West and its global protector requires very little democracy. That is why, when opposition erupts, it's defined as "populist" and anti-democratic. The less democracy the better for many of our rulers. After all, the most dynamic capitalism today (China) is governed by a single-party state. The West doesn't have to go quite as far as this, but the model is appealing to many billionaires. The bulk of mainstream media is an essential pillar of the new order.

It was these intersecting currents that produced WikiLeaks. "Publish and be damned": the Duke of Wellington's famous words were the motto of a few newspaper editors in the last century. WikiLeaks did precisely this and Private Chelsea Manning, a cyber expert in the intelligence wing of the US military, put her life at risk by leaking secret documents that detailed atrocities and tortures (still ongoing) from her post in Iraq to Julian Assange and his WikiLeaks colleagues. It was this that made the outfit world famous and much admired. The liberal papers in the West published extracts from WikiLeaks and, later, Snowden. But they soon retreated as the pressure from the secret state became intense.

Manning was arrested, Snowden was forced to seek asylum and refuge in Putin's Russia, and Assange was subjected to a slanderous campaign to discredit his character. In addition, in Sweden, he was accused of sexual assault and misconduct by two women he had stayed with, which he has always strenuously denied. Swedish prosecutors (both women) fell out on the subject—the chief prosecutor of Stockholm dropped the case, but it was reopened later by another prosecutor. Many believed this was a ploy to lock him up so the US could extradite him. He remained in Sweden for the duration of the initial investigation, and then, when given permission to leave the country, went to Britain to work on the Iraq War Logs release. In November 2010, Sweden issued an international arrest warrant to question Assange—in circumstances where he was offering his testimony anyway. Assange voluntarily presented himself to the UK police that December. After a week in jail, Assange was put under house arrest, taking up residence in the Norfolk countryside. He said that he would voluntarily return to Sweden if the government there guaranteed he would not be delivered to the Americans. The Swedish government declined to give such a reassurance, saying it was a matter for their courts, not a political decision. The UK Supreme Court finally ruled in favor of his extradition to Sweden in May 2012, prompting Assange to seek asylum in the Ecuadorian embassy, which he entered, in disguise, in June 2012.

While Rafael Correa was president, the Ecuadorian embassy felt like liberated territory. Though the cramped space, lack of sunlight and access to health care, as well as various threats to his life and work by a number of people, including governmental representatives in the US, were ever present challenges, Assange was given unlimited access to the Internet and freedom to receive visitors. He got along well with embassy staff. Not to gloss over some disputes, such as Ecuador cutting off Assange's Internet in October 2016 over fears of his alleged interference in the US presidential election, this relatively benign treatment came to an end with the election in 2017 of Correa's successor. Lenín Moreno, despite his name and appearance on a left ticket, capitulated on every level to pressure from the American Empire. The embassy became a prison: Assange's Internet access and visitations were severely restricted, surveillance intensified, and his health rapidly deteriorated. He was in no doubt that Moreno had been asked and had agreed to expel him from the embassy.

The US demand for extradition was no longer a secret by November 2018 when, to the embarrassment of prosecutors, hidden charges against Assange came to light in an unrelated court filing. On April 11, 2019, with permission from the Ecuadorian government, British police entered the embassy and dragged out Assange. He was immediately served with a provisional US extradition request for prosecution for his work with WikiLeaks—the very reason for which he was granted asylum in the first place and about which he had warned since 2010. He was convicted for breaking bail and sent to Belmarsh, a high-security prison in southeast London while the US perfected its extradition request. That same day, programmer and data privacy activist Ola Bini, a friend of Assange's, was arrested in Quito, Ecuador without charges for allegedly hacking the Ecuadorian government. Held for 70 days in what he described as "inhumane conditions," Bini was released on June 20, but at this writing, he is not permitted to leave the country. One need not overspeculate why Bini was targetted.

The superseding indictment announced in late May 2019 against Assange includes numerous charges under the Espionage Act. He now faces 175 years in prison if extradited to the US. If we lived in a world where laws were respected, Assange's charge of failing to attend a bail hearing (a minor offense) would have resulted in a fine or a short prison sentence followed by release and a return to his native Australia. But both the UK and Australia are, effectively, viceroys that will generally bow deeply to US demands. The secret and not-so-secret state in both countries work closely with (or under) their US masters. Why do the Americans want Assange so badly? To set an example. To incarcerate and isolate him as a warning to others not to follow the WikiLeaks path. After being pardoned by Obama following seven years of imprisonment and significant mistreatment in American military prisons, Chelsea Manning was re-arrested and temporarily thrown into solitary confinement once more because she refused to testify before the grand jury that indicted Assange. Released after two months, Manning again refused to cooperate with the second grand jury and, at the time of writing, is back in jail after just a week of freedom. Since the Russian and Chinese intelligence agencies are pretty much aware of what the US is up to in most parts of the world, the threat posed by WikiLeaks was that it made its information available to any citizen globally who possessed a computer. American/European foreign policy and its post-9/11 wars have been based on lies, promoted by global TV and media networks, and often accepted by a majority of the North American and European population. Information contradicting these lies challenges the stated motives for war—human rights, democracy, freedom, etc.

WikiLeaks has been exposing all this by publishing classified documents that shine a light on the real reasons behind military interventions. It is an astonishing record. Since its inception WikiLeaks has published more than 2 million diplomatic cables and other US State Department records, which if printed, the WikiLeaks cofounder has stated, would amount to some 30,000 volumes. It truly "represents something new in the world." This is where the Internet becomes a subversive force, challenging the propaganda networks of the existing order. Assange and his colleagues made no secret of the fact that their principal subject of publication was the American Empire and its global operations. The response of US institutions has been hysterical and sometimes comical. The Library of Congress restricted Internet access to WikiLeaks. The US National Archives even blocked searches of its own database for the phrase "WikiLeaks." So absurd did the taboo become that, like a dog snapping mindlessly at everything, eventually it found its mark—its own tail. As Julian Assange pointed out: "By March 2012, the Pentagon had gone so far as to create an automatic filter to block any emails, including inbound emails to the Pentagon, containing the word 'WikiLeaks.'" As a result, Pentagon prosecutors preparing the case against US intelligence analyst Chelsea Manning found that they were not receiving important emails from either the judge or the defense.

The British government is insisting that it will follow the law. We shall see. Diane Abbott, the shadow home secretary and a leading member of Jeremy Corbyn's shadow cabinet, said in Parliament on the day of Assange's arrest:

> On this side of the house, we want to make the point that the reason we are debating Julian Assange this afternoon—even though the only charge he may face in this country is in relation to his bail hearings—is entirely to do with the whistleblowing activities of Julian Assange and WikiLeaks. It is this whistleblowing activity into illegal wars, mass murder, murder of civilians, and corruption on a grand scale that has put Julian Assange in the crosshairs of the US administration. It is for this reason that they have once more issued an extradition warrant against Julian Assange . . .

Julian Assange is not being pursued to protect US national security, he is being pursued because he has exposed wrongdoing by US administrations and their military forces.

In January 2018, three doctors performed an intensive psychological and physical examination of Assange, then still in the Ecuadorian embassy, and determined "that his continued confinement is dangerous physically and mentally to him, and a clear infringement of his human right to healthcare." After his May 2019 visit to Belmarsh Prison, the UN special rapporteur on torture, Nils Melzer, reported that Assange "has been deliberately exposed, for a period of several years, to progressively severe forms of cruel, inhuman or degrading treatment or punishment, the cumulative effects of which can only be described as psychological torture." Melzer continued:

> *In 20 years of work with victims of war, violence and political persecution I have never seen a group of democratic States ganging up to deliberately isolate, demonize and abuse a single individual for such a long time and with so little regard for human dignity and the rule of law ... The collective persecution of Julian Assange must end here and now!*

On May 30, Assange was moved to the hospital wing in Belmarsh for treatment of drastic weight loss and other problems with his physical and mental health. Unable to engage in a normal conversation, he could not appear via video link to the Westminster Magistrate Court for his initial extradition hearing, which will now take place in February 2020. In this fragile condition, Assange now waits for the courts to decide on his extradition to the United States, as UK home secretary Sajid Javid has already given the request his thumbs-up. If the court rules in favor of it, Assange could then appeal to the High Court, and from the High Court to the Supreme Court, where the tides of his fate end.

Amnesty International has decided that it will not adopt Assange as a prisoner of conscience. If anyone fits the bill it's him, but the fact that it's the US, Britain, and Australia nexus that must be confronted worries the bureaucrats who head Amnesty. Might their money be cut off and bank accounts frozen? Whatever the reason, it's a disgrace.

On a more optimistic note, in late July the DNC's lawsuit brought against WikiLeaks, Assange, the Russian government, and the Trump campaign on April 20, 2018 was officially thrown out. Rejecting the DNC's contention that Assange and WikiLeaks illegally "furthered the prospects" of the Trump campaign by publishing and disseminating allegedly Russia-stolen materials, Judge John Koeltl granted no small victory in our momentous project to defend First Amendment rights. The judge ruled that the prosecution of Assange would render "any journalist who publishes an article based on stolen information a co-conspirator in the theft." Onward.

* * *

The following are some of the most significant challenges we face in our global mission to support and defend Julian Assange.

I. A Decade-Long Character Assassination

The US espionage indictment against Assange shows that he has been the victim of psychological operation warfare—rumor, disinformation, and false news—designed to destroy his reputation and defame his character. While Assange and his lawyers have consistently maintained that the primary reason he sought protection in the Ecuadorian embassy was to avoid extradition on espionage, the media has insisted otherwise, downplaying the threat from the US. For seven years, while Assange remained in the embassy under worsening conditions, this big lie provided the corporate media with a blind from which to issue myriad attacks on Assange. Segments of a contribution by Caitlin Johnstone appearing throughout this anthology explore and debunk the accusations designed to isolate Assange and mute the opposition to US efforts to close down national security journalism. This character assassination greatly hinders the public's understanding that his persecution under espionage charges will open the door for anyone, anywhere around the world, to suffer the same fate.

II. Swedish Rape Allegations

Another reason for the lack of support for Assange, especially in the US and the UK, is the rape investigation in Sweden. The manipulation of the Swedish sexual assault investigation began in 2010 in the immediate wake of WikiLeaks' release of Chelsea Manning's cache of damning US war secrets. Two of the lesser allegations have been dismissed because the statute of limitations has run. The most serious accusation, that Assange did not receive prior consent for unprotected sex from his partner, is again under investigation. One of the reasons for the heated criticism of Assange was the belief that his primary motive for fleeing to the Ecuadorian embassy was to avoid the rape investigation rather than to escape extradition to the US, which, it was widely contended, was never a serious threat.

The recently unsealed US indictment dispels that assertion. In addition, documents secured by Stefania Maurizi, a well-respected Italian journalist and contributor to this anthology, under a series of hard fought FOIA requests concerning the Swedish allegations, reveal that: 1. The UK advised the Swedes against interviewing Assange at the embassy to carry out the first stage of the investigation even though Sweden had carried out extra-territorial interviews in the past; 2. The UK attempted to dissuade Sweden from dropping the investigation in 2013, and wrote to the Swedish prosecutor, "Please do not think that the case is being dealt with as just another extradition request"; 3. A cover-up was implied because both UK and Swedish prosecutors destroyed some of their email exchanges during the course of the investigation.

Included in this collection are an article and an unpublished letter from Women Against Rape which more fully discuss this issue. At the time of writing, the Swedish prosecutor has decided to reopen the investigation, though Assange has never been charged and may never be. It should be noted that not only were the allegations dismissed once, but the prosecutor who took over the case and reinstated the investigation successfully filed for the original European Arrest Warrant without the imprimatur of a judicial authority, despite the seeming requirement in the treaty then in force, because the UK authorities decided that the word of the Swedish prosecutor was sufficient.[2] This time carefully following the law, the prosecutor applied to the Swedish court for an arrest warrant and was surprised when her request was denied. For now, Sweden will not seek Assange's extradition. As Craig Murray astutely noted, "This is a desperate disappointment to the false left in the UK, the Blairites and their ilk, who desperately want Assange to be a rapist in order to avoid the moral decision about prosecuting him for publishing truths about the neo-con illegal wars which they support." Assange's lawyers always believed that it would be easier for the US to extradite him from Sweden, which has rarely, if ever, refused a US extradition request. There would be a benefit in Assange finally facing those accusing him of sexual assault in a court of law, if that is what they want and it is warranted by the investigators, but it now seems unlikely that this will ever happen. Even if the case did go to court,

---

[2] The UK treaty currently in force clarifies the requirement of the necessity for judicial oversight. It also requires that the accused party be charged with a crime, and that an investigation is not sufficient. These changes were made after the UK Supreme Court decision in the Assange case, designed to protect against individuals being extradited in the same circumstances in the future.

Swedish law often dictates that such hearings are held in private, so the public might be denied the possibility of hearing the evidence presented.

III. Redactions and Reckless Endangerment

Perhaps with the intention of undermining the revelations of WikiLeaks disclosures, politicians and media have regularly focused on one assertion concerning WikiLeaks' practices, namely that its publication of uncensored materials has been irresponsible, reckless, and harmful to the national security of countries and innocent individuals named in the documents. This narrative began after WikiLeaks released the Afghan War Logs without redacting some source names, something even WikiLeaks' staunchest supporters, including a number that appear in this book, criticize to this day. After much pushback, the organization dedicated itself to carefully protecting the names of innocents in its subsequent disclosures. But the controversy burgeoned again in 2011 following a breach of WikiLeaks' full, unredacted trove of Cablegate files, which the organization had originally been releasing with numerous media outlets over the course of months. A blame game ensued between WikiLeaks, which unintentionally kept an accessible yet hidden folder on its server containing the Cablegate files, and *Guardian* writers David Leigh and Luke Harding, who published in their book, *WikiLeaks: Inside Julian Assange's War on Secrecy*, a password to the files Assange gave them that they allegedly believed was temporary. Both parties are clearly responsible to some degree for the unwanted release of the documents but, predictably, WikiLeaks suffered disproportionate condemnation and its name and work have since been smeared by the lie that they nefariously endangered innocent people— that Assange has blood on his hands. One clear fact remains, however, and will be repeated throughout this text: there exists no evidence that WikiLeaks' releases have caused the death or persecution of a single individual—globally. Even the Pentagon has confirmed, after review, that no one has been killed as a result of being named in the documents leaked by Chelsea Manning.[3]

Assange and his colleagues have argued before that complete transparency, the publication of raw, unredacted files, would generate a far greater good than leaving decisions about what is in the public interest, and subsequently published, to journalists, a circumstance prone to benefitting and protecting governments and corporations. This original element of WikiLeaks' philosophy, one which it has not entirely adhered to itself, is a contentious issue, including among fervent supporters of Assange and WikiLeaks' mission. What are indisputable, however, are the truths that the organization's disclosures brought to light. As Glenn Greenwald remarked at the time:

> As usual, many of those running around righteously condemning WikiLeaks for the potential, prospective, unintentional harm to innocents caused by this leak will have nothing to say about these actual, deliberate acts of wanton slaughter by the US. The accidental release of these unredacted cables will receive far more attention and more outrage than the extreme, deliberate wrongdoing these cables expose.[4]

IV. Russia, Assange, and the Clinton Loss

Another aspect of Assange's limited support in the US may be that the ideological divide between those in the US and other Western countries and the developing world is not sufficiently acknowledged. Assange's

---

[3]   Ed Pilkington, "Bradley Manning leak did not result in deaths by enemy forces, court hears," *The Guardian*, July 31, 2013, https://www.theguardian.com/world/2013/jul/31/bradley-manning-sentencing-hearing-pentagon.

[4]   Glenn Greenwald, "Facts and myths in the WikiLeaks/Guardian saga," *Salon*, September 2, 2011, https://www.salon.com/2011/09/02/wikileaks_28/.

global perspective is shaped by a cosmopolitanism that is more commonly found among those who originate or reside outside the US. In her contribution to this anthology, Margaret Kimberley, editor and senior columnist at Black Agenda Report, touches on what she calls a "naïveté" of Assange about the American view of the world. He is more concerned with the international aspects of US policy and less concerned with American domestic issues. He is less acquainted with internal North American history than he might be. His interest in who is elected to be the US president is colored by this.

Many American liberals cannot forgive Assange for, in their mind, helping Donald Trump become president of the United States in 2016. The accusation is that Assange was Russia's surrogate. But this claim does not stand up to closer examination. Consider the charges concerning Hillary Clinton's private server: her emails were revealed through a *FOIA request* filed in 2012 by the nonprofit Citizens for Responsibility and Ethics in Washington (CREW). They were made searchable by both WikiLeaks *and* by the *Wall Street Journal*. The Podesta emails were retrieved as the result of a simple spear-phishing operation—and not by WikiLeaks. No elaborate collusion by a cartoon criminal mastermind, Trump, or the Russian government, was needed. As journalist Chris Hedges points out in these pages, James Comey himself said that WikiLeaks probably received the emails via an intermediary. In general, WikiLeaks merely receives information from sources. As for the DNC documents, WikiLeaks was not the only publication to allegedly communicate with Guccifer 2.0 and receive and publish the material. The Intercept, Politico and others did as well, and the Hill openly admitted to communicating with Guccifer 2.0. But it was Assange and WikiLeaks that were the focus of the Mueller investigation, and only Assange and WikiLeaks who were sued by the DNC.

The finding that the DNC documents were hacked from seven separate accounts by agents of the Russian state rests on the assertions of private cybersecurity companies, CrowdStrike, Fidelis, and Mandiant, rather than of the FBI, which was denied access to the DNC server. As will be discussed in this anthology, no factual basis has been supplied for the accusation that Assange knew the DNC emails derived from a Russian source, and especially not the Russian government. Assange himself has repeatedly stated that the leaks came from an individual, not from a state actor. In July 2019, CNN reported that the embassy was Assange's "command post for election meddling," where he collaborated with Russians to ensure Trump's victory in 2016. But in what is now a Russiagate media trope, the outlet presented only circumstantial evidence. Regardless, WikiLeaks' explicit goals include exposing the deceits of both governments—US and Russian. Its mission has always been to publish what is true and important for the historical record.

A common refrain by Assange critics is the contention that he released the Podesta emails on the spur of the moment, immediately after the release of the Trump *Access Hollywood* tape in order to counter its public impact. However, according to Stefania Maurizi, who worked on the release, the disclosure was not a sudden decision but was planned some time in advance. Assange, like many others in the early part of 2016, did not believe Trump had a chance of winning. He has also said publicly that he disdained both of the 2016 presidential candidates. But because the releases were helpful to Trump, and because there exists an expressed hostility between Assange and Clinton, many have inferred that Assange intended to help Trump win. Clearly a number of factors were at play in Trump's surprise victory. But to place significant responsibility at the door of Assange for the defeat of Clinton, widely regarded as a lackluster candidate who was handicapped by being seen as "inside the beltway" and responsible for major campaign errors, including describing Trump supporters as "deplorable" and failing to campaign in key Midwestern states where a working class vote was critical to the Democrats, seems wide of the mark.

* * *

The various contributors to this book together confront these challenges—albeit with different emphases and occasional disagreements. For instance, Craig Murray's essay on the Mueller Report's distortions and failures to fill information gaps about the DNC leak argues that an *insider leak*, not a *Russian hack* preceded WikiLeaks' publication of the emails, while Caitlin Johnstone, though sympathetic to the holes Murray underlines in the Russiagate narrative, contends that neither theory presents conclusive evidence. Other differences arise elsewhere in the collection concerning Assange's sexual dealings in Sweden, his political ideology, and WikiLeaks' publication methods. It's important to note however that these disagreements do not override that which unites the contributors' writings, activism, legal interventions, art, diplomacy, reporting, and speeches: namely a clear desire to defend Julian Assange.

The anthology is broken into five sections. It begins with Assange's expulsion from the Ecuadorian embassy, including what immediately preceded and followed: Chris Hedges, Noam Chomsky, Alan MacLeod, Charles Glass, and Geoffrey Robertson describe the urgency, the dangers, the precedent of his persecution, and the shameful response of mainstream media; Katrin Axelsson and Lisa Longstaff set out their position as participants in the organization Women Against Rape who simultaneously reject Assange's extradition; Kevin Gosztola outlines the Democratic Party's responsibility in Assange's current situation, while Margaret Kimberley puts Americans criticisms of the publisher into better context. Daniel Ellsberg and Matt Taibbi establish the implications of the Espionage charges against Assange; Vivienne Westwood confronts the misrule of law that is Assange's plight; and Pamela Anderson describes the upsetting circumstances she encountered when visiting Assange in Belmarsh Prison.

Next, we meet Assange during the time he felt compelled to take up residence in the Ecuadorian embassy. We learn of the details surrounding his confinement from Fidel Narváez, one of the former Ecuadorian ambassadors under Rafael Correa, followed by Julian Assange's appeal to Correa for asylum; we hear from Srećko Horvat, John Pilger, Sister Teresa Forcades, and Angela Richter on their bittersweet meetings with Assange; and Ai Weiwei's 2015 interview unlocks the mind of the imprisoned WikiLeaks visionary.

Following this are the philosophical underpinnings of WikiLeaks, beginning with Assange in his own words in 2012 under house arrest in the UK. Slavoj Žižek underscores the revelations of nefarious and bloody connections between private corporations and state agencies brought out by Assange, while Franco "Bifo" Berardi ponders WikiLeaks' foundational premise of combatting state secrecy; Sally Burch contextualizes the persecution of Assange within the war for a people's Internet, and against surveillance capitalism; Nozomi Hayase mines the anti-imperial and democratizing potential of WikiLeaks' scientific and revolutionary journalism, and Geoffroy de Lagasnerie applauds Assange and his organization for developing and adhering to utopian principles.

The last section of this book covers the legacy of Assange and WikiLeaks: Patrick Cockburn waves off the irrelevant coverage of Assange and uncovers the vital contributions of his work to governmental and corporate transparency; Jennifer Robinson unpacks the opportunities for justice that Assange gave to the planet, while Naomi Colvin spotlights the heroic operations and influence of WikiLeaks in 2010–2011; Mark Curtis shifts the focus from US disclosures to those of the UK, and, following the espionage charges, John C. O'Day discusses how the corporate media designates who is, and who is not, a journalist; Craig Murray dismantles the Russiagate scandal that implicates Assange, and Renata Avila dives into a personal who-and-what of the publisher; Stefania Maurizi and Natália Viana both recount their journalistic work with WikiLeaks. After hearing from the optimistic outlook of the late Michael Ratner, Assange's widely respected defense attorney, the collection ends with the 18-count superseding indictment against Assange—disturbing yet essential reading for its potential to crush press freedom around the world.

This book is the initiative of Colin Robinson at OR Books. It has been assembled and edited with the critical input of Teddy Ostrow. Its aim is simple. To declare our solidarity with Julian Assange and the WikiLeaks publishing organization. The contributors are many and varied. What unites them is the view that Assange must be defended against the secret state and its friends. Punishments meted out to Manning and Assange will fail in their objective. As long as the West initiates and supports the wars of recolonization (of which Yemen is the latest example) there will always be those who will resist in all ways they can. Providing information to the citizens of this world has become a dangerous act, but it cannot be stopped, as every authoritarian regime understands. The courageous people who provide this information must be defended. It is impossible to foresee who next in official circles or secret state institutions, disgusted by what is going on, is going to say: "Enough! No more. I'm going to tell the truth." That precedents exist, not least the vital and extraordinary work of Julian Assange and WikiLeaks, is not unimportant.

Tariq Ali and Margaret Kunstler

August 2019

CHRONOLOGY OF MAJOR EVENTS

October 4, 2006—The wikileaks.org domain name is registered in Iceland.

December 2006—WikiLeaks publishes its first document: a secret decision to assassinate government officials, signed by Sheikh Hassan Dahir Aweys, a Somali rebel leader then a part of the Islamic Courts Union.

November 2007—WikiLeaks publishes a copy of the US Army's 2003 *Standard Operating Procedure for Camp Delta*, the protocol manual for soldiers stationed at Guantánamo Bay.

February 2008—WikiLeaks publishes allegations of illegalities by the Swiss bank Julius Baer in the Cayman Islands. Shortly thereafter Julius Baer sued WikiLeaks and obtained an injunction that temporarily shut down wikileaks.org.

September 2008—WikiLeaks publishes leaked emails from then Republican VP contender Sarah Palin's Yahoo account, just two months before the US presidential election of 2008.

September 2009—Shortly before Iceland's financial crisis of 2008–2012, WikiLeaks publishes leaked internal documents from Kaupthing Bank

May 2017—Swedish prosecutors drop their investigation against Julian Assange, but he still faces arrest for jumping bail, and, subsequently, extradition to the United States.

September 2017—WikiLeaks begins publishing the Spy Files Russia, a continuation of the Spy Files of 2011, which consists of over 650,000 documents on Russia's surveillance activities, including its work with private contractors.

December 2017—Julian Assange receives Ecuadorian citizenship.

January 2018—Three doctors examine Julian Assange's mental and physical health in the Ecuadorian embassy, prompting them to call on the UK to allow him safe passage to hospital for treatment.

March 2018—The newly elected Ecuadorian president, Lenín Moreno, imposes harsh restrictions on Julian Assange's Internet access, electronic communications, and visitations in the embassy.

November 2018—US prosecutors mistakenly reveal the existence of a sealed indictment against Julian Assange in an unrelated court filing.

April 11, 2019—Ecuador revokes Julian Assange's asylum and allows the UK authorities to come into the embassy to arrest him. A US grand jury unseals an indictment charging Julian Assange with conspiracy to crack a password on a Department of Defense computer with Chelsea Manning in 2010.

May 1, 2019—A British court sentences Julian Assange to 50 weeks in Belmarsh Prison for jumping bail in 2012 to take refuge in the Ecuadorian embassy.

May 23, 2019—In a superseding indictment, the US charges Julian Assange with an additional 17 counts of violating the Espionage Act, prompting international unrest among media outlets and press freedom activists.

May 30, 2019—Julian Assange is moved into the hospital wing of Belmarsh Prison amid his deteriorating health.

May 31, 2019—UN special rapporteur on torture, Nils Melzer, declares that Julian Assange shows all typical signs of prolonged exposure to psychological torture.

June 2019—The Swedish judiciary rejects prosecutors' request for an arrest warrant on Julian Assange, effectively striking down his possible extradition to Sweden. A British court pushes Assange's full US extradition hearing to February 2020.

July 30, 2019—In defense of press freedom, a US federal judge dismisses the Democratic National Committee's lawsuit brought against Julian Assange, WikiLeaks, the Russian government, and members of the Trump campaign on April 20, 2018. The judge upheld Assange's, WikiLeaks', and effectively all journalists' right to publish illegally acquired materials.

RESPONDING TO ASSANGE'S CRITICS 1-3[5]

Caitlin Johnstone, April 2019

Have you ever noticed how whenever someone inconveniences the dominant Western power structure, the entire political/media class rapidly becomes very, very interested in letting us know how evil and disgusting that person is? It's true of the leader of every nation which refuses to allow itself to be absorbed into the blob of the US-centralized power alliance, it's true of anti-establishment political candidates, and it's true of WikiLeaks founder Julian Assange.

Corrupt and unaccountable power uses its political and media influence to smear Assange because, as far as the interests of corrupt and unaccountable power are concerned, killing his reputation is as good as killing him. If everyone can be placed into viewing him with hatred and revulsion, they'll be far less likely to take WikiLeaks publications

---

[5] This piece, portions of which are broken up between sections of this anthology, was originally published April 19, 2019, with added sections on April 25, 2019. Read it in its entirety here: Caitlin Johnstone, "Debunking All the Assange Smears," *Medium*, last modified April 25, 2019, https://medium.com/@caityjohnstone/ debunking-all-the-assange-smears-a549fd677cac.

seriously, and they'll be far more likely to consent to Assange's imprisonment, thereby establishing a precedent for the future prosecution of leak-publishing journalists around the world. Someone can be speaking 100 percent truth to you, but if you're suspicious of him you won't believe anything he's saying. If they can manufacture that suspicion with total or near-total credence, then as far as our rulers are concerned it's as good as putting a bullet in his head.

Those of us who value truth and light need to fight this smear campaign in order to keep our fellow man from signing off on a major leap in the direction of Orwellian dystopia, and a big part of that means being able to argue against those smears and disinformation wherever they appear. Unfortunately I haven't been able to find any kind of centralized source of information which comprehensively debunks all the smears in a thorough and engaging way, so with the help of hundreds of tips from my readers and social media followers I'm going to attempt to make one here. What follows is my attempt at creating a tool kit people can use to fight against Assange smears wherever they encounter them, by refuting the disinformation with truth and solid argumentation.

Smear 1: "He is not a journalist."

Yes he is. Publishing relevant information so the public can inform themselves about what's going on in their world is the thing that journalism is. Which is why Assange was just awarded the GUE/NGL Award for "Journalists, Whistleblowers and Defenders of the Right to Information," why the WikiLeaks team has racked up many prestigious awards for journalism, and why Assange is a member of Australia's media union. Only when people started seriously stressing about the very real threats that his arrest poses to press freedoms did it become fashionable to go around bleating, "Assange is not a journalist."

The argument, if you can call it that, is that since Assange doesn't practice journalism in a conventional way, there's no way his bogus prosecution for his role in the Manning leaks could possibly constitute a threat to other journalists around the world who might want to publish leaked documents exposing US government malfeasance. This argument is a reprisal of a statement made by Trump's then CIA director Mike Pompeo, who proclaimed that WikiLeaks is not a journalistic outlet at all but a "hostile non-state intelligence service," a designation he made up out of thin air the same way the Trump administration designated Juan Guaidó the president of Venezuela, the Golan Heights a part of Israel, and Iran's military a terrorist organization. Pompeo argued that since WikiLeaks was now this label he made up, it enjoys no free-press protections and shall therefore be eliminated.

So they're already regurgitating propaganda narratives straight from the lips of the Trump administration, but more importantly, their argument is nonsense. As I discuss in a recent essay,[6] once the Assange precedent has been set by the US government, the US government isn't going to be relying on your personal definition of what journalism is; they're going to be using their own, based on their own interests. The next time they want to prosecute someone for doing anything similar to what Assange did, they're just going to do it, regardless of whether you believe that next person to have been a journalist or not. It's like these people imagine that the US government is going to show up at their doorstep saying, "Yes, hello, we wanted to imprison this journalist based on the precedent we set with the prosecution of Julian Assange, but before

---

[6] Caitlin Johnstone, "The US Government Won't Care About Your Definition of Journalism After The Assange Precedent is Set," *Medium*, April 14, 2019, https://medium.com/@caityjohnstone/the-us-government-wont-care-about-your-definition-of-journalism-after-the-assange-precedent-is-set-66ae974d23fe.

doing so we wanted to find out how you feel about whether or not they're a journalist."

Pure arrogance and myopia.

Smear 2: "He's a rapist."

The feedback I've gotten while putting together this article indicates that this is the one Assange defenders struggle with most, and understandably so: it's a complex situation involving multiple governments, a foreign language, a foreign legal system, lots of legal jargon, many different people, some emotionally triggering subject matter, and copious amounts of information. These layers of complexity are what smearers rely upon when circulating this smear; most people don't understand the dynamics, so it's not evident that they're ingesting disinfo.

But just because the nature of the allegation is complex doesn't mean the argument is.

The strongest, simplest, and most obvious argument against the "rapist" smear is that it's an unproven allegation which Assange has always denied, and you'd have to be out of your mind to believe a completely unproven allegation about a known target of US intelligence agencies. It's just as stupid as believing unproven claims about governments targeted for US regime change, like believing Saddam had WMD. The fact of the matter is that if you go up against America's opaque and unaccountable government agencies, they have "six ways from Sunday of getting back at you," to quote from the Gospel of Schumer.[7]

---

[7] Johnstone is referencing US Senate Minority Leader Chuck Schumer's comments. See Daniel Chaitin, "Schumer warns Trump: Intel officials 'have six ways from Sunday at getting back at you,'" *The Washington Examiner*, January 3, 2017, https://www.washingtonexaminer.com/schumer-warns-trump-intel-officials-have-six-ways-from-sunday-at-getting-back-at-you.

I know we've all been told that we have to unquestioningly believe all women who say they've been raped, and as a general practice it's a good idea to tear away our society's patriarchal habit of dismissing anyone who says they've been raped. But as soon as you make that into a hard, rigid rule that can't have any room for questioning the agendas of the powerful, you can be 100 percent certain that the powerful will begin using that rule to manipulate us.

The people aggressively promoting the "rapist" narrative and saying "You have to believe women!" do not care about rape victims any more than all the Hillary supporters saying "Bernie says you have to behave!" after the 2016 convention cared about Bernie. Earlier this month I had my Twitter privileges suspended when I went off on a virulent Assange hater who said I was lying about having survived multiple rapes myself, *while* continuing to bleat his "believe all women" schtick. The political/media class of the Western Empire, which never hesitates to support the violent toppling of sovereign governments and all the death, destruction, chaos, terrorism, suffering, and yes, rape which necessarily comes along with those actions, does not care about rape victims in Sweden.

You could spend days combing through all the articles that have been written about the details of the Swedish preliminary investigation, but let me try to sum it up as concisely as possible:

Laws about consent and rape are significantly different in Sweden from most other societies. Assange had consensual sex with two women, "SW" and "AA," in Sweden in August 2010. SW and AA were acquainted with each other and texted about their encounters and, after learning about some uncomfortable sexual experiences SW said she'd had with Assange, AA convinced SW to go to the police together to compel Assange to take an HIV test. AA took her to see her friend and political ally who was also a police officer. SW said one of the times Assange had initiated sex with her happened while she was "half-asleep" (legally and literally very different from asleep) and without a condom, and AA said Assange had deliberately damaged his condom before using it. SW freaked out when she learned the police wanted to charge Assange with rape for the half-asleep incident, and refused to sign any legal documents saying that he had raped her. She sent a text that she "did not want to put any charges against JA but the police wanted to get a grip on him," and said she had been "railroaded by police and others around her." AA went along with the process.

To gain a basic understanding of the events through 2012, I highly recommend taking ten minutes to watch the animated video footnoted here.[8]
More info:

- This all occurred just months after Assange enraged the US war machine with the release of the "Collateral Murder" video, and he was already known to have had US feds hunting for him.

- It's obvious that there were some extreme government manipulations happening behind the scenes of the entire ordeal. More on that in subsequent bullet points.

- The condom AA produced as evidence that Assange had used a damaged condom had no DNA on it, hers or Assange's.

- Assange has consistently denied all allegations.

- Neither accuser alleged rape. AA's accusation wasn't an accusation of rape and SW repeatedly refused to sign off on a rape accusation.

- AA once authored an article on how to get revenge on men who "dump" you.[9]

---

[8] InfobytesTV, "The WikiLeaks, Julian Assange Diplomatic Standoff – Animated," *YouTube*, November 29, 2012, https://www.youtube.com/watch?v=PZOUgJRPhx-w&feature=youtu.be.

[9] Celia Farber, "Exclusive New Docs Throw Doubt on Julian Assange Rape Charges in Stockholm," *Observer*, February 5, 2016, https://observer.com/2016/02/exclusive-new-docs-throw-doubt-on-julian-assange-rape-charges-in-stockholm/.

- Sweden has strict laws[10] protecting the confidentiality of the accused during preliminary investigations of alleged sexual offenses, but some convenient leaks circumvented this law and allowed Assange to be smeared as a rapist ever since. Assange learned he'd been accused from the headlines of the local tabloid *Expressen*, where AA happens to have interned.

- After an arrest warrant was issued a senior prosecutor named Eva Finne pulled rank and canceled it, dropping the matter completely on August 25, saying the evidence "disclosed no crime at all."

- Out of the blue it was restarted again on August 29, this time by another prosecutor named Marianne Ny.

- On August 30, Assange voluntarily went to the police to make a statement. In the statement, he told the officer he feared that it would end up in the *Expressen*. How do I know that? The full statement was leaked to the *Expressen*.

- Assange stayed in Sweden for five weeks waiting to be questioned, then went to the UK after a prosecutor told him he's not wanted for questioning.

- After leaving, Interpol bizarrely issued a Red Notice[11] for Assange, typically reserved for terrorists and dangerous criminals, not alleged first-time rapists. This exceedingly disproportionate response immediately raised a red flag with Assange's legal team that this was not just about rape accusations, and they decided to fight his extradition to Sweden fearing that he was being set up to be extradited to the United States, a country that WikiLeaks

---

[10] WikiLeaks, Twitter post, January 13, 2016, 3:08 p.m., https://twitter.com/wikileaks/status/687365705457598466.

[11] Interpol stands for the International Criminal Police Organization, an international body that facilitates cooperation between police forces in its 196 member countries. A Red Notice is a request by Interpol to global law enforcement for the arrest of an individual pending extradition or other similar legal actions.

had recently embarrassed with extremely damaging leaks about war crimes.

- In December 2010 Assange went to a UK police station by appointment and was arrested. He spent ten days in solitary confinement and was released on bail, then spent 550 days under house arrest with an electronic ankle bracelet.

- We now know that a grand jury had been set up in the Eastern District of Virginia already at this time to try and find a crime to hang him for, or at least put him away 'til the end of his life. Assange's lawyers were aware of this.

- The UK Supreme Court decided Assange should be extradited to Sweden, the Swedes refused to give any assurances that he would not be extradited on to the US, and the US refused to give any assurances that they would not seek his extradition and prosecution. If either country had provided such an assurance as urged by Amnesty International, Assange would have traveled to Sweden and the ordeal would have been resolved.

- This was never resolved because this was never about rape or justice. It was about extraditing Assange to the United States for his publications.

- As the window until extradition to Sweden closed, in 2012 Assange sought and won asylum at the Ecuadorian embassy as a journalist who risked unfair prosecution.

- A few days ago we learned that the FBI affidavit supporting Assange's arrest at the embassy asserts that, "Instead of appealing to the European Court of Human Rights, in June 2012, Assange fled to the embassy." But according to Assange, Marianne Ny had actually worked to cancel his window to apply to appeal the matter at the European Court of Human Rights, reducing it from 14 days to zero days and thereby shutting that door in his face.

- In 2013, Sweden attempted to drop extradition proceedings but was dissuaded from doing so by UK prosecutors, a fact we wouldn't learn until 2018.

- In 2017 we learned that the UK's Crown Prosecution Service had dissuaded the Swedes from questioning Assange in London in 2010 or 2011, which could have prevented the entire embassy standoff in the first place, and that the CPS had destroyed crucial emails pertaining to Assange.

- We also learned that Marianne Ny had deleted an email she'd received from the FBI, claiming it could not be recovered.

- In May 2017, Marianne Ny closed her investigation, strangely on the very day she was due to appear in Stockholm court to face questions on why she had barred Assange's defense lawyer and other irregularities during his questioning in the embassy the previous November, and rescinded the extradition arrest warrant.

- Contrary to popular belief in the UK press, the case is unlikely to be reopened now that Assange is theoretically available again because she formally closed the case under Sweden's prosecutorial code Ch 23, Section 4,[12] which dictates that preliminary investigations must be run so as to put the suspect to a minimum of suspicion, inconvenience, and cost.[13] After seven years of foot-dragging on Ny's part it was obvious to all—including Sweden's courts—that hers had become disproportionate.

---

[12]   Marianne Ny, "Decision," *Aklagare*, May 19, 2017, https://www.aklagare.se/globalassets/dokument/ovriga-dokument/decision-20170519.pdf.

[13]   Contrary to Johnstone's prediction, the preliminary investigation was reopened on May 13, 2019, but in June 2019, the Swedish courts rejected a renewed request for Assange's arrest warrant, ruling against his extradition to Sweden. This section was written a month prior on April 19, 2019. "Preliminary investigation in the Assange case to be reopened," *Aklagare*, May 13, 2019, https:// www.aklagare. se/en/news-and-press/press-releases/?newsId=3256997.

- Assange was never charged, despite having been thoroughly interviewed at the embassy by Swedish prosecutors before the investigation was closed.[14] Some smearers claim that this is due to a technicality of Swedish law which made the government unable to charge him in absentia, but Sweden can and has charged people in absentia. They did not do so with Assange, preferring to keep insisting that he come to Sweden without any assurances against onward extradition to the US instead, for some strange reason.

- Shortly after Assange's embassy arrest the Intercept's Charles Glass reported that "sources in Swedish intelligence told me at the time that they believed the US had encouraged Sweden to pursue the case."[15]

- It cannot be denied that governments around the world have an extensive and well-documented history of using sex to advance strategic agendas in various ways, and there's no valid reason to rule this out as a possibility on any level.

- Sometimes smearers will try to falsely claim that Assange or his lawyers admitted that Assange committed rape or pushed its boundaries during the legal proceedings, citing mass media reports on a strategy employed by Assange's legal team of arguing that what Assange was accused of wouldn't constitute rape *even if true*. This conventional legal strategy was employed as a means of avoiding extradition and in no way constituted an admission that events happened in the way alleged, yet mass

---

[14]   Esther Addley and David Crouch, "Julian Assange faces Swedish prosecutor in London over rape accusation," *The Guardian*, November 14, 2016, https://www.theguardian.com/media/2016/nov/14/julian-assange-to-face-swedish-prosecutors-over-accusation.

[15]   A version of this cited piece by Charles Glass, "Prizes For Some, Prison For Assange," can be found in the following section of this collection.

media reports deliberately twisted it to appear that way. Neither Assange nor his lawyers have ever made any such admission.[16]

For more information on the details of the rape accusation, check out the following resources:

- A 2012 *Four Corners* segment titled "Sex, Lies, and Julian Assange"[17]
- A 2016 *Observer* article titled "Exclusive New Docs Throw Doubt on Julian Assange Rape Charges in Stockholm"[18]
- A timeline of events by Peter Tatchell titled "Assange: Swedes & UK obstructed sex crime investigation"[19]
- A John Pilger article titled "Getting Julian Assange: The Untold Story"[20]
- A Justice Integrity Report article titled "Assange Rape Defense Underscores Shameful Swedish, U.S. Tactics"[21]
- The aforementioned ten-minute YouTube video.

---

[16] Tom Peck, "Discourteous and disrespectful, but not rape: the Assange defence," *The Independent*, July 13, 2011, https://www.independent.co.uk/news/uk/home-news/discourteous-and-disrespectful-but-not-rape-the-assange-defence-2312641.html.

[17] "Sex, Lies, and Julian Assange," *ABC*, last modified April 24, 2019, https://www.abc.net.au/4corners/sex-lies-and-julian-assange/4156420.

[18] Celia Farber, "Exclusive New Docs Throw Doubt on Julian Assange Rape Charges in Stockholm," *Observer*, February 5, 2016, https://observer.com/2016/02/exclusive-new-docs-throw-doubt-on-julian-assange-rape-charges-in-stockholm/.

[19] "Assange: Swedes & UK obstructed sex crime investigation," *Peter Tatchell Foundation*, April 17, 2019, https://www.petertatchellfoundation.org/assange-swedes-uk-obstructed-sex-crime-investigation/.

[20] John Pilger, "Getting Julian Assange: The Untold Story," *John Pilger*, May 20, 2017, http://johnpilger.com/articles/getting-julian-assange-the-untold-story.

[21] Andrew Kreig, "Assange Rape Defense Underscores Shameful Swedish, U.S. Tactics," *Justice Integrity Project*, https://www.justice-integrity.org/1170-assange-rape-defense-underscores-shameful-swedish-u-s-tactics.

For some feminist essays on the infuriating hypocrisy of the entire patriarchal empire suddenly caring so, so deeply about the possibility that a man might have initiated sex in an inappropriate way, check out:

- A Naomi Wolf essay titled "J'Accuse: Sweden, Britain, and Interpol Insult Rape Victims Worldwide" [22]
- A *Guardian* article by Women Against Rape titled "We are Women Against Rape but we do not want Julian Assange extradited—For decades we have campaigned to get rapists caught, charged and convicted. But the pursuit of Assange is political" [23]

I see a lot of well-meaning Assange defenders using some very weak and unhelpful arguments against this smear, suggesting for example that having unprotected sex without the woman's permission shouldn't qualify as sexual assault or that if AA had been assaulted she would necessarily have conducted herself differently afterward. Any line of argumentation like that is going to look very cringey to people like myself who believe rape culture is a ubiquitous societal illness that needs to be rolled back far beyond the conventional understanding of rape as a stranger in a dark alley forcibly penetrating some man's wife or daughter at knifepoint. Don't try to justify what Assange is accused of having done, just point out that there's no actual evidence that he is guilty and that very powerful people have clearly been pulling some strings behind the scenes of this narrative.

Finally, the fact remains that even if Assange were somehow to be proven guilty of rape, the argument "he's a rapist" is not a legitimate reason to support a US extradition and prosecution which would set a precedent that poses a threat to press freedoms everywhere. "He's a rapist" and

[22] Naomi Wolf, "J'Accuse: Sweden, Britain, and Interpol Insult Rape Victims Worldwide," *HuffPost*, December 13, 2010, https://www.huffpost.com/entry/jaccuse-sweden-britain-an_b_795899.

[23] This piece is reprinted elsewhere in this anthology.

"It's okay that the Western legal system is funneling him into the Eastern District of Virginia for his publishing activities" are two completely different thoughts that have nothing whatsoever to do with each other, so anyone attempting to associate the two in any way has made a bad argument and should feel bad.

Smear 3: "He was hiding from rape charges in the embassy."

No he wasn't, he was hiding from US extradition. And his arrest this month under a US extradition warrant proved that he was right to do so.

People who claim Assange was "hiding from rape charges" are necessarily implicitly making two transparently absurd claims: one, that Assange had no reason to fear US extradition, and two, that Ecuador was lying about its official reasons for granting him asylum—that in fact the Correa government was just in the business of protecting people from rape charges for some weird reason.

For its part, the Ecuadorian government was crystal clear in its official statement about the reasons it was providing Assange asylum, saying that "there are serious indications of retaliation by the country or countries that produced the information disclosed by Mr. Assange, retaliation that can put at risk his safety, integrity and even his life," and that "the judicial evidence shows clearly that, given an extradition to the United States, Mr. Assange would not have a fair trial, he could be judged by a special or military court, and it is not unlikely that he would receive a cruel and demeaning treatment and he would be condemned to a life sentence or the death penalty, which would not respect his human rights."

A lot of the rank-and-file Assange haters you'll encounter on online forums are just completely clueless about what political asylum is and how it works, because they receive their information from the same mass media which led 70 percent of Americans to still believe Saddam was behind 9/11 six months after the Iraq invasion. They either believe that (A) Assange found some strange loophole which enabled him to hide from all criminal charges simply by staying in an embassy, without any permission from that embassy's government, or that (B) the Ecuadorian government hands out political asylum willy-nilly to anyone who's been accused of sexual assault. These beliefs can only be maintained by a rigorous determination not to think about them too hard.

Assange wasn't hiding from justice, he was hiding from injustice. His sole concern has only ever been avoiding extradition and an unjust trial, which was why he offered to go to Sweden to be questioned if they would only provide assurances that he wouldn't face onward extradition to the US. Sweden refused. America refused. Now why would they do that? If Sweden were really only interested in resolving a rape investigation, why wouldn't they provide assurances that they wouldn't extradite him to the United States in order to accomplish that?

The fact that Assange was perfectly willing to travel to Sweden and see the investigation through is completely devastating to the "he's hiding from rape charges" smear, and it casts serious doubt on the "he's a rapist" smear as well.

The US government tortured Chelsea Manning.[24] Trump's current CIA director was called "Bloody Gina" because of her fondness for torture on CIA black sites. Assange had every reason to be mortally afraid of extradition, and to remain so. The correct response to anyone claiming Assange should have done anything which could have allowed him to be extradited is, "How well do you think you'd fare under torture, tough guy?"

---

[24] Caitlin Johnstone, "Reminder: Chelsea Manning Was Twice Driven To Suicide By a Regime That Tortures Whistleblowers," *Medium*, May 17, 2017, https://medium.com/@caityjohnstone/reminder-chelsea-manning-was-twice-driven-to-suicide-by-a-regime-that-tortures-whistleblowers-43a053aff7b4.

PART I: EXPULSION

1. THE MARTYRDOM OF JULIAN ASSANGE[25]

Chris Hedges, April 11, 2019

The arrest of Julian Assange eviscerates all pretense of the rule of law and the rights of a free press. The list of illegalities, embraced by the Ecuadorian, British, and US governments, in the seizure of Assange are ominous. They presage a world where the internal workings, abuses, corruption, lies, and crimes, especially war crimes, carried out by corporate states and the global ruling elite will be masked from the public. They presage a world where those with the courage and integrity to expose the misuse of power will be hunted down, tortured, subjected to sham trials and given lifetime prison terms in solitary confinement. They presage an Orwellian dystopia where news is replaced with propaganda, trivia, and entertainment. The arrest of Assange, I fear, marks the official beginning of the corporate totalitarianism that will define our lives.

Under what law did Ecuadorian president Lenín Moreno capriciously terminate Julian Assange's rights of asylum as a political refugee?

[25] A version of this essay was originally published online. Chris Hedges, "The Martyrdom of Julian Assange," *TruthDig*, April 11, 2019, https://www.truthdig.com/articles/the-martyrdom-of-julian-assange/.

Under what law did Moreno authorize British police into the Ecuadorian embassy—diplomatically sanctioned sovereign territory—to arrest a naturalized citizen of Ecuador? Under what law did Prime Minister Theresa May order the British police to grab Assange, who has never committed a crime? Under what law did Donald Trump demand the extradition of Assange, who is not a US citizen and whose news organization is not based in the United States?

I am sure government attorneys are skillfully doing what has become de rigueur for the corporate state, using specious legal arguments to eviscerate enshrined rights by judicial fiat. This is how we have the right to privacy with no privacy. This is how we have "free" elections funded by corporate money, covered by a compliant corporate media and under iron corporate control. This is how we have a legislative process where corporate lobbyists write the legislation and corporate indentured politicians vote it into law. This is how we have the right to due process with no due process. This is how we have a government, whose fundamental role is to protect citizens, which orders and carries out the assassination of its own citizens such as the radical cleric Anwar al-Awlaki and his 16-year-old-son. This is how we have a press legally permitted to publish classified information and a publisher sitting in jail in Britain awaiting extradition to the United States and a whistleblower, Chelsea Manning, in a jail cell in the United States.

Great Britain will use as its legal cover for the arrest the extradition request from Washington based on conspiracy charges. This legal argument, in a functioning judiciary, would be thrown out of court. Unfortunately, we no longer have a functioning judiciary. We will soon know if Great Britain lacks one as well.

Assange was granted asylum in the embassy in 2012 to avoid extradition to Sweden to answer questions about sexual offense allegations that were eventually dropped. Assange and his lawyers always argued that if he was put in Swedish custody he would be extradited to the United States. Once he was granted asylum and Ecuadorian citizenship the British government refused to grant Assange safe passage to the London airport, trapping him in the embassy for seven years as his health steadily deteriorated.

The Trump administration will seek to try Assange on charges that he conspired with Manning in 2010 to steal the Iraq and Afghanistan War Logs obtained by WikiLeaks. The half-million internal documents leaked by Manning from the Pentagon and the State Department, along with the 2007 video of US helicopter pilots nonchalantly gunning down Iraqi civilians, including children, and two Reuters journalists, provided copious evidence of the hypocrisy, indiscriminate violence, routine use of torture, lies, bribery, and crude tactics of intimidation by the US government in its foreign relations and wars in the Middle East. Assange and WikiLeaks allowed us to see the inner workings of empire—the most important role of a press—and for this it became empire's prey.

US government lawyers will attempt to separate WikiLeaks and Assange from the *New York Times* and the *Guardian*, which also published the leaked material from Manning, by implicating Assange in the theft of the documents. Manning was repeatedly and often brutally pressured during her detention and trial to implicate Assange in the seizure of the material, something she steadfastly refused to do. She is currently in jail because of her refusal to testify, without her lawyer, in front of the grand jury assembled for the Assange case. President Barack Obama granted Manning, who was given a 35-year sentence, clemency after she served seven years in a military prison.

Once the documents and videos provided by Manning to Assange and WikiLeaks were published and disseminated by news organizations such as the *New York Times* and the *Guardian* the press callously, and foolishly, turned on Assange. News organizations that had run WikiLeaks material over several days soon served as conduits in a black propaganda campaign to discredit Assange and WikiLeaks. This coordinated smear campaign was detailed in a leaked Pentagon document prepared by the Cyber Counterintelligence Assessments Branch dated March 8, 2008. The document called on the US to eradicate the "feeling of trust" that is WikiLeaks' "center of gravity" and destroy Assange's reputation.

Assange, who with the Manning leaks had exposed the war crimes, lies, and criminal manipulations of the Bush administration, soon earned the ire of the Democratic Party establishment by publishing 70,000 hacked emails belonging to the Democratic National Committee (DNC) and senior Democratic officials. The emails were copied from the accounts of John Podesta, Hillary Clinton's campaign chairman. The Podesta emails exposed the donation of millions of dollars from Saudi Arabia and Qatar, two of the major funders of Islamic State, to the Clinton Foundation. It exposed the $657,000 Goldman Sachs paid to Hillary Clinton to give talks, a sum so large it can only be considered a bribe. It exposed Clinton's repeated mendacity. She was caught in the emails, for example, telling the financial elites that she wanted "open trade and open borders" and believed Wall Street executives were best-positioned to manage the economy, a statement that contradicted her campaign statements. It exposed the Clinton campaign's efforts to influence the Republican primaries to ensure that Trump was the Republican nominee. It exposed Clinton's advance knowledge of primary-debate questions. It exposed Clinton as the primary architect of the war in Libya, a war she believed would burnish her credentials as a presidential candidate. You can argue that this information, like the war logs, should have remained hidden, but you can't then call yourself a journalist.

The Democratic leadership, intent on blaming Russia for its election loss, charges the Podesta emails were obtained by Russian government hackers, although James Comey, the former FBI director, has conceded that the emails were probably delivered to WikiLeaks by an intermediary.[26] Assange has said the emails were not provided by "state actors."

WikiLeaks has done more to expose the abuses of power and crimes of the American Empire than any other news organization. In addition to the war logs and the Podesta emails, it made public the hacking tools used by the CIA and the National Security Agency, their surveillance programs, and their interference in foreign elections, including in the French elections. It disclosed the internal conspiracy against British Labour Party leader Jeremy Corbyn by Labour members of Parliament. It intervened to save Edward Snowden, who exposed the wholesale surveillance of the American public by our intelligence agencies, from extradition to the United States by helping him flee from Hong Kong to Moscow. The Snowden leaks also revealed that Assange was on a US "manhunt target list."

A haggard looking Assange, as he was dragged out of the embassy by British police, shook his finger and shouted: "The UK must resist this attempt by the Trump administration . . . The UK must resist!"

We must all resist. We must, in every way possible, put pressure on the British government to halt the judicial lynching of Assange. If Assange is extradited and tried it will create a legal precedent that will terminate the ability of the press, which Trump repeatedly calls "the enemy of the people," to hold power accountable. The crimes of war and finance, the persecution of dissidents, minorities, and immigrants, the pillaging by corporations of the nation and the ecosystem and the ruthless impoverishment of working men and women to swell the bank accounts of the rich and consolidate the global oligarch's total grip on power will not only expand, but will no longer be part of public debate. First Assange. Then us.

---

[26] "Full transcript: FBI director James Comey testifies on Russian interference in 2016 election," *The Washington Post*, March 20, 2017, https://www.washingtonpost.com/news/post-politics/wp/2017/03/20/full-transcript-fbi-director-james-comey-testifies-on-russian-interference-in-2016-election/?utm_term=.b242f9f7c3dl.

2. THE SCANDAL OF ASSANGE'S ARREST[27]

Noam Chomsky, April 12, 2019

The arrest of Assange is scandalous in several respects. One of them is just the show of government power—and it's not just the US government. The British are cooperating. Ecuador, of course, is now cooperating. Sweden, before, had cooperated. These are efforts to silence a journalist who was producing materials that people in power didn't want the rascal multitude to know about. WikiLeaks was producing things that people ought to know about the people in power. But they don't like that, so therefore they have to silence it. This is the kind of scandal that unfortunately takes place over and over.

Take another example, right next door to Ecuador: Brazil. Brazil is the most important country in Latin America, one of the most important in the world. Under the Lula government early in this millennium, Brazil was perhaps the most respected country in the world. It was the voice for the

---

[27] This is an excerpt from Chomsky's interview with Amy Goodman. "Chomsky: Arrest of Assange is 'Scandalous' and Highlights Shocking Extraterritorial Reach of U.S.," *Democracy Now!*, April 12, 2019, https://www.democracynow. org/2019/4/12/chomsky_arrest_of_assange_is_scandalous.

Global South under the leadership of Lula da Silva. Notice what happened. There was a coup, a soft coup, to eliminate the nefarious effects of the labor party, the Workers' Party. The Lula years are described by the World Bank—not me, the World Bank—as the "golden decade" of Brazil's history: a radical reduction of poverty, a massive extension of inclusion of marginalized population. Large parts of the population—Afro-Brazilian, indigenous people, a large segment of the Brazilian population was brought into the functioning society. There was a new sense of dignity and hope for the general population. That couldn't be tolerated.

After Lula left office, a kind of a "soft coup" took place. He was put in jail, solitary confinement, essentially a death sentence of 25 years (since reduced), banned from reading the press, and, crucially, barred from making any public statements—to silence the person who was likely to win the election. He is the most important political prisoner in the world. But do you hear anything about him?

Assange is a similar case: We've got to silence this voice. You go back to history. Some of you may recall when Mussolini's fascist government put Antonio Gramsci in jail. The prosecutor said, "We have to silence this voice for 20 years. Can't let it speak." That's Assange. That's Lula. There are other cases. That's one scandal.

Another scandal is the shocking extraterritorial reach of the United States. Why should the United States—or any other country for that matter—have the power to control what others are doing elsewhere in the world? It's an outlandish situation. It goes on all the time, unnoticed, without comment.

Take the trade agreements with China. The Trump administration doesn't like the Chinese development model so let's undermine them. Ask yourself: What would happen if China did not observe the rules that the United States is trying to impose? If US companies Boeing and Microsoft don't like the trade agreements in place, they don't have to invest in China.

Nobody has a gun to their heads. If anybody really believed in capitalism, corporations should be free to make any arrangement they want with China. Even if it involves technology transfer. The United States wants to block that so that China can't develop.

Take what are called intellectual property rights under the World Trade Organization—they create exorbitant patent rights for medicines and monopolies for corporations like Microsoft to control operating systems and so on. Suppose China didn't observe these. Who would benefit, and who would lose? Consumers would benefit.

Well, you might ask yourself: What lies behind all of these discussions and negotiations? Why is this bullying accepted on just about any issue you pick across the board? In this case, why is it acceptable for the United States to have the power to even begin to extradite a foreign journalist for exposing materials about US actions in all parts of the world—information that people in power don't want you to see? That's basically what's happening.

3. THE MEDIA CHEER ASSANGE'S ARREST[28]

Alan MacLeod, April 18, 2019

Julian Assange was arrested inside the Ecuadorian embassy in London on April 11. The Australian-born cofounder of WikiLeaks had been trapped in the building since 2012 after taking refuge there. He was immediately found guilty of failing to surrender to a British court, and was taken to Belmarsh Prison. An extradition to the United States is widely seen as imminent by corporate media, who have, by and large, strongly approved of these events.

A *Washington Post* editorial (4/11/19) claimed Assange was "no free-press hero" and insisted the arrest was "long overdue." Likewise, the *Wall Street Journal* (4/11/19) demanded "accountability" for Assange, saying, "His targets always seem to be democratic institutions or governments."

Other coverage was more condemnatory still. *The View*'s Meghan McCain (4/11/19) declared she hoped Assange "rots in hell." *Saturday Night Live*'s Colin Jost (4/13/19) said it was "so satisfying to see an Internet

---

[28] This piece was originally published by Fairness & Accuracy In Reporting (FAIR). Alan MacLeod, "Media Cheer Assange's Arrest," FAIR, April 18, 2019, https://fair. org/home/media-cheer-assanges-arrest/.

troll get dragged out into the sunlight." But it was perhaps the *National Review* (4/12/19) that expressed the most enthusiastic approval of Assange's arrest, condemning him for his "anti-Americanism, his anti-Semitism and his raw personal corruption" and for harming the US with his "vile spite."

Both the United Nations and the ACLU have denounced Assange's arrest, with the former condemning Sweden and the UK for depriving him of liberty and freedom, ordering them to pay compensation for the many years he was confined to the embassy. Despite this, establishment media have overwhelmingly described this situation with a euphemism: Mr. Assange's "self-imposed isolation" (CNN, 4/11/19; *USA Today*, 4/11/19; *New York Times*, 4/11/19), a phrase that conjures a very different image of the situation and the responsibilities of the various parties involved. The Daily Beast (4/11/19) made this implication explicit, describing Assange's predicament as "voluntary confinement."

Assange is a controversial character who originally took refuge in the Ecuadorian embassy after England's High Court ruled to extradite him to Sweden to face allegations of rape. Yet most of the media coverage downplayed or even did not mention this (e.g., Bloomberg, 4/11/19; *Nation al Review*, 4/12/19; Daily Beast, 4/11/19), suggesting they did not consider it relevant.

The universal charge of narcissism

Celebrating his arrest, *The Week* (4/11/19) attacked Assange as a "delusional, childish narcissist" who undermined the security of every nation. A host of other media outlets across the spectrum (*Washington Post*, 4/12/19; *New York Times*, 4/12/19; London *Times*, 4/7/19) similarly framed him as a "narcissist," one with an "outsized view of his own importance," despite his poor "personal hygiene," according to the *New York Times* (4/11/19).

The narcissist accusation is a common trope thrown at enemies of the US establishment, including Venezuelan president Hugo Chávez (*National Review*, 6/27/07; *Economist*, 3/9/13; *Miami Herald*, 7/25/15), Vladimir Putin (*Atlantic*, 4/15/14; *Guardian*, 3/10/18) and even Bernie Sanders (*Huffington Post*, 2/9/16; *New York*, 11/25/18). It was also exactly the same line of attack the media used against Edward Snowden, the whistleblower who leaked NSA documents (*New Yorker*, 6/10/13; Bloomberg, 11/1/13; *Chicago Tribune*, 12/23/14), and how the prosecution portrayed Chelsea Manning at her trial, suggesting it is a convenient putdown rather than a good-faith description of anti-establishment figures.

Manning had offered the files that came to be known as the Iraq War Logs to both the *Washington Post* and the *New York Times*. However, only WikiLeaks decided to publish them. The files showed evidence of US war crimes in the Middle East, and shot both Manning and Assange onto the world stage.

The UK press reaction

The infamously acerbic British press responded to Assange's arrest with undisguised glee. The *Daily Mail*'s front-page headline (4/12/19) read, "That'll Wipe the Smile Off His Face," and devoted four pages to the "downfall of a narcissist" who was removed from "inside his fetid lair" to finally "face justice." The *Daily Mirror* (4/11/19) described him as "an unwanted guest who abused his hospitality," while the *Times* of London (4/12/19) claimed "no one should feel sorry" for the "overdue eviction."

The *Mirror* (4/13/19) also published an opinion piece from Labour member of Parliament Jess Phillips that began by stating, "Finally Julian Assange, everyone's least favorite squatter, has been kicked out of the Ecuadorian embassy." She described the 47-year-old Australian as a "grumpy, stroppy teenager."

At the far-left of the corporate media spectrum, the *New Statesman* (4/12/19) described Assange as a "demented-looking gnome." The *Glasgow Herald* editorial board (4/13/19) summed up the press reaction: "Julian Assange is not a journalist, and he's not a hero, and his day in court is long overdue."

Is Assange a journalist?

The central question of whether Assange is a journalist has been discussed at great length this week in corporate media. The resounding response has been "no."

The *National Review* (4/12/19) declared him a "petty, biased, hostile foreign actor"; CNN (4/11/19) described him as an activist, not a journalist, demanding he "face justice." Fox News (4/12/19) also labeled him an activist, one who is using journalism as a "fig leaf for his reckless conduct." Other outlets (Bloomberg, 4/11/19; *Washington Post*, 4/11/19) have also been eager to insist Assange is not a journalist.

The *New York Times* editorial board (4/11/19) writes that while Assange's arrest will likely raise questions about press freedom, for now, the Trump administration has "done well" by charging the "scraggly-bearded refugee" with an "indisputable crime." They argue that there is currently technically no First Amendment issue because he is no journalist but a "foreign agent seeking to undermine the security of the United States through theft," who highlights the "sharp line between legitimate journalism and dangerous cybercrime."

Veteran journalist and supporter of Assange John Pilger disagrees, contending that his arrest is a historically important warning to "real journalists," who are few and far between at establishment media, who resent him for highlighting their subservience to the elite.

Whatever your view of Assange might be, it seems clear he shares virtually nothing in common with those in positions of influence in big media outlets, who have been only too happy to watch his demise.

4. PRIZES FOR SOME, PRISON FOR ASSANGE[29]

Charles Glass, April 14, 2019

While Julian Assange languishes in south London's maximum-security Belmarsh Prison, a British court is weighing his fate. The 47-year-old Australian founder of WikiLeaks is serving time for the minor crime of jumping bail by seeking asylum in the Ecuadorian embassy in 2012 to avoid extradition to Sweden. His fear at the time was that the Swedes, with a track record of assisting rendition of suspects sought by the US, would send him straight across the Atlantic. Now that he has lost his diplomatic refuge, 70 British members of Parliament have petitioned to dispatch Assange to Sweden if prosecutors there reopen the case they closed in 2017. The greater threat to his liberty is the US Department of Justice's extradition demand for him to stand trial in the US for conspiring with Chelsea Manning to hack a government computer.

[29] A version of this piece was originally published online. Charles Glass, "Julian Assange Languishes in Prison as His Journalistic Collaborators Brandish Their Prizes," *The Intercept*, April 14, 2019: https://theintercept.com/2019/04/14/julian-assange-languishes-in-prison-as-his-journalistic-collaborators-brandish-their-prizes/

The US insists that Assange will not face the death penalty. If he did, Britain, in common with other European states, would not be able to send him there. The maximum sentence for the hacking offense is five years, but there is no guarantee that once he arrives in the US, he will not face additional charges under the Espionage Act of 1917 that former president Barack Obama used against nine individuals for allegedly leaking secret information to the public. The sentence for that offense could be death or life in prison. If Assange ends up in the US federal judicial system, he may never be seen again.

His most likely destination is the "Alcatraz of the Rockies," otherwise known as the United States Penitentiary Administrative Maximum Facility, or ADMAX, in Florence, Colorado. Among its 400 inmates are Unabomber Ted Kaczynski, Boston Marathon terrorist Dzhokhar Tsarnaev, FBI agent-turned-Russian spy Robert Hanssen, and Oklahoma City co-bomber Terry Nichols. The prison's regime is ruthless: 23-hour daily confinement in a concrete box cell with one window 4 inches wide, six bed checks a day with a seventh on weekends, one hour of exercise in an outdoor cage, showers spraying water in one-minute spurts and "shakedowns" at the discretion of prison staff.

If Trump's Justice Department ups the ante to charge Assange under the Espionage Act, a journalist-publisher who has not committed homicide may spend the rest of his life at ADMAX.

I have visited Assange often over the past eight years, first at the Norfolk farmhouse of Vaughan Smith, a former British Army officer and news cameraperson, where Assange lived under house arrest for a year and a half. The next place I saw him was in the dreary recesses of an embassy that is a little more than a 630-square-foot converted apartment with no outside space. It was not ideal, but better than ADMAX. Lawyers, supporters, and friends dropped in to keep him company. John Pilger, a few other friends, and I took him more than one Christmas dinner. As each month passed, his skin grew paler from lack of sunlight and his health deteriorated. Dr. Sean Love, who is part of a medical team, with Dr. Sondra Crosby of the Boston Medical Center and British psychologist Dr. Brock Chisholm, that has conducted regular evaluations of Assange since 2017, said, "He had no ability to access medical care." Love complained that the physicians were under constant electronic surveillance, a violation of the doctor–patient relationship, and the British government would not allow Assange safe passage to a hospital for urgent dental surgery. While the British tabloid press scorned Assange's hygiene, it ignored what Love called "the deleterious effects of seven years of confinement, whose risks include neuropsychological impairment, weakened bones, compromised immune function, increased risk of cardio-vascular disease and cancer." Reacting to the stories about Assange not washing, Love insisted, "This is a complete smear. This is meant to degrade his humanity." He believes that the "cumulative effect of pain and suffering inflicted on him is most definitely in violation of the 1984 Convention on Torture, specifically Articles 1 and 16."

At my last meeting this year with Assange, the energy I recall at our first encounter in January 2011 was undiminished. He made coffee, glancing up at surveillance cameras in the tiny kitchen and every other room in the embassy that recorded his every movement. We talked for about an hour, when an embassy official ordered me to leave. In between, we discussed his health, his strategy to stay out of prison, his family, and the Democratic National Committee's accusation that he colluded with President Donald Trump and Russia to hack its emails and publish them. The DNC was alleging that Assange revealed its "trade secrets," a reference to the methods the DNC used to deprive Bernie Sanders of the presidential nomination. The DNC is using the 1970 Racketeer Influenced and Corrupt

Organizations Act, meant to control organized crime, to pursue a journalist-publisher. If successful, it will set a precedent that should worry media everywhere.

Trump's personal lawyers insist that no crime was committed and therefore, no criminal conspiracy took place. That won't stop the DOJ under Trump's attorney general from pursuing criminal charges against Assange, not only for working with Manning to gain access to government secrets, but also to examine how Assange obtained confidential Defense and State Department documents, as well as the CIA's hacking program that WikiLeaks published in 2017 under the name Vault 7. London's *Guardian* newspaper, which had once cooperated with Assange, had accused him of meeting Trump's former campaign manager Paul Manafort in the embassy. Assange said, "I have never met or spoken to Paul Manafort." The embassy's logbook, signed by all visitors, had no record of Manafort.

Assange said that the restrictions and surveillance had become punitive, as there was now nowhere in the apartment that was out of range of cameras and microphones. "It's *The Truman Show*," he joked. We knew the Ecuadorians were watching, but he believed that they supplied the recordings to the US. Someone monitoring the cameras must have seen me taking notes, because an embassy official came into the room and ordered me to leave. "No journalists," Assange explained. That was our last conversation. It was Friday evening. When I left, the embassy closed, the staff left, and Assange was wholly alone until Monday morning.

The road to Belmarsh began in 2006, when WikiLeaks exposed a Somali rebel leader's attempt to assassinate government officials. Next came details of the shocking procedures at America's detention facility at the Guantánamo Bay Naval Base in Cuba. That prompted the US to shut down the WikiLeaks site, which bounced back. Assange then exposed activities of the Church of Scientology and, in 2010, the illegal misbehavior of the US armed forces in Afghanistan and Iraq—through documents in which the parties indicted themselves.

WikiLeaks' collaborators were a consortium of the world's leading newspapers: the *New York Times*, the *Guardian, El Pais* of Spain, and Paris's *Le Monde*. If Assange violated the law, they were in it with him. While redacting thousands of WikiLeaks documents to avoid identifying sensitive intelligence sources, the newspapers presented the Afghan and Iraq wars in ways that deviated from the official line. One of the best-remembered disclosures was a military video of an American helicopter crew taking delight in shooting dead two Reuters journalists and ten other civilians on the streets of Iraq. When US investigators discovered that the source of the leaks was an intelligence analyst named Bradley Manning, they arrested him in May 2010. Bradley, a transgender soldier who became Chelsea, received a 35-year sentence for espionage in August 2013. Obama commuted Manning's sentence in January 2017, leaving the Assange case open.

Among Assange's subsequent disclosures were the emails of Syrian president Bashar al-Assad, no friend of Washington. Assange was becoming a rock star of free speech. Like a rock star, he attracted groupies. So far, so normal. Then he went to Sweden, where two women denounced him to police for sexual misconduct.

Swedish police dropped the case and allowed him to leave the country, but Swedish prosecutors revisited the case and demanded that Assange return to Sweden for an interview. Sources in Swedish intelligence told me at the time that they believed the US had encouraged Sweden to pursue the case. Assange offered to be interviewed in London, where he felt safer from US extradition than in Sweden. The Swedes, while never officially charging Assange with a crime, demanded extradition. British police arrested him pending a court hearing.

Assange was placed first in jail, then under house arrest at Vaughan Smith's farm. When the court at last determined to send him to Sweden, he requested and received asylum in Ecuador's embassy. Conditions were not ideal, but the Ecuadorian president and ambassador gave him full support. Visitors, including myself, came and went. In the meantime, Sweden dropped its investigation into the women's claims. This left Assange facing only a charge of evading bail in Britain, for which he would receive only a small fine. However, if he left the embassy to report to the court, he feared the US would unseal its indictment against him and demand his extradition.

On May 24, 2017, Lenín Boltaire Moreno Garcés became president of Ecuador, and Assange's life changed. An ally of Trump in need of IMF loans, Moreno replaced the ambassador with a functionary hostile to Assange's presence in the embassy. Although the previous regime had granted Assange citizenship, based on five-plus years on what is legally Ecuadorian soil, the new government cut his Internet and telephone access and restricted his number of visitors. Embassy staff changed. The new functionaries became less cordial to visitors like myself and were visibly hostile to Assange. Then, last Thursday, Moreno cast aside the principle of political asylum and told the British police to come and get him. The US presented the indictment that Assange had said all along was waiting for him. And so Assange waits to know whether he will ever be free again, while journalists who published his leaked documents continue working without fear of prosecution and, in some cases, brandish their journalism prizes while denouncing the man who made them possible.

5. WE ARE WOMEN AGAINST RAPE BUT WE DO NOT WANT ASSANGE EXTRADITED[30]

Katrin Axelsson and Lisa Longstaff,
August 23, 2012

When Julian Assange was first arrested, we were struck by the unusual zeal with which he was being pursued for rape allegations.

It seems even clearer now that the allegations against him are a smokescreen behind which a number of governments are trying to clamp down on WikiLeaks for having audaciously revealed to the public their secret planning of wars and occupations with their attendant rape, murder, and destruction.

Justice for an accused rapist does not deny justice for his accusers. But in this case justice is being denied both to accusers and accused.

The judicial process has been corrupted. On the one hand, the names of the women have been circulated on the Internet; they have been trashed,

---

[30] This piece was originally published in the *Guardian*. Katrin Axelsson and Lisa Longstaff, "We are Women Against Rape but we do not want Julian Assange extradited," the *Guardian*, August 23, 2012, https://www.theguardian.com/commentisfree/2012/aug/23/women-against-rape-julian-assange.

accused of setting a "honey trap," and seen their allegations dismissed as "not real rape." On the other hand, Assange is dealt with by much of the media as if he were guilty, though he has not even been charged. It is not for us to decide whether or not the allegations are true and whether what happened amounts to rape or sexual violence—we don't have all the facts and what has been said so far has not been tested. But we do know that rape victims' right to anonymity and defendants' right to be presumed innocent until proven guilty are both crucial to a just judicial process.

Swedish and British courts are responsible for how the women's allegations have been handled. As with every rape case, the women are not in charge of the case, the state is.

Whether or not Assange is guilty of sexual violence, we do not believe that is why he is being pursued. Once again women's fury and frustration at the prevalence of rape and other violence is being used by politicians to advance their own purposes. The authorities care so little about violence against women that they manipulate rape allegations at will, usually to increase their powers, this time to facilitate Assange's extradition or even rendition to the US. That the US has not presented a demand for his extradition at this stage is no guarantee that they won't do so once he is in Sweden, and that he will not be tortured as Bradley Manning and many others, women and men, have. Women Against Rape cannot ignore this threat.

In over 30 years working with thousands of rape victims who are seeking asylum from rape and other forms of torture, we have met nothing but obstruction from British governments. Time after time, they have accused women of lying and deported them with no concern for their safety. We are currently working with three women who were raped again after having been deported—one of them is now destitute, struggling to survive with the child she conceived from the rape; the other managed to return to Britain and won the right to stay, and one of them won compensation.

Assange has made it clear for months that he is available for questioning by the Swedish authorities, in Britain or via Skype. Why are they refusing this essential step to their investigation? What are they afraid of?

In 1998 Chilean dictator Augusto Pinochet was arrested in London following an extradition request from Spain. His responsibility for the murder and disappearance of at least 3,000 people, and the torture of 30,000 people, including the rape and sexual abuse of more than 3,000 women, often with the use of dogs, was never in doubt. Despite a lengthy legal action and a daily picket outside Parliament called by Chilean refugees, including women who had been tortured under Pinochet, the British government reneged on its obligation to Spain's criminal justice system and Pinochet was allowed to return to Chile. Assange has not even been charged, yet the determination to have him extradited is much greater than ever it was with Pinochet. (Baltasar Garzón, whose request for extradition of Pinochet was denied, is representing Assange.) And there is a history of Sweden (and Britain) rendering asylum seekers at risk of torture at the behest of the US.

Like women in Sweden and everywhere, we want rapists caught, charged, and convicted. We have campaigned for that for more than 35 years, with limited success. We are even having to campaign to prevent rape victims being accused of making false allegations and imprisoned for it. Two women who reported visibly violent attacks by strangers were given two- and three-year prison sentences.

But does anyone really believe that extraditing Julian Assange will strengthen women against rape? And do those supporting his extradition to Sweden care if he is then extradited to the US and tortured for telling the public what we need to know about those who govern us?

6. UNPUBLISHED LETTER ON ARREST OF ASSANGE

Lisa Longstaff, May 20, 2019

Dear Editor,

Whether or not Assange is guilty of a sexual offense, it is shocking that 70-plus MPs calling for his extradition to Sweden in the name of justice refuse to take a position on his possible extradition to the US and the torture and even death he may face there.

We agree with Shadow Home Secretary Diane Abbott: Assange's current detention is not about "the rape charges, serious as they are, it is about WikiLeaks and all of that embarrassing information about the activities of the American military and security services that was made public." And so it was from the beginning.

Chelsea Manning (currently reimprisoned despite President Obama having commuted her sentence) was able to use WikiLeaks to expose the extensive cover-up of rape, other sexual violence and murder, including of women and children, by the US military in Afghanistan, Bosnia, and Iraq. Do these victims not count?

At the time of the original allegations against Assange, we pointed to the unusual zeal with which he was being pursued (*Guardian* December 19, 2010, and August 23, 2012). The UK's low conviction rate—6 percent of reported rapes, and falling—resulting largely from negligent and biased investigations, speaks volumes about how rape is generally downgraded.

The MPs' letter claims that Sweden dropped their investigation because of Assange's "unavailability." Untrue. We and others urged the Swedish authorities to question him at the Ecuadorian embassy so his accusers would not be denied the investigation they were entitled to and justice could be done. They refused until December 2015, when they finally did. They then dropped the case. No charge was ever made.

Where is the letter demanding justice for the rapes and murders WikiLeaks exposed? Who will speak up for these victims if whistle-blowers are silenced? In 2004, together with Black Women Rape Action Project, we wrote to women MPs about the war crimes and torture, including rape, that were being committed in Iraq and Afghanistan. We received no reply.

Yours sincerely,

Lisa Longstaff,

Women Against Rape

Since this letter was submitted to the Guardian, *the US government has initiated extradition proceedings against Assange for "espionage," and the Swedish authorities have reopened their investigation into one of the women's allegations.*

7. WIKILEAKS AND THE DEMOCRATS

Kevin Gosztola, May 2019

The Democratic Party's contempt for WikiLeaks reinforces a political consensus, which enables the targeting of WikiLeaks and its editor in chief Julian Assange by President Donald Trump's Justice Department. Most Democrats believe Assange and the organization's staff conspired with the Russian government against Hillary Clinton by publishing emails from her presidential campaign. In 2018, the Democratic National Committee (DNC) sued WikiLeaks, along with the Russian Federation and the Trump campaign.

Since 2018, Democrats and Republicans have considered intelligence authorization bills with the following language: "It is the sense of Congress that WikiLeaks and the senior leadership of WikiLeaks resemble a non-state hostile intelligence service often abetted by state actors and should be treated as such a service by the United States."

This language is rooted in attitudes shared by officials in US intelligence agencies, but alleged Russian election interference did not turn Democrats against WikiLeaks. Hostility from Democrats initially developed when the media organization published over a half-million documents from the Pentagon and State Department disclosed by Pfc. Chelsea Manning in 2010.

Back then, Democrats and many individuals connected to the Clinton campaign did not think WikiLeaks could possibly be a legitimate media organization. Most US media organizations typically do not publish entire caches of leaked documents for the entire world to read. And those same media organizations often identify with the foreign policy agenda of the US government. Journalists may question how the government pursues wars and how officials maintain geopolitical dominance. But they rarely subject the entire imperial project to scrutiny, questioning whether America's actions are just and appropriate.

WikiLeaks' publication of documents on the wars in Afghanistan and Iraq took matters the Democratic Party leadership did not want to debate and opened Democrats up to pressure from their progressive base. Historically, Democrats are far more willing to tolerate right-wing criticism from Republicans, who often argue that they are not tough enough on national security. Yet, the party establishment deplores challenges from the left that force them to openly consider an antiwar agenda.

Cold War liberalism dominates the party. Though Democrats may have won a wave of election victories in 2006 by opposing the Iraq War, party leaders never intended to end the war. They merely wanted a shift in policy that would help the nation-building operation run more smoothly, and by the 2008 presidential election, Democratic candidates were unwilling to put forward a timetable for troop withdrawals.

This ideology fueled a Democratic presidential administration's response to WikiLeaks—one which viewed their publications as an attack on the national security of the United States. President Barack Obama called WikiLeaks' actions "deplorable." Vice President Joe Biden argued if Assange "conspired to get these classified documents with a member of the US military, that's fundamentally different than if someone drops [documents] on your lap" and says, "you're a press person. Here's classified material."

Biden agreed with Republican Senate Majority Leader Mitch McConnell that Assange was much closer to a "high-tech terrorist" than a journalist.

Responding to the release of US diplomatic cables as secretary of state, Hilary Clinton declared "This disclosure is not just an attack on America's foreign policy interests. It is an attack on the international community—the alliances and partnerships, the conversations and negotiations, that safeguard global security and advance economic prosperity."

Attorney General Eric Holder said this was not "saber-rattling" and announced an "active, ongoing, criminal investigation" into WikiLeaks. He treated the organization as if it was different from traditional radio, television, or newspaper organizations that are protected by the First Amendment of the US Constitution. Senator Dianne Feinstein, a powerful Democrat who was elected in California in 1992 and chaired the Senate Select Committee on Intelligence, wrote a column for the *Wall Street Journal*, where she called for Assange to be "vigorously prosecuted for espionage."

"The law Mr. Assange continues to violate is the Espionage Act of 1917," she contended. Feinstein also claimed it was a felony to not "return such materials to the US government," and "courts have held that 'information relating to the national defense' applies to both classified and unclassified material." It was a terribly extreme interpretation of the law.

Like Holder, Feinstein refused to accept Julian Assange's deserved First Amendment protections. "He is no journalist. He is an agitator intent on damaging our government, whose policies he happens to disagree with, regardless of who gets hurt."

"I agree with the Pentagon's assessment that the people at WikiLeaks could have blood on their hands," said Senator Joe Lieberman, an influential, centrist independent who caucused with the Democrats and chaired the Senate Homeland Security Committee. "It sure looks to me that Assange and WikiLeaks have violated the Espionage Act."

Lieberman waged a campaign to shut down WikiLeaks. Staff for Lieberman contacted Amazon, and the company removed WikiLeaks from its servers. He hoped Amazon would "send a message to other companies that might host WikiLeaks that it would be irresponsible to host the site." Visa, Mastercard, and PayPal followed Amazon's lead and cut off donations to WikiLeaks submitted through their payment processors. As activists engaged in denial of service attacks or digital sit-ins against the websites of these corporations, Lieberman praised their censorship.

"We offer our admiration and support to those companies exhibiting courage and patriotism as they face down intimidation from hackers sympathetic to WikiLeaks' philosophy of irresponsible information dumps for the sake of damaging global relationships," Lieberman stated.

According to a "Manhunting Timeline,"[31] which was revealed by NSA whistleblower Edward Snowden, security agencies under Obama even encouraged Australia, the United Kingdom, Germany, and other countries to file criminal charges against Assange.

There were a few voices of reason, however. Democratic Representative John Conyers, chair of the House Judiciary Committee, held a hearing on December 16, 2010, on the Espionage Act and WikiLeaks.

"The repeated calls from members of Congress, the government, journalists, and other experts crying out for criminal prosecutions, or other

---

[31] Kevin Gosztola, "'Manhunting Timeline' Further Suggests US Pressured Countries to Prosecute WikiLeaks Editor-In-Chief," *Shadowproof*, February 18, 2014, https://shadowproof.com/2014/02/18/manhunting-timeline-further-suggests-us-pressured-countries-to-prosecute-wikileaks-editor-in-chief/.

extreme measures, cause me some consternation," Conyers said. "Indeed, when everyone in this town has joined together calling for someone's head, it's a pretty sure sign that we might want to slow down and take a closer look."

In July 2010, Democratic Representatives Dennis Kucinich and Lynn Woolsey saw the Afghan War Logs as reason to cut off funding for the war. Yet, overwhelmingly, Democrats were unmoved by the contents of the documents. They remained committed to pursuing war and occupation in Afghanistan and Iraq. They stayed silent as the Obama administration pursued action against WikiLeaks.

Democrats maintained that WikiLeaks publications were not like the Pentagon Papers disclosed by Daniel Ellsberg, a whistleblower who worked for the Rand Corporation and exposed how US government officials were lying to Americans about the Vietnam War. Ellsberg disagreed. "That's just a cover for people who don't want to admit that they oppose any and all exposure of even the most misguided, secretive foreign policy," Ellsberg declared. "The truth is that *every* attack now made on WikiLeaks and Julian Assange was made against me and the release of the Pentagon Papers at the time."

Eventually, the Obama administration realized in 2013 that it had what it called the *"New York Times* problem." Prosecutors at the Justice Department could not prosecute Assange without exposing journalists at the *Times* or *Washington Post* to potential prosecutions for publishing classified information. But this realization within the Justice Department barely tempered the zeal in which Obama administration officials fought to protect secrets on behalf of the national security apparatus.

As journalist Jonathan Alter recounted in his book, *The Promise: President Obama, Year One,* Obama "made a point of saying" during his first Cabinet meeting that he did not want to "litigate" policy "through the *New York Times* and the *Washington Post.*" When officials spoke to journalists about the Afghanistan War later in 2009, he once again complained about leaks.

In 2009, President Obama had provisions of a drafted shield law[32] removed that would have protected journalists from jail if they refused to reveal confidential sources who leaked information related to "national security." The move effectively killed the shield law.

The Obama administration took the rare step of renewing a subpoena against *New York Times* reporter James Risen a year later. They attempted to force him into revealing and testifying against one of the alleged sources of information for his book, *State Of War: The Secret History of the CIA and the Bush Administration*. Risen fought the subpoena and took his case all the way to the Supreme Court. When the Supreme Court rejected his appeal, he was faced with potential jail time.[33]

For leaking, the Justice Department under Obama charged a record number of individuals with Espionage Act violations. They believed that anyone leaking classified information was engaged in espionage, even if that person was not a spy working on behalf of a foreign power. Officials turned violating the Espionage Act into a strict liability offense. It did not matter if one intended to cause injury to the US or not. A Defense Department strategy document from June 1, 2012, stated, "Leaking is tantamount to aiding the enemies of the United States." Simply disclosing classified information made one a felon who could be jailed for up to ten years for each offense.

---

[32] Donal Brown, "Obama administration wants national security exemption in federal shield law," *First Ammendment Coalition*, October 2, 2009, https://firsta-mendmentcoalition.org/2009/10/obama-administration-wants-national-securi-ty-exemption-in-federal-shield-law/.

[33] James Risen, "My Life as a New York Times Reporter in the Shadow of the War on Terror," *The Intercept*, January 3, 2018, https://theintercept.com/2018/01/03/my-life-as-a-new-york-times-reporter-in-the-shadow-of-the-war-on-terror/.

Former NSA employee Thomas Drake, former CIA officer John Kiriakou, former FBI linguist Shamai Leibowitz, and former CIA officer Jeffrey Sterling, as well as Manning and Snowden, were among the individuals targeted.

WikiLeaks' publications in 2010 led the Obama administration to launch an "insider threat" program. It was described in McClatchy Newspapers as an "unprecedented initiative" that extended "beyond the US national security bureaucracies." The program relied upon a "catchall definition" of "insider threat" to enable agencies to "pursue and penalize a range of other conduct" in addition to classified information leaks.

Manning became a prime example of an "insider threat," according to a file from 2014.[34] She wrote, "The broad sweep of the program means officials have been given a blank check for surveillance. Agencies implementing the Insider Threat program could examine anyone who has motives of 'greed,' 'financial difficulties,' is 'disgruntled,' has 'an ideology,' a 'divided loyalty,' an 'ego' or 'self-image,' or 'any family/personal issues'—the words used to describe my motives. Such subjective labeling could easily be applied to virtually every single person currently holding a security clearance."

Senator Ron Wyden was a lone voice in the Democratic Party, who warned, "Any monitoring of employees' 'electronic behavior on the job as well as off the job' needs to include safeguards to prevent the chilling of legitimate whistleblower communications and protect the confidentiality of any legally privileged information."

All along Democrats allowed a climate of fear to grow within federal agencies. Instead of keeping fewer secrets, they panicked over a breach of the secrecy system and encouraged national security officials to expand

---

[34] Ed Pilkington, "Chelsea Manning: government anti-leak program a 'blank check for surveillance,' *The Guardian*, March 18, 2016, https://www.theguardian.com/us-news/2016/mar/18/chelsea-manning-insider-threat-surveillance-government-employees.

their capabilities to control the free flow of information. That also meant more tools would be available to shield officials from scrutiny for abuses of power.

WikiLeaks published emails from individuals who worked for the DNC in July 2016. Months later, in October, the organization followed that publication with the release of emails from Clinton campaign chairman John Podesta's account. Staff of Clinton's presidential campaign immediately contended the publication was part of a Russian plot, and several campaign individuals said WikiLeaks had published "forged" emails without providing any evidence. Jennifer Palmieri, the campaign's director of communications, warned, "Friends, please remember if you see a whopper of a WikiLeaks in [the] next two days—it's probably a fake."

WikiLeaks was "dribbling" the emails out in the run-up to Election Day because the Russians were intervening on behalf of Trump, Podesta claimed.

As of March 2019, there was nothing but circumstantial evidence[35] that tied WikiLeaks to Russia. Seventeen US intelligence agencies claimed the emails were connected to Russian hacking, however, in January 2017, Assange raised doubts. "The US intelligence community is not aware of when WikiLeaks obtained its material or when the sequencing of our material was done or how we obtained our material directly. So there seems to be a great fog in the connection to WikiLeaks," he asserted.

"The Podesta emails that we released during the election dated up to March [2016]," Assange added. "US intelligence services and consultants for the DNC say Russian intelligence services started hacking DNC in 2015. Now, Trump is clearly not on the horizon in any substantial manner in 2015."

---

[35] John Kruzel, "Is WikiLeaks Russia's 'useful idiot,' its 'agent of influence,' or something else?" *PolitiFact*, March 18, 2019, https://www.politifact.com/truth-o-meter/article/2019/mar/18/wikileaks-russias-useful-idiot-its-agent-influence/.

That did not stop former Clinton campaign officials like Zac Petkanas, who was the rapid response director, from stating in April 2017, "WikiLeaks is not journalism. It's an arm of the Russian intelligence service." Neera Tanden, the president of the Center for American Progress who was part of Clinton's circle of aides during her campaign, asserted in January 2018, "Every reporter who gleefully trafficked in stolen emails via WikiLeaks abetted a crime. Not illegal activity by itself but unethical and immoral."

Representative Hakeem Jeffries, who appeared on news programs as a surrogate for Clinton, stated during a congressional hearing, "WikiLeaks has repeatedly published information designed to damage the United States," and later added, "WikiLeaks is the *enemy* of the state."

In early 2017, Assange was willing to "provide technical evidence and discussion regarding who did not engage in the DNC releases."[36] He also was willing—before the release of "Vault 7" materials[37] from the CIA—to help US agencies address "clear flaws in security systems" that led the US cyber weapons program to be compromised. When Democratic Senator Mark Warner learned Justice Department official Bruce Ohr was negotiating some kind of a deal for limited immunity and a limited commitment from Assange, he urged FBI Director James Comey to intervene.

A potential deal with Assange was killed, and no testimony was ever collected that would have helped the public better understand what happened with the DNC and Clinton campaign email publications.

The Podesta emails exposed excerpts of Clinton's paid speeches to Goldman Sachs, efforts to rig parts of the Democratic primary in favor of Clinton, proposals for turning voters against Democratic presidential

---

[36] John Solomon, "How Comey intervened to kill WikiLeaks' immunity deal," *The Hill*, June 25, 2018, https://thehill.com/opinion/white-house/394036-How-Comey-intervened-to-kill-Wikileaks-immunity-deal.

[37] "Vault 7: CIA Hacking Tools Revealed," *WikiLeaks*, March 7, 2017, https://wikileaks.org/ciav7p1/.

candidate Bernie Sanders, and Clinton's duplicity when it came to key progressive issues, like trade, clean energy, and raising the minimum wage. It opened the Democratic Party establishment to a sharp backlash from their base of voters, particularly when Trump was gaining momentum in the polls, and for that reason, former Clinton campaign officials were compelled to slander WikiLeaks.

Following Assange's expulsion from the Ecuador embassy and arrest on April 11, the Justice Department unsealed an indictment that generally criminalized his involvement in publishing classified US government documents. It alleged that Assange committed a computer crime but incorporated parts of the Espionage Act into the charge against him—the same law the Obama administration wielded aggressively to crackdown on leaks.

Democrats like Warner were pleased. "Assange has long professed high ideals and moral superiority. Unfortunately, whatever his intentions when he started WikiLeaks, what he's really become is a direct participant in Russian efforts to undermine the West and a dedicated accomplice in efforts to undermine American security." Warner added, "It is my hope that British courts will quickly transfer him to US custody so he can finally get the justice he deserves."

Although Assange is not an American, Democratic senator Joe Manchin imperiously declared, "It will be really good to get him back on United States soil. He is our property, and we can get the facts and the truth from him." On *Pod Save The World*, Ben Rhodes, former deputy national security advisor for strategic communications for the Obama administration, articulated his opposition to Assange and provided the clearest articulation of why Democrats endorse prosecution.

"The motivation [to release cables] was just to embarrass the United States and the United States government," Rhodes contended. "Even if you're not a fan of US foreign policy or the United States government, that's just a different motivation than a journalist wanting to shine a light on abuse or corruption, and it's something that we have to reckon with, that it endangers people's lives."

In other words, because Assange has never identified with the foreign policy agenda of the US government, his motives are "anti-American" and aligned with any US adversaries. It is an alarming perspective that casually dismisses the threat prosecuting Assange poses to dissident journalism around the world.

Ten days before Assange's expulsion and arrest, Holder appeared on MSNBC's *The Beat* hosted by Ari Melber. He was asked whether the government, particularly the Trump administration, should be in the business of deciding whether an organization like WikiLeaks is a legitimate media organization when the *Times* publishes similar information. Holder insisted WikiLeaks had "operated in concert with the Russian government." He argued if someone is acting at the behest of a foreign power, that person is in a fundamentally different position and should not be treated as a journalist.

Widespread and largely unsubstantiated allegations that WikiLeaks was a Russian asset have nothing to do with the journalism in 2010 that is targeted by the Trump administration. Nevertheless, Democrats hold out hope they can extradite Assange and avenge Clinton's loss in the 2016 election.

If the Trump Justice Department succeeds in prosecuting Assange, or any other staff member of WikiLeaks, it will be made possible by the complicity or rhetorical support from Democrats.

8. THE NAÏVETÉ OF JULIAN ASSANGE

Margaret Kimberley, April 2019

The importance of Julian Assange's role as a journalist, publisher, and whistleblower cannot be overstated. He and the WikiLeaks organization consistently revealed information that powerful interests all over the world wanted to hide. Assange challenged the United States at a moment when its military power was preeminent. The invasion of Iraq in 2003 was the evil yet logical consequence of the collapse of the Soviet Union twelve years earlier. The old rules of spheres of influence were over in what temporarily became a unipolar world. There was no place on the planet that the United States didn't claim as its own. That meant anyone who took meaningful action against the hegemon would be declared an enemy and treated as harshly as possible.

The invasion of Iraq was carried out under a humanitarian guise and was covered by media "embedded" with the military. By definition they were compromised and complicit in the aggressions of the United States and other nations dubbed "the coalition of the willing."

The embedding process meant that the public were deprived of the ability to see war as the hell that it is. Julian Assange brought to light an atrocity which would have been unknown without the involvement of WikiLeaks. The "Collateral Murder" video showed in brutal detail the killing of twelve people, including two journalists, an attack on a family with small children and gloating, vicious American servicemen laughing at the killings they committed.

The vendetta and persecution of Chelsea Manning and Assange following the release are horrific examples of abuse by the state. But these actions are not at all surprising at this juncture in history. The imperative of an empire dictates that Assange would be targeted by the United States and by its vassals like the United Kingdom who will brook no opposition to their rule. The peculiarities of American politics result in Assange and Manning being vilified by people who ought to be their defenders.

Assange presents a paradox. He was obviously aware of the corruption and the inherent dangers presented by the state during late stage capitalism and the inevitable resurgence of imperialist policies. There would be no reason for a WikiLeaks to exist at all if Assange didn't know that the corporate media have very direct connections with elites and with intelligence agencies. They have no intention of divulging anything the public really needs to know or allowing anyone else to do so if they can possibly prevent it.

But apparently Assange didn't understand the true nature of corruption in the United States. He didn't realize what it meant for him to say that the difference between Hillary Clinton and Donald Trump was a choice between "cholera or gonorrhea." Those words created an enmity which exists to this day and prevents people whose politics would otherwise make them his defenders from speaking on his behalf.

True collusion began with the Democratic National Committee (DNC). The DNC violated its own rules of neutrality when it placed its thumb on the scale for Hillary Clinton as Bernie Sanders made his surprisingly strong showing against her. The depths of corruption in the supposedly democratic United States were exposed when WikiLeaks revealed the contents of DNC emails. The emails showed a party that rigged its system and ensured that Clinton would win the Democratic Party nomination even as Sanders's ascendance indicated a loss of support for her.

Hillary Clinton's defeat in November 2016 was not the fault of the Russian government, Julian Assange, or anyone else outside of the party apparatus. Trump's victory was the day of reckoning after years of the Democrats sabotaging their voters' interests. They had already suffered a calamitous loss of more than 1,000 seats in state legislatures and Congress during Barack Obama's administration. Thanks to Democratic Party fealty to corporate interests, they made little effort to win anything except the presidency, which they primarily view as a deal-making apparatus. In his last term Obama presided over a Senate and House of Representatives that were under Republican control. Neither he nor the rest of the party leadership were particularly concerned about what should have been a scandalous turn of events. The idea that they really want change is a story they tell the people who are deliberately kept uninformed.

America is a country that runs on political sleight of hand meant to engender popular support while not doing very much to address the needs of the people. It is ruled by a far-right party and a center-right party who are willing to work together while making millions of people believe otherwise. Anyone who calls this arrangement into question is attacked and demonized and the condemnation is more likely to come from Democrats than from Republicans. That is because their image as the party of fairness and inclusivity is most at risk when the truth is told.

The surveillance state is an integral part of these insider dealings. The illusion of a free press in a democracy is assiduously maintained, especially when the lie becomes more and more important to cultivate. Once Assange involved himself in the 2016 presidential election he was doomed. It isn't clear if he predicted a Trump victory, but having already gained the enmity of the Democrats he was a sitting duck as he sat helpless in the Ecuadorian embassy.

The United States is very protective of its illusion of democracy. The system won't work well if anyone is permitted to lift the veil of lies. Assange was partly correct when he said there was no difference between Trump and Clinton. There was certainly no difference between them in their view of keeping America in charge of foreign policy decisions which impact the rest of the world. Hillary Clinton had a long history of stating her belief that American might made right. During her 2008 presidential campaign she spoke of Iran's non-existent nuclear weapons and said, "We would obliterate them," if Israel, the country that actually has nukes, were under her imaginary Iranian attack.

Hillary Clinton not only led the United States and NATO destruction of Libya in 2011, but she bragged about her efforts. She famously and shamelessly laughed about the brutal murder of Libyan president Muammar Gaddafi which was recorded and viewed around the world. She said, "We came, we saw, he died," as she cackled at her own bad joke.

Donald Trump was the unknown quantity who gave conflicting accounts of his world view. He spoke of his desire to keep America the world's foremost military power. He often boiled down complex foreign policy decisions to simple words such as, "We should take the oil." He claimed he would withdraw troops from Syria and said he wouldn't support regime change efforts. Yet as president he was dissuaded from undertaking a Syria troop withdrawal plan and he is attempting a coup against Venezuela.

Hillary Clinton was and is a true believer in the empire, and during the 2016 campaign she spoke of establishing a no-fly zone over Syria, a country allied with the other major nuclear power, the Russian Federation. Her willingness to provoke conflict made her no better than Trump in this regard. Her history as a United States senator and as secretary of state proved that a Clinton presidency would have had disastrous consequences for the world. Assange was correct in this aspect of their policy positions.

But the issues of concern to Julian Assange are not the only issues of concern to American voters. Donald Trump's victory was a shock and a trauma to millions of people. The vagaries of the very undemocratic Electoral College system gave the presidency to the person who actually garnered fewer votes. Trump's open racism, xenophobia, Islamophobia, and misogyny make him perhaps the most despised president of the modern era. More than half of the country hates him and still can't understand how he ended up in the White House. Tales of foreign intrigue are comforting to people still in a state of shock and anger that the impossible scenario became a reality.

This hostility to Trump is now extended to Julian Assange. Assange fell victim to the deep links between the Democratic Party, corporate media, and intelligence agencies. Former CIA director Michael Morell publicly endorsed Hillary Clinton in a *New York Times* op-ed. She was the choice of the *New York Times*, the *Washington Post*, CNN, and MSNBC and they did not take her defeat lying down. They certainly didn't reveal how Democratic Party corruption and the resulting incompetence allowed Trump to squeak through. They joined in the propaganda campaign to absolve the Democrats of guilt in the debacle they made for themselves. Julian Assange became one of their favorite targets.

It is partially true that there are no differences between the Republicans and the Democrats. Both parties are capitalist and imperialist. Both favor the needs of ruling class interests. While the issues which separate them are fewer and fewer, there is enough difference to mark Assange as an enemy when his revelations were directed against the Democrats.

The Democratic Party is the one which markets itself as the party of inclusion. Its record in regard to fighting for equality and justice has been rather sparse since the days of the Black American-led liberation movement in the 1960s. But the Republicans reacted to that movement by becoming the white people's party and openly courting racist voters. They work to undermine legislation and policies that are meant to provide protection against discrimination. They gain office with voter suppression tactics and outright vote theft which nullify black citizens' preference for Democratic candidates.

Declaring that there ought to be a pox on both houses made Assange an enemy not just of the elites who hate him, but of ordinary people as well. The time when Assange gained some admiration from liberals who believe in the cause of the whistleblower is now over. Three years of lies have convinced them that he is to blame for the very existence of a Trump presidency.

Many leftist and leftish Americans are well aware of the Democratic Party's shortcomings. They hold true to the old dictum, "Hold your nose and vote," for Democratic candidates. It is easy for an outsider like Assange to miss this contradictory but very real impulse. He may not have cared who won the election, but millions of people did and have now vented their anger at anyone who is seen as being responsible for Clinton's loss.

Democrats often treat politics like some sort of religion. Because they are constantly fooled by duplicity from the political duopoly they are forced to boil down their allegiance to seeing their side as the good one. It isn't hard to see how that happens. Republicans welcome the racists and the homophobes. They are open about wanting to end immigration from the global south. Democrats can then have it both ways. Bill Clinton ended a 60-year right to federal public assistance and yet was lauded as the last bulwark against the right wing. Barack Obama made the Bush-era temporary tax cuts to the wealthy permanent and bailed out the banks who caused the 2008 financial crisis. In his case, racist attacks from those further to the right cemented his position as the savior that Democrats wanted him to be.

The charge that Assange hacked into the DNC computers with the help of Russian assets has been repeated endlessly and is often stated as fact and not allegation. There is no independent corroboration of the DNC version of events and also compelling evidence that WikiLeaks gained access to the documents from an individual within the DNC who leaked them. Former British diplomat Craig Murray has publicly stated that he has spoken to the person who is responsible. The Veterans Intelligence Professionals for Sanity (VIPS) corroborate Murray's version of events. VIPS members are former Central Intelligence Agency and National Security Agency staffers. They make the case that download speeds prove that the DNC emails were loaded onto a flash drive and were not stolen via hacking of a computer system. But the professional credibility of individuals means nothing if the corporate media exclude this information from their readers and viewers.

Despite three years of charges that Trump colluded with Russia, it is the Democratic Party which brought domestic and foreign intelligence assets into the presidential campaign. The DNC paid for former MI6 asset Christopher Steele to produce opposition research to discredit Trump and they did so before their computer systems were compromised. That fact gets little attention from Assange's enemies in the corporate media and deprives him of much needed public support.

Hillary Clinton had her own secrets to keep. As secretary of state she refrained from using her agency's server system and instead secretly kept a server in her home. She wanted to hide her own double-dealing with the international-influence-peddling slush fund known as the Clinton Foundation. She needed to find or create dirt on Donald Trump in order to hide her own.

The investigation overseen by special counsel Robert Mueller is over without any American being indicted for colluding with Russia during the 2016 campaign. But that finding was reached without any attempt to speak to Assange. One can only conclude that Mueller and his associates know that neither Assange nor Russian agents hacked anything. Speaking to Assange in person would have revealed what intelligence assets like Mueller want to keep hidden.

So Assange remains a public enemy in the eyes of millions of people. He is cut off from the world and is unable to mount a public defense. Only people determined to seek out independent sources of information know that the story of a hack is the very definition of a big lie. The deception is by design. The investigation of Trump campaign collusion is over but not the demonization of Russia. Now the story can morph into a claim that Russia acted independently to undermine the United States and that it did so with the help of a man who can't speak for himself.

Manning and Assange are not just targets of the government. They have exposed the hollowness of American liberalism. The same people who make a great show of supporting rights for transgender people give Chelsea Manning the back of their hand and call her a traitor. Concerns about the rights of whistleblowers and journalists are forgotten in the case of Julian Assange because he is blamed for Hillary Clinton's loss.

Assange has not helped himself with his uninformed musings that offended many people. While he still had Internet access he would pose controversial questions on the Twitter platform. In one instance he questioned the need to fight the American Civil War. "Surely more tools to kill slavery than killing 2.3% of the pop [sic]."[38] He apparently was unaware that the Confederacy started the war and steadfastly refused to end slavery. He

---

[38]   Defend Assange Campaign, Twitter post, September 22, 2017, 8:45 a.m., https://twitter.com/DefendAssange/status/911209732060233728.

received mostly negative responses which not only corrected his lack of knowledge, such as from this writer, but which also called him a Putin puppet and a Trump supporter.

For five years the Ecuadorians allowed Assange access to the Internet. But he didn't seem to understand that his asylum was still a kind of imprisonment. The leak of the DNC emails was entirely defensible and would have been a historical footnote if Hillary Clinton had won. But she didn't win and Assange became entangled in something far greater than he anticipated.

What little is left of American democracy depends upon the existence of a free and independent press. Julian Assange must be defended for that reason. He must be defended precisely because the ruling elites want him locked up. His willingness to show us what war looks like or how trade agreements deprive millions of people of their rights make him an ally not just as a person but an ally of the principles Americans claim to care about.

The extradition effort must be vigorously opposed by anyone who claims to care about press freedom or democracy. Assange cannot get a fair trial in this country. Whistleblowers never do. They and their attorneys are deprived of any meaningful defense and the court of public opinion is stacked against them.

But future whistleblowers must beware. The continued persecution of Assange and Manning is akin to the medieval warning of a head stuck on a post. They are made examples to anyone who considers following in their footsteps. This system is brutal and unforgiving and good intention won't save anyone. Perhaps the Assanges of the world are by nature naïve and idealistic. They must know that we live at a moment when ideals will be punished if they anger the wrong people and that wrong people are the ones who are in charge.

9. IF JULIAN GOES . . .

Vivienne Westwood, June 2019

Misrule of law is now global; all governments use it for their own protection. The American government has charged Julian Assange; the charge is that it is a crime to publish American war crimes. They have invented a sentence of 175 years in concrete. Public opinion is crucial in demolishing this situation. I have known Julian for all the nine years he's been trapped, first by the Swedish government and then the British government, who have contrived to hold him for America while America prepared its case.

My job as an activist is to demolish the narrative that has been constructed by spin and the media. The smear has been fabricated by allegation on allegation and innuendo. The establishment control the narrative. Maybe they would like to tell a different story; how about the truth?

The UN construes the time Julian was entrapped as torture—the lack of space, air, and sunshine—during which his health was undermined. They also consider destruction of someone's reputation as torture. His treatment is not only a crime against Julian, but a loss for society. Julian is a noble freedom fighter and an aspiration. If Julian goes then responsible journalism goes with him.

10. JULIAN ASSANGE MUST NEVER BE EXTRADITED[39]

Matt Taibbi, May 30, 2019

WikiLeaks founder Julian Assange today sits in the Belmarsh high-security prison in southeast London. Not just for his sake but for everyone's, we now have to hope he's never moved from there to America.

The United States filed charges against Assange early last month. The case seemed to have been designed to assuage fears that speech freedoms or the press were being targeted.

That specific offense was "computer hacking conspiracy" from back in 2010. The "crime" was absurdly thin, a claim that Assange agreed (but failed, apparently) to try to help Chelsea Manning develop an administrative password that could have helped her conceal her identity as she downloaded secrets. One typewritten phrase, "No luck so far," was the damning piece of evidence.

---

[39] This column was originally published in Rolling Stone. Matt Taibbi, "Julian Assange Must Never Be Extradited," Rolling Stone, May 30, 2019, https://www. rollingstone.com/politics/politics-features/wikileaks-julian- assange-extradited-taibbi-842292/.

The troubling parts of that case lurked in the rest of the indictment, which seemed to sell normal journalistic activity as part of the offense. The government complained that Assange "took measures to conceal Manning as the source of the disclosure." Prosecutors likewise said, "Assange encouraged Manning to provide information and records from departments and agencies of the United States."

The indictment stressed Assange/Manning were seeking "national defense information" that could be "used to the injury of the United States." The indictment likewise noted that the pair had been guilty of transmitting such information to "any person not entitled to receive it."

It was these passages that made me nervous a month and a half ago, because they seemed to speak to a larger ambition. Use of phrases like "national defense information" given to persons "not entitled to receive it" gave off a strong whiff of Britain's Official Secrets Acts,[40] America's Defense Secrets Act of 1911 (which prohibited "national defense" information going to "those not entitled to receive it") and our Espionage Act of 1917, which retained many of the same concepts.

All of these laws were written in a way that plainly contradicted basic free speech protections. The Espionage Act was revised in 1950 by the McCarran Internal Security Act,[41] sponsored by Nevada Senator Pat McCarran (who incidentally was said to be the inspiration for the corrupt "Senator Pat Geary" character in *The Godfather*). The change potentially removed a requirement that the person obtaining classified information had to have intent to harm the country.

---

[40] "Official Secrets Act 1889," *Wikipedia*, https://en.wikipedia.org/wiki/Official_Secrets_Act_1889.

[41] "McCarran Internal Security Act," *Wikipedia*, https://en.wikipedia.org/wiki/McCarran_Internal_Security_Act.

There was a way to read the new law that criminalized what the *Columbia Law Review* back in 1973 (during the Pentagon Papers controversy) called the "mere retention" of classified material.

This provision buried in subsection 793 of the Espionage Law has, since passage, been a ticking time bomb for journalism. The law seems clearly to permit the government to prosecute anyone who simply obtains or receives "national defense" information. This would place not only sources who steal and deliver such information at risk of prosecution, but also the journalists who receive and publish it.

If the government ever decided to start using this tool to successfully prosecute reporters and publishers, we'd pretty quickly have no reporters and publishers.

I'm not exaggerating when I say virtually every reporter who's ever done national security reporting has at some time or another looked at, or been told, or actually received copies of, "national defense" information they were technically "not entitled to receive."

Anyone who covers the military, the intelligence community, or certain congressional committees, will eventually stumble—even just by accident—into this terrain sooner or later. Even I've been there, and I've barely done any reporting in that space.

This is why the latest indictment handed down in the Assange case has been met with almost universal horror across the media, even by outlets that spent much of the last two years denouncing Assange as a Russian cutout who handed Trump the presidency.

The 18-count indictment is an authoritarian's dream, the work of attorneys who probably thought the Sedition Act was good law and the Red Scare-era Palmer raids a good start. The "conspiracy to commit computer intrusion" is there again, as the eighteenth count. But counts 1–17 are all subsection 793 charges, and all are worst-case-scenario interpretations of the Espionage Act as pertains to both the receipt and publication of secrets.

Look at the language:

Count 1: Conspiracy to *Receive* National Defense Information. Counts 2–4: *Obtaining* National Defense Information. Counts 5–8: *Obtaining* National Defense Information. And so on.

The indictment is an insane tautology. It literally charges Assange with conspiracy to obtain secrets for the purpose of obtaining them. It lists the following "offense":

> To obtain documents, writings, and notes connected with the national defense, for the purpose of obtaining information respecting the national defense...

Slowly—it's incredible how slowly—it is dawning on much of the press that this case is not just an effort to punish a Russiagate villain, but instead a deadly serious effort to use Assange as a pawn in a broad authoritarian crackdown.

The very news outlets that have long blasted Donald Trump for his hostility to press freedoms are finally coming around to realize that this case is the ultimate example of all of their fears.

Hence even the *Washington Post*, no friend of Assange's of late, is now writing this indictment could "criminalize investigative journalism." CNN wrote, "What is at stake is journalism as we know it."

It became clear that this is a genuine effort to expand the ability of the US government to put a vice-grip on classified information, scare whistleblowers into silence, and scare the pants off editors across the planet.

The Assange case is more than the narrow prosecution of one controversial person. This is a crossroads moment for the whole world, for speech, reporting, and transparent governance.

It is happening in an era when the hegemonic US government has been rapidly expanding a kind of oversight-free zone within its federal bureaucracy, with whole ranges of activities—from drone killings to intelligence budgets to surveillance—often placed outside the scope of either Congress or the courts.

One of the few outlets left that offered any hope of penetrating this widening veil of secrecy was the press, working in conjunction with the whistleblower. If that relationship is criminalized, self-censorship will become the norm, and abuses will surely multiply as a result.

Add to this the crazy fact that the Assange indictment targets a foreigner whose "crimes" were committed on foreign soil, and the British government now bears a very heavy responsibility. If it turns Assange over to the United States and he is successfully prosecuted, we'll now reserve the right to snatch up anyone, anywhere on the planet, who dares to even try to learn about our secret activities. Think of all the ways that precedent could be misused.

Britain is in a box. On the one hand, thanks to Brexit, it's isolated itself and needs the United States more than ever. On the other hand, it needs to grow some stones and stand up to America for once, if it doesn't want to see the CIA as the World's Editor in Chief for a generation. This case is bigger than Assange now, and let's hope British leaders realize it.

11. THE "ASSANGE PRECEDENT":

The Threat to the Media Posed by the Trump Administration's Prosecution of Julian Assange[42]

The Courage Foundation, March 2019

A precedent with profound implications for press freedom

New York Times:

"An indictment centering on the publication of information of public interest ... would create a precedent with profound implications for press freedoms."[43] "Mr. Assange is not a traditional journalist, but what he does

---

42 This article was originally published online. "The 'Assange Precedent': The Threat to the Media Posed by the Trump Administration's Prosecution of Julian Assange," *Defend WikiLeaks*, March 2019, https://defend.wikileaks.org/2019/03/18/the-assange-precedent-the-threat-to-the-media-posed-by-trumps-prosecution-of-julian-as-sange/.

43 Adam Goldman, Charlie Savage, and Michael S. Schmidt, "Assange Is Secretly Charged in U.S., Prosecutors Mistakenly Reveal," *The New York Times*, November 16, 2018, https://www.nytimes.com/2018/11/16/us/politics/julian-assange-indict-ment-wikileaks.html.

at WikiLeaks has also been difficult to distinguish in a legally meaningful way from what traditional news organizations, like the *New York Times*, do every day: seek out and publish information that officials would prefer to be kept secret, including classified national security matters."[44]

David McCraw, lead lawyer for the *New York Times*:

"I think the prosecution of him [Assange] would be a very, very bad precedent for publishers. From that incident, from everything I know, he's sort of in a classic publisher's position and I think the law would have a very hard time drawing a distinction between the *New York Times* and WikiLeaks."[45]

The Atlantic:

"If the US government can prosecute the WikiLeaks editor for publishing classified material, then every media outlet is at risk."[46]

Introduction

The Trump administration has confirmed that it has charged WikiLeaks' publisher Julian Assange and that it seeks his extradition from the United

---

[44] Charlie Savage, "Julian Assange Charge Raises Fears About Press Freedom," *The New York Times*, November 16, 2018, https://www.nytimes.com/2018/11/16/us/politics/julian-assange-indictment.html#click=https://t.co/iQHSxEcX25.

[45] Maria Dinzeo, "Judges Hear Warning on Prosecution of WikiLeaks," Courthouse News, July 24, 2018, https://www.courthousenews.com/judges-hear-warning-on-prosecution-of-wikileaks/.

[46] Bradley P. Moss, "Julian Assange Isn't Worth It," The Atlantic, November 19, 2018, https://www.theatlantic.com/ideas/archive/2018/11/prosecuting-julian-assange-puts-free-press-risk/576166/?utm_term=2018-11-19T14%3A42%3A34&utm_content=edit-promo&utm_campaign=the-atlantic&utm_medium=social&utm_source=twitter.

Kingdom.[47] The charges relate to WikiLeaks' 2010–2011 joint publications on war, diplomacy, and rendition with a range of media organizations; these were published in Europe while Julian Assange was in Europe.[48] In the US, Assange faces life in prison.

The alleged source, Chelsea Manning, who was granted a commutation by President Obama, was re-jailed on March 8, 2019 by the Trump administration to coerce her to testify in secret against WikiLeaks over the 2010 publications. On her jailing, she stated that "I stand by my previous public testimony."[49] In her 2013 trial, Manning stated that "the decisions that I made to send documents and information" to WikiLeaks "were my own."[50]

The Trump administration's actions are a serious threat to freedom of expression and freedom of the media.

1. **The Trump administration is seeking to use its case against WikiLeaks as an "icebreaker" to crush the rest of the press.**

   The administration is seeking to end the rash of leaks about it by using the case against WikiLeaks as an "icebreaker" against the rest of the media. The administration has been plagued by hundreds of

47   https://pacerdocuments.s3.amazonaws.com/179/399086/18919235200. pdf. https://www.apnews.com/21288cb5819b49dd9042c0cf19ff2734. https://www.washingtonpost.com/world/national-security/julian-assange-has-been-charged-prosecutors-reveal-in-inadvertent-court-filing/2018/11/15/9902e6ba-98bd-48df-b447-3e2a4638f05a_story.html?utm_term=.9f54fa7bdcec

48   Rachel Weiner, "Chelsea Manning fights subpoena in WikiLeaks probe," *The Washington Post*, March 5, 2019, https://www.washingtonpost.com/local/legal-issues/chelsea-manning-fights-subpoena-in-wikileaks-probe/2019/03/05/8351dafa-3eb8-11e9-9361-301ffb5bd5e6_story.html?utm_term=.40d88115e473.

49   Chelsea E. Manning, Twitter post, March 8, 2019, 1:58 p.m., https://twitter.com/xychelsea/status/1104094170950578177.

50   "Bradley Manning's personal statement to court martial: full text," *The Guardian*, March 1, 2013, https://www.theguardian.com/world/2013/mar/01/bradley-manning-wikileaks-statement-full-text.

government leaks, on everything from Trump's conversations with the leaders of Australia and Mexico to Jared Kushner's security clearance to an upcoming meeting with Kim Jong Un to his personal diary etc. In fact, the Trump administration has already threatened to prosecute journalists publishing classified leaks.[51] The Trump administration is hostile to the press and will not stop at WikiLeaks; WikiLeaks is the desired precedent-setter to hobble the rest of the press.

2. **Prosecuting WikiLeaks is a severe precedent-setting threat to press freedoms.**

If the US succeeds in prosecuting the publisher and editor of WikiLeaks, for revealing information the US says is "secret," it will open the flood gates to an extremely dangerous precedent. Not only will the US government immediately seize on the precedent to initiate further prosecutions, states the world over will follow suit and claim that their secrecy laws must apply globally too. Assange's copublishers at *Der Spiegel, Le Monde, New York Times, Espresso,* and the *Guardian,* among others, will also risk immediate prosecution in (and extradition to) the US. The prosecution of Assange will have a profound chilling effect on the press and national security reporting. Publishers should not be prosecuted, in the US or elsewhere, for the "crime" of publishing truthful information.

---

[51] In August 2017, then Attorney General Sessions threatened to prosecute media outlets publishing classified information. Julia Edwards Ainsley, "Trump administration goes on attack against leakers, journalists," *Reuters,* August 4, 2017, https://www.reuters.com/article/us-usa-trump-sessions-leaks/trump-administration-goes-on-attack-against-leakers-journalists-idUSKBN1AK1UR.

3. **The Trump administration should not be able to prosecute a journalist in the UK, operating from the UK and the rest of Europe, over claims under US laws.**

   The extradition and prosecution of Julian Assange would post an invitation to other states to follow suit, severely threatening the ability of journalists, publishers, and human rights organizations to safely reveal information about serious international issues. If the Trump administration can prosecute an Australian journalist in Europe for publishing material on the US, why can't Russia prosecute an American journalist in Washington revealing secrets about Moscow? Why can't Saudi Arabia prosecute a Turkish journalist for revealing secrets about the Khashoggi murder?

   With the Assange precedent established, foreign states will have grounds to insist journalists and publishers are extradited for their reporting. Even in states that bar the extradition of their citizens, as soon as the journalist goes on holiday or on assignment, they can be arrested and extradited from a third state using the Assange precedent.

4. **The Trump administration seeks to turn Europe and the rest of the world into a legal Guantánamo Bay.**

   The US seeks to apply its laws to European journalists and publishers and at the same time strip them of constitutional rights, effectively turning Europe into a legal Guantánamo Bay, where US criminal laws are asserted, but US rights are withheld. In April 2017, CIA director Mike Pompeo said that "Julian Assange has no First Amendment privileges. He is not a US citizen." He stated:

   We have to recognize that we can no longer allow Assange and his colleagues the latitude to use free speech values against us. To give

them the space to crush us with misappropriated secrets is a per-
version of what our great Constitution stands for. It ends now.[52]

But while rejecting any rights under the the First Amendment, which guarantees free speech and freedom of the media under the US Constitution, the US believes it still has a right to prosecute a non-US publisher in Europe.

Alan Rusbridger, former editor of the *Guardian*:
"Journalists—whatever they think of Julian Assange—should defend his First Amendment rights."[53]

James Goodale, the lawyer representing the *New York Times* in the Pentagon Papers case, put it succinctly:
"... the prosecution of Assange goes a step further. He's not a source, he is a publisher who received information from sources. The danger to journalists can't be overstated ... As a matter of fact, a charge against Assange for 'conspiring' with a source is the most dangerous charge that I can think of with respect to the First Amendment in almost all my years representing media organizations. The reason is that one who is gathering/writing/distributing the news, as the law stands now, is free and clear under the First Amendment. If the government is able to say a person who is exempt under the First Amendment then *loses* that exemption because that person has "conspired" with a source who is subject to the Espionage Act or other law, then the government has succeeded in applying the standard to all news-gathering. That will mean that the press' ability to get newsworthy classified information from government sources will be severely curtailed, because every story that is based on leaked info will theoretically be

---

[52] "Director Pompeo Delivers Remarks at CSIS," *Central Intelligence Agency*, April 13, 2017, https://www.cia.gov/news-information/speeches-testimony/2017-speeches-testimony/pompeo-delivers-remarks-at-csis.html.

[53] Alan Rusbridger, Twitter post, November 30, 2018, 6:32 p.m., https://twitter.com/arusbridger/status/1068648931301584896.

subject to legal action by the government. It will be up to the person with the information to prove that they got it without violating the Espionage Act. This would be, in my view, the worst thing to happen to the First Amendment—almost ever."[54]

Which other publishers and journalists are also in the frame?
WikiLeaks copublished the Afghanistan and Iraq files in 2010 with a range of media organizations. The copublishers of the Afghanistan material were *Der Spiegel*, the *New York Times*, the *Guardian*, and *Espresso*. The copublishers of the Iraq material were *Der Spiegel*, the *Guardian*, the *New York Times*, *Al Jazeera*, *Le Monde*, the Bureau of Investigative Journalism, Channel 4's Dispatches, the Iraq Body Count project, RUV (Iceland), and SVT (Sweden). The individual journalists reporting the Afghanistan and Iraq material are identified below.

Copublishers with WikiLeaks of the Afghanistan War Logs	Journalists who reported the material
Espresso	Gianluca Di Feo, Stefania Maurizi[55]
Guardian	Nick Davies, David Leigh, Declan Walsh, Simon Tisdall, Richard Norton-Taylor, Rob Evans[56]

---

[54] Goodale led the paper's legal team in the Pentagon Papers case. Trevor Timm, "Former New York Times Chief Lawyer: Rally to Support Julian Assange – Even If You Hate Him," *Medium*, November 21, 2018, https://medium.com/s/oversight/former-new-york-times-chief-lawyer-rally-to-support-julian-assange-even-if-you-hate-him-639b2d89dd92.

[55] Examples: http://espresso.repubblica.it/internazionale/2010/10/14/news/tra-gli-italiani-l-incubo-di-teheran-1.24754. http://espresso.repubblica.it/internazionale/2010/10/14/news/dove-finiscono-le-donazioni-occidentali-1.24762. http://espresso.repubblica.it/dettaglio/afghanistan-ecco-la-verita/2136377

[56] Examples: Nick Davies and David Leigh, "Afghanistan war logs: Massive leak of secret files exposes truth of occupation," *The Guardian*, July 25, 2010, https://www.theguardian.com/world/2010/jul/25/afghanistan-war-logs-military-leaks. "Afghanistan: the war logs," *The Guardian*, https://www.theguardian.com/world/the-war-logs.

11. THE "ASSANGE PRECEDENT"

New York Times	Mark Mazzetti, Jane Perlez, Eric Schmitt, Andrew W. Lehren, C. J. Chivers, Carlotta Gall, Jacob Harris, Alan McLean[57]
Der Spiegel	Matthias Gebauer, John Goetz, Hans Hoyng, Susanne Koelbl, Marcel Rosenbach, Gregor Peter Schmitz[58]

Declan Walsh, "Afghanistan war logs: Clandestine aid for Taliban bears Pakistan's fingerprints," *The Guardian*, July 25, 2010, https://www.theguardian.com/world/2010/jul/25/pakistan-isi-accused-taliban-afghanistan. Declan Walsh, "Afghanistan war logs: Clandestine aid for Taliban bears Pakistan's fingerprints," *The Guardian*, July 25, 2010, https://www.theguardian.com/world/2010/jul/25/taliban-tapped-mobile-phones-afghanistan. Rob Evans and Richard Norton-Taylor, "Afghanistan war logs: Reaper drones bring remote control death," *The Guardian*, July 25, 2010, https://www.theguardian.com/world/2010/jul/25/reaper-drone-missions-afghanistan-flights.

[57] Examples: "The War Logs," The New York Times, https://archive.nytimes.com/www.nytimes.com/interactive/world/war-logs.html. Andrew Lehren, Mark Mazzetti, Jane Perlez, and Eric Schmitt, "Pakistan Aids Insurgency in Afghanistan, Reports Assert," *The New York Times*, July 25, 2010, https://www.nytimes.com/2010/07/26/world/asia/26isi.html. C.J. Chivers et al. "View Is Bleaker Than Official Portrayal of War in Afghanistan," *The New York Times*, July 25, 2010, https://www.nytimes.com/2010/07/26/world/asia/26warlogs.html. Eric Schmitt, "In Disclosing Secret Documents, WikiLeaks Seeks 'Transparency,'" *The New York Times*, July 25, 2010, https://www.nytimes.com/2010/07/26/world/26wiki.html. C.J. Chivers, "Strategic Plans Spawned Bitter End for a Lonely Outpost," *The New York Times*, July 25, 2010, https://www.nytimes.com/2010/07/26/world/asia/26keating.html.

[58] Examples: "Explosive Leaks Provide Image of War from Those Fighting It," *SPIEGEL*, July 25, 2010, http://www.spiegel.de/international/world/afghanistan-explosive-leaks-provide-image-of-war-a-708314.html. Matthias Gebauer et al., "War Logs Illustrate Lack of Progress in Bundeswehr Deployment,"*SPIEGEL*, July 26, 2010, http://www.spiegel.de/international/germany/the-helpless-germans-war-logs-il-lustrate-lack-of-progress-in-bundeswehr-deployment-a-708393.html. Matthias Gebauer et al., "US Elite Unit Could Create Political Fallout for Berlin," *SPIEGEL*, July 26, 2010, http://www.spiegel.de/international/germany/task-force-373-and-targeted-assassinations-us-elite-unit-could-create-political-fallout-for-berlin-a-708407.html.

**Copublishers with WikiLeaks of
the Iraq War Logs**

Bureau of Investigative Journalism	Writers not named[59]
Channel 4 (UK TV)	Anna Doble, Kris Jepson[60]
Guardian	Nick Davies, Jonathan Steele, David Leigh, James Meek, Jamie Doward, Mark Townsend, Maggie O'Kane[61]
Iraq Body Count	Writers not named[62]
Al Jazeera	Gregg Carlstrom[63]

---

[59] Example: "Iraq War Logs: The Real and Uncensored Story of the War," *The Bureau of Investigative Journalism*, November 3, 2010, https://www.thebureauinvestigates. com/stories/2010-11-03/iraq-war-logs.

[60] Examples: Anna Doble, "Iraq secret war files, 400,000 leaked," *Channel 4 News*, October 22, 2010, https://www.channel4.com/news/iraq-secret-war-files. Kris Jepson, "Iraq's secret war logs: Iraqi torture," *Channel 4 News*, October 22, 2010, https://www.channel4.com/news/iraqs-secret-war-logs-iraqi-torture.

[61] Examples: "Iraq: The war logs," *The Guardian*, https://www.theguardian. com/world/iraq-war-logs. David Leigh, "Iraq war logs: An introduction," *The Guardian*, October 22, 2010, https://www.theguardian.com/world/2010/oct/22/ iraq-war-logs-introduction. Nick Davies, "Iraq war logs: Secret order that let US ignore abuse," *The Guardian*, October 22, 2010, https://www.theguardian.com/ world/2010/oct/22/iraq-detainee-abuse-torture-saddam. Jonathan Steele, "Iraq war logs: Civilians gunned down at checkpoints," *The Guardian*, October 22, 2010, https://www.theguardian.com/world/2010/oct/22/iraq-checkpoint-kill-ings-american-troops. James Meek, "Iraq war logs: How friendly fire from US troops became routine," The Guardian, October 22, 2010, https://www.theguard-ian.com/world/2010/oct/22/american-troops-friendly-fire-iraq.

[62] Example: "Iraq War Logs: What the numbers reveal," *Iraq Body Count*, October 23, 2010, https://www.iraqbodycount.org/analysis/numbers/warlogs/.

[63] Example: Gregg Carlstorm, "WikiLeaks releases secret Iraq file," *Aljazeera*, October 24, 2010, https://www.aljazeera.com/secretiraqfiles/2010/10/ 2010102217631317837.html.

Le Monde	Patrice Claude, Yves Eudes, Rémy Ourdan, Damien Leloup, Frédéric Bobin[64]
New York Times	Michael R. Gordon, Andrew W. Lehren, Sabrina Tavernise, James Glanz[65]
RUV (Icelandic state TV)	Kristinn Hrafnsson
Der Spiegel	Writers not named[66]
SVT (Swedish state TV)	Susan Ritzén, Örjan Magnusson[67]

[64] Examples: "Irak: l'horreur ordinaire révélée par WikiLeaks," *Le Monde*, October 22, 2010, https://www.lemonde.fr/proche-orient/article/2010/10/22/irak-l-horreur-ordinaire-revelee-par-wikileaks_1429990_3218.html. Frédéric Bobin, "WikiLeaks: le jeu trouble de l'Iran sur le théâtre afghan," *Le Monde*, December 2, 2010, https://www.lemonde.fr/documents-WikiLeaks/article/2010/12/02/WikiLeaks-le-jeu-trouble-de-l-iran-sur-le-theatre-afghan_1448301_1446239.html

[65] Examples: "The War Logs: An archive of classified military documents offers views of the wars in Iraq and Afghanistan," *The New York Times*, 2012, https://archive.nytimes.com/www.nytimes.com/interactive/world/war-logs.html. Michael R. Gordon and Andrew W. Lehren, "Leaked Reports Detail Iran's Aid for Iraqi Militias," *The New York Times*, October 22, 2010, https://www.nytimes.com/2010/10/23/world/middleeast/23iran.html. Sabrina Tavernise and Andrew W. Lehren, "Detainees Fared Worse in Iraqi Hands, Logs Say," *The New York Times*, October 22, 2010, https://www.nytimes.com/2010/10/23/world/middleeast/23detainees.html?mtrref=archive.nytimes.com&mtrref=www.nytimes.com&gwh=C3A5D1F76C1C0E615D4A2030D1A32EF8&gwt=pay. James Glanz and Andrew W. Lehren, "Use of Contractors Added to War's Chaos in Iraq," *The New York Times*, October 23, 2010, https://www.nytimes.com/2010/10/24/world/middleeast/24contractors.html?mtrref=archive.nytimes.com&mtrref=www.nytimes.com&gwh=3C81E847FC108DCD56D23054FB59C9A0&gwt=pay

[66] Example: "The WikiLeaks Iraq War Logs: Greatest Data Leak in US Military History," *SPIEGEL*, October 22, 2010, http://www.spiegel.de/international/world/the-wikileaks-iraq-war-logs-greatest-data-leak-in-us-military-history-a-724845.html

[67] Example: Susan Ritzén, "New Documents are Revealed from the Iraq war," *svt nyheter*, October 22, 2010, https://www.svt.se/nyheter/utrikes/nya-dokument-avslojas-fran-irak-kriget

The *Guardian* published hundreds of documents in full, in various sets, often using those exposés as major headlines, as did the other papers.[68] The *New York Times* published WikiLeaks "war logs," as "An archive of classified military documents offers views of the wars in Iraq and Afghanistan."[69]

Re-reported coverage of WikiLeaks files by other media organizations is of course even more extensive. Hundreds of outlets reported on the files, often quoting from them extensively. Some of these news organizations published dozens of files in full, with interactive maps and facilities to search the documents, such as the *Telegraph* in the UK.[70]

All major newspapers prominently covered the WikiLeaks publication of thousands of CIA files in March 2017, the biggest leak in the history of the CIA and the stimulus for the Trump administration to shut down WikiLeaks.

The fact that media freedom under threat is recognized by a raft of organizations:
Dinah PoKempner, general counsel, Human Rights Watch:
"No one should be prosecuted under the antiquated Espionage Act for publishing leaked government documents. That 1917 statute was designed to punish people who leaked secrets to a foreign government, not to the media, and allows no defense or mitigation of punishment on the basis that

---

[68] "US embassy cables: the documents," *The Guardian*, https://www.theguardian.com/us-news/series/us-embassy-cables-the-documents

[69] "The War Logs: An archive of classified military documents offers views of the wars in Iraq and Afghanistan," *The New York Times*, 2012, https://archive.nytimes.com/www.nytimes.com/interactive/world/war-logs.html?module=inline

[70] "The WikiLeaks Files Cables," *The Telegraph*, https://www.telegraph.co.uk/news/wikileaks-files/

public interest served by some leaks may outweigh any harm to national security."[71]

David Kaye: UN special rapporteur on freedom of opinion and expression:
"Prosecuting Assange would be dangerously problematic from the perspective of press freedom ... and should be strongly opposed."[72]

Kenneth Roth, director of Human Rights Watch:
"Deeply troubling if the Trump administration, which has shown little regard for media freedom, would charge Assange for receiving from a government official and publishing classified information—exactly what journalists do all the time."[73]

David Bralow, an attorney with the Intercept:
"It's hard to see many of WikiLeaks' activities as being different than other news organizations' actions when it receives important information, talks to sources and decides what to publish. The First Amendment protects all speakers, not simply a special class of speaker."[74]

71 Dinah PoKempner, "UK Should Reject Extraditing Julian Assange to US: Faces Possible Indictment under Outdated Espionage Act," *Human Rights Watch*, June 19, 2019, https://www.hrw.org/news/2018/06/19/uk-should-reject-extraditing-julian-assange-us

72 David Kaye, *Twitter*, November 16, 2018, https://twitter.com/davidakaye/status/1063445428337864706

73 Kenneth Roth, *Twitter*, November 15, 2018, https://twitter.com/KenRoth/status/1063335936031899653?s=03

74 Avi Asher-Schapiro, "By suing WikiLeaks, DNC could endanger principles of freedom," *Committee to Project Journalists*, May 29, 2018, https://cpj.org/blog/2018/05/by-suing-Wikileaks-dnc-could-endanger-principles-o.php

Alexandra Ellerbeck, Committee to Protect Journalists, North America program coordinator:
"We would be concerned by a prosecution that construes publishing government documents as a crime. This would set a dangerous precedent that could harm all journalists, whether inside or outside the United States."[75]

Trevor Timm, director of Freedom of the Press Foundation:
"Any charges brought against WikiLeaks for their publishing activities pose a profound and incredibly dangerous threat to press freedom."[76]

Bruce Shapiro, contributing editor to *The Nation*:
"The notion of sealed charges against a publisher of leaked documents ought to have warning sirens screaming in every news organization, think tank, research service, university, and civil-liberties lobby . . . The still-secret Assange charges, if unchallenged, could burn down the scaffolding of American investigative reporting."[77]

Ben Wizner, ACLU:
"Any prosecution of Mr. Assange for WikiLeaks' publishing operations would be unprecedented and unconstitutional and would open the door to criminal investigations of other news organizations."[78]

---

[75] "US has filed secret charges against Julian Assange, reports say," *Committee to Protect Journalists*, November 16, 2018, https://cpj.org/2018/11/us-has-filed-secret-charges-against-julian-assange.php

[76] "Prosecuting WikiLeaks for publishing activities poses a profound threat to press freedom," *Freedom of the Press Foundation*, November 16, 2018, https://freedom.press/news/prosecuting-wikileaks-publishing-activities-poses-profound-threat-press-freedom/

[77] Bruce Shapiro, "The Indictment of Julian Assange Is a Threat to Press Freedom," *The Nation*, November 20, 2018, https://www.thenation.com/article/julian-assange-Wikileaks-indictment-press-freedom/

[78] Jamil Dakwar, *Twitter*, November 16, 2018, https://twitter.com/search?q=from%3Ajdakwar%20statement&src=typd

High-ranking Trump administration officials have issued a series of threats against Assange and WikiLeaks to "take down" the organization, asserting that "Julian Assange has no First Amendment privileges. He is not a US citizen" (then CIA director Mike Pompeo)[79] and stating that arresting Assange is a "priority" for the US (then US attorney general Jeff Sessions).[80]

The key reason for this approach is WikiLeaks' release of thousands of files on the CIA in 2017, which revealed the CIA's efforts to infest computers, smartphones, TVs, routers, and even vehicles with CIA viruses and malware. The US government arrested a young US intelligence officer as WikiLeaks' source who now faces 160 years in prison and is being held in harsh conditions. The media reported in 2017, just after the Vault 7 publications, that the US was expanding the investigation against Assange and had prepared charges against him.[81] All the while, it has never been questioned that WikiLeaks simply published truthful information.

Julian Assange's contribution to journalism

Julian Assange and WikiLeaks have won numerous major journalism prizes, including Australia's highest journalistic honor (equivalent to the Pulitzer), the Walkley prize for "The Most Outstanding Contribution to

---

[79] Andrew Blake, "CIA 'working to take down' WikiLeaks threat, agency chief says," *The Washington Times*, October 20, 107, https://www.washingtontimes.com/news/2017/oct/20/cia-working-take-down-wikileaks-threat-agency-chie/. Scott Shackford, "CIA Chief Pompeo Takes Aim at the Free Press," *Newsweek*, April 23, 2017, https://www.newsweek.com/cia-chief-pompeo-takes-aim-free-press-587686

[80] David Smith, "Arresting Julian Assange is a priority, says US attorney general Jeff Sessions," *The Guardian*, April 21, 2017, https://www.theguardian.com/media/2017/apr/21/arresting-julian-assange-is-a-priority-says-us-attorney-general-jeff-sessions

[81] Evan Perez, Pamela Brown, Shimon Prokupecz, and Eric Bradner, "Sources: US prepares charges to seek arrest of WikiLeaks' Julian Assange," *CNN*, April 21, 2017, https://edition.cnn.com/2017/04/20/politics/julian-assange-wikileaks-us-charges/index.html

Journalism," The Martha Gellhorn Prize for Journalism (UK), the Index on Censorship and the *Economist*'s New Media Award, the Amnesty International New Media Award, and has been nominated for the UN Mandela Prize (2015) and the 2019 Nobel Peace Prize (nominated by Nobel Laureate Mairead Maguire). WikiLeaks has been repeatedly found by courts to be a media organization.[82]

WikiLeaks receives censored and restricted documents anonymously after Julian Assange invented the first anonymous secure online submission system for documents from journalistic sources. For years it was the only such system of its kind, but secure anonymous dropboxes are now seen as essential for many major news and human rights organizations.

WikiLeaks publications have been cited in tens of thousands of articles and academic papers and have been used in numerous court cases promoting human rights and human rights defenders. For example, documents published by WikiLeaks were recently successfully used in the International Court of Justice over the UK's illegal depopulation of the Chagos Islands, which were cleared to make way for a giant US military base at the largest island, Diego Garcia. The islanders have been fighting for decades for recognition.

Julian Assange pioneered large international collaborations to secure maximum spread and contextual analysis of large whistleblower leaks. For "Cablegate," WikiLeaks entered into partnerships with 110 different media organizations and continues to establish partnerships in its publications. This model has since been replicated in other international media collaborations with significant successes, such as the Panama Papers.

[82]   Ewen MacAskill, "WikiLeaks recognised as a 'media organisation' by UK tribunal," The *Guardian*, December 14, 2017, https://www.theguardian.com/media/2017/dec/14/wikileaks-recognised-as-a-media-organisation-by-uk-tribunal

Conclusion

All media organizations and journalists must recognize the threat to their freedom and ability to work posed by the Trump administration's prosecution of Assange. They should join human rights organizations, the United Nations, and many others in opposing Assange's extradition. They should do so out of their own self-interest given that their ability to safely publish is under serious threat.

12. ASSANGE'S ESPIONAGE CHARGES[83]

Daniel Ellsberg, May 23, 2019

DANIEL ELLSBERG: I was sure that the Trump administration would not be content with keeping Julian Assange in prison for five years, which was the sentence for the one charge of conspiracy that he was charged with earlier. So I was sure they would go after him with a much longer sentence under the Espionage Act. I was charged with 12 counts, including one of conspiracy, in 1971, for a possible sentence of 115 years. In this case they brought 17 counts under the Espionage Act, plus the one conspiracy. So they're facing him with 175 years. That's, frankly, not that different from 115. It's a life sentence. And it'll be enough for them.

They weren't anxious, I think, to bring it while he was still in Britain because it's so clearly a political offense, and Britain isn't compelled to extradite under the treaty for a political offense. And that's what they're charging here now, as well as a politically motivated charge. But apparently they had to bring the charges now rather than after he is back in the States,

[83]   This is a transcript from an interview with Ellsberg by Sharmini Peries. Daniel Ellsberg, interview by Sharmini Peries, *The Real News Network*, May 23, 2019, https://thereal-news.com/stories/daniel-ellsberg-on-julian-assanges-espionage-charges.

which was what I had expected, because they have to tell Britain, in deciding whether to extradite him to the US or not, the full scale of the charges that he would be facing. In particular, both Sweden and the US, I think, are reluctant to extradite people on charges that hold the death penalty. That's true I think for Sweden in particular, which is also trying to extradite him. They're not going to charge him with the death penalty. Just a life sentence, as I was facing.

This does, however, complicate somewhat their extradition. And I thought that Trump would hold off on declaring war on the press until the extradition matter had been settled. But no, the declaration of war came today. This is a historic day, and a very challenging one for American democracy.

Sharmini Peries: Now, Daniel, Ecuador, at the time they released him or revoked his stay at the embassy, made it a condition that Julian Assange be not extradited to a country where there is the death penalty. You said that there could be a lifelong sentence here in terms of prison. So the fact that there is a death penalty in the United States is insignificant, as far as you're concerned?

DE: My understanding is that Sweden, which is trying to extradite him as well, cannot extradite somebody to a country that has a death penalty. But I think they would probably try to get around that if the prosecutors said we're not seeking the death penalty, and that's surely the case right now. Actually, the death penalty under the Espionage Act only applies in certain circumstances; probably not the paragraphs of 18 USC 793, paragraphs D and E, which I was charged under, which didn't carry a death penalty. That was essentially for people who were spies in wartime against an enemy country. So they'll say they're not seeking the death penalty. But the problem remains that these are very clearly political offenses. And the question whether they should extradite him for that, that will complicate the appeals in the extradition process, and probably make it longer. So I don't expect him in the US very quickly, unless the UK, with their special friendship, just ships him off very quickly, instead of to Sweden.

But the challenge is on as of now, right now. Every journalist in the country now knows for the first time that she or he is subject to prosecution for doing their job as journalists. It cuts out the First Amendment, essentially. That eliminates the First Amendment freedom of the press, which is the cornerstone of our American democracy and of this republic. So there's an immediate focus, there should be an immediate concern not just for journalists over here and publishers, but for everyone who wants this country to remain a democratic republic.

SP: As journalists we engage with states all the time. We engage and we ask questions, and we try to assess and ascertain information. How does it actually specifically affect journalists working?

DE: John Demer for the Department of Justice, I notice just now, is trying to distinguish Julian from journalists. In fact, he's saying he's not a journalist, although the *New York Times*, to whom he gave Chelsea Manning's information initially, as I did, is saying very frankly that what he does is what the *New York Times* does. And clearly if he's prosecuted and convicted, that confronts the *New York Times*, the *Washington Post*, and you, and every other journalist, with the possibility of the same charges. A second DOJ is saying he didn't act like a responsible journalist. Well, people who are responsible journalists often do what Julian criticized, actually, and that is they give their stuff to the Department of Defense, or the Department of Justice, or the White House, before it's printed. That's a very questionable practice, really, and he certainly doesn't do that. And it was not done, for example, in the case of the Pentagon Papers, because they knew they would get an injunction before they published instead of an injunction after they had started publishing.

So this shows, in other words, that they're saying, well, we won't prosecute responsible journalists. But that assurance is worth nothing, aside from the question of who they'll consider responsible or not. Remember that President Trump's unprecedented charge here is that the American press, the mainstream press, is the enemy of the people. That's a phrase that was used under Stalin, and also under Hitler, to describe people who were to be eliminated. It's a very, very ominous historical phrase. But he has now declared war on the enemy of the people. And by saying that, for example, that he requested information, classified information, from Chelsea Manning, and that's what distinguishes him from the press, or the responsible press, well, let me tell you, I can't count the number of times I have been asked and urged to give classified information to the responsible press. The *New York Times*, the *Washington Post*, AP. Anything you can name.

So that is journalism. And the idea that they're distinguishing that should not reassure any journalists. I'm sure it won't, actually. So they're feeling the chill right now, before the prosecution actually begins. These indictments are unprecedented. And I would say they are blatantly unconstitutional, in my opinion. Which is not worth that much, except it's a subject I've been close to for a long time. This is an impeachable offense, to carry on a prosecution this blatantly in violation of the Constitution, which the president and the attorney general are sworn to uphold. They are not doing that at this moment.

SP: Daniel, the 17 counts of violating the Espionage Act, what are they, as far as you know?

DE: What is most ominous to me, by the way—it's not obvious—is that they referred to 2010, when he was dealing with Chelsea Manning. Now, I followed those charges, and the material that was released by the *Times*, *Le Monde*, the *Observer* in London, and several, a number of other papers.

I followed that fairly closely, including in the Chelsea Manning trial. That clearly was shown to result in no damage, no harm to any individual, which was precisely what they're charging him now with having risked. And they weren't able to come up with a single instance in these hundreds of thousands of files which were released in which a person had, in fact, been harmed. Now, I thought they would probably bring charges under his very recent revelations of various kinds, of which I don't know the substance, entirely, what he had or what he released, and they might have come up with something that looked very questionable. I know that for 2010 we now know that what he released was in no violation of national security, did not harm any individuals, and is indeed what journalists do all the time.

His releasing himself, in contrast to some of the newspapers he gave it to, of unredacted material was questionable at that time, including by me, and raised questions of whether that was the right way to do it. As I say, though, that was tested over a matter of years in terms of not having done any harm, given the sources from which that was drawn, and that reassured me about the judgment of both Chelsea and Julian in having released at that time. But in any case, there's no question that the 2010 material is material that should have been protected by the First Amendment. And he is. And if the current court fairly judges the intent and effect of the First Amendment, this case would be dropped. As we all know, we can't count on that. And a 5–4 decision now by this Supreme Court is probably another reason why Trump has gone further in attacking the First Amendment than any previous president, because he has an unprecedented court.

13. OUTSIDE BELMARSH PRISON[84]

Pamela Anderson, May 7, 2019

Obviously, it's been very difficult to see Julian here, and to make our way through the prison to get to him was quite shocking and difficult. He does not deserve to be in a supermax prison. He has never committed a violent act. He's an innocent person. He hasn't access to a library, a computer, any information—he's really cut off from everybody. He hasn't been able to speak to his children. And public support is very important. Fundraising is very important. He needs all the support he can get. Justice will depend on public support.

And he's a good man. He's an incredible person. I love him. I can't imagine what he's been going through. And to see him—it was good to see him. It was great to see him. But he's . . . this is just misrule of law and operation. It is an absolute shock that he has not been able to get out of his cell. It's been one month. It's going to be a long fight. He deserves our support—needs our support. So whatever anybody can do to—maybe write to him, encourage him. He's appreciative of any support that he's received,

[84] This is a transcription of Anderson's press statement after visiting Assange in Belmarsh on May 7, 2019. See the full video here: https://vimeo.com/334640055.

and I think he hasn't received too much yet in the way of letters, but I know people have been writing. It's a process for to him to have any kind of communication. It's very difficult. We just have to keep fighting because it's unfair. He's sacrificed so much to bring the truth out, and we deserve the truth. That's all I can say, I'm sorry. I feel sick. I feel nauseous.

14. ASSANGE IN PRISON—FOREVER?[85]

Geoffrey Robertson, June 2019

D-day for Julian Assange came on April 11, 2019: the world watched as he was forcibly ejected from his refuge in the Ecuadorian embassy, his long white beard giving him the look of a disgruntled guru. He re-emerged a few hours later in a courtroom to face an angry magistrate who branded him a "coward" (which he certainly is not) and a "narcissist" (which the judge, not being a psychiatrist, had no business to call him). This was not a good look for British justice, although it was US justice that he most feared and from which he had sought asylum in the Ecuadorian embassy almost seven years before: it had caught up with him now, as he was presented with an extradition warrant accusing him of conspiring with Chelsea Manning to spill American secrets when he released "Cablegate" back in 2010. Soon the full weight of the Espionage Act fell on him—17 charges carrying up to 175 years imprisonment. The United States badly wants to destroy this man for publishing the truth.

---

[85] This essay was adapted from a chapter in Robertson's autobiography, *Rather His Own Man: In Courts with Tyrants, Tarts and Troublemakers* (Biteback, 2018).

I handled his bail and extradition (to Sweden) proceedings back then and visited him in the embassy from time to time. It's a small set of offices in an Edwardian building opposite Harrods, with some reminders of Ecuador—posters of native art, travel magazines on the front desk, a few toy llamas, a portrait of the incumbent president and smatterings of conversational Spanish from the ambassador. The refugee's bedroom at the end of the corridor was converted from a toilet and its space compared in size with that of the "supermax" prison cell to which the US government would wish him consigned for the rest of his life. Here he has done some portentous things like channeling Edward Snowden and exposing how the Democrats rigged the selection process to favor Hilary Clinton over Bernie Sanders (who might have beaten Donald Trump, but never mind). That was in 2016, when the tergiversating Trump was tweeting "I love WikiLeaks"—an organization he now professes to know nothing about ("It's not my thing").

But Mike Pompeo, when CIA director, called it a "hostile foreign intelligence agency" and then Attorney General Jeff Sessions announced that Assange's arrest was "a priority." They had plenty of time to prepare his extradition warrant. Assange told me shortly before his expulsion that he had seen the writing on the wall when Mike Pence visited the new Ecuadorian president and provided him with much-needed loans—Assange thought that he would be the collateral. But his hosts, in an exercise of what can only be described as black propaganda, claimed he was an insufferable guest—rude to staff, mentally unstable, smelly, and given to smearing his excrement on their walls. I can only say that when I visited, Assange was always very rational, quite deferential to staff, clean, and well-mannered. The notion of him smearing feces probably came from PR advisors who thought it clever to associate him with the "dirty protests" of IRA prisoners. When the ambassador invited the tabloids into the embassy to complain about his dirty habits, all they could show was a picture of his unwashed plates in the sink. Still, the world's media reported all this uncritically. When, a few days later, Ecuador's own human rights committee, together with the ACLU and Liberty, condemned his expulsion as contrary to national and international law, no newspaper noticed.

However, the bad behavior of Ecuador is history: Assange must now fight for his life against the Leviathan. His time in the embassy had its bizarre aspects: British bobbies waited to catch him if he toppled over its balcony (whereupon, by a miracle of international law, he would leave South America and land in London). It had unnecessary cruelty of late, when the British government refused him permission to leave for a few hours to have hospital scans and x-rays that specialists required to treat his malfunctioning chest. Now, in prison, he is said to be too ill to be brought to court: he appears by video link, looking old.

He is now in prison for 11 months, punished for breaching his bail conditions back in 2012, when he sought refuge in the embassy, causing his sureties to forfeit the money they had staked (Phil Knightly, the distinguished journalist, said it was worth it). He is likely to remain in a London prison for a further year whilst his US (and/or his Swedish) extradition case winds its way through the courts. The warrant now charges 18 offenses— conspiracy with Chelsea Manning to effectuate her Cablegate leak, and 17 counts of violating the Espionage Act on which he could be jailed for up to 175 years. His co-conspirator, Manning, was sentenced to 35 years but was pardoned by President Obama: Assange is unlikely to be pardoned by President Trump.

* * *

What a long strange trip it has been (and continues to be) for this international man of mystery, whose baby-face first glowed from the newswires in mid-2010, after he produced the "Collateral Murder" tape. Assange's own photo was no shoulder-slumped mugshot, but the visage of a dangerous cherub, beaming beneath a halo of blond hair, which hid a cranium that seemed able to outwit the most powerful country in the world. He had no money nor interest in acquiring any, which gave him a rock-star image among the Internet generation in Europe as he sang his siren song of political transparency, justice, and human rights. Just how mesmeric Assange had become by August of that year may be measured by the front-page reporting, throughout the world, of the allegation that he had raped a woman in Stockholm. Within a few hours 7 million people had clicked on the website of *Expressen*, the tabloid paper to which the story had been leaked. There was much less publicity a day or so later, when the senior prosecutor of Stockholm dropped the charge and said there was virtually nothing else to investigate.

Then, a week later, this baseless charge was reinstated by a "gender prosecutor" in another Swedish city, after an appeal to her by a publicity hungry politician. This "gender prosecutor" had an agenda, which was to put Assange in prison irrespective of the evidence. She refused to interview Assange in London, and insisted he should be arrested and imprisoned by British authorities and then extradited to Sweden. She wants to charge him with what the Swedes call "minor rape" —a contradiction in terms, but in his case, it means having consensual sex without using (as agreed) a condom.

The bail hearing was jam-packed with journalists—hundreds attended from all over the world, straining and craning to see the human embodiment of Internet freedom, captive in the court dock. I supported their request to allow, for the first time, tweeting from a courtroom, and it was granted: Assange's first legal precedent in favor of freedom of speech.

The atmosphere was tense throughout, but the allegations were dismissed and character witnesses refuted any idea that he was some kind of sex pest: bail was granted. But the United States could not cope with his release of a quarter of a million of its diplomatic cables. There was a burst of hysteria against this alien, this peripatetic Australian, this blogosphere Machiavelli. Vice President Biden labeled him "a high-tech terrorist." Mike Huckabee, on Fox News, suggested that he be assassinated. Shock jock Rush Limbaugh yearned for him "to die of lead poisoning—from a bullet in the brain," while Sarah Palin, shooting from the lip, said "he should be hunted down like Bin Laden" (which would at least have given him nine more years of freedom).

Later, visiting him in the Norfolk countryside when he was on bail, I would keep a wary eye open for Navy Seals. I received a few death threats from America for representing him, although since they came by email I did not take much notice. Assange, of course, had many more, one—from the US authorities—frighteningly real. A grand jury had been convened in secrecy in Maryland to consider charges under the Espionage Act, which would jail him in a US "supermax" prison for many years. I was not without contacts high in the Obama White House, and they told me, "We don't want him, but the Pentagon does," adding that the Pentagon usually gets its way. It kept its plans to punish him secret for some years—so successfully that many journalists and commentators in the UK derided Assange's fears—but in 2017 the US finally admitted that his arrest was "a priority." It had been ever since Cablegate.

* * *

It is worth going back, before going forward, to analyze why, exactly, America wants to incarcerate Assange for at least as long as it succeeded (until Obama mercifully interceded) in jailing his source, Chelsea Manning—which was for 35 years.

Ironically, it is to the wisdom of the great Americans that Assange turned for his free-speech arguments: to James Madison, urging for a First Amendment to create a nation "where knowledge will forever govern ignorance, and a people who mean to be their own governors must arm themselves with the power that knowledge brings." To Theodore Roosevelt, who called on "muckrakers" to destroy what he described as "the invisible government"—the corrupt links between business and politics. To the US Supreme Court, when it refused to injunct the publication of a top-secret leak, the Pentagon Papers, because it ruled that the only protection against abuse of power was an enlightened citizenry.

Assange took the American legal aphorism that "sunlight is the best disinfectant" seriously. He invented what might be termed an electronic dead-letter box, where sources could send him secret documents in complete confidence and would remain anonymous because even he could not find out who they were. There would be no problem about protecting his sources—they could waterboard him for weeks and he could not tell because he would not know. All he could do would be to check the authenticity of the document—and WikiLeaks, so far as I know, has never published an inauthentic document.

So Assange became the latter-day Johnny Appleseed of information, scattering it far and wide, watching it inspire revolutions, expose crooked politicians and bent policemen, provoke policy debates, and make us more knowledgeable about history and context. Now, hardly a week goes by without reference in some book or news story to a WikiLeaks revelation.

The organization (using "organization" very loosely—WikiLeaks is basically Julian Assange, an inveterate loner, with a few assistants) began in 2006, publishing documents about the massive corruption in Daniel arap Moi's Kenya. Then documents were leaked exposing tax evasion through the Cayman Island banks, then a document from the Church of Scientology, revealing malpractice. Then documents relating to banking fraud in Iceland; the dangers of a nuclear accident in Iran; and the greedy price-gouging of US and British contractors after the war in Iraq.

All these revelations were of obvious public interest and made him pretty popular. His exposés have not always benefited liberals or the left: WikiLeaks also helped to reveal "Climategate," the apparent rigging of data by scientists. This gave a free kick to climate-change deniers, but it was true and WikiLeaks did not hesitate to host it, as he later did not hesitate to publish emails revealing chicanery at the Democratic National Committee.

After "Climategate" came the material we now know to have been provided by Chelsea Manning. It is difficult to forget "Collateral Murder," the tape that showed the aerial manslaughter of civilians by US forces. Then, in quick succession:

- The Afghan War Logs: revealing far higher civilian casualties from drone attacks than the US had been prepared to admit.
- Iraq-gate: no fewer than 400,000 filed reports, showing many thousands more civilian casualties than the US had admitted, and providing a treasure trove for war historians by revealing how the Iraq War had been fought on the ground, how blind eyes were turned to torture at Abu Ghraib and elsewhere, and how US forces would sometimes hand their prisoners over for torture and murder to pro-government death squads.

At this point, there had been only muted protest from the US government. But a number of other countries had become disturbed and had taken action to block all WikiLeaks-related websites, threatening to jail any of their citizens caught sending material to Assange. These countries were China, Syria, North Korea, Russia, Thailand, and Zimbabwe. Enemies of freedom sensed the danger, because dictators cannot cope with freedom of information.

Then came "Cablegate"—the release of a quarter of a million American diplomatic cables. Hillary Clinton, then secretary of state, warned foreign governments to be prepared for some unpleasant comments among the US government's supposedly private communications. They said, so she reported, "Don't worry. You should see what we say about you."

And so it came to pass that the people of Egypt and Tunisia discovered facts about the endogenous corruption of their rulers. In Tunisia anger erupted among protesters when they read a cable from the US ambassador describing the Ben Ali regime, accurately, as a political kleptocracy. It was headed "Corruption in Tunisia—what's yours is mine." The most virulent attack on WikiLeaks came in the midst of "Cablegate," on January 14, 2011. Assange was accused of leading the protesters in Tunis astray by false claims against their incorruptible president. That attack was made by Colonel Gaddafi.

Once he was on bail in Norfolk, Assange worked to transmit the cables to 90 different countries, alerting their people to misfeasance, hitherto hidden, in their public life. The cables revealed Hillary Clinton's plans to bug diplomats at the UN headquarters, and how Saudi Arabia and other Gulf States had urged the US to "cut off the head of the snake"—the Iranian nuclear program—by bombing Tehran.

But as "Cablegate" unfolded, it revealed, at least in my view, the most surprising secret of all—that US diplomacy is reasonably principled and pragmatic, and better informed and more objective than Western or locally based journalists. What WikiLeaks was doing, in some respects, was promulgating a CIA-sourced view of the world, ironically made to seem all the more credible by the US threats to silence Assange. The "Cablegate" releases certainly showed how the United States was under constant pressure from many "friendly" governments to bomb and brutalize, or at least protect them against their enemies.

Nonetheless, America was upset by dissemination of its diplomatic messages and the shrill, exaggerated voices calling for the messenger to be killed continued unhappily from the land of the First Amendment. American pride had been hurt by a pesky Australian, so they targeted him by grand jury proceedings and the military took out its anger on young Chelsea Manning, treating her abominably in prison until Hillary Clinton's press spokesman, P. J. Crowley, resigned in protest. Manning had been kept for eight months in solitary confinement, naked and without blanket or pillow, awoken every few minutes for a pretended "suicide watch." Her prosecutors hoped she would confess to being "groomed" by Assange, and at one point, according to her lawyer, threatened her with the death penalty if she did not. Then came the CIA pressure on PayPal, Mastercard, and Visa, to which they succumbed, to stop receiving donations for WikiLeaks or Assange. (You can still buy Nazi uniforms and Ku Klux Klan outfits with your Visa card but you can't donate to WikiLeaks.)

On what basis was Assange demonized? There is no doubt that the cables were of manifest public interest, revealing many examples of human rights violations and political corruption that American diplomats (with their CIA sources) were well aware of, but which had not been made public. But his accusers claimed that release of the cables had put "lives at risk," and that he had "blood on his hands." However, over eight years have passed since "Cablegate" began and six since all the cables were released. There has been no fatality causally related to their publication. Several US ambassadors and cable-authoring diplomats have had to be withdrawn because of their comments about their host country, but by August 2013, at the sentencing proceedings for Chelsea Manning, the Pentagon could produce no evidence that release of the cables had put any life in jeopardy and was forced to retract an earlier claim that it had.

The lack of fatalities is unsurprising, and indeed to be expected, because none of the WikiLeaks cables was classified "top secret"—the designation that diplomats must use if release would put lives at risk. The

Pentagon Papers were classified "top secret" and distributed to a small circle of officials, but up to 3 million people, including 22-year-old soldiers, had access to the cables that Chelsea Manning uploaded on a Lady Gaga disc for Julian Assange. The fact that they were not classified as "top secret" meant their authors did not expect any lethal reprisals if they were published, and none was in fact suffered, even after Assange published all the cables, including the parts "redacted" by nervous newspapers.

We can all envisage situations where "leaks" would be wrong and should be severely punished, because of the criminal way in which they are obtained—by bribery or duress or hacking. Custodians of genuine secrets have a duty to classify them as such and to protect them, by "top secret" classification if release would endanger lives or really damage national defense, by encrypting or redacting source names, or simply by keeping them anonymous. It all comes back to a proper classification policy. If a "top secret" class of harmful information does get out, then the first duty of government is to take steps to protect as best it can any persons whom the leak might put at risk, and then to make sure that its top-secret information is better protected in future. There should be no criminal blame attached to journalists or publishers who receive state secrets from those who wish to divulge them, certainly if they reveal abuse of state power. They have an ethical duty to protect their source, although if that source is caught through their own carelessness, he or she will have to suffer the legal consequences. (Chelsea Manning, for example, was caught because she confessed to someone who befriended her in an online chatroom.)

The first charge against Assange leveled by the FBI is that he took forbidden steps to protect his source. That, of course, is an ethical duty for every journalist, and in the UK and Europe, a qualified legal duty after the case of *Goodwin v. UK* in the European Court of Human Rights. Assange is accused that in March 2010 he did "knowingly and intentionally combine, conspire, confederate and agree with Manning to release 'secret' (but not 'top secret') information with 'reason to believe' it could be used to the injury of the United States." The accompanying affidavit from the FBI gives no details of any injury, other than an unlikely claim that a member of the Taliban had telephoned the *New York Times* in 2010 to tell the newspaper it was studying their coverage of WikiLeaks, and two letters found in Bin Laden's compound indicating that he was curious to read newspaper reports of the Afghanistan War Logs distilling WikiLeaks material. More importantly, for press freedom, the US indictment alleges that Assange's acts were unlawful because they helped conceal Manning as his source by removing usernames and deleting chat logs; that he encouraged Manning to provide information and records; that he afforded the facility of a drop-box for Manning to deposit the information and offered advice for Manning to "crack the password" of a Defense Department computer.

These allegations, even if correct, attempt to incriminate normal journalistic relationships with sources. It is hard to see how any reporter, approached by a source eager to report a public interest story, will not in some measure encourage him to do so (in Manning's case, she needed no encouragement). Assange's duty was to protect Manning, and journalists quite often do this by deleting messages and using drop-boxes or dead-letter boxes, and by signals (Watergate's "Deep Throat," Mark Felt, would move a potted plant on his window ledge to signal to Woodward and Bernstein that he was ready to talk). Although the reference to "cracking computer passwords" did sound as if it was above and beyond the demands of source protection, the FBI alleges merely that Manning asked if Assange could help her log in to a computer under a different name: Assange made inquiries but could not offer advice. In other words, this allegation is not of "hacking" a Defense Department computer (as was wrongly reported), it was rather a willingness to help Manning, who had access under her own name to that computer, to log in under a different name and so protect her identity. Did Assange go too far in discussing the possibility with his source of protecting her identity, or in helping her navigate the contents of the Lady Gaga disc into the WikiLeaks electronic letter-box? If the Assange indictment ever goes to trial, it will update the hypotheticals of print journalism for the Internet age. The fact remains that Assange was not forcing or paying or inciting Manning to do what she very much wanted to do in any event, and his advice was directed to protecting his source by helping her hide her identity.

As expected, the US Justice Department's superseding indictment released on May 23 added to the case against Assange 17 counts of violating the Espionage Act. The Pentagon's intention to prosecute journalists for working with sources to obtain and publish classified documents is no longer the thinly veiled truth we've known since the beginning. This is now an open war on publishers. There will be constitutional issues in play in any trial of Assange, most particularly the question of whether, as a foreign publisher, he can claim the protection of the First Amendment, which has historically protected the American media's freedom of speech against which "Congress shall make no law . . ." The White House has a simple answer: he is not protected because he is an Australian and not an American citizen. A ruling to this effect by the Supreme Court would severely cut back free speech, depriving British journalists and any other nationals working for the US media of legal protections so important for newsgathering. Jim Goodale, the real hero of the Pentagon Papers case as lawyer for the *New York Times*, has come out of retirement to warn that no matter how unlikeable Assange was as a person, defending him will be crucial for press freedom.

If the CIA gets its hands on Assange he will die in a US supermax prison, in order to deter other would-be publishers of US diplomatic data and military records. WikiLeaks was not based in America and Assange owed it no national allegiance: he received the information outside the country and shared it with the media at the *Guardian* offices in London. Under the vague but broad provisions of the US Espionage Act of 1917, passed amid hysteria about spies in wartime, can a US grand jury's writ run anywhere in the world? It appears so. He was public enemy number one in Washington after Cablegate in 2010–11 and again in 2016–17 when he published leaked emails exposing chicanery within the Democratic Party. But he is really in no different position to any journalist who receives authentic information of public interest from a source who is willing to go to some lengths to give it, and who goes to some lengths to protect her identity.

It only diminishes US leadership and dims the beacon of the First Amendment to raise that old blunderbuss, the Espionage Act, and to aim it beyond the jurisdiction at a publisher who is a national of a friendly country, who disseminated information of public interest that was not "top secret" and was in any event accessible to 3 million Americans, and who took steps to protect his source. Yet this is what the Trump administration intends, by insisting that its US courts have an exorbitant jurisdiction over nationals of other countries for their publishing operations outside America.

If the CIA were really clever, it would have fed Assange some information about the corruption of Putin and his clique, or that confirmed Putin's order of the death by polonium poisoning in London of his enemy Alexander Litvinenko. This would have tested Assange's integrity, but I guess he would have published it.

* * *

By mid 2019, Assange had served seven years (and still counting) of incarceration of one form or another. He has single-mindedly suffered the loss of his freedom of movement in return for trying to retain his freedom of speech.

In his British prison, Assange might have been comforted by the long-awaited release of the Mueller Report, which acquitted him of any conspiracy with Trump or his team to steal the confidential emails of the Democratic National Committee during the 2016 elections. These had been "spearphished" by Russian army intelligence (the GRU) and distributed anonymously to a number of potential publishers, and Mueller found no evidence that Assange knew from whence they had come. That would probably have not have stopped Assange, as they were of public interest, showing how Democratic officials had rigged the odds against Bernie Sanders—five of them had to resign in disgrace. The Democratic Party was damaged by the leak and Hillary has been unforgiving. There was certainly Russian Government interference in the 2016 US presidential election campaign—but that hardly seems a good reason to shoot the messenger.

At the time of writing, Assange must serve 11 months in prison for bail breach, and then will have a further long wait, probably in prison without bail, while contesting extradition. The Swedish prosecutor has decided that she wants him as well, for "minor rape," no force or violence is alleged, and the maximum penalty is four years (Swedish lawyers tell me that it would not normally carry a jail sentence). The home secretary must decide this tug-of-war over Assange, although the US may defer to Sweden in order to prolong his ordeal. The Swedish courts are more likely, in fact, to grant the US request than the British, which have a better reputation for independence (at least in the higher judiciary). One problem is that in Sweden all sex offense trials are held in secret (to protect witnesses from embarrassment or from being contradicted). This is contrary to the open justice principle in the US and UK, and in all human rights conventions. A secret trial cannot be a fair one, and after it may follow a lengthy trial in America, now under the 17 Espionage charges.

Decrying the case against Assange as "a clear threat to journalism," the *Columbia Journalism Review*, a week after his arrest, argued that all who care for the profession should come out in his defense. For all his faults as a "chaos monster" it sagely pointed out "we don't get to choose the individuals who provide the opportunity for us to defend free speech, and it is hard to argue that Assange is any worse than Larry Flynt or any of the other reprobates who have helped shape First Amendment law." I have tried to explain that Assange is not as bad as he is painted—but even if he were, defending him should be an imperative for those who look to journalism as a means of holding power to account.

* * *

I don't share Assange's politics, but I agree with A. J. P. Taylor's opinion that "All change in history, all advance, comes from the non-conformists. If there had been no trouble-makers, no dissenters, we should still be living in caves." Assange is one of those gifted and mischievous eccentrics that society should learn to treat with a degree of toleration and even appreciation. He is in many respects his own worst enemy and gives little thought to people other than himself, but his legion of critics—mostly journalists who have never met him—continue to overlook his genius and (actually) his courage. He is not a liberal's ideal of a "nice" person when his sarcasm turns nasty or he turns against friends, and snobbish critics in England typically deplore his table manners (they accuse him of eating with his fingers) and always remind readers, as if it makes him the ultimate outsider, that he is an Australian. Without money or freedom, he is in no position to refute the calumnies. When not raging against enemies real and imaginary (but never including himself), he is charming, funny, and auto-didactically erudite.

RESPONDING TO ASSANGE'S CRITICS 4-8

Caitlin Johnstone, April 2019

Smear 4: "He's a Russian agent."

Not even the US government alleges that WikiLeaks knowingly coordinated with the Kremlin in the 2016 publication of Democratic Party emails; the Robert Mueller Special Counsel alleged only that Guccifer 2.0 was the source of those emails and that Guccifer 2.0 was a persona covertly operated by Russian conspirators.[86] The narrative that Assange worked for or knowingly conspired with the Russian government is a hallucination of the demented Russia hysteria which has infected all corners of mainstream political discourse. There is no evidence for it whatsoever, and anyone making this claim should be corrected and dismissed.

But we don't even need to concede that much. To this day we have been presented with exactly zero hard evidence of the US government's narrative about Russian hackers, and in a post–Iraq invasion world there's no good reason to accept that. We've seen assertions from opaque

---

[86] See U.S. v. Viktor Borisovich Netyksho et al., U.S. District Court for the District of Columbia, 1:18-cr-215, https://www.justice.gov/file/1080281/download.

government agencies and their allied firms within the US-centralized power alliance, but assertions are not evidence. We've seen indictments from Mueller, but indictments are assertions and assertions are not evidence. We've seen claims in the Mueller Report, but the timeline is riddled with plot holes, and even if it wasn't, claims in the Mueller Report are not evidence. This doesn't mean that Russia would never use hackers to interfere in world political affairs or that Vladimir Putin is some sort of virtuous girl scout, it just means that in a post–Iraq invasion world, only herd-minded human livestock believe the unsubstantiated assertions of opaque and unaccountable government agencies about governments who are oppositional to those same agencies.

If the public can't see the evidence, then as far as the public is concerned there is no evidence. Invisible evidence is not evidence, no matter how many government officials assure us it exists.

The only reason the majority believes that Russia is known to have interfered in America's 2016 election is because news outlets have been repeatedly referring to this narrative as an established and proven fact, over and over and over again, day after day, for years. People take this repetition as a substitute for proof due to a glitch in human psychology known as the illusory truth effect, a phenomenon which causes our brains to tend to interpret things we've heard before as known truths. But repetitive assertions are not the same as known truths.

For his part, Julian Assange has stated unequivocally that he knows for a fact that the Russian government was not WikiLeaks' source for the emails, telling Fox News in January 2017 that "our source is not the Russian government or any state party." You may be as skeptical or as trusting of his claim as you like, but the fact of the matter is that no evidence has ever been made public which contradicts him. Any claim that he's lying is therefore unsubstantiated.

This is the best argument there is. A lot of people like to bring up the fact that there are many experts who dispute the Russian hacking narrative, saying there's evidence that the DNC download happened via local thumb drive and not remote exfiltration, but in my opinion that's generally poor argumentation when you're disputing the narrative about WikiLeaks' source. It's a poor tactic because it shifts the burden of proof onto you, making yourself into the claimant and then forcing you to defend complicated claims about data transfer rates and so on which most people viewing the argument won't understand, even if you do. There's no reason to self-own like that and put yourself in a position of playing defense when you can just go on the offense with anyone claiming to know that Russia was WikiLeaks' source and just say "Prove your claim," then poke holes in their arguments.

There is no evidence that Assange ever provided any assistance to the Russian government, knowingly or unknowingly. In fact, WikiLeaks has published hundreds of thousands of documents pertaining to Russia,[87] has made critical comments about the Russian government[88] and defended dissident Russian activists, and in 2017 published an entire trove called the Spy Files Russia,[89] exposing Russian surveillance practices.

Of course, the only reason this smear is coming up lately is because people want to believe that the recent imprisonment of Julian Assange has anything to do with the 2016 WikiLeaks email publications. It isn't just the propagandized rank-and-file who are making this false claim all over the internet, but Democratic Party leaders like Senate Minority Leader Chuck

---

[87] See "WikiLeaks: Advanced Search, Russia," *WikiLeaks*, https://search.wikileaks.org/?q=Russia.

[88] Suzie Dawson, "In Plain Sight: Why WikiLeaks Is Clearly Not in Bed With Russia," *steemit*, 2018, https://steemit.com/russia/@suzi3d/in-plain-sight-why-wikileaks-is-clearly-not-in-bed-with-russia

[89] "Spy Files Russia, All Releases, Peter-Service," *WikiLeaks*, September 19, 2017, https://wikileaks.org/spyfiles/russia/

Schumer and Center for American Progress president Neera Tanden. As we should all be aware by now, Assange's completely illegitimate arrest in fact had nothing whatsoever to do with 2016 or Russia, but with the 2010 Manning leaks exposing US war crimes. Anyone claiming otherwise is simply informing you that they are brainwashed by Russia conspiracy theories and have no interest in changing that character flaw.

The smearer may claim, "Well, he toes the Kremlin line!" When you ask them to explain what that means, they'll tell you it means that WikiLeaks speaks out against Western interventionist and war propaganda narratives like Trump's bombing of Syria, or their criticism of the establishment Russia narrative which tries to incriminate WikiLeaks itself. That's not "toeing the Kremlin line," that's being anti-interventionist and defending yourself from evidence-free smears. Nobody who's viewed their 2010 video "Collateral Murder" will doubt that criticism of the US war machine is built into the DNA of WikiLeaks and is central to its need to exist in the first place.

In reality, anyone who opposes western interventionism will see themselves tarred as Russian agents if they achieve a high enough profile, and right-wing empire sycophants were fond of doing so years before the brainwashed Maddow Muppets[90] joined them. Russia, like many sovereign nations, opposes western interventionism for its own reasons, so anyone sufficiently dedicated to their own mental contortions can point at a critic of western imperialism and say, "Look! They oppose this subject, and so does Russia! They're the same thing!" In reality a westerner opposing western interventionism is highly unlikely to have any particular loyalty to Russia, and opposes western interventionism not to protect their own geostrategic agendas as Moscow does, but because western interventionism is consistently evil, deceitful, and disastrous.

---

[90] Johnstone is referring to followers of MSNBC host Rachel Maddow.

The smearer may claim, "Well he had a show on RT in 2012!" So? What other network would air a TV program hosted by Julian Assange? Name one. I'll wait. If you can't name one, consider the possibility that Assange's appearances on RT were due to the fact that western mass media have completely deplatformed all antiwar voices and all criticism of the political status quo, a fact they could choose to change any time and steal RT's entire audience and all their talent. The fact that they choose not to shows that they're not worried about RT, they're worried about dissident thinkers like Assange.

In reality, Assange's 2012 show *The World Tomorrow* was produced separately from RT and only picked up for airing by that network, in exactly the same way as Larry King's show has been picked up and aired by RT. Nobody who isn't wearing a tinfoil pussyhat believes that Larry King is a Russian agent, and indeed King is adamant and vocal about the fact that he doesn't work for RT and takes no instruction from them.

The only people claiming that Assange is a Russian agent are those who are unhappy with the things that WikiLeaks publications have exposed, whether that be US war crimes or the corrupt manipulations of Democratic Party leaders. It's a completely unfounded smear and should be treated as such.

Smear 5: "He's being prosecuted for hacking crimes, not journalism."

No, he's being prosecuted for journalism. Assange is being prosecuted based on the exact same evidence that the Obama administration had access to when it was investigating him to see if he could be prosecuted for his role in the Manning leaks, but the Obama administration ruled it was impossible to prosecute him based on that evidence because it would endanger press freedoms. This is because, as explained by the Intercept's

Micah Lee and Glenn Greenwald, the things Assange is accused of doing are things journalists do all the time: attempting to help a source avoid detection, taking steps to try to hide their communications, and encouraging Manning to provide more material. This is all Assange is accused of; there is no "hacking" alleged in the indictment itself.

Joe Emersberger of FAIR.org notes the following:

> Now Assange could be punished even more brutally if the UK extradites him to the US, where he is charged with a "conspiracy" to help Manning crack a password that "would have" allowed her to cover her tracks more effectively. In other words, the alleged help with password-cracking didn't work, and is not what resulted in the information being disclosed. It has also not been shown that it was Assange who offered the help, according to Kevin Gosztola (Shadowproof, 4/11/19). The government's lack of proof of its charges might explain why Manning is in jail again.

> The indictment goes even further, criminalizing the use of an electronic "drop box" and other tactics that investigative journalists routinely use in the computer age to work with a confidential source "for the purpose of publicly disclosing" information.[91]

The only thing that changed between the Obama administration and the Trump administration is an increased willingness to attack journalism. Assange is being prosecuted for journalism.

Furthermore, there's every reason to believe that this new charge which the Trump administration pulled out of thin air is only a ploy

[91] Joe Emersberger, "Assange's 'Conspiracy' to Expose War Crimes Has Already Been Punished," *FAIR*, April 12, 2019, https://fair.org/home/assanges-conspiracy-to-expose-war-crimes-has-already-been-punished/?fbclid=IwAR3TqJpe6kU_uvJ7Ke9llkyQp6ca6FQ8DAHusW1wgoEEeajhVCloR85uvtg

to get Assange onto US soil, where he can be smashed with far more serious charges, including espionage.[92] Pentagon Papers lawyer James Goodale writes the following:

> Under the US–UK extradition treaty, one cannot be extradited from the United Kingdom if the extradition is for "political purposes." This explains why the indictment does not contain any charges alleging that Assange conspired with the Russians to impact the 2016 presidential election. It may also explain why the indictment focuses on hacking government computers rather than on leaking stolen government information, in as much as leaking could be characterized as being done for political purposes.

> When Assange arrives in the United States through extradition, as many expect he will, the government will then be able to indict him for his participation in that election. It is not out of the question that the government will come up with additional charges against Assange.[93]

If that happens, Assange will not be spending the five years behind bars for computer offenses that his current charge allows, he'll be spending decades.

"I don't think Julian is looking at five years in prison, I think he's probably looking at 50 years in prison," said CIA whistleblower John Kiriakou,

---

[92] In a superseding indictment, the Trump administration charged Julian Assange with 17 counts of violating the Espionage Act on May 23, 2019, after this smear rebuttal was written.

[93] James C. Goodale, "Pentagon Papers lawyer: The indictment of Assange is a snare and a delusion," *The Hill*, April 12, 2019, https://thehill.com/opinion/criminal-justice/438709-pentagon-papers-lawyer-indictment-of-assange-snare-and-delusion#.XLfdre9ecGx.twitter

who was the first person tried in the US for leaking classified materials to a journalist under Obama's crackdown on whistleblowers.

"I think that there are many more charges to be considered for Julian," Kiriakou added. "I would expect a superseding indictment, possibly to include espionage charges."

There is no legitimate reason to feel confident that this won't happen, and there are many reasons to believe that it will.[94] All for publishing truthful documents about the powerful. Assange is being prosecuted for journalism.

It's also worth noting here that President Executive Order 13526, section 1.7[95] explicitly forbids the classification of material in order to hide government malfeasance, meaning it's perfectly reasonable to argue that Manning did not in fact break a legitimate law, and that those prosecuting her did.

"In no case shall information be classified, continue to be maintained as classified, or fail to be declassified in order to: (1) conceal violations of law, inefficiency, or administrative error; (2) prevent embarrassment to a person, organization, or agency," the section reads, while Manning's lawyer has argued the following:

> *The information released by PFC Manning, while certainly greater in scope than most leaks, did not contain any Top Secret or compartmentalized information. The leaked information also did not discuss any current or ongoing military missions. Instead, the Significant Activity Reports (SIGACTs, Guantánamo detainee*

---

[94] On May 23, 2019, the US charged Assange in a superseding indictment with an additional 17 counts of violating the Espionage Act. The full indictment can be found in the Appendix of this collection.

[95] "The President Executive Order 13526: Classified National Security Information," *National Archives,* "https://www.archives.gov/isoo/policy-documents/cnsi-eo.html

assessments, Apache Aircrew video, diplomatic cables, and other released documents dealt with events that were either publicly known or certainly no longer sensitive at the time of release.[96]

There was no legitimate reason for what Manning leaked to have been classified; it was only kept so to avoid US government embarrassment. Which was illegal. To quote Assange: "The overwhelming majority of information is classified to protect political security, not national security."

Smear 6: "He should just go to America and face the music. If he's innocent he's got nothing to fear."

This is the new "He can leave the embassy whenever he wants." Except this one's also being bleated by Trump supporters.

The only way to make it feel true for oneself that Assange stands a chance at receiving a fair trial in America is to believe that the US is a just nation with a fair judicial system, especially in the Eastern District of Virginia when trying the cases of people who expose incriminating information about the US war machine. Anyone who believes this has packing foam for brains.

"No national security defendant has ever won a case in the EDVA [Eastern District of Virginia]," Kiriakou told RT upon Assange's arrest. "In my case, I asked Judge Brinkema to declassify 70 documents that I needed to defend myself. She denied all 70 documents. And so I had literally no defense for myself and was forced to take a plea."

"He will not, he cannot get a fair trial," Kiriakou said on a Unity4J vigil when Assange was still at the embassy. "It's impossible, because the

---

[96] Natasha Lennard, "Manning's lawyer: She didn't receive a fair trial," *Salon*, March 27, 2014, https://www.salon.com/2014/03/27/mannings_laywer_she_didnt_receive_a_fair_trial/

deck is stacked. And everybody knows what's gonna happen if he comes back to the Eastern District of Virginia. This is the same advice I gave Ed Snowden: don't come home, because you can't get a fair trial here. Julian doesn't have the choice, and that's what frightens me even more."

Assange is indeed being extradited to face trial in the Eastern District of Virginia. Manning herself did not get a fair trial according to her lawyer. Anyone who thinks Assange can expect anything resembling justice upon arrival on US soil has their head in something. Power doesn't work that way. Grow up.

Smear 7: "Well, he jumped bail! Of course the UK had to arrest him."

Never in my life have I seen so many people so deeply, deeply concerned about the proper adherence to the subtle technicalities of bail protocol as when Sweden dropped its rape investigation, leaving only a bail violation warrant standing between Assange and freedom. All of a sudden I had establishment loyalists telling me how very, very important it is that Assange answer for his horrible, horrible crime of taking political asylum from persecution at the hands of the most violent government on the planet to the mild inconvenience of whoever had to fill out the paperwork.

This smear is soundly refuted in a lucid article[97] by Simon Floth, which was endorsed by the Defend Assange Campaign. Floth explains that under British law bail is only breached if there's a failure to meet bail "without reasonable cause," which the human right to seek asylum certainly is. The UK was so deeply concerned about this bail technicality that it waited a full nine days before issuing an arrest warrant.

---

[97] "The Breach of Bail Allegation Against Assange," *Medium*, April 6, https://medium.com/@gigest/the-breach-of-bail-allegation-against-assange-934522ba9fa9

After the Swedish government decided to drop its sexual assault investigation without issuing any charges, Assange's legal team attempted last year to get the warrant dropped. The judge in that case, Emma Arbuthnot, just happens to be married to former Tory junior defense minister and government whip James Arbuthnot, who served as director of Security Intelligence Consultancy SC Strategy Ltd with a former head of MI6. Lady Arbuthnot denied Assange's request with extreme vitriol, despite his argument that British law does have provisions which allow for the time he'd already served under house arrest to count toward far more time than would be served for violating bail. The British government kept police stationed outside the embassy at taxpayers' expense with orders to arrest Assange on sight.

This, like America's tweaking the law in such a way that allows it to prosecute him for journalism and Ecuador's tweaking its asylum laws in such a way that allowed it to justify revoking Assange's asylum, was another way a government tweaked the law in such a way that allowed it to facilitate Assange's capture and imprisonment. These three governments all tweaked the law in unison in such a way that, when looked at individually, don't look totalitarian, but when taken together just so happen to look exactly the same as imprisoning a journalist for publishing inconvenient truths.

Smear 8: "He's a narcissist/megalomaniac/jerk."

Assange has been enduring hardships far worse than most people ever have to go through in their lifetime because of his dedication to the lost art of using journalism to hold power to account. If that's what a narcissist/megalomaniac/jerk looks like to you, then whatever I guess.

But really, the primary response to this smear is a simple, "So what?" So what if the guy's got a personality you don't like? What the hell does that have to do with anything? What bearing does that have on the fact that a journalist is being prosecuted in a legal agenda which threatens to set a precedent which is destructive to press freedoms around the world?

So many of the most common Assange smears boil down to simple ad hominem fallacy, in which the person is attacked because the smearer has no real argument. Pointing out the absence of an actual argument is a more effective weapon against this smear than trying to argue that Assange is a nice person or whatever. Plenty of people say Assange has a pleasant personality, but that's ultimately got nothing to do with anything. It's no more material to meaningful discourse than arguing over his physical appearance.

PART II: CONFINEMENT

1. OPEN DOORS FOR JULIAN

Fidel Narváez, May 2019

When the door of my embassy in London was opened to protect Julian Assange, on June 19, 2012, he was not running from justice. Julian was escaping from the injustice of persecution from the most powerful nation in the world, which had been embarrassed by his revelations of war crimes. The United States was on his heels with a grand jury investigation. The cover for arresting him was a Swedish extradition order for a preliminary investigation into alleged sexual misconduct. Julian had exhausted all legal possibilities in the United Kingdom and, faced with imminent arrest, decided to request political asylum, a right enshrined in the Universal Declaration of Human Rights.

Julian did not randomly choose the door of the Ecuadorian embassy. By 2012, Ecuador had its most progressive government to date and was focused on taking back its national sovereignty. The government of Rafael Correa had already removed the largest US military base in South America from its territory, expelled several American diplomats for their direct involvement in Ecuador's police and intelligence services, and taken a firm stand against transnational corporations.

One month before his request for asylum, Julian interviewed President Correa for his TV show *The World Tomorrow*, earning his interest and sympathy. The interview touched on freedom of expression and Correa told Julian that in Ecuador, ". . . the power of the media is much greater than that of politicians." Correa explained that his greatest opposition always came from the media in the service of domestic oligarchs fiercely opposed to the type of structural change his government sought.

Ecuador at this time was the only country to ask WikiLeaks to publish all the diplomatic cables referring to itself, without exception, in a demonstration of transparency that surely contributed to Julian thinking of Ecuador as a potential ally.

On the day that the door of my embassy opened to welcome Julian, we both knew that an asymmetrical geopolitical conflict, and a long diplomatic battle with an uncertain outcome, had begun. A small nation with no great economic weight faced the world's greatest power and two of its unconditional allies with the fate of the world's most persecuted man in the balance.

Ecuador, even before granting political asylum, tried to obtain guarantees from Sweden and the United Kingdom that Julian would not be extradited to the United States for his journalistic activity. An attempt was also made to corroborate the existence of a nascent extradition process from the United States. Australia was invited to offer its protection over its citizen. There were no positive outcomes, not at this time, nor in the following seven years. Rather than act in the interest of justice, these countries instead acted—independently or in coordination—to ensure that Julian's options were restricted. It was a sad reality that was described in May 2019 by the UN special rapporteur on torture, Nils Melzer, in an emphatic statement:

> *In 20 years of work with victims of war, violence and political persecution I have never seen a group of democratic States ganging up*

to deliberately isolate, demonise and abuse a single individual for such a long time and with so little regard for human dignity and the rule of law.

During the first three years, the embassy was surrounded by police—in the street and lobby of the building. In the latter four years, surveillance was covert, but no less intrusive. Cameras and high-range microphones were deployed in the surrounding buildings and phones were tapped. The embassy became the most surveilled place on earth, particularly after the Ecuadorian intelligence services, under the government of Lenín Moreno, installed a system of cameras to outright spy on Julian.

The British even threatened to enter the embassy by force on August 15, 2012, the day before the formal concession of asylum was announced by Ecuador. The threat was delivered in writing and then in person. At night, dozens of policemen closed the street and encircled the building, attempting to intimidate those of us inside. The UK realized the serious precedent they would have set by entering a foreign embassy without authorization—a breach of international diplomatic legislation. Ecuadorian diplomacy secured Latin American–wide condemnation of Britain's threat.

The internment of Julian Assange lasted 2,487 days and nights. The embassy has no more than 200 square meters in total, of which Julian had only a small portion allocated for his exclusive use: a room that served as a bedroom; a bathroom fitted with a shower; and a working space that he shared with diplomats. He also shared a small space adapted as a kitchen and a toilet with all the embassy staff.

The embassy has no interior patio, and scant natural light reaches inside. Subjected to exclusively artificial light, Julian compared his stay in that apartment to living in a spaceship. All of us who worked in that embassy felt a heavy atmosphere and an uncomfortable energy generated by so many people in such a small space, with no fresh air, no outdoor access, and security cameras filming at all times. While everyone else could leave at the end of each day, Julian could not step outside for so much as a cigarette break. The longest distance he could walk continuously was in the only corridor in the embassy. Barely 15 meters long.

Over time, health problems emerged. His already pale skin was more pallid. One of his shoulders needed to be scanned with medical equipment which could not be brought into the embassy. Some dental problems had to be left untreated. Julian began to have difficulty distinguishing colors easily. The British government would not allow him to be taken to a health center. One of the doctors who visited him, Sandra Crosby, sent her diagnosis to the UN Human Rights Council, stating Julian's health care in the embassy was worse than in a conventional prison and that his indefinite and uncertain confinement increased the risk of chronic stress, as well as physical and psychological risks, including suicide.

Under these conditions, Julian's resistance, both physically and psychologically, to surrender was remarkable. I personally thought that he would be emotionally unbreakable. However, the examination carried out by UN experts on torture revealed a shocking result. In the words of aforementioned Nils Melzer:

> It was obvious that Mr. Assange's health has been seriously affected by the extremely hostile and arbitrary environment he has been exposed to for many years. Most importantly, in addition to physical ailments, Mr. Assange showed all symptoms typical for prolonged exposure to psychological torture, including extreme stress, chronic anxiety and intense psychological trauma. The evidence is overwhelming and clear . . . Mr. Assange has been deliberately exposed, for a period of several years, to progressively severe forms of cruel, inhuman or degrading treatment or punishment,

*the cumulative effects of which can only be described as psycho-
logical torture.*

During the first six years, when Ecuador offered genuine protection, his
relationship with the diplomatic staff and the rest of the officials was of
mutual respect. Together we shared countless celebrations, birthdays,
farewells, meals, or cups of coffee over which politics and the world's injus-
tices were discussed.

Julian was always grateful to Ecuador. It was wrongly reported
that he treated Ecuadorians with arrogance. Isolated incidents of dis-
cord occurred only after private security guards hired by Ecuadorian
intelligence services to "protect" the embassy turned out to have their
own agenda and deliberately generated distorted reports about Julian's
behavior. Julian and staff treated the ineptitude and awkwardness of the
security guards as a joke. However, we underestimated the seriousness
of the problem; these false reports leaked to the press and Julian's image
was greatly affected. Public opinion turned against him. The press in
Ecuador had no direct access to Julian at any time so the only available
narrative was the one presented by the hostile security companies in the
embassy.

During the first six years Julian was able to work and express himself
freely. I cannot remember a single occasion when I saw him bored or inac-
tive. He was always busy, always working. During his stay, he published
several books and WikiLeaks continued publishing with the same fervor
as always. He received nearly a thousand visits from all over the world,
from intellectuals, artists, dissidents, journalists, politicians, and activists. He gave many interviews and dozens of conferences via Internet. On
exceptional occasions, as in the 2016 US presidential election, his actions
generated diplomatic tension for Ecuador with other countries, and in
turn, tension between the Ecuadorian government and Julian. Despite

this, the commitment of Rafael Correa's government to respect his asylum and continue his protection remained firm.

The reasons for his asylum and Ecuador's position in guarding it were strengthened over time. In 2014, the extradition law in the United Kingdom changed; if Julian's case began then the Swedish extradition order would not be legal, as he was only wanted for a preliminary investigation. He would never have needed to ask for asylum. In 2015, the United Nations Working Group on Arbitrary Detentions ruled against the United Kingdom and Sweden, describing Julian's situation as arbitrary detention and requesting the two countries to grant his freedom. The United Kingdom appealed against that decision and lost.

Disregard for UN resolutions positioned the United Kingdom and Sweden on the side of lawbreakers, and Ecuador on the side of justice. At the end of 2016, Sweden finally accepted Ecuador's proposal to interview Julian at the Embassy in London. For two whole days, two Swedish prosecutors questioned Julian; months later, in May 2017, Sweden closed the investigation and the Swedish extradition order was withdrawn. At the end of 2017, media confirmed that the Crown Prosecution Service admitted to deleting key communications with its Swedish counterparts. The media disclosed communications from Britain to Sweden urging them to keep the case open and to refuse to interview Julian in London. It was revealed that Sweden had considered closing the case as early as 2013.

Although the extradition request from Sweden was dropped, Britain still insisted on arresting Julian for breaching bail when he sought asylum. Given that the initial reason for his bail in the first place, his imminent extradition to Sweden, was no longer relevant, the British government's interest in his arrest was excessive. That the UK spent more than 20 million pounds of taxpayers' money on a void mission to detain Julian shows just how valuable he was to the government.

In December 2017, Julian was granted Ecuadorian nationality, something to which he was entitled, having lived for more than five years within its jurisdiction. In May 2018, the Inter-American Court of Human Rights (equivalent to the European Court of Human Rights), instructed Ecuador on its diplomatic asylum obligations, ruling that the nation could not allow the extradition of a political refugee. At the end of 2018, due to a publication error in a judicial document in the US, the world learned, as we had warned from the beginning, that there were secret charges against Julian Assange, which would only be made public at the time of his arrest.

Ecuador held all the legal and moral cards to defend Julian's asylum, but the change of our government in May 2017 marked the beginning of the end of its moral position on the wider world stage, and therefore, the end of its moral—and physical—defense of Julian. In Julian's 2012 interview with Rafael Correa, referring to social advances in Ecuador and Latin America, the former president predicted, "This road is not irreversible, everything can be reversed if the same people return to dominate our countries."

The new president, Lenín Moreno, turned Ecuador's international policy upside down, obeying the demands of the United States and surrendering its principled stand on human rights. Julian became a "stone in the shoe" and his head a bargaining chip.

Lenín Moreno never understood the nature of WikiLeaks and called Julian a "hacker." His approach toward him was as crude as it was cruel. He started by isolating him; he cut off his means of communication such that he had no Internet, no phone, and no visits, except from his lawyers. From March 2018, Julian was effectively kept in solitary confinement, according to Human Rights Watch's general counsel, Dinah PoKempner. A new company was employed to provide "security" for the embassy and given explicit instruction to spy on Julian. New audio-enabled cameras were installed in every possible corner. We now know that the guards also carried hidden cameras to follow each of Julian's movements and that, as per government instruction, they recorded all of his meetings, including those with his lawyers and doctors; they even photographed documents used in those meetings. The diplomats were replaced with new officials tasked with provoking Julian in order to generate incidents that would serve as a pretext for the government to expel him from the embassy.

When the government imposed a set of draconian regulations designed to push Julian out, he tried to defend himself with a complaint in the Ecuadorian courts. This was characterized as "biting the hand that feeds him." The Ecuadorian courts, in the pocket of Lenín Moreno, ruled in favor of the government. The Inter-American Commission on Human Rights did not impede the implementation of said regulations in the embassy but did warn Ecuador that it should respect the asylum and not permit the extradition of an asylee.

Julian's life was made unbearable during his last year in the embassy. Ecuador had been the only nation to defend him, and it now joined those that persecuted him. Lenín Moreno only held back his eviction because of the international shame that handing over a political refugee would bring. Forcing Julian to leave voluntarily through abject cruelty had failed, so the government turned to the Americans and the British to strategize an end to his asylum. An alleged verbal confirmation from the US that they would not apply the death penalty for Julian's "crimes" was apparently enough for Ecuador's conscience to be clear.

In February 2019, a case of corruption involving the president and his inner circle emerged in Ecuador, and Parliament initiated an investigation. WikiLeaks tweeted about the inquiry with a link to the website that had published the information. The government then accused Julian of having "hacked" the president's phone and of invading the privacy of his family, and WikiLeaks of leaking embarrassing information. Neither WikiLeaks nor Julian had anything to do with accessing or leaking this information but this was irrelevant to the government who had found a way to scapegoat the "dangerous," "ungrateful" "hacker."

In a surreal episode, the Parliament of Lenín Moreno voted to investigate Julian's "hacking" of the president's private communication. However, all of the information that the Parliament referred to had already been made available in the public domain by the people who found the information in the first place—well before WikiLeaks sent a tweet about it. A junior fact checker would have taken minutes to find that their allegations against Julian were baseless, but the government nonetheless launched a campaign against him with puerile accusations about hygiene, respect, and interference in the affairs of friendly countries. The Ecuadorian media likewise did not waste their time with corroboration of the government's claims. Instead, they printed the official lies as fact.

On April 11, 2019, Lenín Moreno allowed a foreign force into the Ecuadorian embassy to capture the world's most important political refugee. Had a perceived rival nation such as China or Russia been seeking the extradition of Julian for telling the truth about their regimes, he would be treated globally as a hero, rather than reviled as an inconsiderate houseguest.

International legislation on asylum, resolutions from the UN and the Inter-American Court of Human Rights, and the Ecuadorian Constitution that prohibits the extradition of an Ecuadorian citizen were all insufficient to prevent his attack from all sides. The US extradition warrant against Julian was activated as soon as he was dragged from the embassy, proving that Julian was right to request protection, and that Ecuador was right to grant his asylum.

The very same embassy door that I opened on June 19, 2012, to uphold the right to asylum, to defend freedom of expression and equality of nations in the international arena, was opened again after 2,487 days of his arbitrary detention—this time to destroy the concept of national sovereignty and to send a message that fearless journalism used against the self-interest of established powers will not be tolerated.

Julian has been stabbed in the back and is hurt, but he is not broken. Now that there is no nation to protect him, he depends on the solidarity of those of us who understand the value of opening windows on the misuse of power. Julian's freedom is our freedom to tell and know the truth. We must open all doors possible for him.

2. A LETTER TO THE ECUADORIAN PRESIDENT, RAFAEL CORREA, CONCERNING MY APPLICATION FOR ASYLUM

Julian Assange, June 25, 2012

IN DEFENSE OF JULIAN ASSANGE

25th June 2012

President Rafael Correa
Republic of Ecuador

Dear President Correa

Re: Application for Asylum and Protection

1.   I hereby amplify in writing my request made on 19th June 2012 to the Government of Ecuador for diplomatic asylum/protection, including asylum under the UN Convention 1951 relating to the Status of Refugees. This request is made in the belief I will be sent to the United States where as a result of my imputed political opinions, I will be persecuted. This persecution will take place in the form of prosecution for political reasons, and excessive punishment if convicted, and inhumane treatment all contrary to the Convention. I also contend this treatment will be inhuman or degrading and will breach every international convention in that regard including the European Convention on Human Rights and the Inter-American Convention on Human Rights. It is my belief that the country of which I am a national, Australia, will not protect me and the country to which I am due to be extradited imminently from the UK, Sweden, will not prevent my onward extradition to the US. I ask that protection be extended so far as is reasonably possible, to prevent such an occurrence.

2.   I have been made aware that a Grand Jury was convened in the USA in Alexandria, Virginia two years ago, and has sat since that time hearing evidence - its purpose, that I be indicted. It is my belief that there is now a sealed indictment in existence, and that had I succeeded in my appeal to the Supreme Court in the UK, as a result of which any ongoing extradition to Sweden would have been stopped, that the United States would have sought my immediate arrest here. I believe, my extradition having been ordered to Sweden, that upon completion of those

2. A LETTER TO THE ECUADORIAN PRESIDENT

proceedings in Sweden (if not before) a warrant for my arrest for extradition to the USA will be thereupon sought. The basis of my arrest would be in respect of my involvement with WikiLeaks, and the publication of information by WikiLeaks of material said by US prosecutors to have emanated from a serving military officer then in Iraq, Bradley Manning.

3. I have reason to fear that once I am in Sweden, unless I have protection against onward extradition to the USA, it is highly likely that such an onward transfer will be unable to be prevented. Although I have been charged with no offence in Sweden, I am to be imprisoned nevertheless and I am advised if charged I will remain in prison until any trial.

4. Although I am an Australian citizen I am unable to effect any or any adequate protection from my country; information publicly available shows active discussion by senior Australian officials, including by the Australian Police Force (as well as the then Attorney General) as to the cancellation of my passport, as well as close liaison with US officials in relation to my proposed prosecution in that country. Because of the seriousness that surrounds the request I am making to the government of Ecuador and in recognition of the extreme degree of courtesy afforded to me by the Government of Ecuador in considering that request, I set out in a fuller form details that I hope will assist such a consideration.

5. I wish to emphasise that I am entirely innocent; I have committed no crimes in the USA or Sweden. I would have presented myself for trial, and would now present myself in both countries without hesitation if I had not been forced to the view that the inevitability once in Sweden will be that I am placed on an unstoppable course towards a politically engineered show trial in the USA, and imprisonment, in isolation, for life.

Prosecution in the USA

6. The issuing of an indictment by prosecutors in the USA is a certainty (a Grand Jury in Virginia is authoritatively reported to have been empanelled to receive evidence for approximately 2 years for this purpose).

7. A request for my extradition will be made with equal certainty at the latest when legal processes in Sweden are concluded, and possibly before then, utilising a "temporary surrender" procedure permitted in the US/Swedish bilateral extradition treaty.

8. My imprisonment in the USA, pre-trial, is also a certainty in view of the potential charges likely to be brought against me, as is the certainty of conditions of severe isolation in prison in that country.

9. The allegations being canvassed publicly by many senior figures in the USA include allegations of espionage, material support for terrorism, assistance to the enemy, and conspiracy with a serving military officer to carry out acts of computer fraud and abuse incorporated by the USA Patriot Act 2001 into a "Federal Crimes of Terrorism" list. The likely charges, the attitude of the US government towards me and the known circumstances of placement of individuals on comparable charges mean that I will, again with certainty, be imprisoned in conditions that mirror those experienced by my alleged co-accused Bradley Manning, being held in conditions of confinement which violate of Article 3 of the European Convention of Human Rights and UN minimum conditions of imprisonment.

10. If convicted of any of the above charges, the sentences imposed upon me would be enormous, including cumulative sentences on multiple counts should they run consecutively. Any of these would constitute a life sentence.

11. The circumstances in which I would inevitably be held awaiting trial, would be under Special Administrative Measures ("SAMs"), requiring that I would be held in solitary confinement with access to no other prisoner, only to lawyers and in severely limited encounters, confined 23 hours a day in a small single cell, "recreation" taken only in an adjacent enclosed cell area and with no other person.

12. It is certain the US Attorney General will take the position that he has the authority to impose those conditions of detention on me, both pre-trial and, if convicted, post-trial. Under Federal regulations, the Attorney General may authorize the Director of the Bureau of Prisons to implement SAMs for detaining individuals whose communications or contacts pose a substantial risk of death or bodily injury to

persons, "or substantial damage to property that would entail the risk of death or serious bodily injury to persons." The attitude already taken publicly by the Administration is that the communications of WikiLeaks pose such a risk. Federal regulations allow the Attorney General to authorize SAMS that are "reasonably necessary to prevent disclosure of classified information" if such information "would pose a threat to the national security and there is a danger that the inmate will disclose such information." 28 C.F.R. § 501.2(a), again, what is already repeatedly maintained by senior US officials about me and about WikiLeaks.

13. Initially SAMs can be imposed for up to 120 days or, with the Attorney General's approval, for up to a year. Thereafter, "Special restrictions . . . may be extended . . . in increments not to exceed one year" if it is determined "that there continues to be a substantial risk that the inmate's communications or contacts with other persons could result in death or serious bodily injury to persons, or substantial damage to property that would entail the risk of death or serious bodily injury to persons."

14. The Attorney General may even order monitoring of a prisoner's communications with his attorney if it is determined that such communications may be used to facilitate acts of terrorism, a term applied, however extravagantly and wrongly, by US officials in relation to me and to Wikileaks.

15. The legal and human rights communities have repeatedly condemned the U.S. government's use of SAMS as inhumane and violative of human rights protocols: the total isolation of prisoners; the lack of access to visitors or outside communications; and the impact SAMS have on a prisoner's ability to participate in and prepare a defence or his willingness to accept a plea bargain.

16. SAMS aside, the effects of solitary confinement are well-documented. "*Social science and clinical literature have consistently reported that when human beings are subjected to social isolation and reduced environmental stimulation, they may deteriorate mentally and in some cases develop psychiatric disturbances.*" These psychiatric disturbances "*include perceptual distortions, hallucinations, hyper-responsivity to external stimuli, aggressive fantasies, overt paranoia, inability to concentrate, and problems with impulse control.*" These symptoms are especially

prevalent in prisoners held alone in *"small, often windowless cells with solid steel doors for more than 22 hours a day"*.

17. The United Nations Human Rights Committee and the Committee Against Torture have criticized the United States for such conditions pre-trial and post trial. In a 2003 report, the UN Committee Against Torture expressed concern about *"prolonged isolation periods . . . [and] the effect such treatment has on [prisoners'] mental health."* Further, the Committee expressed concern that the purpose of such isolation *"may be retribution, in which case it would constitute cruel, inhuman or degrading treatment or punishment (art. 16)."*

18. The UN Human Rights Committee expressed concern that the conditions of some US "maximum security prisons" are *"incompatible with article 10 of the Covenant and run counter to the United Nations Standard Minimum Rules for the Treatment of Prisoners and the Code of Conduct for Law Enforcement Officials"*.

19. In regard to any international monitoring of my internationally prohibited circumstances of detention in the USA the following factors are relevant:

    (a) The USA is not a party to the American Convention on Human Rights, having signed but never ratified the convention. I would therefore not have recourse to the Convention's enforcement bodies (the Inter-American Commission on Human Rights and the Inter-American Court on Human Rights).

    (b) The USA is party to the International Convention for Civil and Political Rights, but not to the Optional Protocol permitting the right of individual petition to the UN Human Right's Committee (the HRC). I would not have recourse to the HRC.

    (c) The USA is a party to the UN Convention against Torture but has not accepted the right of individual petition under Article 22 of that Convention. I would not have recourse to the UN Committee Against Torture.

    (d) The USA has not signed, much less ratified, the optional protocol to that treaty which establishes a Committee for the Prevention of Torture that would offer protection comparable to the protection offered by the CPT in Europe.

2. A LETTER TO THE ECUADORIAN PRESIDENT

(e)   The USA accepts a different (and lower test) for its definition of torture than the European Court of Human Rights.

(f)   The possibility that I could apply to any competent national or international human rights monitoring body in the event of the real risk of exposure to a violation of my rights materialising is non-existent. I would be without access to any international or effective body. Furthermore it would leave me exclusively in control of the very State at whose hands I fear serious and irreparable harm. (The reality is although applications are made to the Inter American Commission on Human Rights, the US has followed a continuous practice of refusing to acknowledge or act upon any adverse findings by that body). My alleged co-accused Bradley Manning, held in such conditions was refused private access to the UN Special Rapporteur on Torture despite the sustained request of the latter and the normality of the provision of such access by the international community as a whole.

20.   I am highly likely, furthermore, to be detained for a substantial length of time before a trial begins. Although the Speedy Trial Act provides that a defendant is entitled to a trial within seventy days of indictment or first appearance, time may be (and, indeed, routinely is) excluded from the Speedy Trial clock. Thus defendants routinely go many months and even several years before being tried and still have no recourse under the Act (or any Constitutional right to a speedy trial).

21.   Any potential sentences I face in the USA will ensure I am never released from prison. The Centre for Constitutional Rights in the USA stated on 20 June 2012 *"The concrete reality is that he was facing the death penalty or certainly life in jail"*.

22.   I am likely to be charged with a death-eligible offence as is Bradley Manning (although this would not be available if brought through extradition under treaties that prohibit the death penalty) or one punishable by life imprisonment. Title 18 U.S.C. § 794(a) precludes an individual from communicating, delivering, or transmitting (or attempting to do the same) to any foreign government or other party materials or information relating to the national defence where that individual does so with intent or reason to believe that the material or information is to be used to the injury of the U.S. or to the advantage of a foreign nation. Any violation of §

794(a) *"shall be punished by death or by imprisonment for any term of years or for life."*

23. § 793(g) provides that if one *"conspire[s] to violate any of the foregoing provisions of this section, and one or more of such persons do any act to effect the object of the conspiracy, each of the parties to such conspiracy shall be subject to the punishment provided for the offence which the object of such conspiracy."* This provision may be significant in the event of the government seek to establish a conspiracy between me and Bradley Manning, or other individuals accused of actually leaking material related to the national defence.

24. The following are only some of the many statements made by senior figures in the US. They underscore my belief that the allegations levelled against me in the USA are founded on political reactions and motivations rather than on any certain legal basis. There are wild and ever changing public statements, including demands to bring in new laws if necessary to ensure I am neutralised, to categorise WikiLeaks as a foreign terrorist organisation and to eliminate me by any means including assassination.

19.12.2010
Vice President Joseph Biden
Asked whether Mr. Assange was a high-tech terrorist or a whistleblower akin to those who released the Pentagon Papers, Mr. Biden stated: *"I would argue that it's closer to being a high-tech terrorist."* *"This guy has done things and put in jeopardy the lives and occupations of people in other parts of the world,"* Biden said. *"He's made it difficult to conduct our business with our allies and our friends. . . . It has done damage."*

05.12.2010
U.S. Senator Mitch McConnell ((R-KY), Senate Minority Leader)
"I think the man is a high-tech terrorist. He's done an enormous damage to our country, and I think he needs to be prosecuted to the fullest extent of the law. And if that becomes a problem, we need to change the law."

30.11.2010
Tom Flanagan Prof., Univ. of Calgary, and fmr. Chief of Staff to Prime Minister Stephen Harper

In an edition of CBC's Power & Politics with Evan Solomon, Mr. Flanagan said U.S. President Barack Obama *"should put out a contract and maybe use a drone or something"* on Assange.
"I think Assange should be assassinated, actually," Flanagan said with a laugh. When asked to expand on his answer, he added that he *"wouldn't be unhappy"* if Assange *"disappeared."*

2. A LETTER TO THE ECUADORIAN PRESIDENT

03.08.2010
Marc Thiessen (political commentator and fmr. Speech writer to President George W. Bush)

"Let's be clear: WikiLeaks is not a news organization; it is a criminal enterprise. Its reason for existence is to obtain classified national security information and disseminate it as widely as possible -- including to the United States' enemies. These actions are likely a violation of the Espionage Act, and they arguably constitute material support for terrorism."

30.11.2010
Bill Kristol (well known conservative columnist)

"Why can't we act forcefully against WikiLeaks? Why can't we use our various assets to harass, snatch or neutralize Julian Assange and his collaborators, wherever they are? Why can't we disrupt and destroy WikiLeaks in both cyberspace and physical space, to the extent possible? Why can't we warn others of repercussions from assisting this criminal enterprise hostile to the United States?"

30.11.2010
Kathleen McFarland (Fox News national security analyst; served in national security posts in the Nixon, Ford and Reagan administrations)

"WikiLeaks founder Julian Assange isn't some well-meaning, anti-war protestor leaking documents in hopes of ending an unpopular war. He's waging cyber war on the United States and the global world order. Mr. Assange and his fellow hackers are terrorists and should be prosecuted as such."
"The President needs to get on the phone with the Australians (who are eagerly awaiting our call) and ask them to pull WikiLeaks founder Julian Assange's passport. Once he's cornered and can no longer travel, they can find him and charge him with espionage. Then the president can ask the country he's hiding in to extradite him to the United States and try him in a military tribunal."

02.12.2010
Jeffrey Kuhner (Washington Times columnist)
"Julian Assange poses a clear and present danger to American national security. The WikiLeaks founder is more than a reckless provocateur. He is aiding and abetting terrorists in their war against America. The administration must take care of the problem - effectively and permanently."

05.12.2010
Newt Gingrich (Former Speaker of U.S. House of Reps)

"Julian Assange is engaged in warfare. Information terrorism, which leads to people getting killed is terrorism. And Julian Assange is engaged in terrorism." As such, Gingrich suggested, *"He should be treated as an enemy combatant and WikiLeaks should be closed down permanently and decisively."*

IN DEFENSE OF JULIAN ASSANGE

29.11.2010
U.S. Rep. Peter King, (chairman of the House homeland Security
Committee)

Regarding labelling WikiLeaks a terrorist organization: *"The benefit of that is,
we would be able to seize their assets and we would be able to stop anyone
from helping them in any way,"* King said, appearing on MSNBC.
*"I don't think we should write it off that quickly and say we can't do it. They
are assisting in terrorist activity. The information they are giving is being used
by al Qaeda, it's being used by our enemies,"* he said.

28.11.2010
U.S. Rep. Peter King

*"Moreover, the repeated releases of classified information from WikiLeaks,
which have garnered international attention, manifests Mr Assange's
purposeful intent to damage not only our national interests in fighting the war
on terror, but also undermines the very safety of coalition forces in Iraq and
Afghanistan. As the Department of Defence has explicitly recognized,
WikiLeaks' dissemination of classified US military and diplomatic documents
affords material support to terrorist organizations, including Al Qaeda, Tehrik-
e-Taliban Pakistan (TTP) and Al Shabaab."*
*"Given Mr Assange's active role in encouraging the theft and distribution of
classified material, he should be held liable pursuant to section 793(g), which
provides that if more than one person conspire to violate any section of the
Espionage Act and perform an act to the conspiracy, then "each of the parties
to such conspiracy shall be subject to the punishment provided for the
offense which is the object of such conspiracy." In addition, Mr Assange
should be chargeable for obtaining classified documents pertaining to
national defence initially acquired in violation of the Espionage Act and for
wilfully retaining such documents with the knowledge that he was not entitled
to receive them. There should be no misconception that Mr Assange
passively operates a forum for others to exploit their misappropriation of
classified information. He actively encourages and solicits
the leaking of national defence information. He pursues a malicious agenda,
for which he remains totally immune to the consequences of his actions."*

07.12.2010
U.S. Sen. Dianne Feinstein (D-CA)

*"When WikiLeaks founder Julian Assange released his latest document
trove—more than 250,000 secret State Department cables—he intentionally
harmed the U.S. government. The release of these documents damages our
national interests and puts innocent lives at risk. He should be vigorously
prosecuted for espionage."*

01.12.2010
Robert Gibbs (White House Press Secretary)

Referred to Mr. Assange as an *"accomplice."*

2. A LETTER TO THE ECUADORIAN PRESIDENT

06.12.2007
Robert Beckel (Fox News Analyst and Deputy Asst. Sec. of State in Carter Administration)

"A dead man can't leak stuff. This guy's a traitor, a treasonist [sic], and he has broken every law of the United States. And I'm not for the death penalty, so . . . there's only one way to do it: Illegally shoot the son of a bitch."

29.11.2010
Sen. Kit Bond (RMO)

"It is critical that the perpetrator who betrayed his country be brought to justice for this deliberate treason that jeopardizes our national security."

[Date unknown – approx Dec 2, 2010]
Sen. Charles Schumer (D-NY)
"This man has put his own ego above the safety of millions of innocents," Sen. Charles Schumer (D-NY) said in a statement. *"He should be extradited, tried for espionage, and given the most severe penalty possible."*

02.12.2010
Dianne Feinstein (D-CA)
Letter to Attorney General Eric Holder.

"We respectfully urge the Department of Justice (DOJ) to take action to bring criminal charges against WikiLeaks founder Julian Assange and any all of his possible accomplices involved in the unauthorised possession and distribution of vast quantities of classified and unclassified material from the US government. The unauthorised release of this information, including the recent release of approximately 250,000 State Department documents, is a serious breach of national security and could be used to severely harm the United States and its worldwide interests."
We appreciate your statement earlier this week that DOJ has an "active, ongoing, criminal investigation" with regard to the WikiLeaks matter. We also understand that Private First Class Bradley E Manning – who may have been involved in disclosing the most recent set of documents provided to WikiLeaks – has already been charged in military court with eight violations of federal criminal law, including unauthorised computer access and transmitting classified information to an unauthorised third party in violation of a section of the Espionage Act, 18 U.S.C. 793(e).
If Mr Assange and his possible accomplices cannot be charged under the Espionage Act (or any other applicable statute), please know that we stand ready and willing to support your efforts "to close those gaps" in the law, as you also mentioned this week. Thank you very much for your attention to this matter."

29.11.2010
U.S. Rep. Peter King, (chairman of the House homeland Security Committee)

Letter to US Attorney General *"I urge you to criminally charge WikiLeaks activist Julian Assange under the Espionage Act"*.

IN DEFENSE OF JULIAN ASSANGE

29.11.2010
U.S. Rep. Peter King, (chairman of the House homeland Security Committee)

Letter to US Secretary of State Hillary Clinton *"I request you undertake an immediate review to determine whether WikiLeaks cound be designated a foreign terrorist organisation in accordance with section 21D of the Immigration and Nationality Act".*

25. A climate has been set by these remarks, in which any potential juror has been urged in advance of any trial over a number of years to view me as an enemy of the USA. I am forced to believe that despite the fact that I and WikiLeaks have endeavoured only to make the truth available to all, and that the principle of free expression is endorsed by the First Amendment of the US Constitution, that nevertheless any presumption of my innocence has been systematically destroyed in advance of any trial and that no patriotic juror would feel able to acquit me.

26. The National Fair Trial Jury Project in the USA has commented on the inappropriateness of the federal judicial venue reportedly selected for my case and in which the Grand Jury sits. Of all the 94 federal judicial districts in the United States, it reports that the Department of Justice has selected the one district in the country which is uniquely unqualified to afford me a fair trial: the Eastern District of Virginia drawn from a district that has the highest density of government and military contractors in the United States. For that reason espionage trials in particular are conducted there. Grand juries are handpicked from the local area by prosecutors with no screening for bias. (Senior figures, for instance the organisation Stratfor's vice president (the former deputy chief of the Department of State's Counter Terrorism Division for the Diplomatic Security Service) have stated that a secret grand jury investigating me already has a sealed indictment.) Within that relatively small jury catchment area are housed the following federal institutions:

The Pentagon, The Headquarters of the CIA, The United States Department of Homeland Security, The Office of the Director of National Intelligence, The National Counterterrorism Center, The National Geospatial Intelligence Agency, The National Reconnaissance Office, The Quantico Marine Corp Base (with over 8,000 civilian employees). Other major employers in the district servicing the military include Lockheed Martin, General Dynamics, Northrup Gruman, Boeing, and BAE Systems.

2. A LETTER TO THE ECUADORIAN PRESIDENT

27. The combination of all of the above factors make the concept of a fair trial unimaginable. I am aware that the statistic of convictions in the USA is 97%, brought about in large part by pleas of guilt by defendants whether guilty or innocent, in understandable attempts to negotiate for a lesser sentence or conditions short of the most severe, in my case life without any form of parole and in isolation. I have read the comments attributed to the lawyer for Bradley Manning,

    "During the December pre-trial hearing in the case against Bradley Manning, Manning's defense lawyer, David Coombs, claimed that the government was vastly overcharging his client in an attempt to force Manning into making a plea deal and turning evidence against Assange.

    Manning's attorney David E. Coombs opened the morning stating that the Army was overcharging his disturbed but idealistic client and exaggerating the impact of the leaks in order to strong-arm Manning.

    Coombs said the government wants to force his client into making a plea deal and turning evidence against Assange, whom the Justice Department is investigating in a criminal case stemming from the leaks allegedly provided by Manning.

    Coombs asked the court's Investigating Officer to drop the charge accusing Manning of aiding the enemy and to consolidate some of the charges, saying that many were redundant and that Manning shouldn't be facing 100 to 150 years in prison.

    "If the Department of Justice got their way, they would get a plea in this case, and get my client to be named as one of the witnesses to go after Julian Assange and Wikileaks.""

Parallel pressures

28. Beyond the sustained verbal assaults by senior figures in the USA, an even more widespread attack on the WikiLeaks organisation has been orchestrated at all levels by the US administration. I do not set out here the history or detail of information

made available by WikiLeaks on the internet save that information relating to actions primarily of the United States but also of other nations included concrete and unequivocal evidence of serious crimes, including war crimes and crimes against humanity. Despite the publication of that evidence, and despite the publication by others of evidence of closely related unlawful or criminal agreements, actions and statements whereby WikiLeaks was being targeted with the intention of its elimination, I am unaware that anyone or any organisation exposed as a result of those many and various disclosures as having committed unlawful acts has been charged with any criminal offence. Instead, it is WikiLeaks against whom criminal accusations are made for its exposure of State misconduct and the impunity of those state agents and agencies responsible.

29.   A financial blockade has been instituted by the US government and US financial services companies including Bank of America, Visa, MasterCard, PayPal and Western Union; it is illegal, violating competition laws and trade practice legislation in numerous states. Following an announcement that WikiLeaks intended to release material incriminating an American bank in unethical practices, Bank of America commissioned a data intelligence contractor via a Washington law firm to propose a multi pronged attack to take out WikiLeaks. The plans later revealed on the internet, show that it was intended to mount illegal cyber attacks on WikiLeaks' computer systems, attack the public reputation of prominent journalists supporting WikiLeaks and survey and catalogue WikiLeaks' supporters on the internet.

30.   Requests came from US government figures that American banking corporations Visa, Mastercard, Paypal, Western Union and Bank of America impose an illegal financial blockade against the organization, blocking the ability of members of the public to make donations, and thereby shutting off 95% of WikiLeaks' funding. In December 2010 Paypal froze 60,000 euros of WikiLeaks donations held by the Wau Holland charitable foundation. Two days later Swiss bank PostFinance froze my account, containing 31,000 euros, used for WikiLeaks Staff Defence Funds.. In July 2011 WikiLeaks lodged a complaint about the financial blockade with the European Commission for infringement of EU Anti-Trust laws; it is still awaiting an answer.

31.   The UN High Commissioner for Human Rights, Navanethem Pillay, condemned the US government for exerting pressure on private companies to close down the credit

2. A LETTER TO THE ECUADORIAN PRESIDENT

lines for donations to WikiLeaks, and to stop hosting its website. The UN Special Rapporteur Protection of the Right to Freedom of Opinion and Expression as well as the Inter-American Commission on Human Rights' Special Rapporteur for Freedom of Expression issued a joint statement defending WikiLeaks against the blockade and politically motivated attacks. The statement considered that the banking blockade was an unprecedented attack on supporters' freedom of expression. It constitutes a direct interference to people's ability to affect change with no parallel in recent history. It revives the infamous blacklisting of the McCarthy era.

32. WikiLeaks' volunteers and associates have endured constant harassment, being detained at US border points, having their electronic devices seized and secret so-called 2703(d) orders issued for their Twitter records, the latter only coming to light when Twitter challenged the injunction against letting individuals know their records were being turned over to federal authorities. It is not yet known how many other internet service providers received similar 2703(d) orders relating to WikiLeaks - so far, Google and ISP Sonic.net as well have been confirmed. WikiLeaks volunteers and associates continue to be pressured to become "informants" against the organisation and / or against myself.

Australia

33. The contradictory nature of public statements in Australia gives me the gravest concern that agreements have been secretly reached between the US and Australia, my own country. Although Prime Minister Julia Gillard, Foreign Minister Bob Carr and Attorney General Nicola Roxon have all stated that they have seen "no evidence" or "no evidence from the US" that the US government has or intends to charge me with any offence, Australian Diplomatic Cables released to Fairfax Media show the Australian Embassy in Washington as early as 7 December 2010 confirming that the Justice Department was conducting an "active and vigorous inquiry into whether Julian Assange can be charged under US law, most likely the 1917 Espionage Act". The Embassy reported being told by US officials "the WikiLeaks case was unprecedented both in its scale and nature", and reported to Canberra on 22 December 2010 that "the reports that a secret grand jury had been convened in Virginia were "likely true". The Embassy provided Canberra with regular updates through 2011 including reporting on the issuing of subpoenas to

compel WikiLeaks associates to appear before the Grand Jury and Justice Department efforts to access Twitter and other internet accounts to "*cast the net beyond Assange*".

34. I understand that Prime Minister Julia Gillard instigated a federal investigation into whether criminal charges could be brought against me. Before it had been concluded that I have broken no laws, the Prime Minister had already publicly called my actions "illegal" and stated that my passport might be cancelled, the Australian police being commissioned to investigate whether that was possible . A copy of a "WikiLeaks Task Force" Minute released by the Australian Attorney General's Department includes a sentence that indicates the Australian Police Force was considering the "*possibility of cancelling Mr Assange's passport*", consideration was despite the conclusion of the Australian Police Force that I and WikiLeaks had broken no Australian laws by publishing classified US government documents.

35. The Australian government has repeatedly delayed, censored and blocked Freedom of Information (FOI) requests for material that would reveal its internal legal deliberations over my extradition to the US and has refused to answer parliamentary questions about the extent of its co-operation.

36. Meanwhile Australia quietly changed its own extradition laws three months ago. Amongst the amendments is a significant lessening of the restrictions on extradition for "political offences" thereby weakening the security of all Australians, and facilitating my extradition if ever required from my home country. There was no media reporting of the passage of this amendment.

37. In July 2011 the Australian government passed the 'WikiLeaks Amendment', broadening the powers of Australia's ASIO intelligence agency to spy on Australian citizens and anyone associated with WikiLeaks.

38. Australia has given only cursory assistance regarding the highly irregular and politicised Swedish extradition request for me under the European Arrest Warrant (EAW) system and in parallel declassified Australian diplomatic cables show that Australian diplomats have raised no concerns over my possible extradition to the United States, the Australian government having asked only that it be forewarned,

2. A LETTER TO THE ECUADORIAN PRESIDENT

so as to coordinate a media response. Requests have been made on my behalf over a sustained period of time to the Australian government to provide me with protection in a range of ways, yet the Australian government has not felt able to provide any of the forms of protection requested. The following requests remain unanswered:

"1) _Re Sweden:_ Mr Assange asks the Australian government to seek the following undertakings from Sweden:

(a) To seek an undertaking concerning extradition to the USA. It is Mr Assange's understanding as a result of Ms Robinson's recent meeting with the Attorney General, that the Australian government's position is it would prefer any extradition to happen from Australia than from a foreign jurisdiction. This being the case, it would of course be appropriate for the Australian government to be seeking relevant assurances and undertakings through diplomatic channels to ensure that possibility occurs should Mr Assange be extradited from the UK to Sweden.

(b) To enquire of Sweden if it has not already, why Sweden has not made use of customary mutual assistance provisions to interrogate Julian Assange from London or equivalent methods. We understand from Miss Robinson that the Attorney General considered it "odd" that Mr Assange had been held without charge for 18 months and that she found it difficult to understand how this could accord with principles of justice. (It may be that the Australian government has already raised this issue with Sweden, but if so, Mr Assange is not aware of such a request).

(c) To ask that Mr Assange be allowed to remain under similar conditions to those he has been in the UK (curfew), pending the resolution of his case if he is extradited. (He understands from his lawyers in Sweden that prosecutors there have refused to negotiate any alternative to custody, despite the fact that Mr Assange has complied with his bail conditions in England for nearly 18 months).

(d) To obtain undertakings concerning prison detention, for however short a period, including undertakings re access to visitors, computer etc.

(e) To seek an undertaking in relation to serving any potential sentence in Australia under normal prisoner treaty transfer arrangements.

(f) That the Australian government raises a complaint with the Swedish government as to continual adverse public comments from the most senior members of Swedish political and executive, including the Prime Minister, the Minister for Justice and the Foreign Minister, such as to potentially interfere with any chance of a fair trial of Mr Assange, such comments having implications not only for Sweden but thereafter in the USA were there to be an attempt by the US to place Mr Assange on trial there.

(g) That given the uncertain political relationships of intermediate countries Mr. Assange may have to travel through to return to Australia, that the Australian government provide safe passage to Australia for Mr Assange should he be in a position to leave Sweden.

2. *Re United States:* Mr Assange asks that Australia seek the following undertakings from the USA: -

    (a) That the US will not prosecute Mr Assange. It appears to be common diplomatic practice – in particular the US government often seeks an assurance from foreign states not to prosecute its citizens and agents. Ms Robinson understood from the Attorney General that such an assurance can indeed be sought from the US government, and it is entirely appropriate in this case for Australia to do so; the case involves an Australian citizen in relation to matters which engage the First Amendment and free speech protections; it is recognised as being a case of the utmost importance, and one that could set disturbing precedents for the freedom of speech.

    (b) An undertaking from the US that Mr Assange if extradited, be granted bail pending the resolution of his case for the same reasons as above in relation to Sweden; he has complied with bail conditions in England for nearly 18 months which should serve to demonstrate that he is not a flight risk. (The United Kingdom sought a similar assurance for the National Westminster Bank defendants of the United States which was granted).

    (c) To ask that in the event of extradition trial and conviction in the USA, any sentence that might be imposed, be served in Australia under normal prisoner treaty transfer arrangements. (Again such an assurance in advance of extradition can be sought).

    (d) That an undertaking be given that he not be placed under special administrative measures if in custody for however short a time, and be permitted free confidential access to his lawyers and visitors pending trial, as well as to a computer and necessary work/case requirements.

    (e) That prejudicial statements by US officials about Mr. Assange (up to and including the Vice President) be retracted forthwith. Those statements already made seriously jeopardise any potential of a fair trial for Mr Assange.

    (f) An undertaking that individuals associated with WikiLeaks or Mr Assange not be further targeted or harassed by FBI agents, including very recently individuals detained, interrogated and pressured to become informants by FBI officers.

Sweden

39. I am imminently due to be extradited by the UK to Sweden in pursuit of a request that I be questioned by a Swedish prosecutor. I have been permitted a 14-day period which expires on 28 June 2012 to seek a stay from the European Court of Human Rights in relation to my transfer to Sweden. I am advised that although there are issues of importance that the European Court may well be likely in due course to consider constitute a breach, in particular, of the right to a fair trial (as any potential trial in Sweden will be in secret with the public excluded) it is unlikely in conformity with its normal practice, that the European Court would issue a Rule 39

2. A LETTER TO THE ECUADORIAN PRESIDENT

Order preventing extradition, but would only thereafter consider the case if and when such proceedings materialise in Sweden.

40. I set out here what has occurred to date in relation to me in Sweden. I visited that country at the invitation of a Swedish political party dedicated to the free provision of information. Whilst there, I had a brief physical involvement with two women at different times, which was (and has always been said by all concerned, to have been consensual). Thereafter in the absence of receiving an immediate response one of the women contacted a police officer to ask whether I could be required to present myself to be checked to ensure that I did not have any communicable disease. Instead, the police officer, herself linked I understand to a particular political party, took immediate steps to notify a duty prosecutor of an allegation of rape on the basis that a brief interlude of unprotected sex during an encounter otherwise protected constituted a criminal offence. A second allegation was added some days later when the second woman was spoken to by police. I as requested, presented myself to a police officer in Sweden and answered all the questions asked of me.

41. Despite the prohibition in Sweden for a prosecutor to publicly name a suspect, an immediate telephone call was made, I understand by the duty prosecutor, to a non-professional acquaintance at a political event. Publication of an intention to charge me with rape was immediately broadcast in the media. Thereafter a senior prosecutor countermanded the charge, which was withdrawn. She said publicly "*I consider there are no grounds for suspecting he has committed rape.*"

42. A lawyer linked to the same political movement I understand, as the original police officer went to a third prosecutor in a different city with whom he had been involved in political campaigning as a result of which a prosecutorial investigation was reinstated. A complaint has I am informed, been filed with the Ethics Committee of that lawyer's professional body for making statements assigning guilt to me, when I have been neither charged nor tried (*"He is afraid of being sentenced for his crimes"*).

43. Thereafter, and in the absence of any active inquiries being made of me, through my lawyer I requested and obtained from the prosecutor permission to leave

Sweden. Subsequently, and despite my willingness to be questioned by the prosecutor where I was in the UK, or by means of mutual assistance through police or courts in the UK, the prosecutor issued a European Arrest Warrant insisting that I be extradited to Sweden where I would be imprisoned.

44.   I remain without charge. I have exercised my rights through the courts in the UK to challenge my extradition to Sweden. Most recently the judges of the Supreme Court were in agreement that the substitution of a prosecutor for a "judicial authority" to issue European arrests warrants was counter to the intention of the UK parliament, when it brought into force the relevant extradition treaty under which I am to be transferred for questioning in custody to Sweden. The Court nevertheless came to the conclusion that cross-European practice, in which some of the more than 40 member states similarly allow prosecutors to be considered to be a judicial authority for the purpose of issuing extradition warrants, was by now so entrenched, that despite the fact that UK parliament was misled when it approved the enabling legislation, nevertheless my extradition would stand.

45.   In the light of this extraordinary history I believe that I cannot look to any guarantees from Sweden that would prevent my onward extradition to the US. The following factors add to that view:

(a) The way in which the allegation against me in Sweden (that in no way emanated voluntarily from the two alleged complainants but, according to one, was pressured upon her by the police), and which neither reported as a criminal offence at the beginning, has since been affected and driven by extraneous and political purposes.

(b) The case of Agiza v Sweden has given me particular concern; the Swedish authorities in conjunction with the US, arranged for the rendition of two men to Egypt where they would be tortured, in the face of knowledge that that was likely to be their fate, and in the knowledge that the inadequate paper assurances requested of the Egyptian regime, would be unable to protect Agiza. It is in the light of Sweden's proven willingness to cooperate with the US to disregard prohibitions when it is claimed that it is to combat a perceived "war on terror" that reinforces my fears, since this is the categorisation that senior members of the

2. A LETTER TO THE ECUADORIAN PRESIDENT

US Administration have ascribed to the work of WikiLeaks and my role in that work.

(c) On 28 May 2012 lawyers instructed to act for me in Sweden confirmed that they had met with the prosecutor, that their view was that the prosecutor would continue to demand that I remain in custody throughout the legal process, that as I am not a resident in Sweden I will be unlikely to be granted an alternative to prison (effective house arrest), by a Swedish judge; that foreign residents are typically held in custody during the investigation and up to and including trial of crimes such as are alleged against me; that I would be held in a Swedish remand prison, with virtual certainty in isolation. Any trial will be held in secret, in breach of the fair trial provisions of the European Convention on Human Rights.

(d) I have further reason to fear that Sweden would not refuse an extradition request by the USA. It is reliably reported that every extradition request that has been sent to Sweden from the United States since 2000 has been granted.

(e) The European Committee against Torture has directed strong criticism of Sweden for the conditions in its remand prisons, including that Swedish courts impose imprisonment on 42% of individuals suspected (as opposed to convicted) of criminal accusations and that the imprisonment is likely. My Swedish lawyers describe "*Sweden's routine misuse of pre-trial detention and isolation*".

(f) In considering the approach likely to be taken by Sweden in relation to the conditions to which I would be inevitably sent and placed thereafter, indefinitely for life, in US prisons, Sweden's own practices in the use of isolation in its own prisons must be relevant. (By contrast its neighbour Norway, has recently refused to permit an extradition to the USA on the basis of the prison conditions that would await the extraditee there).

(g) It is relevant that the European Court of Human Rights has recently considered that extradition of individuals to the US, where they would face solitary confinement (under Special Administrative Measures) and extreme isolation pre-trial, and indefinite isolation in a supermax prison post-trial to be acceptable. On 10 April 2012 the European Court declined to make a finding that such conditions would constitute a breach of Article 3 of the European Convention on Human Rights, prohibiting torture or inhumane and degrading treatment. Had the Strasbourg Court made such a finding it could have prevented my extradition from Sweden to the US, even if there were no other resistance to any US extradition request.

(h) This recent view of the European Court is rejected by every other international body whose task it is to monitor torture, all of whom consider that the conditions in isolation deployed in US prisons even after a very short period of time, violate every international minimum norm. Although the Strasbourg court is at odds with the international human rights community in this regard, it is only a ruling by the European Court that could prohibit extradition from a European country to such a fate, however certain. The European Court before giving judgment refused to accept a specific opinion on the US conditions by Juan Mendez the UN Special Rapporteur on Torture, and disregarded the findings of the European Committee for the Convention of Torture and every international study and recommendation (including the Istanbul statement).

(i) On 8 December 2010 the Independent newspaper in the UK cited "diplomatic sources" confirming informal talks between Sweden and the US about extraditing Julian Assange

(j) The US/Sweden bilateral treaty has a "temporary surrender" clause which can be used for onward transfer to the US, circumventing the safeguards of a formal extradition.

(k) The Swedish Prime Minister's chief political adviser is Karl Rove, previously adviser to George Bush and an associate of Swedish Foreign Minister Carl Bildt, (revealed as a US informant in a State Department cable from the 1970s).

(l) Senior Swedish political figures have made a number of wrong or misleading public statements highly prejudicial to a fair trial for me. These include Prime Minister Reinfeldt, Swedish Foreign Minister Carl Bildt, Sweden's Prosecutor-General Anders Perklev, investigating prosecutor Marianne Ny and Justice Minister Beatrice Ask, as well as the lawyer for the two women. I point out that I have not been charged in Sweden, let alone for any category of offence.

Nevertheless the following are amongst public statements that have been made:

    (i)   In a parliamentary address, the Prime Minister, Fredrik Reinfeldt said that "*we do not accept sexual abuse or rape*" and said that I and my lawyers had little regard for women's rights.

    (ii)   Swedish National Radio, 8/2/2011 Reinfeldt incorrectly stated that I had been charged for rape in Sweden. He also stated 'we do not accept rape [in Sweden]'. His remarks were published in Dagens Nyheter newspaper.

    (iii)   Mr Reinfeldt's remarks were made on the second day of my extradition hearing in the UK, hours after a defence challenge that the Swedish prosecutor be cross-examined in court.

2. A LETTER TO THE ECUADORIAN PRESIDENT

(iv) In his official blog Foreign Minister Carl Bildt repeated an entirely false claim by Espressen newspaper that "Wikileaks is planning a massive smear campaign against Sweden" and also released a series of tweets about it.

(v) A Chancellor of Justice inquiry into the prejudicial publication of my name by a Swedish prosecutor was summarily closed down without explanation.

(vi) The Public Prosecutor Marianne Ny (also Chief Investigator of this case), 3/12/2010 Marianne Ny justified the use of an Interpol Red Notice and EAW extradition because "we are by law prohibited from conducting hearings via telephone or video link, this was the only legal action left" and "The Swedish embassy in London is not Swedish territory in the sense that we can hold interrogations there without formal approval of British authorities." Both statements were incorrect as the UK and Sweden are both signatories to the Mutual Legal Assistance Treaty.

Ms Ny's statement was later retracted in the Swedish press (5/12/2010) but had already been accepted as true by Justice Riddle during my extradition appeal 8-11 February 2011, thus prejudicing his my due process rights.

46. On Tuesday 19th June I sought refuge at the Ecuadorean Embassy. I was able to explain to the Ambassador some of the constellation of circumstances, immediate and of long standing, that had led me to take so drastic a step. I did so because of my fear, for the reasons I have attempted to set out in some detail in this letter, that I am trapped in an onward progression, which I cannot alter by access to any form of protection, towards imprisonment in isolation in the USA for the remainder of my life.

47. It is not my wish to avoid investigation or indeed trial in Sweden, however unjust I believe the context to date to have been. I would welcome the opportunity after so long, of defending myself and clearing my name. Were I able, as I believe I am not, to know that I had any other route by which I could counter the accusations and the way in which those accusations have been mounted against me by the USA, and the methods by which I will be treated and my conviction inevitably achieved in that country, I would, and in the future will take it.

I wish to register my gratitude for your consideration of my request.

Yours sincerely

Julian Assange

3. WHAT'S THE POINT OF SWIMMING IN THE SEA, IF YOU DON'T BELIEVE IN ANYTHING?

Srećko Horvat, February 2019

Each time I approached the Ecuadorian embassy in London, walking through the streets of Knightsbridge, the feeling was the same.

As soon as one reaches the corner of Hans Crescent Street, one is immediately teleported into a version of postmodern Saudi Arabia, though in the midst of London: golden Lamborghinis and limited-edition Ferraris with Arabian plates are parked in front of Harrods, one of the most luxurious shopping malls in the world, which carries the deeply ironic Latin motto *Omnia Omnibus Ubique* ("all things for all people, everywhere").

When, after passing a memorial to Princess Diana and Dodi Fayed (the eldest son of the billionaire who purchased the store), I enter the famous Harrods Food Halls with its haute cuisine to buy some food for someone who hasn't seen the sea for more than seven years. I wonder how many of the 300,000 customers who visit the shop on busy days know that, only a few meters away, there resides someone—probably the most famous dissident in the West—who hasn't seen the sky or sunlight for more than 3,000 days? Not to mention a sunset somewhere on the beach.

I take the escalator up toward the exit and finally reappear on the street. People are walking with shopping bags of luxurious brands, while others are sitting at the Gran Caffè Londra eating Tagliata di Tonno or fresh Scottish salmon fillet while drinking Sicilian rosé with aromas of spring flowers and strawberries. The street is busy, with those distinctive black London cabs coming and going. I make my way to the embassy.

I have flown in directly from the Croatian coast, carrying not some expensive rosé but a simple bottle of fresh seawater. I wondered whether it means something to the numerous surveillance cameras around Hans Crescent Street. When I enter the Ecuadorian embassy, after the usual detailed inspection of all my belongings, including the bottle of seawater, I switch off my phone and leave it with the guards. Once in, I know, on each occasion, that I am entering a different world. The "white noise" starts . . .

To someone who hasn't been there, the best way to imagine the interior of the embassy is to watch Alfonso Cuarón's *Gravity* about two astronauts stuck in space. A total loss of temporality. Once I was inside for just two hours, yet it lasted an eternity. Once I left the building certain that I had been inside for just two hours, only to realize that it was already six in the morning.

There is no fresh air. No direct sunlight. Each breath you take, every step you make, even *inside* the embassy, is surveilled. Now imagine being inside for almost *seven years*.

"What is the first thing you would do when you would get out of the embassy?" I once asked him during a meeting in the permanently artificial light.

"I would look at the sky," said Julian Assange.

I asked what Julian missed during all these years of what the United Nations back in February 2016 described as "arbitrary detention."

Julian calmly answered: "Nothing."

"Not even the sky?"

139

"No."

This seemingly contradictory answer is probably the best shortcut to understanding the mind of a man who is without a doubt the biggest enemy of all the world's secret services—a man whose organization, WikiLeaks, was described by the new director of the CIA, Mike Pompeo, in his first speech in April 2017, as a "non-state hostile intelligence service."

How is it possible that the very first thing he would do upon leaving the embassy after seven years of imprisonment is look at the sky, but he says he doesn't miss it? I am sure he misses it, the same as someone who comes from Australia misses the ocean. But consider how Julian described his situation during one of our conversations at the embassy:

"This is not a price I have stumbled across, because I didn't understand how the world works. That's the price I knew I would pay, not this particular price, but a price like this. Yes, the situation is tough, but I'm confident there are prices to pay for what you believe in."

I am sure he would repeat this even today. Just recently, three doctors with a combined experience of four decades caring for and about refugees and other traumatized populations spent 20 hours in the embassy with Assange over three days, performing a comprehensive physical and psychological evaluation of his health. They concluded in an open letter published in the *Guardian* that his continued confinement is "dangerous physically and mentally, and a clear infringement of his human right to healthcare."[98]

Omnia Omnibus Ubique, as the Harrods motto says—but not healthcare for Julian Assange. Not even the Hippocratic Oath, except with the

[98] Sondra S. Crosby, Brock Chisholm, and Sean Love, "We examined Julian Assange, and he badly need care—but he can't get it," *The Guardian*, January 24, 2018, https://www.theguardian.com/commentisfree/2018/jan/24/julian-assange-care-wikileaks-ecuadorian-embassy?CMP=twt_gu),.

courageous doctors who visited him and published their report, counts when it comes to Assange.

It is usually the ("communist") East that is portrayed as the universe of persecuted dissidents, from famous communists-turned-harshest-critics of communism like Arthur Koestler or Aleksandr Solzhenitsyn, to contemporary dissenters like Pussy Riot or Ai Weiwei. But isn't the "liberal" and "free" West also producing a growing number of dissidents?

In just the last decade the list is getting ever longer: Julian Assange, Chelsea Manning, Aaron Schwartz, Jeremy Hammond, Barrett Brown, Edward Snowden, Laurie Love . . . Why are all these people either facing life in prison or constant surveillance, living in political asylum, faced with extradition to the US, or are even dead? Precisely because they have been revealing the dirty secrets of the West.

These courageous individuals find themselves in a situation that resembles the alternative history novel by Philip K. Dick, *The Man in the High Castle* (1963), recently popularized by the Amazon TV-series of the same name. It is a fictional scenario of a world divided between Germany and Japan, who are the victors of the Second World War. In this dystopian society every history, except the winner's official history, is forbidden. However, there is a resistance movement whose main weapon is finding and distributing accounts of the factual history (or rather, another parallel universe in which things not only could have been different, but are different). In the original Philip K. Dick story, it is books that serve this subversive role. In the TV-series it is movies. In real life it is WikiLeaks that has been serving this function for the past ten years.

Looking at the valuable material WikiLeaks has been publishing during the last decade, it is undeniable that it already represents an alternative history of the world. What is also evident is that there is unfortunately no reason for optimism. WikiLeaks has shown that our world is moving dangerously in the direction of mass destruction, from ongoing Western interventions in Africa to the Middle East; from the refugee crisis to global secret trade agreements; from terrorism to the militarization of public spaces; not to mention the realistic possibility of a nuclear catastrophe and environmental breakdown.

In one of his most recent works, *Hope without Optimism* (2015), the British literary theorist Terry Eagleton has manifested a much-needed deconstruction of the notion of optimism, showing that it is a typical component of ruling-class ideologies, and that it is precisely in the United States where a special kind of optimistic fatalism is nourished. As Eagleton says, "the US is one of the few countries on earth in which optimism is almost state ideology." Remember Obama's slogan, "Yes, we can!" Of course, WikiLeaks poses a threat to the US establishment for questioning this optimistic fatalism; it is constantly pointing the finger toward the ruling class and saying: "The Emperor is naked!"

Another lesson Eagleton provides us with is precisely the relation between the past and the future. If the establishment always attempts to impose its own version of history in order to govern the future, what we must still do is the opposite—we must keep the past unfinished, and reveal the dirty secrets involved in the construction of what is called official history.

Once, back in the winter of 2015, I was traveling to London from Paris bringing with me a present for Assange: a new installment in the famous Asterix comic series, *Asterix and the Missing Scroll* (in Deutsch, *Der Papyrus des Cäsar*). The central theme of the book is censorship and the battle over information, so the cartoonist decided to create a character inspired by Julian Assange.[99]

When he received my gift from Paris, Julian was obviously thrilled. A glow appeared in his eyes.

---

[99] "New comic in Asterix series to feature Julian Assange character," *The Guardian*, October 14, 2015, https://www.theguardian.com/books/2015/oct/14/new-comic-in-asterix-series-to-feature-julian-assange-character.

I asked him how he felt about ending up as a character in Asterix?

"It's better than receiving the Nobel," he replied. "Many more people received the Nobel Prize, than became characters in Asterix."

And it is precisely this characteristic answer—and Asterix—which can help us to better understand WikiLeaks. In the comic series all of Gaul is under the control of the Roman Empire, except for one small village in present-day Brittany, whose inhabitants are made invincible by a magic drink. In the same manner, WikiLeaks is a tiny organization which has for years published the dirty secrets of the world's leading empires from the United States to Russia, from Saudi Arabia to Syria, from the EU to Google.

I made this point to Julian and asked what was the "magic drink" of WikiLeaks?

"Cryptography," he replied unhesitatingly.

But of course, reality is not always a comic series.

There are some in the West who are fully convinced that Assange deserves to be tried and thrown in jail for "threatening" US national security and "undermining" its democratic processes. Former US presidential candidate Hillary Clinton and former vice president Joe Biden have called him a "terrorist."[100] Former US attorney general Jeff Sessions said prosecuting Assange was a "priority."

Whatever Assange's political leanings, whether you like him as a person or not, the factors are irrelevant: his case is about freedom of the press. As Edward Snowden rightly said: "You can despise WikiLeaks and everything it stands for. You can think Assange is an evil spirit reanimated by Putin himself, but you cannot support the prosecution of a publisher

---

[100] Warren Strobel and Mark Hosenball, "CIA chief calls WikiLeaks a 'hostile intelligence service,'" *Reuters*, April 13, 2017, https://www.reuters.com/article/us-cia-wikileaks/cia-chief-calls-wikileaks-a-hostile-intelligence-service-idUSKBN17F2L8.

for publishing without narrowing the basic rights every newspaper relies on."[101]

If Assange is eventually arrested, extradited to the US, and put on trial there, he is almost certainly going to be found guilty—just as Chelsea Manning was—and he will probably end up in a Guantánamo-like prison. His prosecution and jailing will have global repercussions for whistle-blowers, publishers, and journalists.

According to US lawyer and civil liberties advocate Ben Wizner at the American Civil Liberties Union (ACLU), "Any prosecution of Mr. Assange for WikiLeaks' publishing operations would be unprecedented and unconstitutional, and would open the door to criminal investigations of other news organizations."[102]

In other words, a lawsuit that tries to make it illegal or a form of "espionage" to publish documents as WikiLeaks has done would set a dangerous precedent for publishers and journalists who routinely violate foreign secrecy laws to deliver information vital to the public's interest. It would endanger the very foundation of free press.

We already live in a world in which politics and the distribution of information are being transformed. Not only are dangerous populists and authoritarian leaders coming to power by "manufacturing consent," backed by the use of "perception management" methods by tech companies (Facebook and Cambridge Analytica) or organized fake news campaigns (Trump in US, Bolsonaro in Brazil), but they also come to power by concealing information of public interest.

---

[101] Edward Snowden, *Twitter*, November 16, 2018, https://twitter.com/Snowden/status/1063520583789539328.

[102] "ACLU comment on report of DOJ Preparing to Prosecute Julian Assange," ACLU, November 15, 2018, https://www.aclu.org/news/aclu-comment-report-doj-preparing-prosecute-julian-assange.

While it has become commonplace for politicians to employ such questionable methods to obtain power, it is the job of journalists, the media, and whistleblowers to keep such behavior in check. Punishing journalists for doing their job—uncovering uncomfortable truths that those in power would like to keep away from the public—means removing one of the most important checks on executive political power.

How would we know today of the wiretapping of the Democratic Party headquarters if it hadn't been for the hard work of American investigative reporters uncovering information the Nixon administration wanted to hide? How would we know about all the offshore accounts and money laundering activities of politicians across the world if a whistleblower hadn't leaked the Panama Papers? How would we be aware that innocent civilians and Reuters journalists had been killed by the US Army in Iraq without the "Collateral Murder" video leaked by Chelsea Manning and published by WikiLeaks?

And how would we know that the higher-ups of the Democratic Party discriminated against Bernie Sanders, the most progressive voice seeking its nomination in the 2016 presidential election, if WikiLeaks hadn't released the files from the hacked Democratic National Committee email server? It was the Democrats, by choosing the wrong candidate in the first place (Hillary instead of Bernie), who brought Trump to power—not WikiLeaks.

One can argue about timing and political consequences, but it is hard to deny that it was in the interest of the American public to know these facts. The information was not fake or fabricated; it was the truth.

Back in 1919, Walter Lippmann, the father of modern journalism who coined the phrase "manufacturing consent" (which Noam Chomsky made famous in his 1988 book with Ed Herman), wrote that "there can be no liberty for a community which lacks the means by which to detect lies."

Fighting the extradition of Assange to the US is not just about protecting his individual rights; it is also about protecting the very means by which we are able to detect lies. It is about protecting freedom of the press and our ability to keep checks on political power.

Or as Lippman wrote in *Liberty and the News* a hundred years ago: "Not what somebody says or somebody wishes to be true, but what is so beyond all opinions, constitutes the touchstone of our sanity."

Without WikiLeaks and Julian Assange, without the courageous whistleblowers and journalists who are revealing the dirty secrets and immoral acts of powerful regimes, who are opposing or criticizing authority, truth would quickly lose value. And it would be then that we would also lose the touchstone of our sanity.

Each time I left the Ecuadorian embassy in London, I was struck by the parting look in Julian's eyes. The question was the same. Would this be the last time I will see him there, at this postmodern prison cell in the midst of a Western metropolis? Or would I return once again, bringing fresh seawater and other souvenirs of the freedom which, like the rest of us who can still look to the sky and enjoy the sun, he so fully deserves?

I don't know what Julian did with that bottle of seawater I brought, but I hope it stays forever there at Hans Crescent Street, not so much as a reminder that a prison cell was there, but as a warning that freedom is a precious thing—and that it's worth paying a price for, because what's the point of swimming in the sea if you don't believe in anything?

PS After Julian's arrest, all his belongings were handed over by Ecuador to the United States government, including two manuscripts, legal documents, and perhaps an empty bottle. To make the lives of the intelligence services agents easier—it was seawater!

4. FOR JULIAN ASSANGE[103]

Serge Halimi, December 2018

With an air of triumph and a smile, surrounded by 50 or more photographers and cameramen, CNN correspondent Jim Acosta announced his return to the White House on November 16. Having lost his press pass a few days earlier, a US judge ordered President Donald Trump to reverse the punishment. "This was a test and I think we passed the test. Journalists need to know that in this country their First Amendment rights of freedom of the press are sacred, they're protected in our constitution. Throughout all of this I was confident and I thought that . . . our rights would be protected as we continue to cover our government and hold our leaders accountable." Fade-out, cue music, happy ending.

Julian Assange was probably not able to watch the moving conclusion to this affair live on CNN. Having taken refuge for six years in the Ecuadorian embassy in London, his life has come to resemble that of a prisoner. Barred from leaving, under threat of being arrested by the British authorities, then, probably, extradited to the United States; his access to

[103] This article was originally published in French. Serge Halimi, "Pour Julian Assange," *Le Monde diplomatique*, December 2018, https://www.monde-diplomatique.fr/2018/12/HALIMI/59366.

communications has been reduced and he has faced harassment repeatedly, since, to please Washington, the Ecuadorian president Lenín Moreno has resolved to make conditions less comfortable for his "guest".

The detainment of Mr. Assange, as well as the threat of several decades in prison in an American penitentiary (in 2010 President Trump called for him to be executed), are all due to the website he founded. WikiLeaks has been behind major revelations which have inconvenienced some of the most powerful figures in the world over the last decade: photographic evidence of American war crimes in Afghanistan and in Iraq, American industrial espionage, secret bank accounts in the Cayman Islands. The dictatorship of Tunisian president Zine al-Abidine Ben Ali was shaken by the leaking of a secret communication by the American State Department calling this kleptocratic friend of Washington's a "sclerotic regime" and "quasi-mafia." It was also WikiLeaks that revealed that two senior figures in France's Socialist Party, François Hollande and Pierre Moscovici, had visited the United States embassy in Paris in June 2006, to say they regretted the vigor of president Jacques Chirac's opposition to the invasion of Iraq.

But what the "left" cannot forgive Assange for is the publication by his site of stolen emails from Hillary Clinton's presidential campaign. They deem that this affair favored Russian designs and the election of Trump, and forget that, in this matter, WikiLeaks only unveiled the Democratic candidate's plans to sabotage Bernie Sanders's campaign during their party's primaries. At the time, media around the world did not hesitate to relay the information, as they had done with previous leaks, without editors being compared to foreign agents and threatened with imprisonment.

American authorities' harassment of Assange is encouraged by the cowardice of journalists who have left him to his fate or even revel in his misfortune. Even star anchor Chris Matthews, formerly a heavyweight of the Democratic Party, suggested that the US Secret Service should "pull one of those Israeli numbers and just grab him."

Translated from French by Camille Constanti

5. THE PRISONER SAYS NO TO BIG BROTHER[104]

John Pilger, March 4, 2019

Whenever I visit Julian Assange, we meet in a room he knows too well. There is a bare table and pictures of Ecuador on the walls. There is a bookcase where the books never change. The curtains are always drawn and there is no natural light. The air is still and fetid.

This is Room 101.

Before I enter Room 101, I must surrender my passport and phone. My pockets and possessions are examined. The food I bring is inspected.

The man who guards Room 101 sits in what looks like an old-fashioned telephone box. He watches a screen, watching Julian. There are others unseen, agents of the state, watching and listening.

Cameras are everywhere in Room 101. To avoid them, Julian maneuvers us both into a corner, side by side, flat up against the wall. This is how

---

[104] Pilger gave this speech at a rally in Sydney for Julian Assange, organized by the Socialist Equality Party. John Pilger, "The Prisoner Says No to Big Brother," johnpilger.com, March 4, 2019, http://johnpilger.com/articles/the-prisoner-says-no-to-big-brother.

we catch up: whispering and writing to each other on a notepad, which he shields from the cameras. Sometimes we laugh.

I have my designated time slot. When that expires, the door in Room 101 bursts open and the guard says, "Time is up!" On New Year's Eve, I was allowed an extra 30 minutes and the man in the phone box wished me a happy new year, but not Julian.

Of course, Room 101 is the room in George Orwell's prophetic novel, *1984*, where the thought police watched and tormented their prisoners, and worse, until people surrendered their humanity and principles and obeyed Big Brother.

Julian Assange will never obey Big Brother. His resilience and courage are astonishing, even though his physical health struggles to keep up.

Julian is a distinguished Australian, who has changed the way many people think about duplicitous governments. For this, he is a political refugee subjected to what the United Nations calls "arbitrary detention."

The UN says he has the right of free passage to freedom, but this is denied. He has the right to medical treatment without fear of arrest, but this is denied. He has the right to compensation, but this is denied.

As founder and editor of WikiLeaks, his crime has been to make sense of dark times. WikiLeaks has an impeccable record of accuracy and authenticity which no newspaper, no TV channel, no radio station, no BBC, no *New York Times*, no *Washington Post*, no *Guardian* can equal. Indeed, it shames them.

That explains why he is being punished.

For example:

Last week, the International Court of Justice ruled that the British government had no legal powers over the Chagos islanders, who in the 1960s and '70s were expelled in secret from their homeland on Diego Garcia in the Indian Ocean and sent into exile and poverty. Countless children died, many of them from sadness. It was an epic crime few knew about.

For almost 50 years, the British have denied the islanders' the right to return to their homeland, which they had given to the Americans for a major military base.

In 2009, the British Foreign Office concocted a "marine reserve" around the Chagos archipelago.

This touching concern for the environment was exposed as a fraud when WikiLeaks published a secret cable from the British government reassuring the Americans that "the former inhabitants would find it difficult, if not impossible, to pursue their claim for resettlement on the islands if the entire Chagos Archipelago were a marine reserve."

The truth of the conspiracy clearly influenced the momentous decision of the International Court of Justice.

WikiLeaks has also revealed how the United States spies on its allies; how the CIA can watch you through your iPhone; how presidential candidate Hillary Clinton took vast sums of money from Wall Street for secret speeches that reassured the bankers that if she was elected, she would be their friend.

In 2016, WikiLeaks revealed a direct connection between Clinton and organized jihadism in the Middle East: terrorists, in other words. One email disclosed that when Clinton was US secretary of state, she knew that Saudi Arabia and Qatar were funding the Islamic State, yet she accepted huge donations for her foundation from both governments.

She then approved the world's biggest-ever arms sale to her Saudi benefactors: arms that are currently being used against the stricken people of Yemen.

That explains why he is being punished.

WikiLeaks has also published more than 800,000 secret files from Russia, including the Kremlin, telling us more about the machinations of power in that country than the specious hysterics of the Russiagate pantomime in Washington.

This is real journalism—journalism of a kind now considered exotic: the antithesis of Vichy journalism, which speaks for the enemy of the people and takes its sobriquet from the Vichy government that occupied France on behalf of the Nazis.

Vichy journalism is censorship by omission, such as the untold scandal of the collusion between Australian governments and the United States to deny Julian Assange his rights as an Australian citizen and to silence him.

In 2010, Prime Minister Julia Gillard went as far as ordering the Australian Federal Police to investigate and hopefully prosecute Assange and WikiLeaks—until she was informed by the AFP that no crime had been committed.

Last weekend, the *Sydney Morning Herald* published a lavish supplement promoting a celebration of "Me Too" at the Sydney Opera House on March 10. Among the leading participants is the recently retired minister of foreign affairs, Julie Bishop.

Bishop has been on show in the local media lately, lauded as a loss to politics: an "icon," someone called her, to be admired.

The elevation to celebrity feminism of one so politically primitive as Bishop tells us how much so-called identity politics have subverted an essential, objective truth: that what matters, above all, is not your gender but the class you serve.

Before she entered politics, Julie Bishop was a lawyer who served the notorious asbestos miner James Hardie, which fought claims by men and their families dying horribly with asbestosis.

Lawyer Peter Gordon recalls Bishop "rhetorically asking the court why workers should be entitled to jump court queues just because they were dying."

Bishop says she "acted on instructions...professionally and ethically."

Perhaps she was merely "acting on instructions" when she flew to London and Washington last year with her ministerial chief of staff, who had indicated that the Australian foreign minister would raise Julian's case and hopefully begin the diplomatic process of bringing him home.

Julian's father had written a moving letter to the then prime minister Malcolm Turnbull, asking the government to intervene diplomatically to free his son. He told Turnbull that he was worried Julian might not leave the embassy alive.

Julie Bishop had every opportunity in the UK and the US to present a diplomatic solution that would bring Julian home. But this required the courage of one proud to represent a sovereign, independent state, not a vassal.

Instead, she made no attempt to contradict the British foreign secretary, Jeremy Hunt, when he said outrageously that Julian "faced serious charges." What charges? There were no charges.

Australia's foreign minister abandoned her duty to speak up for an Australian citizen, prosecuted with nothing, charged with nothing, guilty of nothing.

Will those feminists who fawn over this false icon at the Opera House next Sunday be reminded of her role in colluding with foreign forces to punish an Australian journalist, one whose work has revealed that rapacious militarism has smashed the lives of millions of ordinary women in many countries: in Iraq alone, the US-led invasion of that country, in which Australia participated, left 700,000 widows.

So what can be done? An Australian government that was prepared to act in response to a public campaign to rescue the refugee football player, Hakeem al-Araibi, from torture and persecution in Bahrain, is capable of bringing Julian Assange home.

Yet the refusal by the Department of Foreign Affairs in Canberra to honor the United Nations' declaration that Julian is the victim of "arbitrary detention" and has a fundamental right to his freedom is a shameful breach of the spirit of international law.

5. THE PRISONER SAYS NO TO BIG BROTHER

Why has the Australian government made no serious attempt to free Assange? Why did Julie Bishop bow to the wishes of two foreign powers? Why is this democracy traduced by its servile relationships, and integrated with lawless foreign powers?

The persecution of Julian Assange is the conquest of us all: of our independence, our self-respect, our intellect, our compassion, our politics, our culture.

So stop scrolling. Organize. Occupy. Insist. Persist. Make a noise. Take direct action. Be brave and stay brave. Defy the thought police.

War is not peace, freedom is not slavery, ignorance is not strength. If Julian can stand up to Big Brother, so can you: so can all of us.

6. TO MAKE THE WORLD A BETTER AND SAFER PLACE

Teresa Forcades i Vila, March 5, 2019

It was August 29, 2017, and I was not prepared for what I encountered. The beautiful English building I had seen many times in newspaper pictures and on TV was right there in front of me, but the building was not the embassy of Ecuador as I had imagined. The porter directed me to a small door to the left of the main staircase. A civil servant opened the door rather furtively, took my passport in a hurry and then closed it again, leaving me outside, puzzled. I felt heavy. I noticed that the embassy consisted only of a few rather small rooms judging from the two I was finally allowed to enter. The witty and dynamic Assange was very pale, and he looked depressed. It was very hot. *Sorry, but it is not safe to open the windows. Not so long ago a man climbed the wall with the intention of killing me. It was not the first attempt.* I felt heavier.

Our conversation lasted more than an hour. I had originally requested to interview him on behalf of a team of young Spanish filmmakers, but Assange did not want yet another formal interview. Instead, he offered a private conversation with me alone. Just two days prior, I spoke at the

Greenbelt Festival, an annual Christian music festival in England that centers on faith and justice. More than 10,000 people attended. A loud, cheerful festival full of well-meaning Christians committed to social justice. By contrast, the atmosphere in the tiny embassy, and the restrained way Assange talked and moved, felt all the more oppressive. Oppressive and authentic. I was impressed by Assange's sadness and lucidity—by his capacity for self-criticism. *I believed that by revealing to the world the vital information that was being concealed, I would contribute to freedom and to make the world a better and safer place. The contrary has been the case.* His words had a profound effect on me. I was not expecting such a sober, unassuming attitude and was moved.

I believed that by revealing to the world the vital information that was being concealed, I would contribute to freedom and to make the world a better and safer place. The contrary has been the case. Assange argued that the lack of massive and effective condemnation of illegal surveillance—and other criminal offenses perpetrated by governments and corporations—has for all practical purposes been their legitimation. Before WikiLeaks, we—the citizens of established Western democracies—could feign ignorance. But now, thanks to WikiLeaks, we know without a shadow of a doubt that innocent people are regularly targeted in military actions with deficient ethical standards and led by commanders directly accountable to our democratically elected governments; we know that democratically elected governments and their main agencies, notably the CIA in the United States, violate their very own laws, not only in the international arena, but also right at home.

The scandal should have been momentous. So thought and hoped Assange. It was not.

Instead of outrage and decisive collective action, there was generalized apathy and resignation. Impotence disguised as wisdom. It was almost as if the information released by WikiLeaks had granted those responsible for the crimes the confirmation that a generous majority approves of what they do, regardless of what it is and regardless of the degree of violence it might require. Where have we learned such demeaning acquiescence? Maybe we secretly hope that the crimes of governments and big corporations will not affect us personally, and when they finally do—as it is the case for an increasing number of middle-class citizens since the 2007 financial crisis—we then delude ourselves and take refuge in the convenient yet alienating idea that without the criminal actions of "our government," our predicament would be much worse: *Things are not perfect in our country, but think of China!*

To make the world a better and safer place. Shouldn't that be the first priority of the governments of a world that less than 100 years ago experienced the horrors of two consecutive World Wars? Thus far Pope Francis seems to be alone among the world leaders to dare speak openly about a Third World War, not as a nightmarish possibility for the near future, but as an already existing reality. He spoke of it for the first time in 2014 and has repeated it with greater frequency since 2016: *They call it global insecurity, but the real word is war.* Today there are more open armed conflicts, more refugees (65 million worldwide), more commerce of weapons, more military violence, and more militarization of civil societies than during the First and the Second World Wars. There is, though, one crucial difference. During those World Wars, the vision for a better future—however misguided—did inspire and encourage most fighters on all sides. Today the main motivation to wage war seems to be private interest or the avoidance of a greater evil, not to forget those fighting simply to survive. The only ones left with an ideal vision for a better future seem to be in the Third Millennium terrorist movements that, in the name of an ideologized Islam or of any other violent ideology, are ready to kill massively and indiscriminately. So-called global terrorists are ready to kill the innocent and to curtail freedom to a degree most Westerners believe their own democratic governments would never dream to attempt; they strongly believe this despite the revelations of WikiLeaks or—here comes the irony that burdened Assange in our encounter—precisely because of them.

WikiLeaks helped us realize how many decisions are being made daily which run contrary to the standards of justice and respect for the dignity, freedom, and life of human beings, formally and officially upheld by the established democracies of the West. And yet, the overwhelming reaction has been that of turning away. Not everybody, of course: in Latin America, in the Arab countries, in Europe, and in the United States, peaceful and utopic popular movements (be they called La Revolución Bolivariana, Arab Spring, Occupy Wall Street, or the Spanish Indignados) have stood ready to confront the powers that be and their lies. Up to now, they seem to have been mostly defeated.

"Powers that be" is an English idiom that comes from the King James Bible, the authorized translation of the Bible published by the Church of England in 1611. In the letter to the Romans, trying to appease the imperial authorities, the apostle Paul states: *Let every soul be subject unto the higher powers. For there is no power but of God: the powers that be are ordained of God* (Rom 13:1). The letter ominously proceeds: *Therefore whoever resists the authorities resists what God has appointed, and those who resist will incur judgment* (Rom 13:2). The "powers that be" are presented as unquestionable and divinely ordained, but such a strong and definitive Biblical directive has not precluded Christians throughout the ages from opposing and disobeying secular power whenever they found its directives objectionable— take the martyrs of the first centuries who by the hundreds refused to offer sacrifices to the divinized Roman emperors. By doing so, they risked their lives; many lost them, and many more lost their possessions or were indefinitely imprisoned.

So is Assange—indefinitely imprisoned. For having done what? For having revealed that the "powers that be" break the law systematically. If Assange had targeted only one politician or one big company, would it have been easier for the general public to back him, and to force the authorities to bring the perpetrators to justice? WikiLeaks did not focus on one individual, however, nor on a mere few; it revealed criminal corruption of global proportion, existing at the highest levels of governance and power. Who are "the authorities" willing and able to call them to accountability? Where are they?

I am Catalan. I was born in Barcelona, and I live in the beautiful mountain monastery of St. Benet de Montserrat, 60 kilometers away from the city. I am writing these lines in defense of Assange while seven Catalan elected politicians and two mass movement leaders accused of rebellion against the state by the Spanish authorities are being tried in Madrid. The trial began on February 12, 2019, with the state prosecutor asking for sentences between 11 and 25 years, accusing the defendants of having organized the illegal October 1, 2017 referendum on Catalan independence.

Organizing an illegal referendum is not a criminal offense in Spain, however. This is why some of the defendants are also charged with leading an "armed uprising." That there was not a sign of armed uprising in Catalonia is obvious to all who were there. The trial taking place in Madrid right now is outrageous and a sheer abuse of power. The Catalan political prisoners have already spent the last year and a half in preventive detention. I know four of them personally, having shared the podium with them in political discussions and peaceful demonstrations. More than 80 percent of the Catalan population claim the political right to self-determination—more than 2 million voted in favor of independence on the illegal referendum, despite the violent repression; two months later, in the election that followed the suspension of Catalan autonomy, the pro-independence parties revalidated their mandate with an extraordinarily high participation (79 percent of the voting census).

In the fall of 2017, Assange angered Madrid by denouncing Spanish repression of Catalans: he exposed some lies being published in the main Spanish newspapers and defended the right to self-determination of the Catalan population. This, I understand, has caused him grave tensions with the government of Ecuador (who the Spanish diplomats have relentlessly pressured) and an ongoing restriction of his Internet access and activity.

On the day I am writing this text,[105] Colonel Pérez de los Cobos, the commander ultimately responsible for the police deployment and operations during the Catalan referendum, has declared in court without blinking an eye that the policemen under his command used no violence against peaceful voters on October 1—that *their use of force was exquisite* (his literal words). The declarations of the colonel are even more Kafkaesque than those of the Spanish foreign minister Alfonso Dastis in his memorable live BBC appearance in 2017, shortly after the referendum; Minister Dastis tried to convince the journalist interviewing him that the BBC videos showing Spanish policemen using their batons on peaceful voters were fake news.[106] The fact is that in the preliminary stages of the current trial, the judges of the Spanish Supreme Court refused to accept as a witness an expert from Scotland Yard specialized in assessing police violence, and at this writing, they have refused to screen the videos showing police violence presented by the defense attorney in order to call into question the deposition of Colonel Pérez de los Cobos. The trial is being screened live on public TV and the judges have considered that it was more convenient to view the videos later, privately.

[105] March 5, 2019.

[106] *The Andrew Marr Show*, BBC One. October 22, 2017.

Besides being a nun and a theologian, I am a physician specializing in internal medicine and have a doctorate in public health. In 2006 I published a study on the crimes of the big pharmaceutical companies. I was appalled by the degree of cynicism and disregard for human suffering and human life that I discovered.[107] In 2009, I researched and wrote extensively on the swine-flu (H1N1) as a fake pandemic.[108] On December 18, 2009, 14 members of the Parliamentary Assembly of the Council of Europe (PACE)[109] led by the epidemiologist Wolfgang Wodarg, then chair of the Health Committee in the European Council, issued a motion for a recommendation entitled *Faked Pandemics—a threat for health*. This was the main point of the motion:

> *In order to promote their patented drugs and vaccines against flu, pharmaceutical companies have influenced scientists and official agencies, responsible for public health standards, to alarm governments worldwide. They have made them squander tight health care resources for inefficient vaccine strategies and needlessly*

---

[107] Forcades i Vila, T., *Crimes and Abuses of the Pharmaceutical Companies* (Cristianisme i Justícia, Booklet 124, 2006).

[108] Forcades i Vila, T., "Flu Vaccination: The Gap Between Evidence and Public Policy." *Int J Health Serv*; 2015; 45(3): 453-70 PMID: 26077855.

[109] The Parliamentary Assembly of the Council of Europe is dedicated to upholding human rights, democracy, and the rule of law, and oversees the European Court of Human Rights. The parliamentarians who make up PACE come from the national parliaments of the Organization's 47 member states. They meet four times a year to discuss topical issues and ask European governments to take initiatives and report back. These parliamentarians speak for the 800 million Europeans who elected them. They broach the issues of their choice, and the governments of European countries—which are represented at the Council of Europe by the Committee of Ministers—are obliged to respond. They are Greater Europe's democratic conscience. http://website-pace.net/en_GB/web/apce/functioning (accessed 12/10/14).

exposed millions of healthy people to the risk of unknown side-effects of insufficiently tested vaccines.[110]

Wodarg denounced the 2009 pandemic as "one of the greatest medical scandals of the century" and pointed to the change in the definition of "pandemic" implemented by the World Health Organization (WHO) in May 2009: *From June 2009 it is no longer necessary that "an enormous amount of people have contracted the illness or died"—there simply has to be a virus, spreading beyond borders, and one that people have no immunity towards.*[111] On March 23, 2010, the final memorandum of PACE concluded that the H1N1 crisis had been handled without transparency, and that the WHO and other public institutions involved in public decisions regarding the pandemic had "gambled away" the confidence of the European public.[112] It is a serious accusation coming from one of the highest institutions of the European democracies, but it had no practical consequences. Nobody was held accountable.

Learning from these experiences, I must agree with Assange: the unveiling of the crimes of governments and big corporations has thus far failed to lead to effective action, and the tides are now turning against the whistleblowers with a virulence that I did not anticipate. I stand by Julian Assange. We must organize worldwide to block his extradition, and to obtain his acquittal and his release. We are defending not only his freedom and his dignity, but ours as well.

[110] Faked Pandemics—a threat for health. Motion for a recommendation presented by Mr. Wodarg and others. Doc. 12110. 18 December 2009. http://assembly.coe.int (accessed 12/7/14).

[111] Interview in Danish done by Louise Voller and Kristian Villesen for the journal *Information* (www.information.dk/219754). A full English translation of the interview can be found on Dr. Wodarg's personal webpage: http://www.wodarg.de/english/3013320.html (accessed 12/12/14).

[112] "The handling of the H1N1 pandemic: more transparency needed." Memorandum presented by Paul Flynn. AS/Soc (2010) 12. 23 March 2010.

7. ENDGAME FOR ASSANGE[113]

Angela Richter, January 2019

Julian Assange looks very pale. "Pale" isn't quite accurate; his skin looks like parchment, almost translucent. He hasn't seen the sun for almost seven years. He sits opposite me in the so-called Meeting Room of the Ecuadorian embassy in London. His snow-white hair, his trademark, is shoulder-length, and he wears a long beard. We joke about him looking like Santa. He wears a thick down jacket and eats a piece of the sushi I brought for lunch. It is cold in the room and I regret that I left my winter coat at the reception.

It is just before Christmas, and Julian Assange has probably just had the worst time of his stay at the embassy. Since March 2018 he has been de facto in isolation: no telephone, no Internet, and no visits. The Internet ban must be particularly difficult for him; it was not only his field of work, but his only access to the world.

The mood in the embassy is tense; the new ambassador is due to arrive. They turned off the heating and took his bed; he now sleeps on a

---

[113] A version of this piece in German originally appeared in *der Freitag*. Angela Richter, "Endgame for Assange," *der Freitag digital*, January 2019, https://digital.freitag.de/0119/endspiel-fuer-assange/.

yoga mat. I cannot help but get the impression that everything possible is being done to make his stay so difficult that he finally gives in and leaves the embassy voluntarily. But what will await him then?

It's the first time since I've known him that he really looks drained, his former boyish face, which always seemed peculiar with the silver-white hair, adapted to his age. The nine months of isolation have visibly weakened him, he has become leaner, but in our conversation, he seems mentally strong and more determined than ever.

Surrounded by microphones

I ask him how he has endured the isolation for so long, and he replies that he was almost delighted at first. He was sure that such a flagrant violation of his human rights would cause great public outrage and European politicians would stand up for him under pressure from the media. Nothing of the sort happened, however, and as the months passed, he lost faith.

Now, it has been made public that the US authorities have filed criminal charges against Assange—charges that were supposed to remain under lock and key until he could no longer escape arrest. They confirm what Assange has feared for years, and reveal the foolishness of the press that blazoned him paranoid. But even after this revelation, there is no indignation.

WikiLeaks

His stay in the embassy, granted as political asylum in 2012, now resembles more and more a detention with rigid punishments. His isolation has still not been completely lifted: from Friday evening until Monday morning there is still a ban on contact, and anyone who wants to visit him has to submit a formal application to the embassy. There were probably rejections, he tells me. I was lucky and got two of the four requested hours approved.

I visited Julian Assange about 30 times between 2012 and 2017 at the Ecuadorian embassy. The visits inspired three of my theater plays and crafted my friendship with one of the most controversial people of our time. It was not always easy to defend him, especially since the election of Donald Trump as president of the United States, for which many journalists, including former supporters and friends of mine, have made him jointly responsible. Moreover, most journalists seem to agree that there was a mad conspiracy between Trump and Putin, with Assange as an intermediary. In late November, the *Guardian* claimed that Paul Manafort, head of Donald Trump's presidential campaign, had met Assange three times in London: in 2013, 2015, and 2016. Fidel Narváez, then the Ecuadorian consul in London, has formally denied this. WikiLeaks initiated legal proceedings against the *Guardian* and Manafort publicly denied the meetings. His name does not appear in the Ecuadorian embassy's guest book and there are no images of him entering or leaving one of the world's best-monitored buildings.

Assange, of course, followed all this; when I ask him about it, he only says that the story in the *Guardian* is fictitious. As he inquires about my family and we eat sushi, we try to ignore the cameras and microphones surrounding us. Even in the small kitchen in the hallway, there is now a camera installed. It used to be the only corner where we could withdraw from surveillance. Recently, embassy staff has been changed one by one, and they don't know Assange well; only the cleaning lady is the same. The diplomats who sympathized with him are no longer there.

As a distraction I unpack a few presents for him: the German wholemeal bread he loves, fresh fruit, Ovaltine, a letter with a drawing from my eldest son, and a Ukrainian specialty sausage from Crimea that a friend and former dramaturge of Frank Castorf gave me. I try again to direct the conversation toward him and his precarious situation, but that proves difficult. I hardly know anyone who says "I" as reluctantly as Assange, which is amazing considering how often he is described as a narcissist and an egomaniac in the media.

Blueprint for all of us

It is difficult to describe the complex character of Assange. One thing has become clear to me in recent years: it is simply not conveyable to the average intellectual. He is a meticulous archivist, a courageous revelator and uncompromising iconoclast, highly emotional and at the same time factual. In comparison to him, most of the artists and intellectuals I know seem like petty bourgeois who profit off their personal neuroses.

But what does it mean if Assange is the opposite of what we've been told about him—that he is a nefarious unsympath whose egomania is to blame for his situation? Isn't he then an exemplar for all of us? What he has suffered for years in the middle of Europe could happen to anyone who dares to raise his voice and reveal the truth about the powerful. Not in Russia or China, but in the free West.

Assange never gave up his credo "Let's make trouble." He tells me that he hoped during his isolation that he could take a little "holiday from WikiLeaks." But no one was keen to take the helm, which is not surprising given the consequences. He says that he thinks his isolation was a test run for what would happen if he went to prison in the end: WikiLeaks would probably disintegrate slowly.

I think he's right. Ever since I've known Assange, it's been clear that his organization only exists because of his immense persistence. He often cheered me up with the saying, "Courage is contagious." I can confirm this for myself; he has this effect that encourages you to risk more. His insistence on revealing truth by publishing raw, documented facts has not brought him fame and glory; to the contrary. And yet he has never given up. I've experienced some ups and downs with Assange in recent years. I have talked with him and his team in the embassy for hours, sometimes nights, arguing, laughing, eating, drinking, singing, and trembling.

Since I started visiting Assange in the embassy, Ecuador has replaced three ambassadors. The fourth one arrived in London on the day of my visit, and his primary task will probably be to get rid of Assange as quickly as possible, with the least possible political damage to Ecuador's image. The *New York Times* recently reported that there had been several talks in 2017 between Ecuadorian president Lenín Moreno and the now notorious Paul Manafort. Manafort had traveled to Quito to boost China's investment in Ecuador. Allegedly, at the meeting with Moreno, there was also talk about Assange, about a deal to extradite him to the US in exchange for Ecuador's debt relief. Assange jokes, wouldn't it be ironic if the IMF, the International Monetary Fund, of all entities, decided on his fate? He laughs, tormented. In the end, big money always wins.

They allowed me to stay four hours after all. When I say goodbye, we hug each other tightly. It might be the last time we see each other. Outside I talk to some supporters who camp in front of the embassy with self-painted banners and lit candles. They have been holding out for years, alongside Julian.

8. A CONVERSATION WITH JULIAN ASSANGE

Ai Weiwei, September 16, 2015

Ai Weiwei and Julian Assange in the Ecuadorian embassy.

AI WEIWEI: How do you feel today? Now?

JULIAN ASSANGE: Now? I don't know. When you are in a physical space for so long, you create a new normal. You adapt to a new normal. As far as the new normal is concerned, I'm pretty good. But you lose your sense of perspective. Your new normal becomes "detained without charge," which you should be very pissed off about. But that's just life.

AWW: Did you ever predict that life would turn out like this?

JA: I predicted in response to starting WikiLeaks that there would be something like this. I thought it would happen two years earlier actually. Not precisely this situation, but significant conflict. I know how these things work.

What about you? Did you think that you would have significant conflicts?

AWW: I knew I would have conflicts, of course, those things are meant to have conflicts. But the imagination never catches the details. There are so many details, and we live with details. But of course, you learn from those things.

How do you describe your daily life?

JA: I don't. The biggest problem for all people who are in a situation of confinement is the monotony; the visual monotony of confinement. You start to remember all the shapes around you. Once you remember them, you stop seeing them. Because you can just access your memory. That is the biggest difficulty for confined people. To work against this, you try to make sure there is no routine. You try to interject novelty as much as possible. If you're a curious person, you crave novelty anyway. If you're a confined person, you crave novelty to create an environment where it is not easy to answer this question. This is your whole goal.

AWW: When did you create WikiLeaks and how is your situation now?

JA: I had a Rousseauian vision of the world. That the way to make the world more just and interesting is for people to be better educated. Because of the nature of its funding, the academy, universities and formal schooling, have developed along a certain line that tries to avoid conflict. Studying how human institutions actually behave in the modern world, especially examining how armies kill people, or how intelligence agencies corrupt other institutions, is not something the academy will ever touch as a result of its funding sources. You might say, "Oh, but it has looked at the CIA and Greece in the 1950s" or something. Yes, it will sometimes look at things if you go back 50 years or more because all those people studied are now out of power. You can learn some things from what happened 50 years ago, but really the world has been changing fast in this post–WWII period. To understand how the world works now you need to study what is happening now.

This absence of educational investigation into how human institutions behave in present time means that people don't know how to manage the modern world. They don't know how to manage themselves, their organization, their family or their nation, or their civilization. Our ability to affect things is only as good as our understanding. If we make decisions not based on understanding, then what *are* they based on? It is like pulling random sort-outs from a hat. The chance of having a good outcome is slight. That is on the philosophical level.

On the personal level, people have psychological motivations as well as societal motivations. Psychological motivations include the enjoyment of learning, of figuring things out. That's why people like puzzles, for example. A puzzle is trying to prevent you from solving it. Intelligence agencies are actively trying to prevent you from understanding what they're up to. I like the intellectual challenge this presents.

If we look at how WikiLeaks works in practice, it is intellectually very stimulating. You have emotional stimulation from it being a matter of justice, but then intellectually you have to assemble an understanding of how the world works geopolitically just to survive; how to play off one jurisdiction against another, understand the law, the technology involved, the public presentation, understand how to gain support and how the international modern financial system works. This is not just a question of understanding how intelligence agencies work. We need to understand it ourselves because a blockade was directed against us, the same as the blockade against Cuba, and we had to deal with that blockade.

***

AWW: What kind of education did you have?

JA: The most important early part of my schooling was not formal education. That I did later. Rather it was that I was a teenage computer hacker. I was interested in geopolitics as a teenager, partly because of the intellectual challenges it threw up. I was a young person and the most modern thing was the embryonic beginnings of the Internet. It was not yet public. It was just for the military, research universities, and military contractors.

Like many young people, I wanted to be on the cutting edge of civilization. Where were things going? I wanted to be on this edge. In fact, I wanted to get in front of this edge of the development of civilization. Because the old people were not already there. You had an advantage. If you could learn fast you could get in front of where civilization was going. So I tried to do that and I was pretty good at it. The nature of the Internet then was that it was built by the United States military. That was the reality. To see more of it, you had to hack it. I was hacking Pentagon generals' emails when I was a teenager.

AWW: When was that?

JA: In the late 1980s, early 1990s.

AWW: That first generation of hackers?

JA: Yeah, that first generation. And something that existed even before the Internet called X.25.[114]

We were doing that and were quite good at it. And the Australian computer hackers as a community were, at one stage, the best in the world. That was possible because the telephone calls were very cheap. You just paid ten cents and the call would last as long as you liked, three days even. This created a community that exchanged skills and we got quite good.

AWW: Where were you then?

JA: In Australia.

AWW: Australia was so advanced then?

JA: Well, Australia itself is not that advanced in technology. It's not very backwards either. It's somewhere in the middle. But just the fact that phone calls were so cheap meant that many people could afford to use this early Internet which was very expensive otherwise. There was no legal way to access the Internet for a young person back then. Everything was hacked. The only people there were computer hackers, people working for the military or universities.

***

JA: Australia's very isolated. If you're a curious person, you want to travel elsewhere. But if you're a teenager you can't afford to travel. Air flights were expensive. I certainly couldn't afford it; I didn't even have a passport. But using your mind you could travel out.

---

[114] X.25 is a standard protocol suite defined by the International Telegraph and Telephone Consultative Committee. Used primarily before the Internet protocol suite and developed in the 1970s, X.25 uses packet-switched wide-area network communication, or a method of transferring data in "packets" between computer networks over a large geographical distance. "X.25," *Wikipedia*, last modified June 14, 2019, https://en.wikipedia.org/wiki/X.25.

So I traveled out on this new network and started understanding its power structures. I realized these were centered on United States military bases all over the world. That is how I started to see these institutions from the inside. It didn't give me quite the same experiences as I had subsequently when dealing with them as someone managing the organization. Then I was running dozens of legal cases and trying to protect [myself] from different domains. But for a teenager, it was an unusual experience to go through, and I learned a lot about how the world works and how modern institutions behave.

***

AWW: How would you describe your daily life? Can you communicate effectively? Evidently, you can use a computer. We contacted you through it. What do you have and what is missing?

JA: There are a number of interesting things. I'm in the center of London. I have been detained without charge for five years. The law in the United Kingdom is that you are allowed to detain someone without charge for 72 hours maximum. I have been detained without charge for about 40,000 hours. That is interesting. It's interesting that there is a diplomatic conflict. If you look outside, of course, there are all these police and they desperately want to grab me. They have spent now more than $20 million— about $15,000 a day—on surveillance operations around the embassy in the last three years. They are spending a lot of money to avoid the humiliation of me winning. They are willing to spend a lot of money doing that.

Actually, they have all the force. Physically, of course, they could come in anytime they like. They could smash the door down. So, why can't they do that? Well, because there is a magic circle around the embassy and this magic circle is something called the Vienna Convention. It's the convention, the international legal convention—actually the one adhered to the most in terms of international law—that specifies you cannot do that. What enforces that law? Is it the goodness of the heart of the prime minister, David Cameron? Obviously not.

***

AWW: Whose interest is it to get you?

JA: The interest is principally the United States as far as the UK–US relationship is concerned, and the Swedish–US relationship. But over time, other interests have developed. The United States has a huge case that has started as a result of our publications. And additional ones that have commenced subsequently. There is a 120-man WikiLeaks war room in the United States—publicly admitted, including the number of staff—that the Pentagon started with the FBI and DIA (Defense Intelligence Agency), headed up by General Carr to work out what we are going to publish, what we have published, how that affects them, etc.

Over time, that has morphed into what they call a "government investigation" led by the Department of Justice and the FBI—the Department of Justice criminal division and the Department of Justice national security division. They sentenced my alleged co-conspirator, Chelsea Manning, to 35 years in US military prison. They want to do this to me and they say the charges are espionage, conspiracy to commit espionage, general conspiracy, computer hacking, and stealing government documents.

These are serious accusations, resulting, potentially in decades in prison. The United States has pressured a variety of countries to take action against me, for a long time. Other factors have arisen. Now it is also a matter of United Kingdom national prestige. The United Kingdom will never say no to the United States but it also doesn't want to offend its European partners. Because the conflict is very public within the United Kingdom it looks weak. The fact the United Kingdom can't arrest me makes it look weak.

Now we all know about the Vienna Convention and the relationships between embassies so it is no surprise it cannot arrest me. But what is the basic nature of the state? What is the basic definition of the state? The classical definition of the state is an organized group which has a monopoly of violence over a defined territory. That is what the state is.

Once we understand that that is the underpinning of all states, we can see why it is so difficult for the United Kingdom for me to be here. Because perceptually it seems to undermine that notion. The United Kingdom establishment has said, "We want him to be arrested," and the police have said, "Okay, we will take on that task." And so there they are, very publicly outside this building for the last three years, trying to arrest me. But they have failed. This failure demonstrates that a single man can resist the coercive power of the state. It means that the state in the United Kingdom does not have a monopoly on coercive force. This leads to one or two conclusions: one, it is not a state. It does not have a monopoly on violence therefore it is not a state. Or two, those people that claim to represent the state—the prime minister and the police—are not the real establishment. Anyone could say, "Arrest Ai Weiwei, go arrest Ai Weiwei." If you are not arrested, that means they don't have control of the police or that the police don't have control over you. Either there is not a functioning state because it cannot arrest the people it wants to arrest or the people who said "Go arrest Ai Weiwei" are not in control of the state.

***

AWW: Why do you think a person like you, just an individual from Australia, is regarded as so threatening to all those states and superpowers?

JA: They must feel that they are weak. How could this very establishment in the United Kingdom, which has been in power for hundreds of years, feel threatened? It's quite sophisticated after all. It has many different components: the intelligence services, the banks, the landed gentry, the oligarchs from Russia who have come here and invested, the commercial media, it has the BBC which is the big propaganda organism that helps keep the country cohesive. It is quite a sophisticated power structure with these interplaying parts. How could they feel threatened by a wild colonial boy from Australia who has arrived from overseas?

AWW: How? Freedom of speech? Information flow?

JA: They perceive that the cohesiveness of the establishment power structure is maintained by secrecy. That is an interesting question. Are they right in their fear? Maybe they are just paranoid. They perceive it as maintained by secrecy and fear.

AWW: Do you think they hesitated? What made them hesitate to arrest you before you came here?

JA: They did initially arrest me and put me in prison for about 10 days. But there was such overwhelming popular support across multiple countries, and even in this country amongst the public, that they had to release me into house arrest. Albeit a very severe house arrest where I had an electronic monitoring device attached to my ankle, base stations in the house giving signals back to the state all the time, hundreds of thousands of dollars of money that I and my friends had to give to the state, going to the police station all the time for 600 days every day at a certain time. A very aggressive house arrest, but nonetheless not prison.

Because I had that support across the world in various countries, as the situation got worse and the United States started to build up their case and the Swedish started to build up their extradition request, I was able to come here. Now, of course, I can still work. It's a very difficult situation to be surrounded by such surveillance. The UK has spent the equivalent of 100 full-time salary positions per year in surveillance or other direct involvement around this embassy. They've released the figures for the overtime so it's very easy to work out the number of police involved. One hundred full-time police, £12 million spent.

AWW: Do you worry that one day they will get you?

JA: You have to be careful, sure. It's a type of chess. I applied for political asylum. I made a case for political asylum with the Ecuadorian government. I won that case and so there is a formal finding that I was being politically persecuted. Now, Ecuador is a country of only 15 million people. It is obviously a brave country that believes in asylum rights, but it is not alone.

AWW: You are not accepted?

JA: It is not alone as a country. It is in a region of supportive states. The president of Tunisia, Moncef Marzouki, also offered me asylum after the revolution because WikiLeaks was involved in the Tunisian Revolution. Although I admire what is happening in Tunisia a great deal, and President Marzouki, Tunisia is not in a region that is supportive. It is not backed up by supportive states whereas Ecuador is backed up by the rest of South America, which is supportive.

AWW: There is the Internet and the leaking of information, you and Snowden, and maybe somebody else. The confrontation is always there, and the state, of course, builds up ever stronger surveillance, despite you and Snowden and other people who have the conscience and skill to leak this information. So what is the future? How do you see this warfare between the state, which tries to maintain all the secrets and does all those unspeakable things, and the individual?

JA: It's not at all clear which way things are heading. Technology goes through periods of centralization and periods of democratization. If you go back to say the late 1960s or the early 1970s, there was a democratization of radio. Radio components got cheaper and more people could make radio, but then most states began to register all radios. They invented radio direction finders, they invented vans that could track the source of a radio station. They would go to where that radio station was, arrest the people involved, and force them to pay licensing fees and so on. In that manner, they prevented the democratization of radio. They limited the number of people that could use radio.

At the same time, you had major computer systems being held by the United States State Department, by the United States tax office, by one or two of the biggest companies, and what did those computer systems do? They enabled those very large organizations to get larger still; to collect ever more records about individuals. Large organizations have been able to deal with the solitary individual. The power imbalance is so immense between the IRS and a single individual; the federal government computer system with a 100,000 employees and a single individual. There is no bargaining power between these two.

Then computer systems started to become democratized so smaller organizations could have the same organizational capacity as these very large organizations. That meant that smaller organizations could do more, but as a result of connecting the world to itself there is a big question about how all these connections will end up: Will they all end up going through just a few large corporations like Google which have become close to the state? Will everyone have to have a crypto-keycard that can't be fabricated where the iris scan is on the card? As soon as they are a couple years old and they have this identity card, they will not only have a relationship with their family, not only have a relationship with their neighbors or with their little community—suddenly that individual has a relationship with all the large states.

***

JA: Here's the little beast [pulls out Panda to Panda].[115] And where is the chip?

AWW: It's in the right leg, at the front. If you cut off the leg you will see the chip.

JA: Cut off the leg? [laughs] What is the story with the panda? Is it a symbol the state police use?

AWW: In China, particularly in Beijing, when we say, "He's a panda," that means they are undercover. The panda's identity is very obscure. It looks like this and you never know if it is happy or unhappy. It always looks the same. So we call the undercover police a panda. Maybe he is listening.

JA: It was discovered that they were upstairs.

AWW: Yeah?

JA: The pandas live upstairs.

AWW: A lot of pandas there. It seems the police at the front door are quite friendly.

JA: That's the British way. That's why I say it's a sophisticated state.

---

[115] Together with computer security researcher and hacker Jacob Appelbaum, Ai Weiwei created an artistic performance called "Panda to Panda," documented by filmmaker Laura Poitras and designed to discuss the idea of privacy in the digital age. For the project, shredded copies of highly confidential NSA documents leaked by Edward Snowden were stuffed into 20 toy pandas in Ai's studio in Beijing. Each panda also contained a micro-SD memory card with a digital backup of the leaked documents, which Assange refers to shortly. "Panda" is the slang term for China's secret police and functions as a means to avoid censorship because "national security" is a homonym of "national treasure." Pandas are China's "national treasure." Additionally, "Panda to Panda" refers to the decentralized communication architecture, peer-to-peer (P2P) networking, which incentivizes egalitarian resource sharing and cooperation on the Internet. See the performance here: Laura Poitras, "The Art of Dissent," *The New York Times*, June 9, 2015, https://www.nytimes.com/2015/06/09/opinion/the-art-of-dissent.html.

AWW: You look fine, you look good. I'm happy to see you in this state. Your mind, your physical condition, is very good. Do you know how long you can stay here?

JA: In theory, forever. At the end of the day, everything is politics. It's all about people's will. Formally, Ecuador is a party to a number of international conventions, which it has activated in this case, so the legal situation is quite clear. The United Kingdom is not obeying international law. Ecuador has activated international law. Now we just have a process of politics where the United Kingdom needs to be brought into compliance with what the law—both EU and international—demands. Possibly even United Kingdom law, actually. I'll explain something of the situation here.

I was arrested on December 7, 2010, and have been detained in one form or another since then. The particular law they arrested me under came about as a result of the September 11 attacks in the United States. They rushed forward various kinds of legislation in Europe and the United Kingdom to make it easier to arrest people and extradite them, including being able to extradite someone without any charges and without presenting any evidence at all. A very big change compared to the situation before where you at least needed to present evidence to extradite someone, and in most cases charges as well.

AWW: Under the name of anti-terrorism?

JA: Exactly. They said, "This is going to be used for terrorism legislation. Yes, this gives the state power, but don't worry we will pass another set of laws that will protect people's rights." That was never done. Instead, they did radical, extreme redefinitions of people's rights after September 11 where you can arrest someone and extradite them without charges or any evidence whatsoever. It's just a form and you tick boxes.

This led to a lot of abusive extradition cases in this country, not just me but a number of other people also faced abusive extradition cases and were subsequently acquitted. And, of course, the cases started because of terrorism, but the first extradition case actually came from Sweden abusing this new system, for someone who was involved in drunk driving. Immediately, this system was corrupted.

To begin with, they began going after people who are foreigners or immigrants or people just visiting the country or the lower classes who have no power. As time went by, they started extraditing people in higher and higher social classes until they got to medium-sized businessmen. And then there was my case, which drew everyone's attention to this problem of extraditing people without charge. The sons and daughters of the elites started to be scared that they would be extradited without charge to Germany where a lot of United Kingdom bankers had been engaged in various dodgy practices from 2008 onwards in the financial collapse.

So then there was enough political will, coming from the human rights lawyers, from me and those that support me, and the bankers. In 2014, they changed the law to say that there was to be no more extraditing without charge from the United Kingdom. As that law was going toward Parliament, they said, "What about Assange? If we pass this law, we can't extradite Assange." So they made a little qualifier to the law which only applies to me, specifying that this new law saying extradition without charge is now banned in the United Kingdom doesn't apply to someone in my situation. There is only one person in the United Kingdom in my situation, which is me.

AWW: Impressive.

JA: Because this law was pushed most famously by my case, our legal team jokes that it should be called Julian Exception to the Assange Law.

AWW: When I was detained, there is a law in the Chinese judicial system called Article 83, which states that you can make people disappear.[116] People called that the Ai Weiwei Law. In history, there is always somebody that has to be marked with those cases. I think that if you talk about the whole situation, maybe people are becoming ever more conscious of your situation, or mine, or other people's, and I think this makes a difference.

JA: What do you mean?

AWW: About individual's reactions to state power. When I talk to people, they are all in support of or sympathetic toward you. They understand why you are in this situation and all the politics that are attached to it.

JA: Cab drivers are the base barometer. People arrive here all the time by taxi. They explain, "I was talking to my taxi driver. He said, 'Where do you want to go?' I said, 'I want to go to the Ecuadorian embassy.' They respond, 'Oh, do you know that Assange guy?'" And the taxi drivers would give their opinion. It's always positive. The taxi driver usually has a quite balanced opinion. They're not always brilliant people, but they get a wide section of views from their passengers and from the radio while they are waiting for

---

[116] Ai was arrested by Chinese authorities in Beijing Capital International Airport on April 3, 2011, purportedly for economic crimes, but it is widely believed that he was targeted for his outspoken criticism of the Chinese government. He was detained for three months allegedly under conditions that constituted psychological torture. Ai is referencing Article 83 from the Law of the People's Republic of China on Penalties for Administration of Public Security which he believes is used by the Chinese government to justify secret detentions. It establishes that "Immediately after the person who commits an act against the administration of public security answers the summons, the public security organ shall conduct interrogation and investigation, which shall not exceed eight hours; and if the circumstances are complicated and, according to the provisions of this Law, a penalty of administrative detention may be applied, the time for the interrogation and investigation shall not exceed 24 hours. The public security organ shall, without delay, notify the family members of the person summoned of the reasons for the summons and the place of detention." See the full Law here: http://www.china.org. cn/china/LegislationsForm2001-2010/2011-02/11/content_21899252.htm.

people. And the taxi drivers don't need to go into details. "He's pissed off powerful people so he's in trouble."

Often, I'll get people here—journalists—and they'll say, "What have you missed the most?" or "Tell us how you have been suffering in some way." That's such rubbish. Actually, what that is about is what they perceive to be a natural order of things. And the natural order of things is that when the establishment—the state—is after someone that person suffers. Somehow it would be reassuring, comforting, if I was suffering. I came in here because I wanted to have a place where I could continue working. In prison I can't do that. And so I had upset the natural order of things. It's not an easy environment by any stretch of the imagination, but I'm not going to tell you how I'm suffering. That's boring. Actually, I have published three books in here, and more than 5 million documents. The organization continues to function, we have not been driven into bankruptcy, and we are now making our own prosecutions, not simply being prosecuted. This is quite disturbing to that perception of what the natural order of things is.

You see, for example, in this Chelsea Manning case. It's a terrible, terrible case. We say, "Look how unjustly this person has been treated. It is absolutely scandalous and outrageous. The UN special rapporteur on torture formally found that Manning had been treated in a cruel and unusual way. Even the United States government's own courts—military courts—formally found that she had been illegally punished."

So, civil society is saying that. Journalists are saying that. But, at the same time, that is precisely what the United States government wants people to say. It doesn't care about being seen as just, but rather it wants people to be scared of it. It wants to induce fear. And so, people go, "Look how this poor person is being treated." And the government also responds, "Yeah, we are treating them really badly. And if you want to do something similar, that's how you're going to end up being treated too."

So it's important to send out the opposite signal. Sure, they are trying to treat me and WikiLeaks in a corrupt manner in violation of all sorts of laws and standards, but nonetheless they have lost all the major confrontations.

Why has that happened? They certainly have a determination and a lot of money. And they certainly have a lot of people. But they are incompetent, and they don't believe in their own courts. For example, the Pentagon held a public press conference, televised before the whole world, about WikiLeaks. They said WikiLeaks must destroy everything it has published and it is going to publish, and that we must cease dealing with United States military whistleblowers. That was a public demand they made before the whole world. Think about when the Pentagon made such a demand of Iraq. What happens next? The country is destroyed. It needs to keep up that appearance. Every time it makes a big demand and someone doesn't fulfill that demand, then they are killed. So it made that big demand, naming me personally. We didn't destroy anything that we had published. It's still there, you can go read it. In fact, we spread it even more. We didn't destroy anything we were going to publish. We published it. We kept going and we still deal with sources who are presumably within the United States government.

What was the next big confrontation? We then published state department material. Hundreds of thousands of documents from the State Department. We have now published more than a billion words from the State Department. And the State Department said the same thing, the United States attorney general too. We didn't stop publishing, didn't destroy anything. We kept on going. They lost. They said this is the field of combat. They lost. The Pentagon lost. The State Department lost.

What's the next thing? Edward Snowden is in Hong Kong with the walls closing in on him. All elements of the United States government, most conspicuously the National Security Agency, are after him. They wanted to extradite him to the United States. They certainly didn't want him to get asylum. They tried to cancel his passport. What happened? We got him out of the country. We got him asylum. So this head to head contest is very well defined. Are they going to grab Edward Snowden and put him in prison? Or are we going to move him to a place of asylum? They lost.

AWW: Well, I don't think they will ever make a real confrontation with you. They are just trying to either put you away or shut you off. Or make other people scared to not do the same thing.

***

AWW: This is a great chance to sit down and explore your mind a little bit. I am surprised you have thought so broadly and profoundly on the things we've been discussing.

JA: I have to do something.

At some stage, I thought about this embassy situation in a new way. It's an interesting confrontation. I came into this embassy because the situation outside was problematic, and coming in here would allow me to do things that would otherwise be impossible. And I have succeeded in that. Now, a time will come when things are going reasonably well where I am no longer in this embassy. People have it in mind that I want to escape, but it's not like that. I was outside, but then I came inside because I wanted to restructure the nature of the engagement, include a diplomatic and state-level aspect and get a formal finding that WikiLeaks has been politically persecuted. That has been achieved. And then at some stage, the situation will resolve, probably as a result of all these court cases, and then I'll be outside the embassy.

Is there anything I would miss in this situation? That is a very interesting question. If you think about it from a theater or art perspective, it's not simply a matter of diplomatic law and political situation. Here we have some kind of stage. This embassy is a stage. It has an audience out front. It has actors—all those police, me, some extras, crowds that turn up. So what is the nature of the play? If you were a playwright, a theater director, how much would you pay for a stage like that? You would probably pay quite a lot for a stage with a guaranteed international audience. You can go out on that balcony and put on your show and draw attention to some particular artistic thought and have guaranteed attention. There are all sorts of constraints, of course, that have to do with Ecuador as a state which has acted in a dignified way. But there may be some advantages to the situation. And you can see them if you consider this as a stage and your perspective is that of an artist. So what would you do? What would you do with such a stage? If it is true that there are advantages to the situation then we should explore what those advantages are before the situation goes somewhere else.

AWW: That's true. It's very clear. We have to think about that.

RESPONDING TO ASSANGE'S CRITICS 9-15

Caitlin Johnstone, April 2019

Smear 9: "He's a horrible, awful monster for reasons X, Y, and Z . . . but I don't think he should be extradited."

I always mentally translate this one into, "I'm going to keep advancing the same propaganda narratives which manufactured public consent for Assange's current predicament . . . but I don't want people to see my name on the end result."

Even if you hate Assange as a man and as a public figure with every fiber of your being, there is no legitimate reason to turn yourself into a pro bono propagandist for the CIA and the US State Department. If you actually do sincerely oppose his extradition, then you should be responsible with the narratives you choose to circulate about him, because smears kill public support and public demand is what can prevent his extradition. If you're just pretending to truly oppose his extradition in order to maintain your public wokeness cred and you really just wanted to throw in a few more smears, then you're a twat.

When looked at in its proper context, what we are witnessing is the slow-motion assassination of Assange via narrative/lawfare, so by couching your support in smears it's just like you're helping put a few bullets in the gun but loudly letting everyone know that you hope they shoot the blank.

Smear 10: "Trump is going to rescue him and they'll work together to end the Deep State. Relax and wait and see."

Make no mistake, this is a smear, and it's just as pernicious as any of the others. People who circulate this hogwash are hurting Assange just as much as the MSNBC mainliners who hate him overtly, even if they claim to support him. At a time when we should all be shaking the earth and demanding freedom for Assange, a certain strain of Trump supporter is going around telling everyone, "Relax, Trump has a plan. Wait and see."

I've been told to calm down and "wait and see" many times since Assange's arrest. What "wait and see" really means is "do nothing." Don't do anything. Trust that this same Trump administration which issued an arrest warrant for Assange in December 2017, whose CIA director labeled WikiLeaks a "hostile non-state intelligence service" and pledged to destroy it, will do the right thing instead of the wrong thing. Do absolutely nothing in the meantime, and especially don't help put political pressure on Trump to end Assange's persecution.

This strategy benefits someone, and that someone ain't Assange.

Please stop doing this. If you support Assange, stop doing this. Even if you're still chugging the Q-l-Aid and still believe the reality TV star who hired John Bolton as his national security advisor is actually a brilliant strategist making incomprehensibly complex 8-D chess moves to thwart the Deep State, even if you believe all that, surely you'll concede that there's no harm in people pressuring Trump to do the right thing and end the persecution of Assange? If he really is a beneficent wizard, there'd surely be no harm in making a lot of noise telling him he'd better pardon Assange, right? Then why spend your energy running around telling everyone to relax and stop protesting?

One argument I keep encountering is that Trump is bringing Assange to America for trial because he can only pardon him after he's been convicted. This is false. A US president can pardon anyone at any time of any crime against the United States, without their having been convicted and without their even having been charged.[117] After leaving office Richard Nixon was issued a full presidential pardon by Gerald Ford for "all offenses against the United States which he, Richard Nixon, has committed or may have committed or taken part in during the period from January 20, 1969 through August 9, 1974." Nixon had never been charged with anything. If Trump were going to pardon Assange he could have done it at any time since taking office, instead of issuing a warrant for his arrest in December 2017 and executing it on Thursday after a series of international legal manipulations.[118] A pardon is not in the plans.

Another common belief I keep encountering is that Trump is bringing Assange to America to get him to testify about his source for the 2016 Democratic Party emails in exchange for a pardon, thereby revealing the truth about Russiagate's origins and bringing down Clinton and Obama. This is false. Everyone who knows anything about Assange (including the Trump administration) knows that he will never, ever reveal a source under any circumstances whatsoever. It would be a cardinal journalistic sin, a violation of every promise WikiLeaks has ever made, and a betrayal

[117] Robert Longley, "The Rules of Presidential Pardons," *Thought Co*, January 8, 2019, https://www.thoughtco.com/presidential-pardons-legal-guidelines-4070815

[118] Caitlin Johnstone, "The Legal Narrative Funnel That's Being Used to Extradite Assange," *Medium*, April 12, https://medium.com/@caityjohnstone/the-legal-narrative-funnel-thats-being-used-to-extradite-assange-8a2e8f7a53d1

of his entire life's work. More importantly, imprisoning a journalist and threatening him with a heavy sentence to coerce him into giving up information against his will is evil.

But that isn't what Trump is doing. Trump is pursuing the imprisonment of a journalist for exposing US war crimes, so that he can scare off future leak publishers and set a legal precedent for their prosecution.

Smear 11: "He put poop on the walls! Poop poop poopie!"

Of all the Assange smears I've encountered, I think this one best epitomizes the entire overarching establishment narrative churn on the subject. Like the rest of the smear campaign, it's a completely unsubstantiated claim designed not to advance a logical argument about the current facts of Assange's situation but to provoke disgust and revulsion toward him, so that when you think of Julian Assange you don't think about press freedoms and government transparency, you think about poo. In a way it's actually more honest than some of the other smears, just because it's so obvious about what it is and what it's trying to do.

People who advance this smear are literally always acting in very bad faith. As of this writing I've never even bothered trying to engage anyone in debate on the matter, because they're too gross and too internally tormented to make interacting with them anything but unpleasant, so I have no advice to give on how to argue with such creatures. Personally I just block them.

There is no reason to believe that this smear is true (his lawyer flatly denies it), and the Ecuadorian government would have had every incentive to lie in order to try and justify its revocation of asylum which WikiLeaks says is "in violation of international law." However, it's worth taking a minute to consider the fact that if this smear *were* true, the people running around mocking Assange and making poop jokes about him on social media today would be *even more* depraved. Because what would it mean if Assange really were spreading feces on the wall? It would mean that he'd cracked under the pressure of his embassy imprisonment and lost his mind. Which would mean that these people are running around mocking a man who's been driven to psychosis by his abusive circumstances. Which would be despicable.

Smear 12: "He's stinky."

It's amazing how many mainstream media publications have thought it newsworthy to write articles about Assange's body odor. Try advocating for him on any public forum, however, and you'll immediately understand the intention behind this smear. Try to argue against the extradition of a journalist for publishing inconvenient facts about the powerful, and you'll be swarmed by people making scoffing comments about how stinky and disgusting he is. As though that has anything to do with anything whatsoever.

For the record, people who visit Assange commonly report that he's clean and smells normal, but that's really beside the point. Trying to turn a discussion about a journalist who is being prosecuted by the American Empire for publishing truth into a discussion about personal hygiene is despicable, and anyone who does it should feel bad.

Smear 13: "He was a bad houseguest."

What he actually was was a target of the US war machine. The "bad houseguest" narrative serves only to distract from Ecuador's role in turning Assange over to the Metropolitan Police instead of holding to the reasons it granted Assange asylum in the first place, and to seed disgust as in Smear 11 and Smear 12.

What actually happened was that Ecuador's new president, Lenín Moreno, quickly found himself being courted by the US government after taking office, meeting with Vice President Mike Pence and reportedly discussing Assange after US Democratic senators petitioned Pence to push for Moreno to revoke political asylum. The *New York Times* reported last year that in 2017 Trump's sleazy goon Paul Manafort met with Moreno and offered to broker a deal where Ecuador could receive debt relief aid in exchange for handing Assange over, and just last month Ecuador ended up receiving a $4.2-billion loan from the Washington-based IMF.[119] And then, lo and behold, we just so happen to see Ecuador justifying the revocation of political asylum under the absurd claim that Assange had violated conditions that were only recently invented, using narratives that were based on wild distortions and outright lies.

Smear 14: "He conspired with Don Jr."

No he didn't. The email exchanges between Donald Trump Jr. and the WikiLeaks Twitter account reveal nothing other than two parties trying to extract favors from each other, unsuccessfully.[120] Here's what the WikiLeaks account sent:

- Information about a pro-Iraq war PAC which it said was now running an anti-Trump site, with the password to a press review site so he could see it and comment on its content.

- A request for help circulating a story about Hillary Clinton's alleged suggestion to "just drone" Julian Assange.

[119] See "IMF approves $4.2bn loan for Ecuador," *Enca*, March 12, 2019, https://www. enca.com/business/imf-approves-42bn-loan-ecuador?fbclid=IwAR2_3jynzZp-bOh1BEIf4klmwkUV_Gy1sc_Cq7l2PqPKJ2YkAaA67fkzqtAE

[120] See Donald Trump, Jr., *Twitter*, November 13, 2017, https://twitter.com/DonaldJTrumpJr/status/930228239494209536

- A link and a suggestion that Trump get his followers digging through the Podesta emails for incriminating information.

- A solicitation for Trump's tax return which was hot news at the time. The WikiLeaks account reasoned with Don Jr. that they could get the jump on any leaks to the establishment media by leaking it to WikiLeaks first.

- A suggestion that Trump not concede the election he was expected to lose so as to draw attention to the massive problems in America's electoral system, specifically "media corruption, primary corruption, PAC corruption etc."

- A suggestion that Trump ask Australia to make Assange ambassador to DC, knowing they "won't do it," but in order to "send the right signals" to the US allies who'd been collaborating with US power to keep him a de facto political prisoner.

- A couple more links it wanted more attention on.

- A suggestion that Don Jr. publish the information on his Trump Tower meeting with them.

The password to the website is getting a lot of attention as of this writing since the release of the Mueller Report, with Slate going so far as to argue that Don Jr. may be guilty of violating "the Computer Fraud and Abuse Act, which makes it illegal to access a computer using a stolen password without authorization" since he did use the password. This is nonsense. WikiLeaks didn't send Trump a password which enabled him to "access a computer" or do anything other than preview a website that was actively being publicized and viewed by many people using the same password.

The password WikiLeaks gave him was a press pass to preview a Russiagate website which was about to launch. Footnoted here[121] is an

---

[121] Charles C. Johnson, "BREAKING: George Soros-Tied Group Launching Trump-Russia Conspiracy Theory Website," *Archive Today*, September 21, 2016, https://archive.fo/aRDXD

archive of a (now missing)[122] article which discussed the website's launch at the time. The article shares an email that was being passed around clearly showing that many people were being invited to look at the site in the hopes that they'd write articles promoting it. The picture that's being painted of WikiLeaks hacking into the back end of a website is completely inaccurate; there was a password to preview a website whose owners wanted people to look at it, lots of people had that password, and one of them reportedly gave it to WikiLeaks.

Beyond that, what is there? WikiLeaks trying unsuccessfully to get Don Jr. to advance its agendas like giving them Trump's tax return (i.e., soliciting a potential source for leaks), challenging America's broken electoral system, trying to get more eyes on their material, and a Hail Mary suggestion that the Trump administration shake things up by making Assange the Australian ambassador with a full acknowledgement that this will never happen. None of these things occurred, and WikiLeaks never responded to Don Jr.'s request for information about an upcoming leak drop.

Assange has agendas. Whoop dee doo. I have agendas too, otherwise I wouldn't be doing this. All journalists have agendas, it just happens that most of them have the agenda to become rich and famous by any means necessary, which generally means cozying up to the rulers of the establishment and manufacturing consent for the status quo. Assange's agenda is infinitely more noble and infinitely more reviled by the servants of power: to upset the status quo that demands war, corruption, and oppression in order to exist. His communications with Don Jr. are geared toward this end, as is the rest of his life's work.

[122] It previously existed at http://gotnews.com/breaking-george-soros-tied-group-launching-trump-russia-conspiracy-theory-website/

Smear 15: "He only publishes leaks about America."

This is just wrong and stupid. Do 30 seconds of research for God's sake.

PART III: THE INTERNET, CENSORSHIP, AND SCIENTIFIC JOURNALISM

1. A CYPHERPUNK IN HIS OWN WORDS[123]

Julian Assange, March 20, 2012

Increased communication versus increased surveillance

JULIAN ASSANGE: If we go back to this time in the early 1990s when you had the rise of the cypherpunk[124] movement in response to state bans on cryptography, a lot of people were looking at the power of the Internet to provide free, uncensored communications compared to mainstream media. But the cypherpunks always saw that, in fact, combined with this was also the power to surveil all the communications that were occurring. We now have increased communication versus increased surveillance. Increased communication means you have extra freedom relative to the

---

[123] The following are excerpted quotes from conversations originally published in *Cypherpunks: Freedom and the Future of the Internet* (OR Books, 2012).

[124] Cypherpunks advocate for the use of cryptography and similar methods as ways to achieve societal and political change. Founded in the early 1990s, the movement has been most active during the 1990s "cryptowars" and following the 2011 Internet spring. The term *cypherpunk*, derived from (cryptographic) *cipher* and *punk*, was added to the Oxford English Dictionary in 2006.

people who are trying to control ideas and manufacture consent, and increased surveillance means just the opposite.

The surveillance is far more evident now than it was when bulk surveillance was just being done by the Americans, the British, the Russians, and some other governments like the Swiss and the French. Now it is being done by everyone, and by nearly every state, because of the commercialization of mass surveillance. And it's totalizing now, because people put all their political ideas, their family communications, and their friendships on to the Internet. So it's not just that there is increased surveillance of the communication that was already there; it's that there is so much more communication. And it's not just an increase in the volume of communication; it's an increase in the types of communication. All these new types of communication that would previously have been private are now being mass intercepted.

There is a battle between the power of this information collected by insiders, these shadow states of information that are starting to develop, swapping with each other, developing connections with each other and with the private sector, versus the increased size of the commons with the Internet as a common tool for humanity to speak to itself.

***

JA: And yet despite this mass surveillance, mass communication has led to millions of people being able to come to a fast consensus. If you can go from a normal position to a new mass consensus position very quickly, then while the state might be able to see it developing, there's not enough time to formulate an effective response.

Now that said, there was a Facebook-organized protest in 2008 in Cairo. It did surprise the Mubarak government, and as a result these people were tracked down using Facebook.[125] In 2011, in a manual which was one of the

---

[125] This was the April 6, 2008, protest in support of the suppressed strike of the Mahalla al-Kobra textile workers. Shortly before the strike the "April 6 Youth

most important documents used in the Egyptian revolution, the first page says "Do not use Twitter or Facebook" to distribute the manual, and the last page says "Do not use Twitter or Facebook" to distribute the manual.[126] Nonetheless, plenty of Egyptians did use Twitter and Facebook. But the reason they survived is because the revolution was successful. If it had not been successful, then those people would have been in a very, very grim position. And let's not forget that pretty early on President Mubarak cut off the Internet in Egypt. It is actually questionable whether the Internet blackout facilitated the revolution or harmed it. Some people think it facilitated it, because people had to go out on the street to get news about what was happening, and once you're out on the street you're out on the street. And people were directly affected because their cell phone and Internet didn't work anymore.

So if it is going to be successful, there needs to be a critical mass, it needs to happen fast, and it needs to win, because if it doesn't win then that same infrastructure that allows a fast consensus to develop will be used to track down and marginalize all the people who were involved in seeding the consensus.

***

Movement" was formed as a Facebook group, conceived to encourage Egyptians to hold protests in Cairo and elsewhere to coincide with the industrial action in Mahalla. The protests did not go to plan, and the Facebook group's administrators Esraa Abdel Fattah Ahmed Rashid and Ahmed Maher were arrested, along with others. Maher was tortured for his Facebook password. The April 6 Youth Movement went on to play a role in the 2011 Egyptian revolution. See "Cairo Activists Use Facebook to Rattle Regime," *Wired*, October 20, 2008: http://www.wired.com/techbiz/startups/magazine/16-11/ff_facebookegypt?currentPage=all (accessed October 23, 2012).

[126] "How to Protest Intelligently," anonymous authors, distributed at the outset of the 18-day uprising that removed President Mubarak (Arabic): http://www.itstime.it/Approfondimenti/EgyptianRevolutionManual.pdf. Excerpts from the document were translated into English and published as "Egyptian Activists' Action Plan: Translated," *Atlantic*, January 27, 2011: http://www.theatlantic.com/international/archive/2011/01/egyptian-activists-action-plan-translated/70388 (both links accessed October 23, 2012).

The militarization of cyberspace

JA: I see that there is now a militarization of cyberspace, in the sense of a military occupation. When you communicate over the Internet, when you communicate using mobile phones, which are now meshed to the Internet, your communications are being intercepted by military intelligence organizations. It's like having a tank in your bedroom. It's a soldier between you and your wife as you're SMSing. We are all living under martial law as far as our communications are concerned, we just can't see the tanks—but they are there. To that degree, the Internet, which was supposed to be a civilian space, has become a militarized space. But the Internet is our space, because we all use it to communicate with each other and with the members of our family. The communications at the inner core of our private lives now move over the Internet. So in fact our private lives have entered into a militarized zone. It is like having a soldier under the bed. This is a militarization of civilian life.

***

Fighting total surveillance with the laws of man

JA: But are there two approaches to dealing with mass state surveillance: the laws of physics and the laws of man. One is to use the laws of physics by actually building devices that prevent interception. The other is to enact democratic controls through the law to make sure people must have warrants and so on and to try to gain some regulatory accountability. But strategic interception cannot be a part of that, cannot be meaningfully constrained by regulation. Strategic interception is about intercepting everyone regardless of whether they are innocent or guilty. We must remember that it is the core of the Establishment carrying such surveillance. There will always be a lack of political will to expose state spying. And the technology is inherently so complex, and its use in practice so secret that there cannot be meaningful democratic oversight.

***

JA: Once you have erected this surveillance, given that it is complex, given that it is designed to operate in secret, isn't it true that it cannot be regulated with policy? I think that except for very small nations like Iceland, unless there are revolutionary conditions it is simply not possible to control mass interception with legislation and policy. It is just not going to happen. It is too cheap and too easy to get around political accountability and to actually perform interception. The Swedes got through an interception bill in 2008, known as the FRA-lagen, which meant the Swedish signals intelligence agency the FRA could legally intercept all communication traveling through the country in bulk, and ship it off to the United States, with some caveats.[127] Now how can you enforce those caveats once you've set up the interception system and the organization doing it is a secret spy agency? It's impossible. And in fact cases have come out showing that the FRA had on a variety of occasions broken the law previously. Many countries simply do it off-law with no legislative cover at all. So we're sort of lucky if, like in the Swedish example, they decided that for their own protection from prosecution they want to go legal by changing the law. And that's the case for most countries—there is bulk interception occurring, and when there is a legislative proposal it is to protect the ass of those who are doing it.

This technology is very complex; for example in the debate in Australia and the UK about proposed legislation to intercept all metadata, most

---

127 See "Sweden approves wiretapping law," BBC, June 19, 2008: http://news.bbc.co.uk/1/hi/world/europe/7463333.stm.
For more on the FRA-lagen, see Wikipedia: http://en.wikipedia.org/wiki/FRA_law (both links accessed October 10, 2012).

people do not understand the value of metadata or even the word itself.[128] Intercepting all metadata means you have to build a system that physically intercepts all data and then throws everything but the metadata away. But such a system cannot be trusted. There's no way to determine whether it is in fact intercepting and storing all data without having highly skilled engineers with authorization to go in and check out precisely what is going on, and there's no political will to grant access. The problem is getting worse because complexity and secrecy are a toxic mix. Hidden by complexity. Hidden by secrecy. Unaccountability is built-in. It is a feature. It is dangerous by design.

***

Fighting total surveillance with the laws of physics

JA: I think that the only effective defense against the coming susrveillance dystopia is one where you take steps yourself to safeguard your privacy, because there's no incentive for self-restraint by the people that have the capacity to intercept everything. A historical analogy could be how people learned that they should wash their hands. That required the germ theory of disease to be established and then popularized, and for paranoia to be instilled about the spread of disease via invisible stuff on your hands

---

[128] Metadata is "data about data." In the context of this discussion, metadata refers to data other than the "content" of the electronic communication. It is the front of the envelope, rather than the contents. Surveillance of metadata does not target the contents of emails, but rather all the information surrounding the contents— who the email was sent to or from, the IP addresses (and therefore location) from which it was sent, the times and dates of each email, etc. The point is, however, that the technology to intercept metadata is the same technology as the technology to intercept the contents. If you grant someone the right to surveil your metadata, their equipment must also intercept the contents of your communications. Besides this, most people do not realize that "metadata in aggregate is content"— when all the metadata is put together it provides an astonishingly detailed picture of a person's communications.

that you can't see, just as you can't see mass interception. Once there was enough understanding, soap manufacturers produced products that people consumed to relieve their fear. It's necessary to install fear in to people so they understand the problem before they will create enough demand to solve the problem.

There is a problem on the opposite side of the equation as well, which is that programs that claim to be secure, that claim to have cryptography in them, are often frauds, because cryptography is complex, and the fraud can be hidden in complexity.[129]

So people will have to think about it. The only question is in which one of the two ways will they think about it? They will either think, "I need to be careful about what I say, I need to conform," the whole time, in every interaction. Or they will think "I need to master little components of this technology and install things that protect me so I'm able to express my thoughts freely and communicate freely with my friends and people I care about." If people don't take that second step then we'll have a universal political correctness, because even when people are communicating with their closest friends they will be self-censors and will remove themselves as political actors from the world.

***

Censorship

JA: If we go back to 1953 and we look at the great Soviet encyclopedia, which was distributed everywhere, that encyclopedia sometimes had

---

[129] For example, a member of the LulzSec group that exposed flaws in Sony's security practices by releasing Sony customers' personal data was arrested after his identity was gained from the proxy site HideMyAss.com, via a court order in the US. See, "Lulzsec hacker pleads guilty over Sony attack," BBC, October 15, 2012: http://www.bbc.com/news/technology-19949624 (accessed October 15, 2012).

amendments as politics changed in the Soviet Union. In 1953 Beria, the head of the NKVD, the Soviet secret police, died and fell out of political favor and so his section, which described him in glowing terms, was removed by the encyclopedia authority, which posted an amendment that was to be pasted into all of those encyclopedias. It was extremely obvious. I'm mentioning this example because it was so obvious and so detectable that the attempt became part of history. Whereas in the UK we have the *Guardian* and the other major newspapers ripping out stories from their Internet archives in secret without any description. You go to those pages now and you try to find them, for example stories on the fraud case of the billionaire Nadhmi Auchi, and you see "Page not found," and they have also been removed from the indexes.

Let me tell you my involvement with the Nadhmi Auchi story. In 1990, Iraq invaded Kuwait, and that led to the first Gulf War. The Kuwaiti government in exile, and also during its return, needed cash, so it started to sell off various assets including several oil refineries outside Kuwait. A UK businessman, Nadhmi Auchi, who had immigrated to the UK in the early 1980s from Iraq, where he used to be a figure in Saddam Hussein's regime, was a broker in that deal and was subsequently accused of being involved in channeling $118 million of illegal commissions. That investigation was the largest corruption investigation in European postwar history. In 2003, Auchi was convicted of fraud in what was to become known as the Elf Aquitaine scandal. Nevertheless, nowadays he has over 200 companies registered through his Luxembourg holding outfit, and others through Panama. He is involved in postwar Iraqi cellular contracts and many other businesses around the world.[130]

---

[130] See the WikiLeaks page on Nadhmi Auchi: http://wikileaks.org/wiki/Nadhmi_Auchi (accessed October 24, 2012).

In the United States Tony Rezko, a fundraiser for Barack Obama's Senate campaign, was a long-term pal of Auchi's, who had been his financier. Similarly Auchi and Rezko became involved with the former governor of Illinois, Rod Blagojevich. Both Rezko and Blagojevich were convicted of corruption, Rezko in 2008 and Blagojevich in 2010–11 (after the FBI recorded him in telephone intercept trying to sell Obama's former Senate seat). In 2007–8, when Obama was running to be the Democrats' presidential candidate, the US press started to investigate Obama's connections. They investigated Rezko and reported some links in relation to the purchase of Barack Obama's house. In 2008, shortly before his trial, Rezko received a $3.5-million transfer from Auchi, which he didn't report to the court, despite being required to—for which he was jailed. So US press scrutiny turned to Auchi, and at that moment he instructed UK lawyers Carter-Ruck to wage an aggressive campaign on much of the 2003 reportage about the Elf Aquitaine scandal and his conviction in France. This was very successful. He targeted the UK press, and even US blogs, and had nearly a dozen articles removed that we know about. Most of those articles, including in UK newspaper archives, simply disappeared. It was as if they had never even existed. There was no, "We have received a legal complaint and decided to remove the story." They also disappeared from the indexes. WikiLeaks dug these out and republished them.[131]

***

JA: History is not only modified, it has ceased to have ever existed. It is Orwell's dictum, "He who controls the present controls the past and he who controls the past controls the future." It is the undetectable erasure

---

[131] "The stories can be found on WikiLeaks here: "Eight stories on Obama linked billionaire Nadhmi Auchi censored from the Guardian, Observer, Telegraph, and New Statesman," *WikiLeaks*, September 26, 2008, http://wikileaks.org/wiki/Eight_stories_on_Obama_linked_billionaire_Nadhmi_Auchi_censored_from_the_Guardian,_Observer,_Telegraph_and_New_Statesman (accessed October 24, 2012).

of history in the West, and that's just post-publication censorship. Pre-publication self-censorship is much more extreme but often hard to detect. We've seen that with Cablegate as WikiLeaks works with different media partners all over the world, so we can see which ones censor our material.[132]

For example the *New York Times* redacted a cable that said that millions of dollars were distributed to covertly influence politically connected Libyans via oil companies operating in Libya. The cable didn't even name a specific oil company—the *New York Times* simply redacted the phrase "oil services companies."[133] Probably the most flagrant was the *New York Times'* use of a 62-page cable about North Korea's missile program, and whether they had sold missiles to the Iranians, from which the *New York Times* used two paragraphs in order to argue, in a story, that Iran had missiles that could strike Europe, whereas elsewhere in the cable just the opposite was argued.[134]

---

[132] As a general note both http://cables.mrkva.eu/ and http://cablegatesearch.net provide excellent ways of comparing redacted versions of cables with full versions, in order to see what WikiLeaks' media partners redacted.

[133] "Qaddafi's Son Is Bisexual and Other Things the *New York Times* Doesn't Want You to Know," Gawker, September 16, 2011: http://gawker.com/5840809/qaddafis-son-is-bisexual-and-other-things-the-new-york-times-doesnt-want-you-to-know-about.

The specific example cited refers to cable reference ID 06TRIPOLI198, WikiLeaks: https://wikileaks.org/cable/2006/05/06TRIPOLI198.html.

The redactions can be seen visually on the Cablegatesearch website which shows the revision history, with the redactions shaded in pink: http://www.cablegatesearch.net/cable.php?id=06TRIPOLI198&version=1291757400 (all links accessed October 22, 2012).

[134] For the original cable see cable reference ID 10STATE17263, WikiLeaks: http://wikileaks.org/cable/2010/02/10STATE17263.html.

For the *New York Times* story see "Iran Fortifies Its Arsenal With the Aid of North Korea," *New York Times*, November 29, 2010: http://www.nytimes.com/2010/11/29/world/middleeast/29missiles.html?_r=0.

The same cable was also used by David Leigh of the *Guardian* for his story, "WikiLeaks cables expose Pakistan nuclear fears," *Guardian*, November 30, 2010: http://www.guardian.co.uk/world/2010/nov/30/wikileaks-cables-pakistan-nuclear-fears. The redacted version of the cable published by the *Guardian*, without a cable reference number, reduced it to just two paragraphs relating to Pakistan.

The *Guardian* redacted a cable about Yulia Tymoshenko, the former prime minister of Ukraine, which said that she might be hiding her wealth in London.[135] It censored out allegations that the Kazakhstani elite in general was corrupt—not even a named person—and an allegation that both ENI, the Italian energy company operating in Kazakhstan, and British Gas were corrupt.[136] Essentially the *Guardian* censored instances where a rich person was accused of something in a cable, unless the *Guardian* had an institutional agenda against that rich person.[137] So, for example, in a cable

"US embassy cables: XXXXXXXXXXXX," *Guardian*, November 30, 2010: http://www.guardian.co.uk/world/us-embassy-cables-documents/250573. The extent of the redaction can be seen visually on the Cablegatesearch website which shows the revision history, with the redaction of nearly the whole document shaded in pink: http://www.cablegatesearch.net/cable.php?id=10STATE17263&version=1291486260 (all links accessed October 22, 2012).

[135] For the original cable see cable reference ID 08KYIV2414, WikiLeaks: http://wikileaks.org/cable/2008/12/08KYIV2414.html.

For the *Guardian* redacted version see, "US embassy cables: Gas supplies linked to Russian mafia," December 1, 2010: http://www.guardian.co.uk/world/us-embassy-cables-documents/182121?INTCMP=SRCH.

The redaction can be seen visually on the Cablegate search website which shows the revision history, with the redactions shaded in pink: http://www.cablegatesearch.net/cable.php?id=08KYIV2414&version=1291255260 (all links accessed October 22, 2012).

[136] For the original cable see cable reference ID 10ASTANA72, WikiLeaks: http://wikileaks.org/cable/2010/01/10ASTANA72.html.

For the *Guardian* redacted version see, "US embassy cables: Kazakhstan—the big four," *Guardian*, November 29, 2010: http://www.guardian.co.uk/world/us-embassy-cables-documents/245167?INTCMP=SRCH.

The redaction can be seen visually on the Cablegatesearch website which shows the revision history, with the redactions shaded in pink: http://www.cablegatesearch.net/cable.php?id=10ASTANA72&version=1291113360 (all links accessed October 22, 2012).

[137] See, for example, cable reference ID 09TRIPOLI413 about Western energy companies operating in Libya. The visual representation on the Cablegatesearch website, with the *Guardian*'s redactions shaded in pink, shows that the *Guardian* removed all references to the names of energy companies and their executives, except for references to Russian energy company Gazprom. Even though some of the content is somewhat mitigating for the Western companies, the redactions are elaborate, and the redacted version gives quite a different picture: http://www.cablegatesearch.net/cable.php?id=09TRIPOLI413&version=1296509820 (accessed October 22, 2012).

about Bulgarian organized crime there was one Russian, and the *Guardian* it made it look like the whole thing was about him, but he was just one person on a long list of organizations and individuals associated with Bulgarian organized crime.[138] *Der Spiegel* censored out a paragraph about what Merkel was doing—no human rights concern whatsoever, purely political concerns about Merkel.[139] There are lots of examples.[140]

***

JA: My experience in the West is that it is just so much more sophisticated in the number of layers of indirection and obfuscation about what is actually happening. These layers are there to give deniability to the censorship that is occurring. You can think about censorship as a pyramid. This pyramid

---

[138] In this example the original cable contained 5,226 words. The redacted version published by the *Guardian* had only 1,406 words.

For the original cable see cable reference ID 05SOFIA1207, WikiLeaks: http://wikileaks.org/cable/2005/07/05SOFIA1207.html.

For the *Guardian* redacted version see, "US embassy cables: Organised crime in Bulgaria," December 1, 2010: http://www.guardian.co.uk/world/us-embassy-cables-documents/36013.

For the *Guardian* news story based on the cable see, "WikiLeaks cables: Russian government "using mafia for its dirty work"," *Guardian*, December 1, 2010: http://www.guardian.co.uk/world/2010/dec/01/wikileaks-cable-spain-russian-mafia.

The extent of the redaction can be seen visually on the Cablegatesearch website which shows the revision history, with the redactions shaded in pink: http://www.cablegatesearch.net/cable.php?id=05SOFIA1207&version=1291757400.

This Bulgarian example is discussed by WikiLeaks' Bulgarian media partner Bivol in, "Unedited cable from Sofia shows the total invasion of the state by organized crime (Update: Cable Comparison)," WL Central, March 18, 2011: http://wlcentral.org/node/1480. In addition see, "The *Guardian*: Redacting, censoring or lying?" WL Central, March 19, 2012: http://wlcentral.org/node/1490. Also of note below both WL Central stories is the comment from *Guardian* journalist David Leigh and the responses (all links accessed October 22, 2012).

[139] This refers to cable reference ID 09BERLIN1108. The redactions can be seen visually on the Cablegatesearch website which shows the revision history, with the redactions shaded in pink: http://www.cablegatesearch.net/cable.php?id=09BERLIN1108&version=1291380660 (accessed October 22, 2012).

[140] For more examples, see the cabledrum website: www.cabledrum.net/pages/censorship.php.

only has its tip sticking out of the sand, and that is by intention. The tip is public—libel suits, murders of journalists, cameras being snatched by the military, and so on—publicly declared censorship. But that is the small- · est component. Under the tip, the next layer is all those people who don't want to be at the tip, who engage in self-censorship to not end up there. Then the next layer is all the forms of economic inducement or patronage inducement that are given to people to write about one thing or another. The next layer down is raw economy—what it is economic to write about, even if you don't include the economic factors from higher up the pyramid. Then the next layer is the prejudice of readers who only have a certain level of education, so therefore on one hand they are easy to manipulate with false information, and on the other hand you can't even tell them something sophisticated that is true. The last layer is distribution—for example, some people just don't have access to information in a particular language. So that is the censorship pyramid. What the *Guardian* is doing with its Cablegate redactions is in the second layer.

Now, such censorship is deniable because it either takes place out of the light, or because there is no instruction to censor a particular claim. Journalists are rarely instructed, "Don't print anything about that," or, "Don't print that fact." Rather they understand that they are expected to because they understand the interests of those they wish to placate or grow close to. If you behave you'll be patted on the head and rewarded, and if you don't behave then you won't. It's that simple. I'm often fond of making this example: the obvious censorship that occurred in the Soviet Union, the censorship that was propagandized about so much in the West—jackboots coming for journalists in the middle of the night to take them from their homes—has just been shifted by twelve hours. Now we wait for the day and take homes from journalists, as they fall out of patronage and are unable to service their debts. Journalists are taken from their homes by taking homes from the journalists. Western societies specialize in laundering censorship and structuring the affairs of the powerful such that any remaining public speech that gets through has a hard time affecting the true power relationships of a highly fiscalized society, because such relationships are hidden in layers of complexity and secrecy.

***

Rats in the opera house

JA: I posed the question of what the most positive trajectory for the future would look like. Self-knowledge, diversity, and networks of self-determination. A highly educated global population—I do not mean formal education, but highly educated in their understanding of how human civilization works at the political, industrial, scientific, and psychological levels—as a result of the free exchange of communication, also stimulating vibrant new cultures and the maximal diversification of individual thought, increased regional self-determination, and the self-determination of interest groups that are able to network quickly and exchange value rapidly over geographic boundaries. And perhaps that has been expressed in the Arab Spring and the pan-Arab activism which was potentiated by the Internet. In our work with Nawaat.org, who created Tunileaks, pushing the State Department cables past the regime's censorship into pre-revolutionary Tunisia, we saw firsthand the terrific power of the network for moving information to where it is needed, and it was tremendously rewarding to have been in a position, because of our efforts, to contribute to what was starting to happen there.[141] I do not perceive that struggle for self-determination as distinct from our own.

---

[141] Nawaat.org is an independent collective blog in Tunisia launched in 2004: http://nawaat.org/portail.
Tunileaks was launched by Nawaat in November 2010, publishing cables from WikiLeaks related to Tunisia: https://tunileaks.appspot.com.

This positive trajectory would entail the self-knowing of human civilization because the past cannot be destroyed. It would mean the inability of neo-totalitarian states to arise in practice because of the free movement of information, the ability for people to speak to each other privately and conspire against such tendencies, and the ability for micro-capital to move without control away from such places which are inhospitable to human beings.

From those underpinnings you can build a wide variety of political systems. Utopia to me would be a dystopia if there was just one. I think utopian ideals must mean the diversity of systems and models of interaction. If you look at the churning development of new cultural products and even language drift, and sub-cultures forming their own mechanisms of interaction potentiated by the Internet, then yes I can see that that does open this possible positive path.

But I think in all probability tendencies to homogenization, universality, the whole of human civilization being turned into one market, mean you will have normal market factors such as one market leader, one second, a third niche player, and then stragglers that don't make any difference at all, for every service and product. I think it will perhaps mean massive language homogenization, massive cultural homogenization, massive standardization in order to make these rapid interchanges efficient. So I think the pessimistic scenario is also quite probable, and the transnational surveillance state and endless drone wars are almost upon us.

Actually, I'm reminded of a time when I smuggled myself into Sydney Opera House to see *Faust*. Sydney Opera House is very beautiful at night, its grand interiors and lights beaming out over the water and into the night

For more on Tunilinks and the Ben-Ali government's censorship efforts against it see, "Tunisia: Censorship Continues as WikiLeaks Cables Make the Rounds," Global Voices Advocacy, December 7, 2010: http://advocacy.globalvoicesonline.org/2010/12/07/tunisia-censorship-continues-as-wikileaks-cables-make-the-rounds (all links accessed October 24, 2012).

sky. Afterwards I came out and I heard three women talking together, leaning on the railing overlooking the darkened bay. The older woman was describing how she was having problems with her job, which turned out to be working for the CIA as an intelligence agent, and she had previously complained to the Senate Select Committee for Intelligence and so on, and she was telling this in hushed tones to her niece and another woman. I thought, "So it is true then. CIA agents really do hang out at the Sydney opera!" And then I looked inside the Opera House through the massive glass panels at the front, and there in all this lonely palatial refinement was a water rat that had crawled up into the Opera House interior, and was scurrying back and forth, leaping on to the fine linen-covered tables and eating the Opera House food, jumping onto the counter with all the tickets and having a really great time. And actually I think that is the most probable scenario for the future: an extremely confining, homogenized, postmodern transnational totalitarian structure with incredible complexity, absurdities and debasements, and within that incredible complexity a space where only the smart rats can go.

That's a positive angle on the negative trajectory, the negative trajectory being a transnational surveillance state, drone-riddled, the networked neo-feudalism of the transnational elite—not in a classical sense, but a complex multi-party interaction that has come about as a result of various elites in their own national countries lifting up together, off their respective population bases, and merging. All communications will be surveilled, permanently recorded, permanently tracked, each individual in all their interactions permanently identified as that individual to this new Establishment, from birth to death. That's a major shift from even ten years ago and we're already practically there. I think that can only produce a very controlling atmosphere. If all the collected information about the world was public that might rebalance the power dynamic and let us, as a global civilization, shape our destiny. But without dramatic change it will not. Mass surveillance applies disproportionately to most of us, transferring power to those in on the scheme who nonetheless, I think, will not enjoy this brave new world much either. This system will also coincide with a drones arms race that will eliminate clearly defined borders as we know them, since such borders are produced by the contestation of physical lines, resulting in a state of perpetual war as the winning influence-networks start to shake down the world for concessions. And alongside this people are going to just be buried under the impossible math of bureaucracy.

How can a normal person be free within that system? They simply cannot, it's impossible. Not that anyone can ever be completely free, within any system, but the freedoms that we have biologically evolved for, and the freedoms that we have become culturally accustomed to, will be almost entirely eliminated. So I think the only people who will be able to keep the freedom that we had, say, twenty years ago—because the surveillance state has already eliminated quite a lot of that, we just don't realize it yet—are those who are highly educated in the internals of this system. So it will only be a high-tech rebel elite that is free, these clever rats running around the opera house.

2. ASSANGE HAS ONLY US TO HELP HIM![142]

Slavoj Žižek, April 12, 2019

It finally happened—on April 11 2019, Julian Assange was dragged from the Ecuadorian embassy and arrested. It was no surprise: many signs pointed in this direction. A week or two ago, WikiLeaks predicted the arrest, and the Ecuadorian foreign ministry responded with what we now know is a blatant lie (that there were no plans to cancel Assange's asylum), peppered with further lies (about WikiLeaks publishing photos of the Ecuadorian president's private life—why would Assange be interested in doing this and thus endangering his asylum?). The recent arrest of Chelsea Manning (largely ignored by the media) was also an element in this game. Her confinement, designed to force her to divulge information about her links with WikiLeaks, is part of the prosecution that awaits Assange when (if) the US gets hold of him.

[142] A version of this article was originally published in the *Independent*. Slavoj Žižek, "Assange helped teach the people about our tarnished freedom—now we are all he has left to defend him," *Independent*, April 12, 2019, https://www.independent.co.uk/voices/julian-assange-extradition-us-wikileaks-google-slavoj-zizek-a8866741.html.

A further hint of his impending arrest was given when the UK said it will not extradite Assange to a country where he could face the death penalty (rather than saying he will not be extradited to the US because of WikiLeaks)—this practically confirmed the possibility of his extradition to the US. Not to mention the long, slow, well-orchestrated campaign of character assassination which reached the lowest level imaginable a couple of months ago with unverified rumors that the Ecuadorians wanted to get rid of him because of his bad smell and dirty clothes. In the first stage of attacks on Assange, his ex-friends and collaborators went public with claims that WikiLeaks began well but then it got bogged down with Assange's political bias (his anti-Hillary obsession, his suspicious ties with Russia). This was followed by more direct personal defamations: he is paranoid and arrogant, obsessed by power and control ... Now we have reached the level of bodily smells and stains.

Assange paranoid? When you live permanently in an apartment that is bugged from above and below, a victim of constant surveillance organized by secret services, who wouldn't be that? Megalomaniac? When the (now ex-) head of the CIA says your arrest is his priority, does not this imply that you are a "big" threat to some, at least? Behaving like the head of a spy organization? But WikiLeaks IS a spy organization, although one that serves the people, keeping them informed on what goes on behind the scenes.

So let's move to the big question: Why now? I think one name explains it all: Cambridge Analytica—a name which stands for all that Assange is about, for what he fights against: the links between the great private corporations and government agencies. Remember how big an obsession was the Russian meddling in the US elections? Now we know it was not the Russian hackers (with Assange) who nudged the people toward Trump, but our own data-processing agencies who joined up with political forces. This doesn't mean that Russia and their allies are innocent: they probably did try to influence the outcome in the same way that the US does so in other countries (only in this case, it is called helping democracy). But it means the big bad wolf who distorts our democracy is here, not in the Kremlin—and this is what Assange was claiming all the time.

But where, exactly, is this big bad wolf? To grasp the whole scope of this control and manipulation, one should move beyond the link between private corporations and political parties (as is the case with Cambridge Analytica), to the interpenetration of data-processing companies like Google or Facebook and state security agencies. We shouldn't be shocked at China but at ourselves who accept the same regulation while believing that we retain our full freedom, and that our media just help us to realize our goals. In China people are fully aware that they are regulated. The overall image emerging from it, combined with what we also know about the link between the latest developments in biogenetics (the wiring of the human brain, etc.), provides an adequate and terrifying image of new forms of social control which make the good old twentieth-century "totalitarianism" a rather primitive and clumsy machine of control.

The biggest achievement of the new cognitive-military complex is that direct and obvious oppression is no longer necessary: individuals are much better controlled and "nudged" in the desired direction when they continue to experience themselves as free and autonomous agents of their own life. This is another key lesson of WikiLeaks: our unfreedom is most dangerous when it is experienced as the very medium of our freedom— what can be freer than the incessant flow of communications which allows every individual to popularize their opinions and form virtual communities of their own free will? Because in our societies permissiveness and free choice are elevated into a supreme value, social control and domination can no longer appear as infringing on a subject's freedom: it has to appear as (and be sustained by) the very self-experience of individuals as free. What can be more free than our unconstrained surfing on the web? This is how "fascism which smells like democracy"[143] really operates today.

This is why it is absolutely imperative to keep the digital network out of the control of private capital and state power, and to render it totally accessible to public debate. Assange was right in his strangely ignored book *When Google Met WikiLeaks* (New York: OR Books, 2014): to understand how our lives are regulated today, and how this regulation is experienced as our freedom, we have to focus on the shadowy relation between private corporations which control our commons and secret state agencies.

Now we can see why Assange has to be silenced: after the Cambridge Analytica scandal exploded, all the effort of those in power goes into reducing it to a particular "misuse" by some private corporations and political parties—but where is the state itself, the half-invisible apparatuses of the so-called "deep state"?

Assange characterized himself as the spy of and for the people: he is not spying on the people for those in power, he is spying on those in power for the people. This is why his only assistance will have to come from us, the people. Only our pressure and mobilization can alleviate his predicament. One often reads how the Soviet secret service not only punished its traitors (even if it took decades to do it), but also fought doggedly to free them when they were caught by the enemy. Assange has no state behind

---

[143] Žižek is referring to a 2019 far-right campaign ad by Israeli justice minister Ayelet Shaked that depicts a mock advertisement for a perfume called "Fascism." In the commercial, Shaked pushes back against those who call her a fascist in saying to the camera, "To me, [the perfume] smells like democracy." See https://www.theguardian.com/world/2019/mar/19/far-right-israeli-campaign-ad-jokes-of-fascism-perfume-ayelet-shaked?CMP=aff_1432&utm_content=The+Independent&awc=5795_1560184350_4e65e226ed1cc83787c9c8f3bb4f821d

him, just us—so let us do at least what the Soviet secret service was doing, let's fight for him no matter how long it will take!

WikiLeaks is just the beginning, and our motto should be a Maoist one: Let a hundred WikiLeaks blossom. The panic and fury with which those in power—those who control our digital commons—reacted to Assange, is a proof that such an activity hits the nerve. There will be many blows below the belt in this fight—our side will be accused of playing the enemy's hands (like the campaign against Assange for being in the service of Putin), but we should get used to it and learn to strike back with interest, ruthlessly playing one side against each other in order to bring them all down.

3. TRUTH AND CHAOS

Franco "Bifo" Berardi, February 2019

You taught me language, and my profit on 't
Is, I know how to curse. The red plague rid you
For learning me your language!
(William Shakespeare, *The Tempest*)

1. Why the persecution?

Why the persecution of Julian Assange? What reproachable act did he commit? Why are some of the most powerful actors of the world's political scene so angry with him that they suggest he may be eliminated by a drone?

The fault of Julian Assange is in the following: he has taken seriously many of the words which are at the foundation of liberal democracy and of the Western political culture at large: truth, transparency, and democracy.

The long-lasting legal aggression against Assange is an act of hypocrisy, and it violates the ethical rules of information freedom.

The philosophy of WikiLeaks and the personal adventure of Julian Assange are based on the unshakable confidence in transparency and the effectiveness of the act of supplying information.

Here is the force of WikiLeaks, here is its weakness.

I say that confidence in transparency is the weak point of WikiLeaks because in the current regime of connective semio-power, the relation between signs and things becomes blurred, such that minds are overwhelmed by the flow of info-neural stimulations, and transparency is subsumed by the trap of white noise.

The old darkness that Europeans used to call the Middle Ages was the effect of an extreme rarefaction of social interactions, a kingdom of pervasive silence. Contemporary darkness, on the other hand, is the result of boundless proliferation of information sources, of the intensification of info-neuro stimulation.

The new age of darkness is the dazzling effect of an excess of glowing: the proliferation of screens and the relentless glimmering of visual stimuli lead to the overall blurred image of the world—like James Williams suggests in his book *Stand Out of Our Light*, the faculty of critical understanding is paralyzed and the shit-storm prevails.

Censorship, once upon a time the essential feature of the authoritarian regime, is replaced today by an explosion of public enunciations, saturating the space of attention up to the point of white noise.

Dark Enlightenment is the formula that best captures the current perception that the future promises the cancellation of the humanist prospect.

2. Power and Secrecy

The assumption that lies beneath the acts of disclosure that WikiLeaks has performed in the last decade is that media-political power is based on hiding information, and therefore truth is subversive. Disclosing the secret, making transparent the workings of power, is the way to democracy: the action of WikiLeaks is grounded here.

The problem is that this philosophical premise is questionable. What is a secret in fact? A secret is the content of an act of occultation. Somewhere there is a truth, hidden in a box. If you have the key, if you can open the box, you can dissolve the secret and disclose the truth.

The history of modern political entities like nation states, armies, and political parties has actually been based on plots, lies, cover-ups, simulations...

But the intricacies of political will scramble the linear relation between strategies and outcomes; the political adroitness has always been based on the ability to mix meticulous tactical awareness and readiness to accept the unpredictable.

Social power in the present world is no more based on secrets.

One of the prominent theoreticians of modern power, Niccolò Machiavelli, in his most celebrated book, *The Prince*, describes political action as the ability to submit to *Fortuna*, the unpredictability of historical events. Actually, the art of government has long been identified with the reduction of the social world's infinite complexity to some few lines of control, subordination, and predictability. Politics may be considered the art of probability, and probability implies the reduction of social discourse's chaotic complexity to a pattern of repetition. This paradigm, however, less and less corresponds to the reality of the late modern world. Because of media proliferation, and of semiotic exchange acceleration, the lines of connection multiply, their speed increases, and the effect is white noise.

If the occultation of truth has played an important (albeit never exclusive) role in the classical forms of sovereignty, contemporary power is essentially based on the explosion of truth. Secrets are finally replaced by enigmas.

If a secret can be defined as the effect of hiding the truth in a site that is known exclusively by those who belong to the circle of power, an enigma is based instead on the infinite complication of the relation between enunciation and truth.

3. King of Fake

In his career as media-activist, Julian Assange has accomplished his mission of reestablishing truth with exceptional effectiveness, denouncing the misconduct and the crimes of power in fields like economic corruption, military aggression, and so on. He has managed to jeopardize the plans of political leaders who deserved to be denounced. But simultaneously, and against his own intentions, he has played into the hands of Chaos, which is the only emperor of the post-rational world in which we dwell.

The cultural background of WikiLeaks activity is based on the Puritanical presumption that language is an instrument of truth or an instrument of falseness, and enunciations can be unambiguously qualified as correct or incorrect, as true or false, and as good or evil.

But this presumption is seldom useful in finding some meaning in the contemporary landscape of social discourse.

The mere identification of true and false in information leads to misjudgments and political mistakes. For instance, disclosing the hidden frauds of the Democratic Party during the electoral campaign in 2016 was morally legitimate, abstractly speaking. But the actual political context in which the disclosure happened changed the sign of that revealing action, and turned truth into a service to the King of Fake, Donald Trump, whose final aim was to attack the very foundations of American democracy.

American democracy is not my main concern, as I think that the United States of America is an entity based on violence, exploitation, and warmongering, so that the ongoing dismantling of American potency is a source of hope rather than of dismal, for me. But this is not the point. The point is that sometimes the abstract worship of truth is leading to paradoxical effects: for the sake of purity, WikiLeaks has apparently played into the hands of the most cynical people who ever entered the political fray.

The cultural landscape of the semio-capitalist society, flooded by uncountable flows of info-stimulation, may be described as a hyper-Baroque riddle. In the relation between Puritanism and Baroque, Baroque is unavoidably prevailing, because Chaos wins against order, and artificial noise wins against human voices. Those who wage war against Chaos are defeated, because Chaos feeds upon war: in the whirlwind of acceleration, Chaos takes hold of the social mind, and transparency and democracy are powerless.

4. EXPOSING ABUSE OF POWER: FOR THE PEOPLE

Sally Burch, April 2019

In a democratic society, governments have the obligation to protect human rights—among them the privacy and security of their citizens. They are also expected to practice transparency and accountability with regard to public policy, since their mandate emanates from the people, the electorate, and their budgets are funded with the public's taxes. Yet it seems that today's surveillance society turns these principles upside-down. When governments and corporations act in collusion to flagrantly violate people's privacy and security, they seek to conceal many of their own actions under a blanket of secrecy.

It is clear today that the massive violations of privacy and loopholes in digital security that are coming to light are not due to accidents or a malfunctioning of the system. On the contrary, they are an integral and essential part of the present financial model of Internet development. A model based on massive collection and monetization of data—with or without the consent of those who provide the data—via the development of mega platforms that offer "free" services. These are controlled by private corporations that are thus able to eliminate competition and concentrate monopoly power in a constantly expanding array of areas. Meanwhile, governments, security agencies, political groups, and others enter into agreements with these corporations to gather data for surveillance purposes, including for political manipulation[144] and the containment of social protest and political dissent.

This is the context in which WikiLeaks and Julian Assange have rendered a great service to humanity—by demonstrating that this digitalized society can also work the other way around, precisely in favor of more democratic governance. They have enabled people to monitor the actions of those who exercise power and have exposed abuses of that power, among other things by providing opportunities for whistleblowers to reveal irregularities in public and private institutions where adequate protective mechanisms are lacking. Where the surveillance society spies on people for those in power, WikiLeaks claims to liberate information so that it is available to the people.

Noam Chomsky explains[145] that, since the early years of the past century, the democratic freedoms won in countries such as the US and the UK meant that those in power could no longer maintain social control mainly by force. They had to change their power strategy to implement control by manipulating opinion through the media and public relations: what the academic refers to as "manufacturing consent." But that implies that whatever is incapable of generating consent must be kept in the dark. Thus—he underlines— the unpardonable "crime" of Assange and WikiLeaks is that they have lifted the veil of secrecy that protects the powerful from scrutiny; and by doing so, they could evaporate power. Chomsky points out that the declassified document archives reveal that official secrecy has little to do

---

[144] As is evident in the Facebook-Cambridge Analytica case and in the massive use of data for targeting segmented political messages and fake news, in both the US and Brazilian elections.

[145] Video intervention by Noam Chomsky at the event: "Julian Assange: 4 years of freedom denied", CIESPAL, Quito, June 20 2016.

with state security (given as the pretext) and a lot to do with hiding from the public decisions that could affect their interests or their livelihoods; ultimately, the archives undermine support for their governments.

Examples include the publication by WikiLeaks of several chapters of trade agreements such as the Trans-Pacific Partnership, when they were being negotiated in secret primarily for the benefit of large corporations—revelations that enabled opposition movements to respond in a timely manner. Or the Iraq and Afghanistan War Logs, released by military whistleblower Chelsea Manning, which detail the indiscriminate killing of civilians during the US invasion and occupation of those countries. But what most aroused the US government's fury was probably the publication, as of March 2017, of the Vault-7 CIA files, that detail the activities and capabilities of the Central Intelligence Agency (CIA) to perform electronic surveillance and cyber warfare.

For these contributions to public knowledge, WikiLeaks and Julian Assange have received numerous awards and tributes[146] that recognize their journalistic input, their defense of human rights and freedom of expression, and their political courage.

The Internet in dispute

The clash between those two distinct visions of how our societies can utilize digital technologies for surveillance or transparency is, to our understanding, part of a broader contradiction in the digital era. There is an underlying dispute between the concentrated corporate project of surveillance capitalism, frequently allied with security agencies and the military on the one hand, and what we call the people's Internet, or the Internet of citizens, that proposes a decentralized project based on distributed technology and the commons, where information, technology, and power tend

---

[146] https://defend.wikileaks.org/wikileaks/#awards

to be shared. A project where the Internet is developed, for example, to strengthen democratic participation, promote freedom of expression, and defend human rights—rather than to manipulate elections, disseminate fake news, and violate privacy.

Both projects have been present under different expressions since the origins of the Internet and continue to coexist, sometimes in cooperation, often in conflict; though clearly in recent years the corporate model has taken the upper hand.[147]

If this sounds like an exaggeration, it is enlightening to read what the security forces are saying about the matter. Andre Damon summarizes a publication of the Atlantic Council, an influential right-wing think tank, which outlines the content of a conference held in March 2018, on "Sovereignty in the Information Age." Organized with the United States Special Operations Command, the meeting brought together Special Forces officers with domestic police forces and representatives from technology companies such as Microsoft.

Damon refers to the explanation of John T. Watts, a former Australian Army officer and consultant to the US Department of Defense and Department of Homeland Security, of why, from the viewpoint of the participants, censorship is necessary to preserve sovereignty—understood as the state's ability to impose its will upon the population (a curious definition, we might say). He continues:

> This "sovereignty," Watts writes, faces "greater challenges now than it ever has in the past," due to the confluence between growing political opposition to the state and the Internet's ability to quickly spread political dissent.

---

[147] See, for example, Sally Burch, "An agenda for the people's internet," *alai*, August 11, 2017, https://www.alainet.org/en/articulo/189104

Watts cites the precedent of the invention of the printing press, which helped overthrow the feudal world order. In the Atlantic Council's estimation, however, this was an overwhelmingly negative development, ushering in "decades, and arguably centuries, of conflict and disruption" and undermining the "sovereignty" of absolutist states. The "invention of the Internet is similarly creating conflict and disruption," Watts writes. [...]

He continues: "Technology has democratized the ability for substate groups and individuals to broadcast a narrative with limited resources and virtually unlimited scope." By contrast, "In the past, the general public had limited sources of information, which were managed by professional gatekeepers."[148]

The Atlantic Council, along with the German Marshall Fund (funded by the US government and NATO), have been key partners in the social media companies' recent censoring of left-wing views. In October 2018, Facebook and Twitter wiped out hundreds of user accounts in the US, including many alternative media outlets. Among those deleted were popular sites that scrutinize police brutality and US interventionism, such as the Free Thought Project, Anti-Media, Cop Block, and the web pages of several journalists. Jamie Marshall of the German Marshall Fund commented at that time, in an interview, that "this is just the beginning," while complaining that "all you need is an email" to set up a Facebook or Twitter account, sites he considers too easily accessible to members of the general public.[149]

---

[148] Andre Damon, "The US military's vision for state censorship," 5 October 2018. https://www.wsws.org/en/articles/2018/10/05/pers-o05.html

[149] Max Blumenthal and Jeb Sprague, "Facebook Censorship of Alternative Media 'Just the Beginning,' Says Top Neocon Insider," October 31 2018. https://www.alainet.org/en/articulo/196274

Clearly, the offensive against WikiLeaks and Julian Assange is not an isolated occurrence, but part of a broader concerted effort to constrain the potential of the Internet to facilitate broader democratic participation, public expression of dissent by the people, and the monitoring and critique of their governments. Nevertheless, Assange, who considers himself a publisher, has become a global symbol of the struggle for freedom of expression. As such, support for his freedom has taken on a special relevance and can be considered part of the struggle to preserve and develop the people's Internet.

A war on a single human being

The level of persecution and the campaign of defamation unleashed against this journalist-publisher are devastating. The UK government spent millions of pounds to keep him under permanent vigilance, under the supposed pretext of the Swedish investigation for possible sexual offenses (later dropped), something that is completely disproportionate. It has always been clear that other interests are at stake.

The UK has paid no heed to the recommendations (normally considered obligatory) of the United Nations Working Group on Arbitrary Detention (WGAD), that in December 2015 concluded in its opinion No. 54/2015[150] that Assange—who at the time had a European Arrest Warrant issued against him—was being arbitrarily deprived of his freedom and demanded that he be released. That would have meant the UK rescinding its own arrest warrant for evading bail and allowing Assange free passage or a safe-conduct to leave the country. In December 2018, in a new statement on the case, the WGAD reiterated its demand and expressed that

---

[150] "United Nations General Assembly: Human Rights Council, Working Group on Arbitrary Detention," April 6,2016, https://documents-dds-ny.un.org/doc/UNDOC/GEN/G16/070/51/pdf/G1607051.pdf?OpenElement

"States that are based upon and promote the rule of law do not like to be confronted with their own violations of the law, that is understandable. But when they honestly admit these violations, they do honor the very spirit of the rule of law, earn enhanced respect for doing so, and set worldwide commendable examples." This fell on deaf ears.

Meanwhile, the media campaign underway to discredit Assange is also completely disproportionate. But this is no coincidence, as Australian journalist John Pilger recounts:

> In 2008, a plan to destroy both WikiLeaks and Assange was laid out in a top-secret document dated 8 March, 2008. The authors were the Cyber Counter-intelligence Assessments Branch of the US Defence Department. They described in detail how important it was to destroy the "feeling of trust" that is WikiLeaks' "centre of gravity."
>
> This would be achieved, they wrote, with threats of "exposure [and] criminal prosecution" and an unrelenting assault on reputation. The aim was to silence and criminalise WikiLeaks and its editor and publisher. It was as if they planned a war on a single human being and on the very principle of freedom of speech.
>
> Their main weapon would be personal smear. Their shock troops would be enlisted in the media—those who are meant to keep the record straight and tell us the truth.[151]

Even so, Pilger expresses astonishment at the journalists who gleefully took on this task against a colleague—without anyone having to tell them

---

[151] John Pilger, "The Urgency of Bringing Julian Assange Home," *johnpilger.com*, June 18, 2018, http://johnpilger.com/articles/the-urgency-of-bringing-julian-assange-home.

what to do; and they have indeed succeeded, to a considerable extent, in undermining public support.

Ecuador caves in to pressure

In 2012, when Julian Assange requested political asylum in the Ecuadorian embassy in London, winds of change were blowing in Latin America, proposing a new balance in the power relations with the global North, especially the United States, and affirming greater regional autonomy. Among other things, these projects contemplated new approaches and policies in communications and initiatives for technological sovereignty.

The government of President Rafael Correa of Ecuador, a relatively small Latin American country, taking the decision to grant asylum to Assange in defiance of world powers has been considered a very courageous act; and indeed, it has been increasingly hard to maintain, over the years, due to strong pressure from the UK, Sweden, and (more directly since 2018) the US.

At that time, Ecuador justified this decision in an extensive document, based on international conventions, that includes the following motives:

That Julian Assange is a communication professional internationally awarded for his struggle on freedom of expression, freedom of press and human rights in general; [. . .]

That there are serious indications of retaliation by the country or countries that produced the information disclosed by Mr. Assange, retaliation that can put at risk his safety, integrity, and even his life; [. . .]

That the judicial evidence shows clearly that, given an extradition to the United States, Mr. Assange would not have a fair trial, he

could be judge by a special or military court, and it is not unlikely
that he would receive a cruel and demeaning treatment and he
would be condemned to a life sentence or the death penalty, which
would not respect his human rights . . .[152]

However, the new Ecuadorian government of Lenín Moreno that took office in May 2017 has resumed the international policy of former decades (as have a number of other Latin American governments), prioritizing relations of cooperation with the global North and seeking a trade agreement with the United States. Significantly, after US vice president Mike Pence visited Moreno in June 2018, the White House confirmed they had discussed the issue of Julian Assange and had agreed to remain in close coordination for the "next steps."

From the outset, the Moreno government made it clear that they consider the asylum an undesired inheritance from their predecessors and Assange an unwelcome guest. Initially, with María Fernanda Espinosa (the present UN general assembly president) as foreign minister, it continued the efforts underway with the UK government to try to obtain a *laissez passer* for Assange to leave the country; they even gave him Ecuadorian citizenship in an attempt to get him diplomatic immunity.

But after that failed, since early 2018 there was growing evidence that the government intended to find a way to expel the unwanted "guest" from the embassy and hand him over to the British authorities, or to force him to decide to abandon the premises. The conditions of virtual isolation as of March 2018, the protocol imposed in October by Ecuador for his inhabitance at the embassy, restriction of his visits and of Internet access and

---

[152] "Statement of the Government of the Republic of Ecuador on the asylum request of Julian Assange," *Ministerio de Relaciones Exeriores y Movilidad Humana*, https://www.cancilleria.gob.ec/statement-of-the-government-of-the-republic-of-ecuador-on-the-asylum-request-of-julian-assange/.

freedom of speech, all point to this goal. If the expulsion of Julian Assange from the embassy did not occur earlier, it was most likely due to the resolution of the Inter-American Court, emitted in July 2018, which stipulates that once asylum has been granted, Ecuador has an international legal obligation not only to guarantee its continuation, but also to adopt positive measures to avoid the surrender of the asylum seeker. Meanwhile, internal pressure to guarantee the asylee's rights was virtually absent, given media hostility and the political atmosphere in the country that demonizes anything or anyone identified with the former process of the Citizens' Revolution led by Rafael Correa.

It is unclear whether the Ecuadorian government will face legal sanctions for its action; but it has already received widespread international condemnation. But that is now secondary to the extradition demands Assange faces in the British (and eventually Swedish) courts, and the accusations he could face in the US. In this context, it would seem that only strong international pressure, particularly from within those three countries, combined with actions by multilateral institutions that defend human rights, could influence the outcome.

If Assange's project is to liberate information for the people, his own liberation depends primarily on pressure from the people on those in power.

5. IMPRISONED LIGHT OF OUR CIVILIZATION THAT KINDLED THE HEART OF DEMOCRACY

Nozomi Hayase, January 2019

George Orwell once wrote, "Who controls the past controls the future: who controls the present controls the past."[153] With increasing government secrecy, censorship, and surveillance, our society seems to be quickly moving into the dystopian future of *1984*.

In April 2010, the world saw a man with remarkable intelligence and passion eloquently articulate Orwell's dictum that has now come true. Julian Assange took the stage at the Oslo Freedom Forum and outlined how this control of history is carried on in the digital age:

> *He who controls the Internet servers controls the intellectual record of mankind, and by controlling that, controls our perception of who we are, and by controlling that, controls what laws and regulations we make in society.*[154]

[153] George Orwell, *1984* (New York: Signet Classic, 1949), 32.

[154] "Julian Assange—The Whistleblower," YouTube video, posted by Oslo Freedom Forum, 7:18, May 18, 2010, https://youtu.be/qDvfQ5gZ-Jw?t=440.

Once it was priests, hereditary aristocrats, and wealthy men who put the masses under monarchical rule. In the modern day, those who seek to control the population hide behind a façade of democracy. Using the media as a weapon, the powerful exert authority over the narrative of history. Claiming objectivity, journalists engage in propaganda, restricting and molding information that challenges the official story.

Assange not only shared his understanding of this problem, but also put forward the concrete means to solve it. WikiLeaks is the solution. When Assange was once asked to describe what exactly he does in life, he answered, "I am an activist, journalist, software programmer, expert in cryptography, specialized in systems designed to protect human rights defenders."[155] With his unique talents and skills, he created a new form of journalism that uses transparency to return suppressed and distorted information back to the historical record—a new journalism for justice.

"Collateral Murder," our forgotten memory

Over its 12-year existence, WikiLeaks published over 10 million documents, at a speed and scale that is unprecedented. With a pristine record of accuracy, the organization released materials that exposed the crimes and corruption of powerful institutions and governments.

Among its many groundbreaking disclosures, the publication of the "Collateral Murder" video had a profound global effect, and it radically changed my life. On April 5, 2010, WikiLeaks burst onto the global stage with the upload of classified US military footage depicting an Apache helicopter gunship in a suburb of New Baghdad, Iraq on July 12, 2007, opening fire and killing more than a dozen civilians. Two Reuters journalists were among the dead.

---

[155] "Julian Assange, homme de l'année pour 'Le Monde'," *Le Monde*, December 24, 2010, https://www.lemonde.fr/documents-wikileaks/article/2010/12/24/julian-assange-homme-de-l-annee-pour-le-monde_1456426_1446239.html.

The sensational 17-minute, 47-seconds video shattered the insulated reality of the American middle-class. It showed the face of war as perpetrated by a country that had over the last ten years become my home. WikiLeaks' emergence in the public limelight instigated my own process of liberation through remembering; to find the oppressed voices in my own history; to witness and free those who have been consigned to oblivion.

I was born in Japan during the postwar era, at a time when my country had opened its doors to democracy. Growing up, I admired the United States and its promise of equality and liberty for all people. It stood in the world as a beacon of light. As a young adult, I moved to America. In crossing the Pacific Ocean, I took the ideals in the Declaration of Independence to heart.

In the aftermath of 9/11, the magnificent light of America that I had seen back in my homeland suddenly disappeared. With the Bush era's "war on terror," and the enactment of the PATRIOT Act, American society quickly moved toward authoritarianism. It was as if the darkness emanating from this nation's unredeemed past had grown, and was swallowing up its future.

By publishing raw footage of a US Army attack in Iraq, a country with no threat to the United States, WikiLeaks informed us about America's troubled beginning and the violation of its own ideals. As the uncensored view of modern warfare laid bare, I began to see something that had escaped our memory—a course of events in American history that has not been fully recognized and continues to cast a shadow on the present.

Scientific journalism

The carnage that visually unfolded of brutal US military occupation in the oil-rich Middle East brought out the forgotten past. There, I saw the Anglo's mission of territorial expansion, with the military might that had once crushed the First Nations. Embodied in the cynical naming of the Apache helicopter is the memory of the genocide of indigenous peoples on American soil. The unveiled wickedness of America's wars in Iraq and Afghanistan confronted civil society with the centuries of terror found in the encounters between European settlers and Native Americans before and after the United States' founding.

WikiLeaks lifted the floodgate of information that suppressed our memory. By using cryptography as a tool for social change, Assange created scientific journalism—an objective method for publishing information, and to build an accurate record of history. Assange explains, "It is our philosophy that raw source material must be made available so that conclusions can be checkable."[156] As the website's submission criteria indicates, WikiLeaks accepts "classified, censored or otherwise restricted material of political, diplomatic, or ethical significance."[157] It authenticates the received documents and always releases the primary source material related to the stories.

Through this rigorous scientific practice, WikiLeaks replaced journalism's source of legitimacy—its creed of objectivity—with the verified documents themselves. Revealed in the raw materials provided by WikiLeaks is a new objectivity, one that allows marginalized perspectives to come forward and challenge the claims of professional journalists.

Barbarians within

Now, the conscience of ordinary people once suppressed by institutional hierarchies can freely engage in the quest for forgotten memory; to recover

---

[156] "Julian Assange: Is WikiLeaks Biased?," YouTube video, posted by "FORA.tv", 3:57, June 24, 2010, https://www.youtube.com/watch?v=wBENlJfZ-f8&feature=youtu.be&t=235.

[157] "WikiLeaks: Submissions." n.d. WikiLeaks. Accessed January 28, 2019. https://wikileaks.org/wiki/WikiLeaks:Submissions.

images buried deep in our history and make sense of the world. The courageous act of whistleblower Chelsea Manning allowed those who have been
systematically labeled "enemy combatants" by the military industrial
complex to speak their side of the story.

The freed images disrupted the monologue narrative of Western
civilization. In the display of US soldiers' callousness toward defenseless
Iraqis—in the congratulation they extended each other for killing innocent people—we now were able to see the barbarians within our culture.
In the destruction of a civilization much older than our own, we can see
colonizers of the past. Clothed in the rhetoric of civility, they continue to
enact Manifest Destiny.

Ambivalent past of Japan

In the scenery shot from a US military gun-sight on that one fatal day in
New Baghdad, I saw the tragic history of my own country. I saw the ambiv-
alent past of Japan, frozen in time, the first and only nation to experience
the horrors of nuclear weapons.

Japan recovered quickly from its devastation after World War II.
Enjoying an economic miracle, the nation achieved First World status and
became a key ally of the United States. As I watched the "Collateral Murder"
video and heard a soldier in the copter shout, "Let's shoot. Light 'em all up.
Come on, fire!"[158] my country's past appeared in my mind for a moment.

I saw blurry faces of Japanese soldiers invading neighboring countries, waving the flag of the Land of the Rising Sun. I saw imperial Japan, its
bloody lust for power, dominating East Asia. At the same time, as I watched
Reuters driver Saeed Chmagh crawl away from the first barrage of muni-
tions, I slowly began to witness Japan's own tormented past.

[158] WikiLeaks, "Collateral Murder," April 5, 2010, https://collateralmurder.wikileaks.
org/.

In the shadow of the Bradley tank driving over one of the Iraqi victims' dead bodies, ghosts of Japan's atomic bombings began to appear. As I watched the medic on the scene try to evacuate wounded children from the bongo truck, I saw Hiroshima vanish from the cockpit of the US B-29 bomber aircraft on August 6, 1945. I found lost images of my history in those colorless reflections of modern warfare. I was able to bear witness to the events that had occurred over half a century ago.

As blips and whirs of radio distortion slowly occupied silence, smothered voices in history suddenly began to speak. What was unveiled in the unfiltered images of "Collateral Murder" was the naked power of Anglo-America, the conquest of natives' land, and its so-called "democratizing" occupation of my mother country.

Supreme power of truth

The past without witness keeps us paralyzed in a cycle of abuse. By restoring the historical archive, WikiLeaks helped me retrieve the unclaimed memory of my ancestors that continues to haunt people of Japan.

In 1945, after the US atomic bombings of two cities, Japan surrendered and put an end to its emperor worship. Two years later, the constitution written under US general Douglas MacArthur was ratified. Article 9 of the constitution—known as the "peace constitution"—solidified Japan's renunciation of war, its pacifist stance toward international conflicts. Under the security treaty signed in 1951 between the US and Japan, my nation was placed under protection of the US military. In reality, Japan was stripped of its right to self-defense.[159]

In July 2003, against the opinion of more than half of the Japanese public, the Parliament approved the deployment of its defense forces to aid

---

[159] Beina Xu, "The U.S.-Japan security alliance," Counsel on Foreign Relations, July 1, 2014, https://www.cfr.org/backgrounder/us-japan-security-alliance.

American troops in Iraq.[160] Here, the country that suffered horrific tragedy by the world's first use of nuclear power, joined the combat zone and fueled the American Empire's war of aggression—the very empire that had once brought destruction to our own land.

Unable to reconcile its past, the island nation cannot assert its own autonomy. Instead, it must bow down to a Western power. With obedience forged in the name of alliance, I saw Japan blindly match the steps of US military action and worship the glory of this new emperor from across the ocean.

Speaking about war, Assange once noted, "Populations don't like wars. They have to be lied into it. That means we can be 'truthed' into peace."[161] By publishing the "Collateral Murder" video, the WikiLeaks founder unleashed the supreme power of truth within history. A power that can overcome military might.

We can now see the truth about us. We saw that, as Manning described, "We're human . . . and we're killing ourselves . . ."[10] In the moment of "Collateral Murder"'s publication, life of all people became sacred. In the recollection of our memory—of who we truly are—the pronouncement of equality in the Declaration of Independence finally became a self-evident truth.

Imagination of ordinary people

Up until WikiLeaks' publication of the "Collateral Murder" video, access to this truth of equality—that all men are created equal—had been denied to us. The Western hegemony in the form of US imperialism expelled all from the original harmonious state of the world. It divided the globe into

---

[160] Jonathan Watts, "End of an era as Japan enters Iraq," *Guardian*, July 25, 2003, https://www.theguardian.com/world/2003/jul/26/iraq.japan.

[161] Julian Assange, *When Google Met WikiLeaks* (New York: OR Books, 2014), 137.

First-Class nations and the Third World. We were made to believe that we are separate. We were placed in racial hierarchies that have us define one another as superior or inferior. We were lied to about each other and made to see our brothers and sisters as enemies and terrorists to fight against.

Assange's gift of the Fourth Estate to the world awakened the creative power embedded in our history. By unleashing the imagination of ordinary people to the authors of their own histories, he resuscitated the heart of democracy. For this great contribution to humanity, Assange was made the enemy of the most powerful government in the world, and of the media that act as stenographers to power.

This award-winning journalist, who published material exposing illegal wars and wrongdoings of governments and corporations, should not be prosecuted. He, who inspired life back into this dying civilization, must not be extradited to the US and faced with possible life in prison, or worse, execution.

Assange sacrificed his own freedom to guard the sacred rights of mankind. He ignited the torch of liberty in our hearts, and as a consequence, he has been made to suffer profound solitude. Now, we must lift our lamp of liberty to free Assange, an imprisoned light of our civilization.

6. JULIAN ASSANGE FOR THE FUTURE

Geoffroy de Lagasnerie, January 2019

WikiLeaks, the utopia we need.

When I started writing about whistleblowers a few years ago, there was genuine sympathy for them across international public opinion, and one sensed a common feeling of indignation at the repression whistleblowers suffered. But during the last few months, something seems to have changed. There now seems to be a mistrust —if not outright hostility—with regard to Julian Assange. The same cannot be said for Edward Snowden and Chelsea Manning, for example: they each continue to receive widespread support from journalists, academics, and various advocates for human rights and freedom of the press. But support for Assange is now much more distanced and qualified. Indeed, I get the impression that a kind of "WikiLeaks bashing" has taken hold: journalists, academics, and politicians have not only begun to distance themselves from Assange; they now question, attack, and try to discredit him on the slightest pretext. While Snowden and Manning remain popular exemplars in the fight for democratic ideals, Assange is described as much more suspect, and there's widespread uncertainty as to whether he's still committed to the progressive project he undertook several years ago. History is replete with disquieting figures. It is often difficult to know whether they deserve our support or mistrust. Julian Assange seems increasingly to be one of these figures.

This shift in Assange's reputation has been punctuated by several important moments. Following the July 14, 2016, terrorist attacks in Nice, France, for example, WikiLeaks posted a video to its Twitter account of Nice's seaside promenade littered with the dead and wounded. This video was deeply disturbing for the French public. But nothing seems to have been more damaging for his reputation than the 2016 US presidential election campaign. Assange's well-known dislike of Hillary Clinton, combined with WikiLeaks' publication of leaked emails from the Democratic National Committee (DNC), has led to the perception that Assange is moving away from progressive politics and democratic struggles, and moving closer to the political circles around Donald Trump and even authoritarian regimes such as Russia.[162]

I am struck by the fact that people always judge Julian Assange's actions and declarations abstractly, without considering the situation he deals with, the threat on his life and freedom. Julian Assange has been living alone in a small room for several years, he can't see the sun and can't go out, he's afraid to end his life in prison. And each of his actions must also be understood in this context. He's not like most of us sitting behind a desk—free. His life is at stake. He can go to jail for the rest of his life. So yes, of course he hesitates, he tries to get out of it, he tries alliances, he makes mistakes. Sometimes I have the impression that those who judge his actions forget this context. If we take this context into account we must

---

[162] Carole Cadwalladr, "Trump, Assange, Bannon, Farage... bound together in an unholy alliance," *The Guardian*, October 29, 2017, https://www.theguardian.com/commentisfree/2017/oct/28/trump-assange-bannon-farage-bound-together-in-unholy-alliance.

acknowledge that Assange has a right to make mistakes. He has a right to error. And for me, all is forgiven.

One can, of course, disagree with one or many of Julian Assange's actions or choices. But what we mustn't overlook is the fact that important historical figures, like Assange, always embody or represent certain principles or values that transcend the particular actions of the historical figure itself. WikiLeaks is an institution based on generalizable principles. And I argue it is precisely these principles that we need in politics today. We often hear that we live in a world where there is no utopia anymore, that we lack a vision of what could be a counter-model for the future. But I think it is a mistake. The future we should fight for is already emerging in our present times and WikiLeaks is one of its incarnations. WikiLeaks' principles are notably in direct opposition to the reactionary sentiments and impulses fueling today's populist backlash and the entire political system that made Donald Trump's or Jair Bolsonaro's electoral victory possible for example.

It's a fundamental political error—and a shame—to try to establish a relationship, a connection between Julian Assange, WikiLeaks, and neo-conservatism or reactionary populism as is often done to discredit him and his actions. No affinity between these two worlds is possible; the political ideals brought to life by WikiLeaks are a crucial form of resistance not only to reactionary populism but also, and perhaps more importantly, to the larger political culture in which reactionary populism thrives. Many people criticize Julian Assange by associating him with populism or with populist leaders or ideologists. But they do so *within* the system that has made the rise of populism possible. While Julian Assange, on the contrary, brings to life an alternative model, a counter-culture, a form of resistance.

I want to enumerate some of the political principles WikiLeaks brings to life and that we need to affirm and support.

1. **WikiLeaks is based on the value of knowledge.** The organization functions almost like a group of historians of the present. Its institutional mission is to reveal the secret activities of political leaders and, in the process, show the public how states actually function and what they actually do. From this point of view, Assange inaugurated a culture of truth, a politics of the archive and of knowledge, that is diametrically opposed to the logic of opinion, fake news, and the echo-chamber ideology of contemporary populism.

2. **WikiLeaks is anti-authoritarian.** Its struggle for transparency is dedicated to opening the black box of government so the public may no longer live in ignorance of the logics that guide the governments they routinely elect or live beneath. This opposition to all forms of authoritarianism places WikiLeaks in a long and vigilant democratic tradition that opposes the centralized powers of the strong state.

3. **WikiLeaks is firmly committed to fighting censorship and the feelings of alienation that a culture of censorship produces.** And it is precisely this kind of culture of alienation that gives rise to reactionary populism in the first place. Today's reactionary populism is largely anchored in a not-unreasonable mistrust of the media, and the disproportionate power the media exerts over the selection, circulation, and interpretation of information. WikiLeaks has consistently attacked the power that traditional media gatekeepers exert over the kinds of information or stories journalists are allowed to pursue and publish. Assange's statements about the publication of the Panama Papers are a perfect example of this.[163] WikiLeaks is an advocate of *total transparency.* WikiLeaks' standard practice is to publish everything: they prefer to release the raw information they receive and let the public

---

[163] Julian Assange, interview by Richard Gizbert of *Al Jazeera, The Listening Post,* April 9, 2016, http://www.aljazeera.com/programmes/listeningpost/2016/04/qa-julian-assange-panama-papers-160409121010398.html.

conduct their own analyses and come up with their own interpretations. Their opposition to media censorship and their refusal to see the public as merely passive spectators aligns with their belief in a vibrant public space, and this conviction has given rise to practices that concretely combat the widespread feeling of alienation that is too often channeled in populist directions.

4. **WikiLeaks nurtures an ethic of *unconditionality*.** Julian Assange has been relentlessly criticized for publishing leaked DNC emails during the 2016 US presidential election, and then for weakening Hillary Clinton's chances of electoral success. But shouldn't we turn this criticism around? Our democracy is in decline today precisely because of our repeated tendency to suspend and defer democratic principles in the interest of achieving short-term practical objectives (such as in the "War on Terror"). Doesn't this suspension of democratic principles ultimately damage democracy by undermining its basic unconditional character? And isn't this tendency to play fast and loose with democratic principles eroding our faith in the rule of law? Assange and WikiLeaks publish the documents they receive when they receive them—no matter where they come from or what the short-term political fallout may be. This ethic of unconditionality is especially important today for reviving our faith in the democratic ideal.

5. **WikiLeaks believes in a non-submissive culture.** The culture of leaking and anonymous denunciation encourages people to distance themselves from the institutions to which they belong, to question their institutional identification, and to maintain an attitude of perpetual institutional skepticism so that they may denounce any potential wrongdoings or crimes. This culture of non-submissiveness, of non-allegiance, is in radical opposition to authoritarian forms of government and forms of nationalistic identification.

6. Lastly, **WikiLeaks amounts to a practical critique of all of forms of nationalism**, insofar as its concrete practice actively promotes an international conception of politics and belonging. WikiLeaks assembles people from all over the world who are fighting for a shared ideal that extends beyond national boundaries and affiliations. WikiLeaks, in other words, is a project that transcends the idea of nations, and it works to dissolve the nationalistic basis at the root of all conservatisms. But more importantly, Assange is one of those rare contemporary political figures to adopt a truly global perception of the world. In all my public discussions with Assange, I was always struck by his ability to take a global perspective on the world, and his consistent capacity to think that whatever is happening in Great Britain is no more important than events in South Africa, Ecuador, Yemen, or Russia. Someone once told me that if Snowden enjoys greater sympathy than Assange in Western Europe or the United States, it's because Snowden's leaks involved predominantly white Westerners, while much of the information WikiLeaks publishes involves Yemenis, Afghans, or Iraqis. I think there is much truth to this.

Populism, nationalism, conservatism, and authoritarianism can't be fought with ready-made speeches. These systems of power and ideologies can only be fought by new practices and new subjectivities created within new political systems. The rise of contemporary reactionary populism isn't an accident or an aberration, nor is it simply a case of manipulated public opinion: it is the logical product of our dominant political and media systems. Yet we are somehow expected to critique populism from within the confines of the very system that made it possible. This is the singular impasse facing progressive politics today, and this is precisely why we need to defend Julian Assange and support WikiLeaks' project today more than ever. The principles upon which WikiLeaks is based are the very same principles that are needed today to create a new political culture: principles of transparency, anti-authoritarianism, internationalism, non-submission, and unconditionality. The principles with which WikiLeaks acts inscribes the organization in a long history of struggle committed to enlarging the democratic horizon. At a moment in history when the CIA has explicit plans to terminate WikiLeaks,[164] WikiLeaks deserves support from progressives. By defending Julian Assange, we defend and protect the future of democracy. It could be that Assange embodies for the twenty-first century a character as important as Nelson Mandela was in the twentieth century, even if we do not yet realize it.

Translation from the French by Matthew MacLellan

---

[164] Andrew Blake, CIA 'working to take down' WikiLeaks threat, agency chief says," *The Washington Times*, October 20, 2017, http://www.washingtontimes.com/news/2017/oct/20/cia-working-take-down-wikileaks-threat-agency-chie/.

RESPONDING TO ASSANGE'S CRITICS 16–22

Caitlin Johnstone, April 2019

Smear 16: "He's an anti-Semite."

Yes, yes, we all know by now that everyone who opposes the imperial war machine in any way is both a Russian agent and an anti-Semite. Jeremy Corbyn knows it,[165] Ilhan Omar knows it,[166] we all know it.

This one's been around a while, ever since headlines blared in 2011 that Assange had complained of a "Jewish conspiracy" against him after an account of a conversation by *Private Eye* editor Ian Hislop. Assange responded to this claim as follows:

---

[165] See Caitlin Johnstone, "How (and How Not) To Beat A Smear Campaign," *Medium*, March 2, https://medium.com/@caityjohnstone/how-and-how-not-to-beat-a-smear-campaign-74e4e95c9306

[166] See Caitlin Johnstone, "Israel Lobby Rebuts Omar's Claims About Its Immense Influence By Exerting Its Immense Influence," *Medium*, March 4, https://medium.com/@caityjohnstone/israel-lobby-refutes-omars-claims-about-its-immense-influence-by-exerting-its-immense-influence-2997d343377e. .

Hislop has distorted, invented, or misremembered almost every significant claim and phrase. In particular, "Jewish conspiracy" is completely false, in spirit and in word. It is serious and upsetting. Rather than correct a smear, Mr. Hislop has attempted, perhaps not surprisingly, to justify one smear with another in the same direction. That he has a reputation for this, and is famed to have received more libel suits in the UK than any other journalist as a result, does not mean that it is right. WikiLeaks promotes the ideal of "scientific journalism"—where the underlying evidence of all articles is available to the reader precisely in order to avoid these types of distortions. We treasure our strong Jewish support and staff, just as we treasure the support from pan-Arab democracy activists and others who share our hope for a just world.[167]

"We treasure our strong Jewish support and staff." Man, what a Nazi.

But that wasn't what cemented this smear into public consciousness. Two related events punched that ticket, and bear with me here:

The first event was the WikiLeaks account tweeting and then quickly deleting the following in July 2016: "Tribalist symbol for establishment climbers? Most of our critics have 3 (((brackets around their names))) & have black-rim glasses. Bizarre." The triple brackets are known as echoes,[168] which are a symbol that anti-Semites often put around words and names to hatefully indicate Jewishness in online discourse. In 2016, some Jewish people began putting the triple brackets around their own names on social media as a way of pushing back against this behavior, so if you

---

[167] Ben Quinn, "Julian Assange 'Jewish Conspiracy' comments spark row," *The Guardian*, March 1, 2011, https://www.theguardian.com/media/2011/mar/01/julian-assange-jewish-conspiracy-comments

[168] See "Echo: General Hate Symbols," *ADL*, https://www.adl.org/education/references/hate-symbols/echo#.V5ZHI_mANBc.

really want to it's possible for you to interpret the tweet as saying, "All our critics are Jewish. Bizarre."

But does that make sense? Does it make sense for the guy who announced, "We treasure our strong Jewish support and staff" to then go making openly anti-Semitic comments? And if he really did suddenly decide to let the world know that he believes there's a Jewish conspiracy against WikiLeaks, why would he delete it? What's the theory there? That he was like, "Oh, I just wanted to let everyone know about my Jewish conspiracy theory, but it turns out people get offended when an account with millions of followers says things like that"? That makes no sense.

If you look at the account's other tweets at the time, it becomes clear that its operator was actually just trying to communicate an obscure, subtle point that was completely unsuitable for a massive international audience and 140 characters. When a user responded to the tweet before it was deleted explaining that some Jewish people now put triple brackets around their names to push back against anti-Semitism, the account responded, "Yes, but it seems to have been repurposed for something else entirely—a wanna be [sic] establishment in-group designator." When accused of anti-Semitism by another account, WikiLeaks responded, "The opposite. We criticised the misappropriation of anti-Nazi critiques by social climbers. Like Ice Bucket Challenge & ALS."

It looks clear to me that whoever was running the WikiLeaks Twitter account that day was clumsily trying to communicate an overly complicated idea about "social climbers" and establishment loyalism, then deleted the tweet when they realized they'd screwed up and stumbled into a social media land mine.

Now, I say "whoever was running the WikiLeaks Twitter account that day" because it's been public knowledge for years that @WikiLeaks is a staff account shared by multiple people. Footnoted is a tweet of the account saying, "this is a staff account, not Assange." Footnoted is a tweet of the account saying "@WikiLeaks is a shared staff account."[169] This became self-evidently true for all to see when Assange's Internet access was cut off by the Ecuadorian embassy for the first time in October 2016, but the WikiLeaks Twitter account kept making posts during that time without interruption. This takes us to the second event, which helped cement the anti-Semitism smear.

The second event occurred in February 2018 when the Intercept's Micah Lee, who has had a personal beef with WikiLeaks and Assange for years,[170] published a ghastly article which made the following assertion:

> Throughout this article, The Intercept assumes that the WikiLeaks account is controlled by Julian Assange himself, as is widely understood, and that he is the author of the messages, referring to himself in the third person majestic plural, as he often does.[171]

There is absolutely no reason for Lee to have made this assumption, and the fact that this remains uncorrected in his original article is journalistic malpractice.

The article reveals Twitter DMs from a group chat of which the WikiLeaks account was a member. One of the other accounts in the group chat shared a tweet[172] by journalist Raphael Satter, who was posting a smear

---

[169] See WikiLeaks, *Twitter*, July 21, 2016, https://twitter.com/wikileaks/status/756140050576998400.

[170] See "Being Julian Assange," *ContraSpin*, March 8, 2018, https://contraspin.co.nz/beingjulianassange/.

[171] Micah Lee and Cora Currier, "In Leaked Chats, WikiLeaks Discusses Preference For GOP Over Clinton, Russia, Trolling, and Feminists They Don't Like," *The Intercept* on *archives today*, February 14, 2018, https://archive.fo/e4tQ0#selection-573.137-581.1.

[172] See https://www.documentcloud.org/documents/4378830-Excerpts-From-Private-WikiLeaks-Twitter-Group.html#document/p13/a404460.

piece he'd written about WikiLeaks. The WikiLeaks account responded as follows:

"He's always ben [sic] a rat."

"But he's jewish and engaged with the ((())) issue."

When I first read about this exchange as written down by Micah Lee, I read it as "He's always been a rat, but then, he is Jewish, and engaged with the ((())) issue." Which would of course be gross. Calling someone a rat because they're Jewish would obviously be anti-Semitic. But if you read the DMs, whoever was running the account didn't do that; they said "He's always ben a rat," followed by a full stop, then beginning a new thought.[173]

Now if you look at the date on that exchange and compare it to the date on the deleted ((())) tweet,[174] you'll see that this was one month after the infamous ((())) tweet that had caused such a tizzy. It appears likely to me that the operator of the account (who again could have been any of the WikiLeaks staff who had access to it) was saying that Satter was mad about "the ((())) issue," meaning the tweet so many people were so recently enraged about and were still discussing, hence his attacking them with a smear piece.

There are also claims about an association between Assange and the controversial Israel Shamir, which WikiLeaks denies unequivocally, saying in a statement:

---

[173] See https://www.documentcloud.org/documents/4378830-Excerpts-From-Private-WikiLeaks-Twitter-Group.html#document/p13/a404460.

[174] Johnstone is referring to the deleted WikiLeaks tweet aforementioned that reads, "Tribalist symbol for establishment climbers? Most of our critics have 3 (((brackets around their names))) & have black-rim glasses. Bizarre."
    See WikiLeaks, *Twitter*, July 23, 2016, https://archive.is/5g8LF#selection-3671.0-3671.21.

Israel Shamir has never worked or volunteered for WikiLeaks, in any manner, whatsoever. He has never written for WikiLeaks or any associated organization, under any name and we have no plan that he do so. He is not an "agent" of WikiLeaks. He has never been an employee of WikiLeaks and has never received monies from WikiLeaks or given monies to WikiLeaks or any related organization or individual. However, he has worked for the BBC, Haaretz, and many other reputable organizations.

It is false that Shamir is "an Assange intimate." He interviewed Assange (on behalf of Russian media), as have many journalists. He took a photo at that time and has only met with WikiLeaks staff (including Asssange) twice. It is false that "he was trusted with selecting the 250,000 US State Department cables for the Russian media" or that he has had access to such at any time.

Shamir was able to search through a limited portion of the cables with a view to writing articles for a range of Russian media. The media that subsequently employed him did so of their own accord and with no intervention or instruction by WikiLeaks.[175]

Now, we're on Smear #16. There's still a ways to go. If you've been reading this article straight through it should be obvious to you by now that there's a campaign to paint Assange as literally the worst person in the world by calling him all the worst things you can possibly call someone. Is it possible that he's some kind of secret Jew hater? Sure, theoretically, but there's certainly no good argument to be made for that based on the facts at hand,

---

[175] WikiLeaks, *TwitLonger*, March 1, 2011, http://www.twitlonger.com/show/92ichb.

and given the extent the narrative shapers are going to paint him in a negative light, it's a mighty big stretch in my opinion.

Smear 17: "He's a fascist."

Unlike most Assange smears this one is more common on the political left than the center, and it totally baffles me. Demanding that governments be transparent and powerful people held to account is not at all compatible with fascism. In fact, it's the exact opposite.

Italian investigative journalist and longtime WikiLeaks collaborator Stefania Maurizi told Micah Lee the following on Twitter last year:

> I've worked as a media partner since 2009, I can bring my experience: I've NEVER EVER seen misogyny [sic] or fascism, rape apology, anti-semitism. I've anti-fascism deep in my DNA, due to the consequences for my family during Fascism.[176]

I really don't know how people make this one work in their minds. "You guys know who the *real* fascist is? It's the guy who's locked behind bars by the most violent and oppressive government on the planet for standing up against the war crimes of that government." I mean, come on.

When I question what's behind this belief I get variations on Smear 18 and Smear 22, and the occasional reference to one odd tweet[177] about birth rates and changing demographics that could look like a white nationalist talking point if you squint at it just right and ignore the fact that it appears

---

[176] Stefania Maurizi, Twitter post, February 19, 2018, 3:28 am, https://twitter.com/SMaurizi/status/965503438133096448.

[177] The tweet reads "Capitalism+atheism+feminism = sterility = migration. EU birthrate = 1.6. Replacement = 2.1. Merkel, May, Macron, Gentiloni all childless."
See Defend Assange Campaign, Twitter post, September 2, 2017, 11:41 am, https://twitter.com/DefendAssange/status/904006478616551425.

on its own surrounded by a total absence of anything resembling a white nationalist worldview, and ignore the tweet[178] immediately following it criticizing "emotional imperialism" and the theft of caregivers from less powerful nations. You have to connect a whole lot of dots with a whole lot of imaginary red yarn and ignore a huge mountain of evidence to the contrary in order to believe that Assange is a fascist.

Whenever I run into someone circulating this smear I usually just say something like, "You know there are powerful government agencies with a vested interest in making you think that, right?" Painting Assange as a right-winger has been immensely successful in killing Assange's support on the left, leaving only his support on the right, which can often be largely worthless when it comes to the Trump administration's war on WikiLeaks. Divide and conquer works.

Smear 18: "He was a Trump supporter."

No he wasn't. He hated Hillary "Can't we just drone this guy?"[179] Clinton for her horrible record and her efforts as secretary of state to shut down WikiLeaks, but that's not the same as supporting Trump. His hatred of Clinton was personal, responding to a complaint by a lead Clinton staffer about his role in her defeat with the words, "Next time, don't imprison and kill my friends, deprive my children of their father, corrupt judicial processes, bully allies into doing the same, and run a seven year unconstitutional grand jury against me and my staff."

And he wanted her to lose. Desiring the loss of the woman who campaigned on a promise to create a no-fly zone in the same region that

---

[178] See Defend Assange Campaign, Twitter post, September 2, 2017, 12:11 pm, https://twitter.com/DefendAssange/status/904013928593846272.

[179] See WikiLeaks, Twitter post, October 3, 2016, 7:32 am, https://twitter.com/wikileaks/status/782906224937410562.

Russian military planes were conducting operations is perfectly reasonable for someone with Assange's worldview, and it doesn't mean he wanted Trump to be president or believed he'd make a good one. Preferring to be stabbed over shot doesn't mean you want to be stabbed.

In July 2016, Assange compared the choice between Clinton and Trump to a choice between cholera and gonorrhea, saying, "Personally, I would prefer neither." When a Twitter user suggested to Assange in 2017 that he start sucking up to Trump in order to secure a pardon, Assange replied, "I'd rather eat my own intestines." Could not possibly be more unequivocal.

Assange saw Trump as clearly as anyone at the time, and now he's behind bars at the behest of that depraved administration. Clinton voters still haven't found a way to make this work in their minds; they need to hate Assange because he helped Hillary lose, but when they cheerlead for his arrest they're cheering for a Trump administration agenda. These same people who claim to oppose Trump and support the free press are cheerleading for a Trump administration agenda which constitutes the greatest threat to the free press we've seen in our lifetimes. When I encounter them online I've taken to photoshopping a MAGA hat onto their profile pics.[180]

Assange has never been a Trump supporter. But, in a very real way, those who support his imprisonment are.

Smear 19: "I used to like him until he ruined the 2016 election" / "I used to hate him until he saved the 2016 election."

That's just you admitting that you have no values beyond blind partisan loyalty. Only liking truth when it serves you is the same as hating truth.

---

[180] See Caitlin Johnstone, Twitter post, March 1, 2019, 11:07 pm, https://twitter.com/caitoz/status/1101695376761872384.

Smear 20: "He's got blood on his hands."

No he doesn't. There's no evidence anywhere that WikiLeaks helped cause anyone's death anywhere in the world. This smear has been enjoying renewed popularity since it became public knowledge that he's being prosecuted for the Manning leaks, the argument being that the leaks got US troops killed.

This argument is stupid. In 2013 the Pentagon, who had every incentive to dig up evidence that WikiLeaks had gotten people killed, ruled that no such instances have been discovered.[181]

Smear 21: "He published the details of millions of Turkish women voters."

No he didn't. The WikiLeaks website reports the following:

> Reports that WikiLeaks published data on Turkish women are false. WikiLeaks didn't publish the database. Someone else did. What WikiLeaks released were emails from Turkey's ruling party, the Justice & Development Party or AKP, which is the political force behind the country's president, Recep Tayyip Erdoğan, who is currently purging Turkey's judiciary, educational sector and press.

That "someone else" was Emma Best, then known as Michael Best, who also happens to be the one who published the controversial Twitter DMs used in Micah Lee's aforementioned Assange smear piece. Best wrote an article

---

[181] See Ed Pilkington, "Bradley Manning leak did not result in deaths by enemy force, court hears," *The Guardian*, July 31, 2013, https://www.theguardian.com/world/2013/jul/31/bradley-manning-sentencing-hearing-pentagon.

clarifying that the information about Turkish women was published not by WikiLeaks, but by her.[182]

Smear 22: "He supported right-wing political parties in Australia."

No he didn't. In 2013, Australia's WikiLeaks Party ended up giving preferential votes to right-wing parties in New South Wales as a result of over-delegation on Assange's part while he was busy trying to help Edward Snowden and Chelsea Manning, along with what the WikiLeaks party described as "administrative errors."

In 2012, WikiLeaks announced on Twitter that Assange was running for the Australian Senate, and in 2013 the WikiLeaks Party was formally registered with the Australian Electoral Commission and fielded candidates in the states of Victoria, New South Wales, and Western Australia. The other candidates in the party included a human rights lawyer, an ethicist, a former Greens candidate, a former diplomat, a law professor and a former president of the Ethnic Communities council in WA. It was a very left-wing offering with unusual political ads.[183]

In Australia we have preferential voting, which is also known in the US as ranked-choice voting. You are given two ballots, a small one for the house of representatives and an arm's-length one for the Senate, which you number the candidates in order of your preference, number one being your first preference. Voting for the Senate is an epic task so you are given the ability to number every single candidate in order of preference (which is

---

[182] See Michael Best, "The Who and How of the AKP Hack, Dump and WikiLeaks Release," *Glomar Disclosure* on *archives today*, July 26, 2016, https://archive.fo/0VsQR.

[183] See Spor Haber, "Julian Assange dons mullet to sing You're the Voice," *Youtube*, August 26, 2013, https://www.youtube.com/watch?v=w0oI_8r5nXk&feature=youtu.be.

called "voting below the line"), or back in 2013 you could simply nominate the party who you want to win "above the line" and if they were knocked out in the first round, their preferences were applied to your vote.

These preferences make up what's called a "How To Vote" card. An example is a pamphlet given to voters on the day that suggests how to number your preferences to support your party, but it's also submitted to the electoral commission so that they can assign your chosen flow of preferences in the Senate vote.[184]

Every election there is a shit-storm over the How To Vote cards as parties bargain with each other and play off each other to try and get the flow of preferences to go their way. To make things even more complex, you have to create these cards for every state and seat you are putting up candidates for. The WikiLeaks Party preferences statement in one of the states, New South Wales, somehow wound up having two right-wing parties preferenced before the three major parties. The WikiLeaks Party said it was an administrative error and issued this statement in August 2013:

> Preferences Statement: The WikiLeaks Party isn't aligned with any other political group. We'd rather not allocate preferences at all but allocating preferences is compulsory if your name is to go above the line.
>
> In allocating preferences between 53 other parties or groups in NSW some administrative errors occurred, as has been the case with some other parties. The overall decision as to preferences was a democratically made decision of the full National Council of the party. According to the National Council decision The Shooters & Fishers and the Australia First Party should have been below

---

[184] See Proportional Representation Society of Australia, http://www.prsa.org.au/htv2016_gr.html.

Greens, Labor, Liberal. As we said, we aren't aligned with anyone
and the only policies we promote are our own. We will support
and oppose the policies of other parties or groups according to our
stated principles.[185]

So, in short, the entirety of the WikiLeaks Party gathered and voted to put those right-wing parties down the ballot below Greens, Labor, and Liberal parties but someone fucked up the form. The WikiLeaks Party ended up getting 0.66 percent of the vote and in NSW those preferences went to those right-wing parties who also failed to get the numbers required to win a seat. Was there mismanagement? Yes. Was it deliberate? At least with regard to Assange, there's no reason to believe that it was.

This was all happening at the same time Chelsea Manning's case was wrapping up and Assange was busy helping Edward Snowden.

"I made a decision two months ago to spend a lot of my time on dealing with the Edward Snowden asylum situation, and trying to save the life of a young man," Assange told Australian TV at the time. "The result is over-delegation. I admit and I accept full responsibility for over-delegating functions to the Australian party while I try to take care of that situation."

---

[185] WikiLeaksParty, *Facebook*, August 18, 2013, https://www.facebook.com/WLParty/posts/460119824085585.

PART IV: THE LEGACY OF WIKILEAKS AND ASSANGE

1. CALLING ASSANGE A "NARCISSIST" MISSES THE POINT[186]

Patrick Cockburn, April 12, 2019

"Oh yeah, look at those dead bastards," and "Ha, ha, I hit them," say the pilots of a US Apache helicopter in jubilant conversation as they machine-gun Iraqi civilians on the ground in Baghdad on July 12, 2007.

A wounded man, believed to be the 22-year-old Reuters photographer Namir Noor-Eldeen, crawls toward a van. "Come on buddy, all you have to do is pick up a weapon," says one of the helicopter crew, eager to resume the attack. A hellfire missile is fired and a pilot says: "Look at that bitch go!" The photographer and his driver are killed.

Later the helicopter crew is told over the radio that they have killed 11 Iraqis and a small child has been injured. "Well, it's their fault for bringing their kids into battle," comments somebody about the carnage below.

---

[186] This essay was originally published in the *Independent.* Patrick Cockburn, "Calling Assange a 'narcissist' misses the point—without WikiLeaks we would live in darker, less informed times," *Independent,* April 12, 2019, https://www.independent.co.uk/voices/julian-assange-wikileaks-chelsea-manning-war-democracy-a8867816. html.

Except there was no "battle" and all those who died were civilians, though the Pentagon claimed they were gunmen. The trigger-happy pilots had apparently mistaken a camera for a rocket propelled grenade launcher. Journalists in Baghdad, including myself, were from the start skeptical about the official US story because insurgents with weapons in their hands were unlikely to be standing chatting to each other in the street with an American helicopter overhead. As on many similar occasions in Iraq, our doubts were strong but we could not prove that the civilians had not been carrying weapons in the face of categorical denials from the US Department of Defense.

It was known that a video of the killings taken from the helicopter existed, but the Pentagon refused to release it under the Freedom of Information Act. Plenty of people were being killed all over Iraq at the time and the incident would soon have been forgotten, except by the families of the dead, if a US soldier called Chelsea Manning had not handed over a copy of the official video to WikiLeaks, which published it in 2010.

The exposure of the Baghdad helicopter killings was the first of many revelations which explain why Julian Assange has been pursued for so long by the US and British governments. The claim by Theresa May echoed by other ministers that "in the United Kingdom, no one is above the law" is clearly an evasion of the real reasons why such efforts have been made to detain him on both sides of the Atlantic.

Jeremy Corbyn is correct to say that the affair is all about "the extradition of Julian Assange to the US for exposing evidence of atrocities in Iraq and Afghanistan." But, within hours of Assange's detention, it was clear that nobody much cared about innocent people dying in the streets of Baghdad or in the villages of Afghanistan and Assange has already become a political weapon in the poisonous political confrontation over Brexit with Corbyn's support for Assange enabling Conservatives to claim that he is a security risk.

Lost in this dogfight is what Assange and WikiLeaks really achieved and why it was of great importance in establishing the truth about wars being fought on our behalf in which hundreds of thousands of people have been killed.

This is what Daniel Ellsberg did when he released the Pentagon Papers about the US political and military involvement in Vietnam between 1945 and 1967. Like Assange, he exposed official lies and was accused of putting American lives in danger though his accusers were typically elusive about how this was done.

But unless the truth is told about the real nature of these wars then people outside the war zones will never understand why they go on so long and are never won. Governments routinely lie in wartime and it is essential to expose what they are really doing. I remember looking at pictures of craters as big as houses in an Afghan village where 147 people had died in 2009 and which the US defense secretary claimed had been caused by the Taliban throwing grenades. In one small area called Qayara, outside Mosul, in 2016–17, the US Air Force admitted to killing one civilian but a meticulous examination of the facts by the *New York Times* showed that the real figure was 43 dead civilians including 19 men, 8 women, and 16 children aged 14 or under.

These are the sort of facts that the US and UK governments try to conceal and which Assange and WikiLeaks have repeatedly revealed. Readers should keep this in mind when they are told that Assange has a narcissistic personality or was not treating his cat properly. If his personal vices were a hundred times more serious than alleged, would they really counterbalance—and perhaps even discredit—the monstrosities he sought to unmask?

The US government documents published by WikiLeaks are about the real workings of power. Take the Hillary Clinton emails published in 2016: much of the media attention has plugged into conspiracy theories about

Russian involvement or, until the recent publication of the Mueller Report, the possible complicity of the Trump election campaign with the Russians. Many Democrats and anti-Trump journalists managed to persuade themselves that Assange had helped lose Hillary Clinton the election, though a glance at a history of the campaign showed that she was quite capable of doing this all by herself by not campaigning in toss-up states.

But look at what the emails tell us about the way the world really works. There is, for instance, a US State Department memo dated August 17, 2014—just over a week after ISIS had launched its offensive against the Kurds and Yazidis in Iraq that led to the butchery, rape, and enslavement of so many.

It was a time when the US was adamantly denying that Saudi Arabia and Qatar had any connection with ISIS and similar jihadi movements like al-Qaeda. But the leaked memo, which is drawn from "Western intelligence, US intelligence, and sources in the region" tells us that they really knew different. It says: "We need to use our diplomatic and more traditional intelligence assets to bring pressure on the governments of Qatar and Saudi Arabia, which are providing clandestine financial and logistic support to ISIS and other radical groups in the region."

This is important information about the level of priority the US gave to keeping in with its Saudi and Qatari allies while it was supposedly fighting the "war on terror." This had been true since 9/11 and remains true today. But in much of the British media such issues are barely considered and the debate is focused firmly on the reasons why rape charges were not brought against Assange by Swedish courts and his culpability in taking refuge in the Ecuadorian embassy in London. Anybody who highlights the importance of the work which Assange and WikiLeaks have done is likely to be accused of being light-heartedly dismissive of the accusations of rape.

1. CALLING ASSANGE A "NARCISSIST" MISSES THE POINT

Assange is likely to pay a higher price than Ellsberg for his exposure of government secrets. The Pentagon Papers were published when the media was becoming freer across the world while now it is on the retreat as authoritarian governments replace democratic ones and democratic governments become more authoritarian.

The fate of Assange will be a good guide as to how far we are going down this road and the degree to which freedom of expression is threatened in Britain at a time of deepening political crisis.

2. INJUSTICE AND JUSTICE:

The Injustice Faced by Assange for Giving Us Tools for Justice

Jennifer Robinson, July 2019

Having been a member of the legal team since 2010, I am often asked why I defend Julian Assange and WikiLeaks. My reasons have only become more compelling over time: an award-winning editor and publisher, who has been nominated for the Nobel Peace Prize for nine consecutive years, has had restrictions placed on his liberty, without charge, for almost a decade. As I write, Assange is detained in a high-security prison in south London, housed alongside murderers, for having sought asylum in the Ecuadorian embassy in 2012 to protect himself from the very outcome he now confronts in 2019: extradition to the US where he faces prosecution for his work with WikiLeaks on 18 separate counts and a potential 175 years in prison.

The injustice of this situation is obvious—or should be. It was obvious to us back in 2010. Since 2010 we have warned about the chilling implications of the US grand jury, convened under Obama, a president who prosecuted more whistleblowers than all previous presidents combined. We called upon the mainstream media to stand with WikiLeaks against the criminal investigation and the use of the Espionage Act because it is impossible to distinguish between what WikiLeaks does from the journalistic activity engaged in by journalists every day—a position that has also been put forward by the *New York Times* general counsel, David McCraw. We warned that the precedent set by the WikiLeaks investigation and any prosecution could—and would—be used against the rest of the media.

But for many years, including the period after Assange sought and was granted asylum in the Ecuadorian embassy, many in the media claimed he was paranoid, that the US wouldn't prosecute and—in the sanctimonious words characteristic of journalist James Ball in January 2018— "what's keeping him trapped there is not so much the iniquitous actions of world powers, but pride." How wrong they were.

On April 11, when Assange was arrested and forcefully removed from the embassy by British police with the consent of Ecuadorian president Lenín Moreno, he was immediately served with a US extradition request.

Alongside the decade-long denial of the self-evident risk of US extradition, there was a decade-long effort to vilify and *other* Assange and WikiLeaks—to somehow distinguish him, the organization, and those who work for it from *conventional* journalists and publications, and therefore to mark them as undeserving of journalistic protection. Whether coordinated or not, the mainstream media fed into this vilification by focusing their reporting on a skewed perception of Assange's personality, his personal habits, unsubstantiated allegations of collusion with Donald Trump and Russia, his cat or his alleged mistreatment of other cats, and whether or not Assange is really a "journalist" (however defined).

When Google announced in late 2014 that it had been subpoenaed, and had handed over all of the emails of WikiLeaks journalists Kristinn

Hrafnsson, Sarah Harrison, and Joseph Farrell to US prosecutors, there was barely a whimper from the mainstream media—and certainly not the outrage one would expect if it had happened to CNN or *New York Times* journalists. In 2017, the head of the Central Intelligence Agency (CIA), Mike Pompeo, declared WikiLeaks a "hostile non-state intelligence agency" that would be "taken down," and that Assange should be prosecuted in the US without the benefits of First Amendment protections.

As images of a bearded Assange being dragged out of the Ecuadorian embassy were broadcast around the world, reactions by journalists on Twitter were filled with glee. The images shocked many, but not those of us who had watched his health deteriorate over the years inside that embassy without access to healthcare or outdoor exercise. The British government refused to recognize his asylum, denying him the ability to seek medical treatment without giving up his asylum, and effectively requiring him to choose between his right to health and his right to asylum.

The grand jury criminal investigation opened by the Obama administration is now in the hands of Trump, the president who has described the media as "the enemy of the people." Trump may have said "I love WikiLeaks" during the 2016 US election, but that hasn't stopped his administration from charging Assange with seventeen counts under the Espionage Act, and one charge of conspiracy to commit unauthorized access to a government computer, a violation of the US Computer Fraud and Abuse Act (CFAA).

The free speech concerns we have warned about since 2010 are now apparent to all: the indictment of Assange by the Trump administration has been described as "the most significant and terrifying threat to the First Amendment in the 21st century." The *New York Times* editorial board said the indictment will have "a chilling effect on American journalism as it has been practiced for generations" and is "a threat to freedom of expression and, with it, the resilience of American democracy itself."

The executive editor of the *Washington Post* said it demonstrated that the Trump administration is "now criminalizing common practices in journalism that have long served the public interest."

Despite widespread speculation about charges being made against Assange relating to the 2016 election releases, the indictment relates solely to WikiLeaks' 2010 publications: the Afghan War Logs, the Iraq War Logs and Cablegate—the material allegedly provided by Chelsea Manning. Even before Assange was arrested, Chelsea Manning, WikiLeaks' alleged source, was in jail for her principled refusal to testify in the grand jury against Assange. Manning had already given testimony in her own trial in which she was convicted, jailed, and spent years in prison until her sentence was commuted by Obama. In March 2019—a month before Assange's arrest— she was subpoenaed to appear for questioning and was jailed for contempt for refusing to testify, expressing concern about being pressured by prosecutors to change the testimony she gave during her trial:

> *I stand by my previous testimony. I will not participate in a secret process that I morally object to, particularly one that has been historically used to entrap and persecute activists for protected political speech.*

As I write, she remains in prison indefinitely and is being fined $1,000 for each day she refuses to testify against Assange. In the US—the country which purports to bring democracy to the world—a source can be held indefinitely and fined daily, on pain of giving evidence against a publisher for having published details of war crimes and human rights abuses.

There is also no denying the overwhelming public interest in the information disclosed by WikiLeaks. From Tunisia to Tonga, Canberra to Cairo, and the West Bank to West Papua, WikiLeaks disclosures have provided an unprecedented insight into the conduct of diplomacy and revealed corruption, abuse of power, and human rights violations the world over. And yet the editor and publisher responsible for these important publications, in partnership with newspapers and broadcasters around the world who benefited from the information provided by WikiLeaks, has suffered years of arbitrary detention without charge and sits in a high-security prison in London awaiting the proceedings to fight against US extradition.

The UN special rapporteur on torture, professor Nils Melzer, concluded—after our complaint to his mandate and his investigation—that Assange had been "deliberately exposed . . . to progressively severe forms of cruel, inhuman or degrading treatment or punishment, the cumulative effects of which can only be described as psychological torture." Melzer concluded with the following reflection, which summed up my experience of working on the Assange case over the past nine years:

> In 20 years of work with victims of war, violence and political persecution I have never seen a group of democratic States ganging up to deliberately isolate, demonize and abuse a single individual for such a long time and with so little regard for human dignity and the rule of law . . . The collective persecution of Julian Assange must end here and now!

Assange has suffered this grave injustice because of the work he does with WikiLeaks: an important public service which provides us with the information that we need for justice and accountability.

For this reason, I was following WikiLeaks well before I was approached about representing Assange in the summer of 2010. From their disclosure of the Guantánamo torture manual, to the "Collateral Murder" video, to breaking the super-injunction, which prevented the mainstream media from reporting on the Trafigura toxic waste spill off the Ivory Coast—the importance of WikiLeaks' work for human rights accountability was obvious to me, as a human rights lawyer. Indeed, as Assange has said about the work of WikiLeaks, "the goal is justice, the method is transparency."

Since 2010 we have seen WikiLeaks materials cited in submissions and judgments in courts around the world, including in the UK Supreme Court, the European Court of Human Rights, and international criminal tribunals. For example, WikiLeaks cables were cited as evidence in the case of *El-Masri v. Macedonia* before the European Court of Human Rights, a case about a German citizen who was renditioned by the US from Macedonia to Afghanistan where he was subjected to months of ill-treatment.

WikiLeaks cables were also cited before the British courts in the domestic challenge by Chagos Islanders, led by Olivier Bancoult, against British occupation of the islands to permit their return. The Chagos Islands were excised from Mauritius before its independence, its inhabitants forcefully removed, and the territory was leased to the US for the purposes of establishing the now notorious military basis on Diego Garcia. For decades the Chagossians have fought to return to their homeland in the face of opposition from the UK and US. A US diplomatic cable dated May 2009 revealed that a British Foreign Office official had told the Americans that the decision to set up a "marine protected area"—described in public as a "major step towards ocean protection"—was in fact created in order to "effectively end the islanders' resettlement claims," and represented "the most effective long-term way to prevent any of the Chagos Islands' former inhabitants or their descendants from resettling." The cable, revealing the neo-colonial attitude of UK and US officials towards the Chagossians, made clear that the UK government's "current thinking on the reserve, [was that] there would be 'no human footprints' or 'Man Fridays'" on the British Indian Ocean Territory uninhabited islands.

The UK Supreme Court decided in 2018 that WikiLeaks cables could be admissible before the British courts as evidence (see *R (on the application of Bancoult No 3) v. Secretary of State for Foreign and Commonwealth Affairs* [2018] UKSC 3, para. 30), which I hope will lead to more cases in which WikiLeaks cables are put to use by human rights lawyers. Later that same year, I had the great pleasure of being able to cite that same WikiLeaks cable before the International Court of Justice in our oral submissions on behalf of Vanuatu in support of Mauritius, successfully arguing that the British excision of the Chagos Islands was unlawful and contrary to the right to self-determination under international law, requiring the UK to return the territory to Mauritius. We celebrated the advisory opinion on the steps of the court in the Hague with Olivier Bancoult and the government of Mauritius, which had successfully taken on the world's imperial powers for the Chagos Islands—and won.

WikiLeaks cables have also been put to great effect in human rights advocacy campaigns around the world: from work in Pakistan advocating for an end to US drone strikes to documenting crimes against humanity in Sri Lanka. In publishing the Iraq War Logs, WikiLeaks partnered with the Iraq Body Count, a web-based effort to record civilian deaths resulting from the US-led 2003 invasion of Iraq. Iraq Body Count found that the war logs published by WikiLeaks, "contain[ed] an estimated 15,000 previously unknown civilian deaths," and that addition of the new material suggested that, "over 150,000 violent deaths have been recorded since March 2003, with more than 122,000 (80%) of them civilian." That is, the US and UK governments were not properly reporting civilian casualties as a result of the Iraq War. WikiLeaks materials were also later used in submissions to the International Criminal Court by public interest lawyers, and by the European Center for Constitutional and Human Rights (ECCHR) calling for an investigation into war crimes by the UK in Iraq.

WikiLeaks has also demonstrated its capacity to build power in social movements by assisting, through its publications, in breaking down dominant narratives maintained by the powerful. Information is power—and those in power maintain their position by controlling the narrative.

This was a lesson I learned a decade before WikiLeaks came onto the scene during my time working in West Papua. West Papua is illegally occupied by Indonesia, a fact little-known around the world because journalists and international organizations are banned from the territory, allowing the Indonesian government to control the narrative. Together with local lawyers and activists at a small NGO called Elsham, I worked on political prisoners' trials, investigated and documented systematic human rights abuse by Indonesian security forces, and worked on the first case of crimes against humanity to be heard before the Indonesian human rights courts after East Timor. One of our investigations was into the shooting of two Americans at the US-owned gold mine Freeport. Indonesia blamed *Operasi Papua Merdeka* (OPM), the armed wing of the West Papuan movement for independence from Indonesia. I interviewed witnesses, including one who linked the shooting with Kopassus—the special forces of the Indonesian military—which was known to incite violence around the mine to justify the multimillion-dollar payments for its security. When the *Washington Post* reported his account, they were threatened with defamation suits by the Indonesian military. A US diplomat visited our offices and told us to "be very careful" about what we were reporting. It was clear the matter was to be covered up—trade, the US gold mine, and good relations with Indonesia were apparently more important than the truth.

WikiLeaks disclosures in 2010 on West Papua confirmed what those of us working on human rights there have long known: the Indonesian military is engaging in widespread human rights abuse while on the Freeport gold mine payroll. We learn through the cables that US diplomats know and report on the rampant corruption and human rights abuses by the

Indonesian military. We also learned that Freeport executives acknowledge how the company pays for security services from the Indonesian military and police. Successive Australian governments, as they did with East Timor, continue to turn a blind eye. But the existence of these documents makes it much harder for our governments to deny that it is happening—and gives power to the West Papuan movement for self-determination by breaking down the official narrative.

As Assange has often said, we cannot act if we do not know. In providing the public with information about what governments are doing, WikiLeaks enables and empowers action. Amnesty International credits WikiLeaks publications as having sparked the Arab Spring in 2010, a pro-democracy protest movement. In its 2010 Annual Report, Amnesty said that political activists, "[l]everaging this information . . . used other new communications tools now easily available on mobile phones and on social networking sites to bring people to the streets to demand accountability." An example highlighted was in Tunisia, where WikiLeaks revelations about Ben Ali's corrupt regime combined with rapidly-spreading news of the self-immolation of a disillusioned young man, Mohamed Bouazizi, sparked major protests. Amnesty International concluded that, as a result of WikiLeaks publications,

> The year 2010 may well be remembered as a watershed year when activists and journalists used new technology to speak truth to power and, in so doing, pushed for greater respect for human rights.

Yet the journalist and publisher responsible for these publications—and a new era of transparency—is in prison in London, facing extradition and 175 years in a US prison. Meanwhile Amnesty has refused to recognize Assange as a prisoner of conscience. When Assange first told me that he was about to publish 250,000 US diplomatic cables, he said that the US would make his life hell but that it was his duty to the source—and to the public—to make the information available to the world. Soon after, his bank accounts were frozen, WikiLeaks faced a banking blockade by Visa, Mastercard, Paypal, and others—cutting them off from donations—and Assange himself was soon arrested. Nine years later, as we fight extradition proceedings in the UK, he faces spending the rest of his life in prison.

We are living in a world where the person responsible for giving us the tools we need to achieve justice and accountability is in prison, while those responsible for the war crimes and human rights abuse he exposed continue to enjoy impunity. It is a grave injustice that must be put right.

That's why I defend Assange. And why we all should.

3. A RETURN TO THE WIKILEAKS OF 2010

Naomi Colvin, March 2019

Today WikiLeaks is a political fixture. It publishes anonymously submitted documents, some of genuine historical importance, and coordinates international media partnerships around the same. It has a notably robust attitude to censorship and has resisted numerous demands to withhold material involving powerful political, commercial, and bureaucratic entities. The organization also plays an outsized role in the political imaginary of those who worry about how the advent of social media is changing the business of representative democracy.[187]

This all felt very novel in 2010. Over the course of that year, WikiLeaks worked through a series of publications of epochal importance disclosed by former US Army intelligence analyst Chelsea Manning. Prime among

---

[187] In the wake of surprise polling results on both sides of the Atlantic in 2016, many have sought to identify external actors who can be held responsible. While the possible use of anonymous leaking platforms by motivated actors including nation-states is an issue that deserves serious discussion substantial analyses of online information flows around the US presidential election emphasize the role of long-standing domestic dynamics. See e.g., Benkler, Faris & Roberts (2018), Network Propaganda.

these documents was a large collection of incident reports from the American wars in Afghanistan and Iraq, video footage from a helicopter gunship showing the killing of Iraqi civilians and two Reuters journalists by US military personnel in July 2007 and, of course, a comprehensive collection of US State Department cables touching on relations with practically every country in the world.

The import of Manning's disclosures is no doubt discussed in detail elsewhere in this volume. Given that they served as one of the triggers for the series of revolutions and grass-roots democratic movements that swept the world in 2011–12, it is hard to imagine a set of public interest disclosures achieving a wider resonance or provoking social change on a larger scale. Freely available to the public in a searchable online archive, these documents continue to serve as an important resource for journalists and researchers, as is clear from the regularity with which they are still referenced in news reporting.

During Manning's court-martial in 2013, it emerged that she had approached a series of prominent media organizations, including the *New York Times* and the *Washington Post*, before going to WikiLeaks. The significance of WikiLeaks is amply demonstrated by the fact that, without it, Manning's revelations would likely never have seen the light of day. The same is surely true of much of the series of publications that have followed since, an impressive group of revelations with particular strengths in diplomacy and the mechanics of public and private sector surveillance.

Without wanting to take anything away from those later releases, when considering the significance of WikiLeaks as a political project, it is 2010 that I find myself returning to. It was a moment when technological innovation, intellectual heft, and bullish public presentation combined to produce a dynamic that was profoundly exciting.[188] WikiLeaks in

---

[188] A taste of this can be obtained from the Twitter archive of those years: https://wlcentral.org/twitter-archive.

2010–11 was iconoclastic and engaging. Unlike most phenomena that can be described that way, it was also engaged in work that was profoundly important. An unusual and dangerous combination of traits—one which is liable to inspire others.

As the impact of Manning's revelations cascaded around the globe, occasioning major power shifts that would otherwise have seemed unrealizable, it felt like there was a lifting of the veil about what kind of change could be contemplated in a post-crash world that was badly in need of a reset. Better still, in WikiLeaks it looked like there was an entity that had both the ability and the commitment to amplify the actions of gratuitously courageous individuals and generate the necessary demonstration effects.

When, at her court-martial in 2013, Manning made a statement taking responsibility for her actions, she also posed a rhetorical question. "How could I, a junior analyst, possibly believe I could change the world for the better?" Those words carried a particularly heavy weight, it being obvious to anyone not wearing a uniform that changing the world for the better is precisely what Chelsea had managed to do. How could we dare to hope that such a thing was feasible?

Julian Assange's great contribution to the world is that he made the kind of heroism articulated and enacted by Chelsea Manning possible. Still more than this, he did so *by design*. Informed by a particular intellectual tradition, but with a degree of originality, Assange formulated a theory about how a particular aspect of the world worked and how it might be disrupted.[189] These ideas about the durability of closed bureaucratic structures were set out on paper and are available to read today.[190] When they were given organizational form and put into action, Assange did indeed

---

[189] The intellectual setting for WikiLeaks and many of its founder's perennial concerns is discussed in *Cypherpunks*, also published by OR Books, portions of which are excerpted in an earlier section of this collection.

[190] See *CRYPTOME*, July 31, 2010, http://cryptome.org/0002/ja-conspiracies.pdf.

change the world—by enabling others to do so—in broadly the way he envisioned.

This is a significant achievement and one that is worthy of recognition and respect. That respect should not be interpreted as some kind of blank check that exempts the bearer from criticism. Still less is it a claim for unquestioning obedience. Still, there is a kind of duty that pertains not to let the author of that achievement go down without a fight. This would, I think, hold true even if the wider implications of a criminal prosecution of Assange or other WikiLeaks staff for their publishing activities weren't so utterly dire.

Back in 2010–11, again, this all seemed pretty commonly understood. Not only was there a large degree of consensus, people went to some effort to make the point—some to the extent that they put themselves at risk in the process. By enabling whistleblowers to generate impact on a huge scale, WikiLeaks also created a sense of opportunity that motivated action among a far wider circle. The momentum generated by WikiLeaks produced multiple waves of activism with different focuses and repertoires. Enthusiasm arose, boundless, and loyalty did not need to be demanded.

The activism around and provoked by WikiLeaks took a number of forms. Firstly, WikiLeaks clearly provided the inspiration for further disclosures—the line from Chelsea Manning to Edward Snowden, Antoine Deltour, and others is obvious[191]—and this included the development of a phenomenon Biella Coleman has called the Public Interest Hack.[192] Some of

---

[191] Though not the focus of this essay, this sequence of disclosures has clearly informed developments in the field of whistleblower protection—not least in the recognition of the importance of privacy enhancing technologies. The whistleblower directive currently being negotiated by the EU institutions owes much to the examples of Manning, Snowden, and especially Deltour. As such, it simply would not have happened without Assange.

[192] E. Gabriella Coleman, "The Public Interest Hack," *limn*, https://limn.it/articles/the-public-interest-hack/

these disclosures were in due course released and preserved for the record by WikiLeaks—an act of tremendous value—but others were not. While the catalyzing force of WikiLeaks should not be underestimated, the ecosystem of leaks was always bigger than WikiLeaks itself, something that has become more obvious as time has gone on, particularly in languages other than English.[193]

Others set up tools to broaden the use of anonymous disclosure. Regional leaking sites proliferated after 2010, though not many of these have survived to the present day. However, SecureDrop and GlobaLeaks systems are now used by a host of media organizations, civil society, and even government agencies to enable them to receive anonymous reports. WikiLeaks pioneered the use of this technology and that it continues to evolve and develop in several different incarnations is testament to the strength of that original vision.

Beyond the origination of public interest information, groups emerged for the purpose of analyzing liberated data. Impromptu discussions on social media or supporter forums coexisted with more dedicated structures. Prominent among these was Project PM, whose concerns about the political economy of surveillance pre-empted many of the current debates around platform capitalism and the power of the big internet companies.

Other WikiLeaks-inspired activist projects were intended to improve the accessibility of published data, sometimes to the extent of providing new search interfaces that improved on those WikiLeaks had produced themselves. Then there were independent surveys of news reflected from and refracted through WikiLeaks publications. The WL Central website, which launched at around the same time as the first of the State Department cables was released, was one of many that published supporter-driven

---

[193] The patchiness of preservation efforts for those disclosures not published by WikiLeaks has posed difficulties for researchers. Initiatives to collate and preserve these varied archives are to be welcomed See e.g., DDoSecrets.com

articles on WikiLeaks and its publications. As time went on it also became one of the better sources for information on the wave of demonstrations that followed in Cablegate's wake.

In addition to all this was the explicit activism in defense of WikiLeaks. Late 2010 saw the start of an informal payment blockade as major payment providers were prevailed upon to stop servicing WikiLeaks. In response, Paypal and other sites were targeted by a series of digital sit-ins. The selective and heavy-handed criminal prosecution of the #PayPal14 was just one of many.[194]

With the experience of 2010–2011 in mind, some of what is happening today should not be unduly surprising. Concerns about a possible US criminal investigation were high at the time. Critics tended to argue not that a US prosecution would not be deeply problematic, but rather that it was not likely to materialize or that, at any rate, the US threat should not be linked to the European Arrest Warrant issued against Assange by a Swedish prosecutor in late 2010.[195]

Chelsea Manning was arrested in May 2010. Throughout the second half of that year, at Camp Arifjan in Kuwait and later the Quantico Marine brig in Virginia, she experienced treatment that was later condemned by the UN special rapporteur on torture. At the time, nobody knew.

---

[194] Those currently incarcerated for their support of WikiLeaks or alleged involvement in disclosures later published by WikiLeaks include Jeremy Hammond (https://freejeremy.net), Matt DeHart (https://mattdehart.com), Justin Liverman, Kane Gamble and, of course, Chelsea Manning (https://xychelsea.is).

[195] Assange's battle against extradition to Sweden to face questioning on sexual assault allegations wound its way through the UK courts and was only interrupted by Ecuador's grant of asylum to defend against a US prosecution in 2012. After several years of standoff and shortly before the statute of limitations on the one remaining allegation expired, the investigation was dropped in a way that was unsatisfactory to all sides. A large amount of WikiLeaks' early reputational capital was expended around the Swedish matter, though many forget that as a result of that case, UK law was changed in 2014 and it would likely not be possible for a similar EAW to be issued today.

Information about the circumstances of Manning's detention was only released to the outside world in the last days of December 2010, with some effort. Manning served almost seven years of a 35-year prison sentence for her whistleblowing, in difficult circumstances, before having that "clearly disproportionate" sentence commuted by Barack Obama in one of his last acts in office.

As I write this, Chelsea Manning has again been remanded to solitary confinement in jail after refusing to co-operate with secret grand jury proceedings in the Eastern District of Virginia. The grand jury appears to be a renewed attempt to bring a criminal prosecution against Julian Assange, the same process that was initiated in 2010 and rolled over several times since, now being pursued by renewed vigor under a US administration with few qualms about media freedom.

What, from the high point of 2010–12, is surprising is that now that the threat is undeniable, how subdued the reaction to it is. It would be a mistake to attribute this entirely to negative press coverage, still less secret machinations by shadowy elites. In part, it's a product of a gradual attrition of faith in and goodwill toward WikiLeaks, which has been compounded by an utterly self-defeating refusal to acknowledge that this could conceivably be a bit of a problem. What is particularly striking is not that there might be hostility from some of those who used to care the most—it's that so many have made the journey through disappointment and anger into the realms of utter disengagement. From many quarters that cared deeply—and maybe still do—there is silence.

There is no point denying that support for WikiLeaks at this juncture carries with it a certain amount of baggage, not least an unhealthy proximity to unlovely fellow-travelers on the American far right. This is a red line for many, and understandably so. A diminishing number of social media disciples reciting catechism at user accounts who have had the temerity to draw impermissible interpretations from commonly understood facts is also a tragedy of sorts. It's certainly a strange place for a discursive revolution to find itself in.

Unfortunately, while the clarity and the sense of possibility of 2010–11 may have dissipated, the threats we were all concerned about then have not. A US prosecution of Julian Assange and other WikiLeaks staff for publishing classified information remains a profoundly dangerous prospect. Many of the advances made since 2010 are potentially under threat. Computer crimes laws should not be used to stifle public interest speech. Extradition proceedings should not be used for political purposes. Large-scale leaks have proven an invaluable tool for social change. Anonymous disclosure is important and any motivation behind the submission of that information is secondary to its public interest value.

The threats are real and many of the arguments are not being made effectively, or at all. A lot has happened since 2010 and I appreciate the difficulty this accumulated baggage presents for many good and principled people. Most of those I have had the privilege to work with since then have a clear idea of what inspired them and the values they hold dear, not to mention the importance of Assange's contribution to realizing both. If the evident injustice of Chelsea Manning's re-imprisonment is to have any positive impact, maybe her courage and clear-mindedness can help those who have held back until now to navigate through this difficult and dangerous terrain and tell their truth.

4. WHO IS JULIAN ASSANGE AND WHAT DID WIKILEAKS DO

Renata Avila, March 2019

Julian and I were friends before I started advising him as a lawyer. We met in Budapest in 2008 at a large conference where digitivists attended various workshops with the goal of starting an international movement to oppose censorship and support free speech. In attendance was a wide spectrum of participants—people from Tor, librarians, and activists, some of whom, like Julian, were to become political prisoners.[196] I think we understood how important it was to convene these meetings, but most of

---

[196] The jailing of other activists who attended the Budapest conference should be noted. Alaa Abd El-Fattah (https://en.wikipedia.org/wiki/Alaa_Abd_El-Fattah), was arrested right after the Arab Spring (and an interview with Julian), and has been arbitrarily detained more than five years (his case was also studied by WGAD, which ruled against Egypt). He will soon be released. Hossein Derakhshan (https://medium.com/@h0d3r), who was arrested months after the summit in Iran, spent six years of his life in prison. Ali Abdulemam (https://en.wikipedia.org/wiki/Ali_Abdulemam), from Bahrain, who was also arrested and tortured, now lives in Europe. Luis Carlos Díaz, from Venezuela (https://www.amnesty.org/en/latest/news/2019/03/venezuela-authorities-must-free-luis-carlos-diaz-immediately/), recently arrested and then released in Venezuela. Julian is the only one subject to arbitrary detention by a Western country, the only one who remains in prison after so long.

us didn't really understand the danger, and didn't see what was in store for some.

Waiting in the lobby for the reception to start, we began talking. He was wearing shorts and hiking boots, in his backpack were two computers, and he had a weird foldable phone that I learned later was a Cryptophone. He looked like a mix of Indiana Jones, James Bond, and a boring librarian. We became engrossed in conversation and decided to take a walk. Julian asked me to leave my devices behind. As I would learn, he had reasons to be paranoid. This was long before the Panama Papers and he had just published material that exposed the corruption of a powerful Swiss bank. He was worried about retaliation.

We walked along the empty streets of Budapest all the way to Gellért Hill. We talked about Palestine and about Iran. We talked about the world and the weird twist the Obama administration brought. I confessed that as a young human rights lawyer from Guatemala, I was losing faith in the international justice system, the interest of mainstream media in countries like mine, and efforts to litigate through the court of public opinion to achieve justice. That first talk opened my eyes to new tactics that could attract attention to the work I was doing. I already had a deep interest in tech and independent publishing.

He explained WikiLeaks in detail. Anyone who has conversed with him knows his explanations are long and detailed. Despite being diagnosed with attention deficit disorder, on that day I had no problem following his vivid description of the strategies and goals of the romantic dream—his vision of the liberation tech WikiLeaks would become.

I learned the revolutionary concept of WikiLeaks had different components. The first one, which struck me as brilliant, was to adapt the Wikipedia form of decentralization and apply it to the analysis of documents. Too often the reporting on relevant issues of countries beyond G20 economies was without context, and technical reports were contaminated by lobbyists and flawed information. More often than not, the stories were superficial and given to bombastic headlines. Taking advantage of the growing interest in citizen journalism in the mid-2000s, WikiLeaks began the powerful participatory idea of making full sets of source documents available to the public. An idea that would unlock traditional journalism and overcome the economic centralization of media outlets.

The second concept was security as a liberating force. Not only security for the people involved, but safety for the documents which would become a vast global library with over 11 million files saved from being burned, thrown away, deleted, altered, or hidden. A global resource, resilient, permanent, and uncensorable, for research and publication, available for journalists and activists to restore equality by decolonizing secret knowledge—the knowledge that those making the most critical decisions about our future and our planet had granted themselves access to, while denying it to us for "our own safety." It would provide the perfect answer to media blockades in cases of brutal genocide[197] because the model circumvented fear of economic retaliation and other forms of censorship.

The third feature WikiLeaks offered was the non-traceability of sources. If we could dispel the fear of prosecution by those in power, we could verify chains of command, complicity, and orders. We could prove cases of genocide, complex corruption scandals, and sophisticated networks operating against public interest. The benefits seemed unlimited. Julian's vision for WikiLeaks made it possible to protect witnesses from getting killed, offices raided, and laptops stolen, especially in post-conflict societies. The innovation was the use of anonymous drop-boxes protected by cryptography.

---

[197] During the Civil War in Guatemala, the military destroyed 626 indigenous villages, killed or "disappeared" more than 200,000 people, and displaced an additional 1.5 million. More than 150,000 were driven to seek refuge in Mexico. The Interamerican Court of Human Rights and domestic courts determined that a genocide was perpetrated against the Mayan population.

Accessibility of data in some places is like a miracle. Now there was a peaceful, affordable way to open closed systems controlled by powerful oligarchs, and to conquer violent retaliation and assassination against human rights defenders and activists—those who spoke truth to power.

While sharing his own vision, he was also interested in my work. He asked about Latin America and I related the conflicts within Colombia, the Condor operation, the dirty wars. As I walked with him up the hill in Budapest, at five feet two inches tall, I could barely follow his pace. He is quite tall. He wouldn't stop talking. I wanted to slow down and take notes, but if I did that, I surely would have gotten lost.

During our walk, his geeky librarian side prevailed. It still prevails today, despite everything. The outside world is afraid of the library he defends, and the planet has moved to a darker place.

We called it a night a few hours later. Laughing, we realized that we didn't know where we were. I took a cab back to the hotel. He went out to fish for free Wi-Fi. Julian used to laugh a lot. He doesn't laugh as much now.

I want that laugh back.

***

I know him better now; more than a decade has passed since that night.

***

April 2010. I watched the DC press conference where the "Collateral Murder" video was released from my office in Guatemala. I believed a wave of arrests would follow and I tried to contact Julian to warn him. We reconnected after Chelsea Manning was arrested. I began to explore ways to bring an action in the Inter-American Court, which would at least make the public aware of the exposed abuses, and perhaps lead to some accountability. With Manning's arrest, I saw that the life of my friend would be changed forever. A series of incidents followed, including threats by Australia to retain Julian's passport and keep him there. A storm of challenges followed, including the refusal of Swedish residency and the sexual assault scandal. The typical means of silencing an activist involves the manipulation of a sexual assault scandal, a tax scandal, or a drug scandal. As Julian does not smoke, and is a person of modest means, you can see why the sex route was taken.

***

April 2011. The Guantánamo files are published. The media alliance expands. Journalists from all over the world are collaborating to expose the wrongdoings of the most powerful government on earth.

Summer of 2011. Ellingham Hall. I am back on a short visit to attend Julian's fortieth birthday party. One of my crushes, Slavoj Žižek, was among the group at the celebratory table. Laughter abounded when I remarked that if the brain is the sexiest part of the body, Slavoj was the sexiest man alive. It was a nerve-wracking time because of the uncertainty caused by the court delays. Despite the threats, media scandals, betrayals from staffers, and a growing legal bill, WikiLeaks continued to publish.

***

After a decade of dealing with Julian's cases, directly and indirectly, I can confidently assert that all forms of legal and administrative abuse were levied against him—from inexplicably strict bail conditions for an uncharged man, to long delays from usually efficient justice systems; from missing records at strict British and Swedish prosecution offices, to legal actions that ensnare his financial assets, preventing him from opening a bank account, or hiring the best criminal lawyers. On top of that, intense character assassination was perpetrated by his former allies—the media he partnered with.

Through the years, I visited him often, and I witnessed the gradual reduction of his freedom, the intensification of surveillance and harassment he suffered along with the betrayals from people working very close to him. Not to mention the churnalism of stupid reports about dirty socks.

But solidarity arose from unexpected places—from those who understand the importance of the fight and that what is at stake goes beyond him and WikiLeaks.

During his time under arbitrary detention Julian has authored books, launched over 30 major publications, and given over a hundred talks via the Internet. He continues to be heard challenging electronic surveillance companies and big tech like Google, and putting corporate immorality in the spotlight.

***

December 2018. By this time, I hadn't seen Julian for months. The Ecuadorian embassy blocked my visits because of a false report from a right-wing outlet in Quito saying I was a Catalan member of the independence movement. For months, I was prevented from visiting until Ecuador finally accepted a copy of my Guatemalan passport.

Surveillance and hostility inside and outside were at its peak. My visit coincided with the arrival of a new ambassador from Ecuador, further restrictions to his visits, and a new behavior protocol— "just because they can" do it to a person whose life depends on Ecuador's diplomatic protection.

Our catch-up conversation was detailed. I was, as usual, surprised by his mental clarity, his strategic decisions, his sense of purpose, his endurance and never-dying hope. He asked about my family, about my life. I tell him that I am now heading an office of two-dozen Latin American millennials on the other side of the planet. His curiosity remains intact, his advice is even sharper, but I worry because I do not want his wit to vanish as his laughter did.

It was seven years without walking outside, without holding his family or playing with his kids; never in the company of those he loves. Seven years under constant surveillance. Never alone, but with three guards at his doorstep, and Scotland Yard and the intelligence services surrounding him.

***

He is the most persecuted journalist in Europe. He is also the most innovative one. Few understand how tech and law combined can erect the most sophisticated system of control and oppression.

He has been persecuted for more than ten years and experienced more than a decade of restless nights, of restricted freedom and uncertainty. Yet he is also probably the busiest and most prolific of captives, posing the question of journalism's and humanity's futures through his writings and talks.

The most persecuted journalist in the West is also one of my dearest friends. One who changed my life profoundly, and probably your life too. Directly or indirectly.

We live in a dangerous time in which everyone opposed to great political and financial powers might soon become a target, just like Assange. No one believes the elites anymore. His imprisonment is a symbol of a growing fear of those in power. A Western publisher, a journalist, is gagged in Europe—a symbol of the collapse of the West. Silencing and torturing a journalist—in plain sight—is to cross a limit, and yet no one rioted.

The visit ends.

The saddest feeling: saying goodbye at the door, fearing this will be the last time, fearing I will not see him again, feeling I have failed—that *we* failed to protect our last hope.

5. THE REAL MUELLERGATE SCANDAL[198]

Craig Murray, May 9, 2019

Robert Mueller is either a fool or deeply corrupt. I do not think he is a fool.

I did not comment instantly on the Mueller Report as I was so shocked by it, I have been waiting to see if any other facts come to light in justification. Nothing has. I limit myself here to that area of which I have personal knowledge—the leak of DNC and Podesta emails to WikiLeaks. On the wider question of the corrupt Russian 1 percent having business dealings with the corrupt Western 1 percent, all I have to say is that if you believe that is limited in the US by party political boundaries, you are a fool.

On the DNC leak, Mueller started with the prejudice that it was "the Russians" and he deliberately and systematically excluded from evidence anything that contradicted that view.

Mueller, as a matter of determined policy, omitted key steps which any honest investigator would undertake. He did not commission any forensic examination of the DNC servers. He did not interview Bill Binney.

---

[198] This essay was originally published online. Craig Murray, "The Real Muellergate Scandal," Craig Murray, May 9, 2019, https://www.craigmurray.org.uk/archives/2019/05/the-real-muellergate-scandal/.

He did not interview Julian Assange. His failure to do any of those obvious things renders his report worthless.

There has never been, by any US law enforcement or security service body, a forensic examination of the DNC servers, despite the fact that the claim those servers were hacked is the very heart of the entire investigation. Instead, the security services simply accepted the "evidence" provided by the DNC's own IT security consultants, Crowdstrike, a company which is politically aligned to the Clintons.

That is precisely the equivalent of the police receiving a phone call saying, "Hello? My husband has just been murdered. He had a knife in his back with the initials of the Russian man who lives next door engraved on it in Cyrillic script. I have employed a private detective who will send you photos of the body and the knife. No, you don't need to see either of them."

There is no honest policeman in the world who would agree to that proposition, and neither would Mueller were he remotely an honest man.

Two facts compound this failure.

The first is the absolutely key word of Bill Binney, former technical director of the NSA, the US' $14-billion-a-year surveillance organization. Bill Binney is an acknowledged world leader in cyber surveillance, and is infinitely more qualified than Crowdstrike. Bill states that the download rates for the "hack" given by Crowdstrike are at a speed—41 megabytes per second—that could not even nearly be attained remotely at the location: thus the information must have been downloaded to a local device, e.g., a memory stick. Binney has further evidence regarding formatting which supports this.[199]

---

[199] See "VIPS: Mueller's Forensics-Free Findings," *Consortium News*, March 13, 2019, https://consortiumnews.com/2019/03/13/vips-muellers-forensics-free-findings/

Mueller's identification of "DC Leaks"[200] and "Guccifer 2.0"[201] as Russian security services is something Mueller attempts to carry off by simple assertion. Mueller shows DC Leaks to have been the source of other, unclassified emails sent to WikiLeaks that had been obtained under a Freedom of Information request and then Mueller simply assumes, with no proof, the same route was used again for the leaked DNC material. His identification of the Guccifer 2.0 persona with Russian agents is so flimsy as to be laughable. Nor is there any evidence of the specific transfer of the leaked DNC emails from Guccifer 2.0 to WikiLeaks. Binney asserts that had this happened, the packets would have been instantly identifiable to the NSA.

Bill Binney is not a "deplorable." He is the former technical director of the NSA. Mike Pompeo met him to hear his expertise on precisely this matter. Binney offered to give evidence to Mueller. Yet did Mueller call him as a witness? No. Binney's voice is entirely unheard in the report.

Mueller's refusal to call Binney and consider his evidence was not the action of an honest man.

The second vital piece of evidence we have is from WikiLeaks' Vault-7 release of CIA material, in which the CIA themselves outline their capacity to "false flag" hacks, leaving behind misdirecting clues including scraps of foreign script and language. This is precisely what Crowdstrike claims to have found in the "Russian hacking" operation.

---

[200] DC Leaks is a website that has published a number of leaks, most notably the DNC leak of 2016. It was alleged by a US federal grand jury in 2018 to be a front for the Russian cyber espionage group, Fancy Bear, that US cybersecurity firms claim is run by Russian Main Intelligence Directorate (GRU) units and responsible for the DNC email hack in 2016.

[201] Guccifer 2.0 is a persona which claimed to be solely responsible for the 2016 DNC email hack. The same US federal grand jury that alleged DC Leaks is run by GRU agents also claimed that Guccifer 2.0 is operated by GRU.

So here we have Mueller omitting the key steps of independent forensic examination of the DNC servers and hearing Bill Binney's evidence. Yet this was not for lack of time. While deliberately omitting to take any steps to obtain evidence that might disprove the "Russian hacking" story, Mueller had boundless time and energy to waste in wild goose chases after totally non-existent links between WikiLeaks and the Trump campaign, including the fiasco of interviewing Roger Stone and Randy Credico.

It is worth remembering that none of the charges against Americans arising from the Mueller inquiry have anything to do with Russian collusion or Trump–WikiLeaks collusion, which simply do not exist. The charges all relate to entirely extraneous matters dug up, under the extraordinary US system of "justice," to try to blackmail those charged with unrelated crimes turned up by the investigation into fabricating evidence of Russian collusion. The official term for this process of blackmail is of course "plea-bargaining."

Mueller has indicted 12 Russians he alleges are the GRU agents responsible for the "hack." The majority of these turns out to be real people who, ostensibly, have jobs and lives which are nothing to do with the GRU. Mueller was taken aback when, rather than simply being in absentia, a number of them had representation in court to fight the charges. Mueller had to back down and ask for an immediate adjournment as soon as the case opened, while he fought to limit disclosure. His entire energies since on this case have been absorbed in submitting motions to limit disclosure, individual by individual, with the object of ensuring that the accused Russians can be convicted without ever seeing, or being able to reply to, the evidence against them. Which is precisely the same as his attitude to contrary evidence in his report.

Mueller's failure to examine the servers or take Binney's evidence pales into insignificance compared to his attack on Julian Assange. Based on no conclusive evidence, Mueller accuses Assange of receiving the emails from Russia. Most crucially, he did not give Assange any opportunity to answer his accusations. For somebody with Mueller's background in law enforcement, declaring somebody in effect guilty without giving them any opportunity to tell their side of the story is plain evidence of malice.

Inexplicably, for example, the Mueller Report quotes a media report of Assange stating he had "physical proof" the material did not come from Russia, but Mueller simply dismisses this without having made any attempt at all to ask Assange himself.

It is also particularly cowardly as Julian was and is held incommunicado with no opportunity to defend himself. Assange has repeatedly declared the material did not come from the Russian state or from any other state. He was very willing to give evidence to Mueller, which could have been done by video-link, by interview in the embassy or by written communication. But as with Binney and as with the DNC servers, the entirely corrupt Mueller was unwilling to accept any evidence which might contradict his predetermined narrative.

Mueller's section headed "The GRU's Transfer of Stolen Material to WikiLeaks" is a ludicrous farrago of Internet contacts between WikiLeaks and persons not proven to be Russian, transferring material not proven to be the DNC leaks. It too is destroyed by Binney and so pathetic that, having pretended he had proven the case of Internet transfer, Mueller then gives the game away by adding, "The office cannot rule out that stolen documents were transferred by intermediaries who visited during the summer of 2016." He names Mr. Andrew Muller-Maguhn as a possible courier. Yet again, he did not ask Mr. Muller-Maguhn to give evidence. Nor did he ask me, and I might have been able to help him on a few of these points.

To run an "investigation" with a pre-determined idea as to who are the guilty parties, and then to name and condemn those parties in a report, without hearing the testimony of those you are accusing, is a method of proceeding that puts the cowardly and corrupt Mr. Mueller beneath contempt.

Mueller gives no evidence whatsoever to back up his simple statement that Seth Rich was not the source of the DNC leak. He accuses Julian Assange of "dissembling" by referring to Seth Rich's murder. It is an interesting fact that the US security services have shown precisely the same level of interest in examining Seth Rich's computers that they have shown in examining the DNC servers. It is also interesting that this murder features in a report of historic consequences like that of Mueller, yet has had virtually no serious resources put into finding the killer.

Mueller's condemnation of Julian Assange for allegedly exploiting the death of Seth Rich would be infinitely more convincing if the official answer to the question "Who murdered Seth Rich?" was not "Who cares?"

6. WIKILEAKS AND UK FOREIGN POLICY

Mark Curtis, March 2019

Julian Assange has been praised mainly for revealing the crimes, human rights abuses, and duplicity of US governments, but WikiLeaks' importance goes well beyond highlighting US secrets. My own country, the United Kingdom, is in reality a highly secretive oligarchy in which the policy-making elite doesn't even truly believe in the public's right to know what it is doing, let alone in allowing significant public influence over policy-making. WikiLeaks' publications of classified US cables shed important light on some of the UK's recent foreign policies, and in particular the reality of the "special relationship" between the two states. For this reason alone, Julian Assange's publishing activities are hugely important for anyone concerned with trying to hold unaccountable power to account.

WikiLeaks has revealed many important UK foreign policies—none of which the world would have known about had it not been for its publication of the US cables.

Revelations on the UK and Iraq

The first concerns how the UK government of Gordon Brown undermined the Chilcot Inquiry[202] it launched in 2009 into the Iraq War by immediately making promises to the US. Just as the inquiry was beginning in 2009, the Ministry of Defense's director for security policy, Jon Day, promised a senior US official that his government had "put measures in place to protect your interests."[203] According to the US cable:

> *He [Day] noted that Iraq seems no longer to be a major issue in the US, but he said it would become a big issue—a "feeding frenzy"— in the UK "when the inquiry takes off."[204]*

We don't know what this protection amounted to, but it appears to have been substantial. No US officials were called to give evidence to Chilcot in public. Evidence from some US officials was only heard in private during visits by inquiry members to the US. The inquiry was also refused permission to publish letters between George Bush and Tony Blair written in 2002 in the run-up to the war, even though they were referred to in evidence.[205]

A second policy revealed by WikiLeaks concerns the UK's war in Iraq itself. A UK military report of 2006 published by WikiLeaks damns UK and US war planning, which, it says, "ran counter to potential Geneva Convention obligations" and led directly to the post-invasion collapse

---

[202] Named after its chairman, Sir John Chilcot, the Chilcot Inquiry was a British public inquiry into the UK's role in the Iraq War published in 2016. See "Iraq Inquiry," *Wikipedia*, last modified June 22, 2019, https://en.wikipedia.org/wiki/Iraq_Inquiry

[203] https://.org/plusd/cables/09LONDON2198_a.html.

[204] https://.org/plusd/cables/09LONDON2198_a.html.

[205] Robert Booth, "WikiLeaks cable reveals secret pledge to protect US at Iraq Inquiry," *The Guardian*, November 30, 2010, https://www.theguardian.com/world/2010/nov/30/wikileaks-chilcot-iraq-war-inquiry.

of Iraqi society. It noted: "Leaders should not start an operation without thinking . . . it is not enough just to identify the desired end-state." The report also reveals that Whitehall had been secretly planning the war during 2002 and that the Blair government kept the pending invasion ("Telic") secret from all but an inner circle of officers and officials until three months before the start of hostilities. It stated:

> In Whitehall, the internal OPSEC (operational security) regime, in which only very small numbers of officers and officials were allowed to become involved in TELIC business, constrained broader planning for combat operations and subsequent phases effectively until 23 December 2002.

Although the UK wanted UN Security Council approval, the UK found itself tied to a US ideological agenda and timetable. The report states:

> The UK had to work to a timetable and strong ideological views set in the United States. As one Senior Officer put it: "the train was in Grand Central Station, and was leaving at a time which we did not control."

The combined secrecy and ideology was a planning disaster that directly led to the devastation of Iraqi society. Not only was the military at large kept in the dark until the end of 2002, but contractors vital to the reconstruction and stabilization of the country were not contacted until the end of the invasion in late April 2003:

> The requirements to plan, find resources for, and undertake interim government and reconstruction in Iraq, the non-military tasks, were discussed in outline across Whitehall, but approaches

to potential contractors were not made until combat operations were coming to an end. Planning was not done in sufficient depth, and, at the outset of Phase IV [post combat operations] little finance was requested (and approved) for reconstruction purposes ... [T]he UK Government, which spent millions of pounds on resourcing the Security Line of Operations, spent virtually none on the Economic one, on which security depended.

The report argues that the result was a breach of Geneva Convention obligations, for which coalition governments are legally responsible.[206]

The invasion of Iraq has long been criticized for being a war for oil and for years many commentators sought information on whether Britain would encourage its oil companies to profit from this widely-condemned war. A US cable of April 2009, six years after the invasion of Iraq, shows Peter Mandelson, a chief architect of Tony Blair's election wins and trade secretary in the Brown government, pushing British oil and other corporate interests in Iraq. Mandelson attended the Basrah Investment Conference, which brought together 23 UK-based companies such as Shell, BP, Rolls Royce, and HSBC. The region was significant to the UK since this was the principal area occupied by UK military forces after the 2003 invasion.

The US cable notes: "According to Basrah HMG officials, UK delegates were able to establish or strengthen relationships with key business figures in Basrah." Attendees also included the directors of oil investment in Basrah and the commander of Iraqi security forces in the region alongside "UK Force Commander Tom Beckett and several Basrah-based UK military officials." The cable added:

---

[206] Julian Assange, "Leaked UK report damns Iraq war planning," *WikiLeaks*, August 6, 2008, https://wikileaks.org/wiki/Leaked_UK_report_damns_Iraq_war_planning.

Lord Mandelson opened the conference by looking back at the UK's long relationship with Basrah, and looked forward to closer economic cooperation ahead . . . The conference also demonstrated to local players that there are serious and respected UK multinational companies ready to do business in Basrah.[207]

The special relationship

The UK under the premierships of Tony Blair and Gordon Brown is often seen in the WikiLeaks publications as acting duplicitously at US behest. In September 2006, for example, a US cable notes that the UK government "agreed to our request" to lobby four other governments in support of Guatemala's bid for the Latin American and Caribbean Group seat on the UN Security Council. The reason was specifically to prevent Venezuela, under socialist president Hugo Chavez, from accessing the seat. "Our demarche was timely," the US official in the London embassy notes, since the FCO director for international security, Stephen Pattison, "has been encouraging the Foreign Office leadership to be more aggressive in supporting Guatemala given the stakes. Pattison and several others at the FCO have told us the idea of Venezuela on the Council would be 'ghastly.'"[208]

In one of the most reported WikiLeaks revelations, the UK is shown to have gone to disturbing lengths to support its US ally. The UK has long fought to prevent the Chagos islanders returning to their homeland, and

---

[207] "Public Library of US Diplomacy, Basrah: United Kingdom Hosts Investment Conference," *WikiLeaks*, April 14, 2009, https://WikiLeaks.org/plusd/cables/09BASRAH18_a.html.

[208] "Public Library of US Diplomacy, UK agrees to limited lobbying for Guatemala's UNSC Bid," *WikiLeaks*, September 12, 2006, https://WikiLeaks.org/plusd/cables/06LONDON6591_a.html. Phil Miller, "Britain's dirty war on Venezuela at UN revealed: Diplomats sabotaged socialist country's security council candidacy," Morning Star, February 14, 2019, https://morningstaronline.co.uk/article/splash-venezuela-winning-un-security-council-seat-would-be-ghastly.

its main island, Diego Garcia, after forcibly removing them in the 1960s. A 2009 cable from the US embassy in London notes that a senior UK Foreign Office official informed the US that the UK wanted to establish a "'marine park' or 'reserve'" around the British Indian Ocean Territory, the UK overseas territory which includes Chagos. This was clearly a ruse concocted by Whitehall to keep the islanders from returning. The cable notes that the "former inhabitants would find it difficult, if not impossible, to pursue their claim for resettlement on the islands if the entire Chagos Archipelago were a marine reserve."

However, US interests would be protected. The cable notes that the establishment of such a reserve "would in no way impinge on USG [US government] use of . . . Diego Garcia, for military purposes."[209] In addition, the UK official "agreed that the UK and US should carefully negotiate the details of the marine reserve to assure that US interests were safeguarded."[210]

WikiLeaks' files also challenge the claim that British decision-making on Trident, the UK's nuclear program, is truly independent of the US. In September 2009, Prime Minister Gordon Brown raised the prospect at the UN General Assembly of reducing the number of British nuclear-armed Trident submarines from four to three. Brown stated that "all nuclear weapons states must play their part in reducing nuclear weapons as part of an agreement by non-nuclear states to renounce them" and described his proposal as a "grand global bargain between nuclear weapon and non-nuclear weapons states."[211]

---

[209] "Public Library of US Diplomacy," *WikiLeaks*, https://WikiLeaks.org/plusd/cables/09LONDON1156_a.html.

[210] "Public Library of US Diplomacy, HMG Floats Proposal for Marine Reserve Covering the Chagos Archipelago (British Indian Ocean Territory)," *WikiLeaks*, May 15, 2009, https://WikiLeaks.org/plusd/cables/09LONDON1156_a.html.

[211] "Public Library of US Diplomacy, PM Brown's Decision to Consider Reducing the UK's Trident Nuclear Deterrent," *WikiLeaks*, September 24, 2009, https://WikiLeaks.org/plusd/cables/09LONDON2222_a.html

As ever, any reduction in UK military forces was likely to be bitterly opposed in Washington. A WikiLeaks publication shows that Julian Miller, the deputy head of the Foreign and Defense Policy Secretariat at the Cabinet Office, privately assured US officials that his government "would consult with the US regarding future developments concerning the Trident deterrent to assure there would be 'no daylight' between the US and UK".[212]

The UK and US have also worked together to prevent reform of the world financial system. In May 2009, Douglas Alexander, secretary of state for International Development and John Sawers, then UK permanent representative to the UN who later that year became chief of MI6, held a meeting with US ambassador to the UN, Susan Rice. A US cable notes that:

> *Alexander and Sawers began the meeting by noting their concern that Cuba, Iran, Venezuela and other "radical" G-77 countries would use the upcoming June 1–2 UN Conference on the World Financial and Economic Crisis and its Impact on Development to push for an outcome document that would for the first time give the UN General Assembly a role in negotiations on revamping the Bretton Woods financial institutions and the world financial system.*

To counter this:

> *Sawers urged the United States to work with the UK to monitor preparatory meetings for the conference, quickly push back against the introduction of activist policy language into the outcome document, and split off more moderate G-77 countries who are already G-20 members.*

Rice agreed, stating that:

[212] Ibid. https://WikiLeaks.org/plusd/cables/09LONDON2222_a.html.

It would be important to work with the Netherlands (a co-facilitator for the negotiations on a conference outcome document) to tone down expectations and ensure that moderate G-77 countries continue to see the G-20 discussions as the proper venue for discussing BWI [Bretton Woods Institutions] reform.[213]

Conniving with the Saudis

The WikiLeaks documents additionally reveal something of the sycophantic relationship that the governments of Tony Blair and David Cameron had with Saudi Arabia. No single policy in this area was more controversial that Blair's decision in 2006 to drop the corruption investigation into British defense contractor BAE's £43-billion arms deal with Saudi Arabia, known as Al-Yamamah.

The UK's Serious Fraud Office (SFO) ended the inquiry after intense diplomatic pressure from the Saudis. A US cable published by WikiLeaks, written four months after the collapse of the investigation, shows the SFO had evidence that BAE paid £73 million to a Saudi prince who had "influence" over the arms contract and that there were "reasonable grounds" to believe another "very senior Saudi official" received payments.[214] Sir Sherard Cowper-Coles, then British ambassador in Riyadh who became a BAE Systems director, "had a profound effect" on the decision by Robert Wardle, then SFO director, to end the investigation. The cable also noted the Italian government's view that the UK decision "seemed to be exclu-

---

[213] "Public Library of US Diplomacy, Ambassador Rice Meets with UK Minister For Development Douglas Alexander," *WikiLeaks*, May 5, 2009, https://WikiLeaks.org/plusd/cables/09USUNNEWYORK458_a.html

[214] "Public Library of US Diplomacy, OECD: U.K.'s Briefing on Terminated BAE/Saudi Arabia Foreign Bribery Case to the Working Group on Bribery, January 16, 2007," *WikiLeaks*, March 5, 2007, https://WikiLeaks.org/plusd/cables/07PARIS829_a.html.

sively supported by economic interests," not national security, as claimed by Whitehall. [215]

Another US cable shows that the Canadian delegation to the Organization for Economic Co-operation and Development (OECD) Working Group on Bribery, which discussed the Saudi bribery case, "had serious concerns about the UK's legal framework and adequacy of its corporate criminal liability legislation," while the US delegation

> *asked whether the UK could provide any assurances that BAE was not continuing to make corrupt payments to Saudi officials and that MOD officials were not continuing to participate in the alleged corrupt payments.*[216]

WikiLeaks exposed the Cameron government's special relationship with Saudi Arabia in its release of files on the Saudi Foreign Ministry. An extraordinary cable from 2013 shows that Britain conducted secret vote-trading deals with Saudi Arabia to ensure both states were elected to the UN human rights council—a major diplomatic gain for Riyadh given its notorious human rights abuses.[217] One cable reads:

> *The ministry might find it an opportunity to exchange support with the United Kingdom, where the Kingdom of Saudi Arabia would support the candidacy of the United Kingdom to the membership*

[215] Ibid. https://WikiLeaks.org/plusd/cables/07PARIS829_a.html.

[216] "Public Library of US Diplomacy, OECD: Report of March 12-14, 2007 Meeting of the Working Group on Bribery," *WikiLeaks,* July 25, 2007, https://WikiLeaks.org/plusd/cables/07PARIS3181_a.html.

[217] Owen Bowcott, "UK and Saudi Arabia 'in secret deal' over human rights council place," *The Guardian,* September 29, 2015, https://www.theguardian.com/uk-news/2015/sep/29/uk-and-saudi-arabia-in-secret-deal-over-human-rights-council-place.

> *of the council for the period 2014–2015 in exchange for the support of the United Kingdom to the candidacy of the Kingdom of Saudi Arabia.*[218]

Another cable shows that Saudi Arabia transferred $100,000 for "expenditures resulting from the campaign to nominate the Kingdom for membership of the human rights council for the period 2014–2016."[219] It was unclear where or how this money was spent.

Assange's role in combatting secrecy

The treatment—real and threatened—meted out to Julian Assange by the US and UK governments contrasts sharply with the service WikiLeaks has done their publics in revealing the nature of elite power. One would think that all journalists, in particular, would be on the side of those revealing secrets rather than on the side of those in the state who seek to punish them. But unfortunately, corporate media hostility toward Julian Assange in the UK is extreme, covering both the "liberal" and right-wing media, with the *Guardian* most noticeable in its vilification.[220] This says a lot about in whose interests the elite media functions.

This is all the more extraordinary given how otherwise difficult it is to discover the true nature of UK policy-making. UK governments have regularly destroyed the historical government files that are meant to be

---

[218] Ibid.

[219] Ibid.

[220] Tom Coburg, "Guilty by innuendo: the Guardian campaign against Julian Assange that breaks all the rules," *the Canary*, December 20, 2018, https://www.thecanary.co/global/world-analysis/2018/12/20/guilty-by-innuendo-the-guardian-campaign-against-julian-assange-that-breaks-all-the-rules/.

declassified and open to the public.[221] Freedom of Information requests are routinely turned down on the spurious grounds of "national security." There have been few whistleblowers involved in foreign policy-making who have revealed important secrets. Thus, the WikiLeaks model is especially important for the UK, which desperately needs more of such revelations.

The real importance of Julian Assange's publication activities is that they are consistent with, and promote, the democracy that elites like to say we already enjoy; the same elite's repression of Assange and his activities are in reality consistent with the dictatorships and oligarchies they claim to oppose.

---

[221] "Declassified: Censorship of Documents," *Mark Curtis*, January 19, 2018, http://markcurtis.info/2018/01/19/censorship-of-documents/.

7. INSIDE THE WIKILEAKS REVOLUTION

Stefania Maurizi, February 2019

When the telephone rang it was late at night. I struggled to get out of the bed, but in the end, I answered. "This is WikiLeaks," a voice said on the line. I was barely cognizant when I was told that I had one hour to download an audiofile from the Internet, after which WikiLeaks would remove it to avoid the risk of its download by someone else. The file was a secret recording related to a major Italian scandal. "Could you please help verify whether it is genuine?" WikiLeaks asked me.

At that time in July 2009, I was working for what was one of Italy's most aggressive media outlets: *l'Espresso*, a major progressive weekly with a notable tradition in investigative journalism. Because the audiofile was genuine and newsworthy, I published an article about it in *l'Espresso*,[222] while WikiLeaks published the original audio on its website.[223] That was

---

[222] See Stefania Maurizi, "Dai rifiuti spunta lo 007," *la Repubblica, L'Espresso*, August 6, 2009, http://espresso.repubblica.it/palazzo/2009/08/06/news/dai-rifiuti-spunta-lo-007-1.15163.

[223] See Stefania Maurizi, "Dai rifiuti spunta lo 007," *WikiLeaks*, August 6, 2009, https://wikileaks.org/wiki/Dai_rifiuti_spunta_lo_007.

the first time I published something in partnership with WikiLeaks. This was before Assange's organization revealed bombshells like the "Collateral Murder" video in April 2010. Few had ever heard of WikiLeaks. To say the least, it was the start of an intense professional experience.

Over the past decade, I've worked as a media partner with WikiLeaks, initially for *l'Espresso*, and then for my current newspaper, the major Italian daily *la Repubblica*. I verify, investigate, and publish stories based on all their secret documents, except the very few that WikiLeaks has handled themselves. The disruption and intrigue Julian Assange's organization injected into my journalistic work that night has not yet come to an end.

That bunch of lunatics

But it all started the year prior to that phone call. Back in 2008, one of my journalistic sources had suddenly cut off all contact out of fear of exposure. That episode made me realize how vulnerable my communications with my sources were. Before going into journalism I had obtained a degree in mathematics, so it was natural for me to consider cryptography as a tool for protection. "You should take a look at that bunch of lunatics," one of my sources in the crypto field advised me, with clear sympathy for WikiLeaks, which had been created just two years before.

That tip put "the lunatics" on my radar for the first time, prompting me to venture my first contact with them. They were pioneering a new model of aggressive journalism, in which cryptography was a crucial element. After WikiLeaks exploded into global renown with the publication of "Collateral Murder" and then the Afghan War Logs—91,920 secret files revealing the true face of the war in Afghanistan—I booked a meeting with Julian Assange in Berlin.

I met Assange on September 27, 2010. The Pentagon was furious with him and his organization for publishing those secret documents.

The heroic whistleblower who had leaked the secret files, Chelsea Manning, had been arrested just a few weeks after the release of "Collateral Murder."

WikiLeaks' founder arrived at my hotel in Berlin around 11 p.m. A few minutes later, Kristinn Hrafnsson—then WikiLeaks' spokesperson and now its editor—joined us in the hotel lobby. Assange had no luggage; it had disappeared in his direct flight from Sweden. I later learned that the missing baggage didn't just contain socks: it held encrypted laptops, which never surfaced again.

The next morning, Assange, Hrafnsson, and I walked to an Internet café in Alexanderplatz. Assange put two or maybe three mobile phones on the table, which he had kept disassembled most of the time. Suddenly one of the phones rang—it was his Swedish lawyer. The Swedish prosecutor, Marianne Ny, had issued a warrant for his arrest to question him about rape allegations of two Swedish women. The case had been opened August 20, just four weeks following the publication of the Afghan War Logs, then immediately closed, and reopened again on September 1. I left Assange in Alexanderplatz that first day of September 2010. It was the last time I would see him as a free man.

Fearless journalism

Working with WikiLeaks as a media partner has never been easy, but it has always been compelling. What happens when a media organization has the full force of the State against it—when it publishes millions of secret documents about the "invisible power," and does so consistently, not occasionally like all the other media outlets? That is what WikiLeaks has done throughout its twelve years of existence.

There are different levels of power in our societies. The visible ones are obvious: officials who have a political role, for example, are often involved in crimes like corruption. Usually, investigating the "visible levels" via journalistic activities is fully tolerated in our liberal democracies. Journalists may be hit by libel cases, and exposing political corruption may prove a liability for their careers, but it is widely accepted in our democracies. The problem arises when journalists touch the highest level, where states and intelligence services operate. Thick layers of secrecy protect this level of power from scrutiny and legitimate accountability; power doesn't like the sunlight, it has a terrible phobia of continuous exposure.

WikiLeaks has published numerous secret documents from clandestine entities like the Pentagon, the CIA, and the NSA for years. We can imagine what it meant for the US national security complex to witness the disclosure of 76,000 of its secret documents related to the war in Afghanistan, and then 390,000 secret reports about the war in Iraq, followed by 251,287 US diplomatic cables and 779 secret files on the Guantánamo detainees.

We can imagine how it was perceived in an environment like the United States, where for years even the top US national security reporters didn't dare publish the name of the head of the CIA Counterterrorism Center, Michael D'Andrea, even though his name and the egregious abuses committed by his center were an open secret in journalist circles. His name was finally published by *New York Times* reporter Mark Mazzetti. "People were scared of him," US intelligence officials had told the *Washington Post*, "Roger [D'Andrea's cover name] was 'the undertaker.'"

You need incredible bravery to reveal thousands of secrets about these powerful individuals and entities for over a decade. You need incredible bravery both as a leaker of those secrets and as a publisher with the guts to make them public—and take massive heat.

Risk

During my time as a media partner, I have seen Assange and his entire team of journalists and tech people at WikiLeaks take immense legal and extralegal risks. To protect himself and his organization, Assange has always avoided revealing the inner workings of WikiLeaks, its resources and vulnerabilities, to powerful entities like the CIA or the Pentagon, which see WikiLeaks as an existential threat. This approach has helped project an aura of mystery and menace over WikiLeaks; many media outlets have crafted and used that peculiarity to fuel a vitriolic campaign against Assange and his organization, framing them as James Bond-style villains with something despicable to hide. What is beyond the veil, however, is a willingness to take on powers no other media organization could even begin to shoulder.

We have seen what happened with Edward Snowden, one of the most important journalistic sources of all time. Had it not been for Julian Assange and the WikiLeaks investigations editor at the time, Sarah Harrison, who flew to Hong Kong to assist him, and who remained in Moscow's Sheremetyevo airport for 40 days until he obtained temporary asylum in Russia, Snowden would be in the US right now—in a maximum-security prison.

Journalism and beyond

The impact of WikiLeaks has been considerable. It pioneered a model so effective that it has been copied by many. It started a platform for the anonymous submission of secret or otherwise restricted documents, a concept that has since been adopted by almost all major media outlets. It also established cross-jurisdictional collaborative reporting, now a model for major organizations like the Consortium of Investigative Journalists, which published the Panama Papers.

The publication's strategy has proved successful: the exiled islanders from the Chagos Archipelago, for example, have been using the US diplomacy cables disclosed by WikiLeaks in court to support their struggle to return to their homeland.[224] A German citizen, Khaled el-Masri, used the cables to support his case at the European Court of Human Rights against his extraordinary rendition,[225] while the *Washington Post* recently used the Hacking Team emails to shed light on the assassination of the Saudi journalist, Jamal Khashoggi.[226]

Making millions of secret documents fully available to anyone is a very challenging operation. In fact, no other media partnerships have done so. The Consortium of Investigative Journalists has never made the full documents of its prominent scoops like the Panama Papers available to the public. Unfortunately, it must be admitted that on some occasions WikiLeaks has performed this task very poorly, publishing personal information which should have been redacted and has allowed critics to say that the organization just dumps stuff on the Internet. But it doesn't.

The kremlin's useful idiots?

The talent and bravery of Julian Assange and the WikiLeaks journalists have been tarnished by repeated allegations that they have, willingly or unwillingly, acted as pawns for the Kremlin—that they are Russia's useful

---

[224] "Public Library of US Diplomacy, HMG Floats Proposal for Marine Reserve Covering the Chagos Archipelago (British Indian Ocean Territory)," *WikiLeaks*, May 15, 2009, https://wikileaks.org/plusd/cables/09LONDON1156_a.html.

[225] "Case of El-Masri v. The Former Yugoslav Republic of Macedonia," *European Court of Human Rights*, December 13, 2012, https://hudoc.echr.coe.int/eng#{%22ite mid%22:[%22001-115621%22]}.

[226] "How a chilling Saudi cyberwar ensnared Jamal Khashoggi," The Washington Post, December 7, 2018, https://www.washingtonpost.com/opinions/global-opin ions/how-a-chilling-saudi-cyberwar-ensnared-jamal-khashoggi/2018/12/07/ f5f048fe-f975-11e8-8c9a-860ce2a8148f_story.html?noredirect=on&utm_term=. a01d366aab15.

idiots. These allegations have been regurgitated by the media without any solid evidence. Reports always quote anonymous intelligence officials, who have an obvious interest in destroying WikiLeaks' reputation.

I remember the first time this smear surfaced prominently in the press. It was 2012. Assange appeared on his TV show, *The World Tomorrow*, and the London newspaper the *Guardian* fiercely attacked him for broadcasting it on the Russian state-owned TV channel, Russia Today—currently RT. In reality, the broadcasting license for *The World Tomorrow* was acquired by my newsgroup as well, which publishes *la Repubblica* and *l'Espresso*. In fact, we broadcasted the show. As far as I know, that program was not the product of any unique collaboration between WikiLeaks and RT. Nonetheless, it has been trumpeted endlessly in press reports as produced in direct cooperation with the Kremlin.

It is true that Assange and his staff have appeared on RT many times, but I have only heard of one instance in which RT partnered with WikiLeaks in the publication of confidential files: The "Spy Files,"[227] a leak consisting of the brochures of private companies selling surveillance technologies. When WikiLeaks collaborates with traditional media, the partners know each other and share the workload. Though to my knowledge RT was a media partner of WikiLeaks' just once, it is true that RT quickly jumps on whatever WikiLeaks publishes, running articles on the organization's publications based on press releases and reporting on every development in the Assange/WikiLeaks saga.

Why does Russia ensure Assange receives such wide coverage? Clearly, the Kremlin enjoys some of the WikiLeaks releases, like those exposing the Pentagon or the CIA. For Russia is happy to stick a finger in the eye of the West by highlighting the contradictions in our democracies, which, while preaching aggressive journalism, have put Chelsea Manning

---

[227] "Spy Files," *WikiLeaks*, https://wikileaks.org/spyfiles/.

in prison, forced Snowden to seek asylum, and kept Assange arbitrarily detained in one way or another for the last nine years.

In bed with donald trump?

The allegations against WikiLeaks intensified during the 2016 US elections, after Assange and his staff published the Democratic National Committee emails[228] and those of the chairman of Hillary Clinton's campaign, John Podesta.[229] Many newspapers have accused WikiLeaks of being part of a conspiracy between Russia and the Trump campaign. Once again, no evidence whatsoever has been made public in support of this.

I was a partner in the publication of the Podesta emails. I don't claim to know the truth about what happened. I can only relate the facts as I have witnessed them. As I write, Robert Mueller's investigation into so-called Russiagate is still ongoing. As of today, I have not seen any evidence of conspiracy, and some of the details of the Russiagate narrative clash with what I saw and what I know.

The Podesta emails were published by WikiLeaks in several batches. I vividly remember that after intense criticism for publishing the full DNC emails dataset all at once, and with very little content curation, WikiLeaks wanted to do the right thing: this time the files would be published in waves so that journalists and the public could make sense of the information. Unfortunately, this choice was criticized too; it was perceived as a malicious attempt to make Hillary Clinton bleed for weeks throughout the month before the elections.

The first batch of Podesta emails was released on October 7, 2016, the day before the second presidential debate. Publishing before a crucial event for maximum impact is a typical WikiLeaks strategy. The first Podesta

---

[228] "Search the DNC email database," *WikiLeaks*, https://wikileaks.org//dnc-emails/.

[229] "The Podesta Emails," *WikiLeaks*, https://wikileaks.org/podesta-emails/.

emails were made public shortly after the *Washington Post* published the infamous *Access Hollywood* tape in which candidate Trump made reprehensible remarks about women. Many newspapers reported this timing as one of the most suspicious indications of collusion between WikiLeaks and the Trump campaign to counter the impact of the *Access Hollywood* tape, which had indeed been damaging for Trump. Because I worked on the Podesta emails, I know for a fact that the publication was not a last-second, opportunistic decision. I had been alerted the day before.

I did not appreciate WikiLeaks exchanging direct Twitter messages with Donald Trump Jr., or with Roger Stone, and I did not appreciate WikiLeaks re-tweeting some reactionary individuals connected to the Trump campaign. Regardless, I do believe that publishing the DNC and Podesta emails, which were widely covered by prominent news outlets like the *New York Times*, was the right thing to do. The documents revealed the sabotage of Bernie Sanders by party officials—a revelation which led the chairwoman of the Democratic National Committee, Debbie Wasserman Schultz, to resign—and they revealed Hillary Clinton's speeches to Goldman Sachs behind closed doors. Even the *Times* editorial board had called for Clinton to release those "richly paid speeches to big banks, which many middle-class Americans still blame for their economic pain."

The demonization of julian assange and wikileaks' journalists

Over these last ten years, I have been able to work on all secret WikiLeaks documents without fear of being arrested, threatened or detained for what I have published. For Julian Assange and his staff, on the other hand, things have gone much differently. As I have said, I never saw Assange a free man after that meeting in Berlin in 2010. I have met with him many, many times, but he remains confined; first, under house arrest with an electronic bracelet around his ankle, then within the Ecuadorian embassy in London beginning on June 19, 2012.

As I write, he is still buried in there, with no access to sunlight and no proper medical treatment. With no end in sight, this arbitrary detention would be a hell for anyone, but it is a unique hell for a man who is as rootless and as free like the air as Julian Assange.

He is the most demonized man on the planet. He is doubtlessly a complicated human being, but he is neither a hard man nor a cartoon villain. He is very talented and brilliant, a true strategist who understands power. He is brave and can be warm and funny. It is tragic to see him in seriously declining health, while he spends his days between four walls, most of the time completely alone.

If he and his former and current WikiLeaks journalists Sarah Harrison, Kristinn Hrafnsson, and Joseph Farrell—and many other journalists and tech people whose identities have never emerged publicly—end up imprisoned in the US, it is not hard to imagine how they will be treated. It will be devastating for their human rights and freedom, but also for press freedom; it will be the first time a publisher and a leader of a media organization has been imprisoned in the US for his work.

The prosecution of Julian Assange and WikiLeaks will be used as a picklock to seriously undermine the press' role in exposing the highest levels of power (the CIA, the Pentagon, and the National Security State more generally), just as "fighting terror" has been used since 9/11 to justify erosion of fundamental rights around the globe, and to make them acceptable to the public.

I want to see Julian Assange and his team free and safe because I want to live in a society where journalists and their sources can expose evil without having to flee to Russia or to risk their necks. That is what freedom of the press is to me.

8. ASSANGE AND WHISTLEBLOWERS

Jesselyn Radack, January 2019

The US government has been engaged in a decades-long effort to criminalize both journalism and whistleblowing. The outlet most in the crosshairs today is the transparency organization WikiLeaks, and even more specifically, its controversial founder and publisher, Julian Assange. The squeeze has been felt by everyone—from donors stymied by a financial blockade, to individuals punished for their mere association with them. I know this firsthand. Before one of my visits with Assange, I was detained and interrogated by Border Force at Heathrow Airport about my plans with and connections to him—a blatant violation of the fundamental freedoms of speech and association recognized in both the UK and the US.

WikiLeaks rose to international prominence in April 2010 with its release of the chilling "Collateral Murder" video. It opened a new chapter on government transparency and accountability in the twenty-first century, at a time when the United States, its growing intelligence apparatus, and its counterparts in other countries (both friendly and hostile) were becoming increasingly powerful and secretive.

That same month, President Obama unleashed a heavy-handed criminal campaign against whistleblowers. I represented a number of them.

Former NSA senior executive Thomas Drake became the first person this century to be charged under the draconian Espionage Act for allegedly sharing government secrets with the media. The Espionage Act is a World War I law meant to go after spies, not whistleblowers.

Although the government's case against Drake ultimately collapsed, the prosecution publicly vilified him as an "enemy of the state"—a stigma that still affects his life today. Julian Assange was one of the only publishers on the planet who immediately, vociferously, and without reservation condemned the Drake indictment.

As one of Drake's attorneys, I believe that Assange displayed enormous journalistic integrity and moral courage to speak truth to the most powerful nation in the world, especially when the mainstream media stayed silent. Assange's intervention helped change the conversation in both the courtroom and the court of public opinion. Assange and WikiLeaks amplified by an order of magnitude my argument that the "leaks" being prosecuted consisted of information that was in the public interest to know. Indeed, the leaks punished most harshly revealed some of the government's darkest secrets in modern history: war crimes (Chelsea Manning); NSA's mass secret surveillance (Thomas Drake and Edward Snowden); and CIA torture (John Kiriakou). Assange advocated for all of them and, despite his own increasingly perilous circumstances, continued to be outspoken as recently as 2018 in the criminal case against Air Force veteran and whistleblower Reality Winner.

In the process, Assange pioneered a new model of source protection—not one grounded on the reporter's privilege and fuzzy or elastic definitions of confidentiality, but rather one that married documentary evidence with technology, anonymity, and encryption. Numerous journalists and news outlets now use secure, online, open-source submission systems.

Assange also had the prescience to call out the dangerous war on whistleblowers as a back-door war on journalists—and a free press more generally—which is coming to full fruition under President Trump. It is a tragic irony that Assange himself is now one of the central targets of this misguided and retaliatory campaign.

Assange understood that information is the currency of power, and a free and independent press is not only a pillar of democracy, but also an important feature of civilized society itself. Documents published by WikiLeaks have exposed a secret war in Yemen, illuminated state-sponsored human rights abuses in Iraq and Afghanistan, and revealed presidential complicity in torture and other war crimes. How we treat Assange is a harbinger of how we will treat journalists, sources, activists, and dissidents in the future. If Assange or WikiLeaks is criminally prosecuted, the *New York Times* and its reporters are equally vulnerable. It is tragic that in trying to preserve civil liberties, government accountability, and individual privacy rights for everyone, Assange has lost so many of his own. Only by allowing him to exercise the asylum he has been lawfully granted due to persecution for his political beliefs and expression will we truly preserve the values that are the hallmark of a free and open democratic society.

9. ASSANGE AND THE CORPORATE MEDIA'S DEMARCATION PROBLEM[230]

John C. O'Day, June 5, 2019

After British police arrested Julian Assange on April 11, the first instinct of corporate journalists was to perform a line-drawing exercise. In so doing, corporate media dutifully laid the groundwork for the US Department of Justice's escalating political persecution of the WikiLeaks founder, and set the stage for a renewed assault on a free and independent press by the Trump administration.

Following the philosopher of science Karl Popper,[231] I'll call this the *problem of journalistic demarcation*. Facing his own demarcation problem in 1953, Popper set out "to distinguish between science and pseudoscience." This philosophical exercise had an overtly political purpose: Popper hoped to draw his line in such a way as to specifically exclude Marxism

---

[230] This piece was originally published by Fairness & Accuracy In Reporting. John C. O'Day, "Corporate Media Have Second Thoughts About Exiling Julian Assange From Journalism," FAIR, June 5, 2019, https://fair.org/home/media-cheer-assanges-arrest/.

[231] See "Karl Popper," *Stanford Encyclopedia of Philosophy*, first published November 13, 1997, revision August 7, 2018, https://plato.stanford.edu/entries/popper/.

from the ranks of scientific theory. Stripping Marxism of its claim to scientific status would help undermine the legitimacy of a political movement that, at the time, posed a serious challenge to the ascendancy of Western capitalist powers following World War II.

The problem of journalistic demarcation is no less ideologically motivated and, through their effort to discredit Assange and WikiLeaks, corporate media have snugly aligned themselves with the contemporary brokers of US imperial power against a journalistic movement that, over the last decade, has presented them with their most significant challenge.

As Assange's asylum was violated and he was dragged out of the Ecuadorian embassy in London at the behest of US authorities, the DOJ[232] unsealed an indictment against him carrying one conspicuously minor charge. Despite their much-ballyhooed skepticism toward the Trump administration, corporate media instantly took the bait and drew their line.

Alan McLeod detailed for FAIR.org (4/18/19)[233] that, because the Trump administration had "done well" by only charging Assange with conspiracy to "hack" a government computer, the prevailing corporate media response was to exclude him from the ranks of journalism. "If Assange Burgled Some Computers, He Stopped Being a Journalist," read a paradigmatic headline at Bloomberg (4/11/19). This reaction intersected normal partisan boundaries, with a similar line collectively drawn by the *Washington Post* (4/11/19), *National Review* (4/12/19), and Fox News (4/12/19).

Individual journalists also took to social media to exile Assange from their profession. Katie Benner, a Justice Department reporter for the *New York Times*, tweeted (4/11/19) that true journalists "don't help sources pick the locks on the safes that hold the information." David Corn

---

[232] US Department of Justice.

[233] This article can be found in the first section of this collection.

(Twitter, 4/11/19), the DC bureau chief for *Mother Jones*, similarly drew a line between himself and Assange: "As a journalist, I've been careful to distinguish between accepting info and inducing or helping leakers break laws to obtain information," he declared.

When the US DOJ predictably superseded its initial indictment of Assange on May 23, charging him with 17 additional counts of espionage, corporate media's demarcation problem just as predictably blew up in their faces. As assistant attorney general John Demers announced the new charges, he boldly traced the all-important line, guided by corporate media's hand: "Julian Assange is no journalist," he asserted.

Because the new indictment is significantly more severe and relates to WikiLeaks' publication of classified material, not just with how that material was obtained, corporate media are now unsurprisingly questioning the line they were so eager to draw. The *New York Times* (5/23/19) no longer thinks the Trump administration is doing well by Assange. Bloomberg (5/23/19), the *Washington Post* (5/24/19), and Fox News (5/30/19) are also having second thoughts.

David Corn (Twitter, 5/25/19), for whom the line was so clear a month ago, now sees "a threat to journalists." Katie Benner apparently deleted her previous demarcation tweet and has since contributed to a new article (*New York Times*, 5/23/19) about the "frightening charges" now facing Assange.

It is impossible to accept that corporate media were simply naïve to the inevitability of further charges against Assange. Moreover, we have known all along that, as C. W. Anderson said nearly ten years ago, "it's very hard to draw a line that excludes WikiLeaks and includes the *New York Times*" (CFR, 12/23/10). So why the sudden change of heart?

Here Popper's demarcation question about science becomes relevant, not only formally but also substantively, because WikiLeaks is a vehicle for what Assange calls "scientific journalism"—an approach that threatens corporate journalism.

Assange wrote in a 2010 op-ed that WikiLeaks aspires to "work with other media outlets to bring people the news, but also to prove it is true." "Scientific journalism," he explained,

> allows you to read a story, then to click online to see the original document it is based on. That way you can judge for yourself: is the story true? Did the journalist report it accurately?

This considerably ups the ante in terms of professional accountability for journalists. While corporate media are content with sourcing "people familiar with the documents," for WikiLeaks obtaining and publishing those documents is not just a bonus or a lucky break, it is a requirement.

This documentation-based journalism precludes the blockbuster fabrications that make corporate media boatloads of money, from never-opened bridges in Venezuela[234] to the entire #Russiagate debacle. Readers can't click online to see whether the *Guardian*'s story (11/27/18) about a secret meeting between Paul Manafort and Assange is true, because it simply isn't true.[235]

So long as the persecution of Assange seemed only to do with his particular style of journalism, corporate media were happy to throw him under the bus. Now seeing that their own jobs could get caught up in the

---

[234] Adam Johnson, "Western Media Fail in Lockstep for Cheap Trump/Rubio Venezuela Aid PR Stunt," *FAIR*, February 9, 2019, *https://fair.org/home/western-media-fall-in-lockstep-for-cheap-trump-rubio-venezuela-aid-pr-stunt/*.

[235] Glenn Greenwald, "Five Weeks After The Guardian's Viral Blockbuster Assange-Manafort Scoop, No Evidence Has Emerged—Just Stonewalling," *The Intercept*, January 2, 2019, https://theintercept.com/2019/01/02/five-weeks-after-the-guardians-viral-blockbuster-assangemanafort-scoop-no-evidence-has-emerged-just-stonewalling/.

collateral damage (Consortium News, 6/5/19), all of a sudden corporate media are scrambling to erase their line.

Meanwhile, much has been made, both by corporate media and the US officials pursuing him, of Assange's supposedly inadequate harm-prevention effort in releasing unredacted classified documents. Marc Theissen of the *Washington Post* (5/28/19), for example, reproduced the US's latest indictment at length to illustrate the "unfathomable damage" allegedly caused by WikiLeaks as it revealed actual crimes perpetrated by the US military.

Aside from the fact that there is no harm-prevention proviso in the First Amendment, and the further fact that the Pentagon previously could not demonstrate any harm stemming from the disclosures in question, it was actually the *Guardian* that released the password to the unredacted Cablegate archive (WikiLeaks, 9/1/11). *Guardian* editors disputed WikiLeaks' characterization of this mistake, but not their paper's role in it. Yet no one expects Alan Rusbridger to stand trial, or for the *Washington Post* to clamor to see him in the dock.

Corporate media jealously guard their self-anointed prerogative to set a limit on what the public may know. Ironically, while Popper sought to exclude Marxism from science because it was too occult, corporate media have sought to exclude WikiLeaks from journalism because it is not occult enough. In both cases, however, the division ultimately comes down to ideological rather than semantic lines.

In the wake of the Manning and Snowden leaks, Northeastern University professor Candice Delmas tried to nail down what it is about these events that provokes such uncritical reaction. Government whistle-blowing of the sort WikiLeaks has enabled, she argued, amounts to a kind of "political vigilantism" that "involves violating the moral duty to respect the boundaries around state secrets, for the purpose of challenging the allocation or use of power." This coheres with Assange's own assessment:

"We deal with almost purely political material—I don't mean party-political, I mean how power is delegated," he said in 2011.

Corporate media have made it clear that, Trump or no Trump, they remain ideologically committed to the objectives of US imperialism. Whether inciting war with Iran (FAIR.org, 10/4/18),[236] promoting regime change in Venezuela (FAIR.org, 4/30/19),[237] whitewashing crimes against humanity in Yemen (FAIR.org, 4/9/19),[238] or downplaying the last three decades of occupation in Iraq (FAIR.org, 4/16/19),[239] it is evident that corporate media retain little interest in challenging US imperial power.

Still, one might have thought that, when drawing a line between Pulitzers and prison, corporate media would instinctively err on the side of caution and go to bat for Assange. Instead, their ideological and vocational attachments to US power, along with their professional jealousy and fear of WikiLeaks, rendered him a political target who was simply irresistible ... at least until now.

Corporate media's belated and self-interested reinvestment in the Assange case might have come too late, both legally and with regard to the humanitarian situation. The UN special rapporteur on torture, Nils Melzer, recently reported that Assange's prolonged isolation and crushing political persecution are now manifesting as "intense psychological trauma." Even in a best-case legal scenario, he may never fully recover.

[236] John O'Day, "Trump Admin Follows Corporate Media Playbook for War With Iran," *FAIR*, October 4, 2018, https://fair.org/home/trump-admin-follows-corporate-media-playbook-for-war-with-iran/.

[237] Teddy Ostrow, "Zero Percent of Elite Commentators Oppose Regime Change in Venezuela," *FAIR*, April 30, 2019, https://fair.org/home/zero-percent-of-elite-commentators-oppose-regime-change-in-venezuela/.

[238] Adam Johnson, "Bill to End Yemen Siege Passes—No Thanks to MSNBC," *FAIR*, April 9, 2019, https://fair.org/home/bill-to-end-yemen-siege-passes-no-thanks-to-msnbc/.

[239] Reed Richardson, "Defining Endless War Down," *FAIR*, April 16, 2019, https://fair.org/home/defining-endless-war-down/.

Legally speaking, despite their newfound concern, this isn't the last we will hear of corporate media's demarcation problem. Insofar as the First Amendment issue rides on whether Julian Assange is a journalist, US prosecutors will no doubt introduce the litany of unsympathetic line-drawing exercises provided by corporate media journalists as evidence that he does not qualify for protection. Sadly, this means that, should the Trump administration's campaign succeed, Assange will indeed have been convicted by a jury of his peers.

10. JULIAN AND HIS CREATURES

Natália Viana, February 2019

A couple of years ago, when Julian Assange was still in contact with the outside world from inside the Ecuadorian embassy in London (his Internet was cut off by the government of Lenín Moreno last year), I spoke with him on Christmas Day.

The holiday season has always been a challenge for the leader of WikiLeaks and his staff during his imprisonment in Knightsbridge. With everyone going home to their families and the Internet slowing down significantly, Assange is left alone with his thoughts. I used to hear many of his close friends express concern for his health during this time of the year.

But that afternoon Assange told me he was fine. "I just spent some time looking at the PlusD library," he said. "And I was proud of what I made." PlusD is the huge online archive built by WikiLeaks with US diplomatic cables dating back from the Kissinger era, but also with the 250,000 leaked US embassy cables that brought the organization to worldwide fame—and led to Assange's forced exile in the 30-square-meter premises of the embassy.

His response stuck with me. It was not the self-congratulatory tone one might expect from a man who has been portrayed again and again as an arrogant activist. It was simple and plain. And true. The work that Assange has done in the last decade is, by all means, remarkable.

When I arrived in London on November 18, 2010, I had no clue I was about to take part in the publication of the biggest leak in history—ten days later, Cablegate would change the way the world sees the US, people see their own governments, governments see the disruptive potential of the Internet, and everyone sees journalism. All that I knew was that it was going to be big.

As a freelance investigative journalist from Brazil, I had received an enigmatic phone call four days before. "Hello Natália, I'm with a very influential organization, and I want to offer you a job," said a young lady with a strong British accent. "We are working on a huge project that is going to have enormous repercussions around the world. All my phones are tapped, so it's not safe to tell you details. But I am sure that any journalist would like to be involved," said the staffer, whom I would soon learn worked for WikiLeaks.

In the ten days that followed, I joined a group of youngsters who gathered in the country house in Ellingham Hall in Norfolk to organize, analyze, strategize, and publish the cables relating to almost every country in the world. I was one of a number of independent journalists invited by Assange to help release the cables in different regions. This was Assange's own decision: he knew that no one on his team or at any of the newspapers involved in the first batch of disclosures—the *Guardian*, the *New York Times*, *Le Monde*, *El Pais*, and *Der Spiegel*—had extensive knowledge about local affairs, especially in the global south.

In the smoke screen of news coverage on the US and UK's persecution of Assange, few media organizations reported on his and his team's outstanding accomplishment in the following months: they managed to deliver and publish embassy cables to outlets across dozens of countries—sometimes through intricate digital means, or through much less sophisticated ways like sticking a pen-drive in a bag of dirty clothes.

Independent journalists and activists flocked to Assange from all over the world. Ellingham Hall has ten rooms and four floors linked by a spiral staircase. I shared my room with a Latin American woman who arrived days later. Mostly everyone was busy reading a fantastic amount of information that revealed the inner workings of their own respective governments and elites, but when we took breaks, the discussions were often heated. We worked around the living room fireplace during very cold days and very cold nights. We slept very little: there was so much to do! On the three sofas, up to six people sat engrossed in their laptops.

The situation grew more tense as we approached the release. The Pentagon was well aware of the leak—Private Chelsea Manning had been arrested a couple of months earlier, accused of being the whistleblower. The Pentagon had warned WikiLeaks to return all the secret documents and delete them from its site, or it would "seek alternatives to force them to do the right thing."

A couple of days before the scheduled release, the US State Department scrambled to try to stop us from doing what we knew was the right thing to do. The *New York Times* approached the DOS for comment, and as a pre-emptive measure, then secretary of state Hillary Clinton called every allied government around the world to apologize in advance for the rude comments of her diplomats, and for the secrets that were soon to reach the public eye. The leak would put lives and national interests at risk, said a spokesman. On the days prior to the publication, false "revelations" started sprouting in the media. The strategy was clear: mix misinformation with real information in order to dampen the biggest leak in the history of journalism. Needless to say, it didn't work.

What struck me during those days was a change of paradigm that has since been reinforced again and again: technology changes the structures of power—especially informational power—such that it takes only a small group of people to affect, if not completely change, history.

For me, Cablegate was an eye-opening experience, proof that the information revolution was going to change international politics and the global economy. In summary, you don't need to be rich, or born into aristocracy, to take part in politics and disrupt crucial aspects of our society. In just a decade, we—small groups of young people with laptops sitting in someone's living room—have managed to disrupt everything from the hotel to taxi industries; from the NSA espionage apparatus to electoral systems of several countries.

Of course, not every one of these groups I am referring to acted alone, and for sure, many did not act for the "greater good." Nevertheless, it has never been so easy and so cheap to change the course of history.

This is the new reality of politics, and Assange was without a doubt a visionary. Of course, what we were doing—and what WikiLeaks has made the core of its work—is the exact opposite of what those juveniles were doing in the city of Veles, Macedonia, dishing out pro-Trump fake news during the US election campaign, to mention just one example.

WikiLeaks has always been about spreading *truth*. After countless attempts by the media and a variety of governments and intelligence agencies to discredit WikiLeaks' published materials, whether through intimidation, character assassination, an economic blockade, internal sabotage, fake bait documents, and legal persecution, it is remarkable that the only smear that "stuck" was a narrative in which Assange is somehow entangled in the Russiagate conspiracy theory—that he meddled in the US election by, indeed, exposing the true documents about the failed presidential candidate Hillary Clinton. By exposing the truth!

As Assange completes seven years of imprisonment in the embassy, it is relevant to highlight some of the truths that WikiLeaks has exposed, beyond the DNC emails. To begin with, there was the "Collateral Murder" release of April 2010, showing the US military's unprovoked killing of 12 innocent human beings, including two Reuters employees on July 12, 2007 in Baghdad. Ahead of the release, Reuters had been trying to obtain the video through a Freedom of Information Act request, but to no avail. The US Army investigated the event itself, and unsurprisingly found that their soldiers had done nothing wrong. The WikiLeaks disclosure contradicted the US Army's story with clear, irrefutable evidence.

WikiLeaks also helped shed light on the dealings of Kaupthing bank in Iceland, which was at the heart of the Icelandic financial collapse in 2008. The leaked documents[240] showed that ahead of the collapse, Kaupthing lent more than 6 billion euros to companies connected to just six clients, four of whom were its own shareholders. The revelation caused an uproar in Iceland, and is hailed as a factor in the eventual resignation of the Icelandic government. The protests following the publication were the largest in Icelandic history.

In Tunisia, one of the US government cables released by WikiLeaks exposed the corruption of president Ben Ali and his family. It read: "Whether it's cash, services, land, property, or yes, even your yacht, President Ben Ali's family is rumored to covet it and reportedly gets what it wants."[241] The disclosure humiliated a population crippled by poverty, high inflation, and unemployment. The cables sparked uprisings of millions of

---

[240] See Rowena Mason, "Kaupthing leak exposes loans," *WikiLeaks*, August 4, 2009, https://wikileaks.org/wiki/Kaupthing_leak_exposes_loans.

[241] "Public Library of US Diplomacy, Corruption in Tunisia: What's Yours is Mine," *WikiLeaks*, June 23, 2008, https://wikileaks.org/plusd/cables/08TUNIS679_a.html.

Tunisians in the streets, who then toppled a government that had been in power for 23 years.

No less important was the Cablegate leak that shed light for the first time on the massive surveillance practices of the US government. The cables revealed that the Americans had been spying on UN leaders for years. The Snowden NSA leak, two and a half years later—and inspired by WikiLeaks' work—broadened the world's comprehension of widespread espionage by the US on its allies, enemies, and its own people.

For a Brazilian, the Cablegate trove contained especially important WikiLeaks revelations. A series of six cables[242] sent from Brasilia between 2009 and 2010 detailed how the US embassy and US oil companies were lobbying against legislation by the Lula da Silva government relating to oil exploration. An offshore oil reserve situated below a 2,000-meter-thick layer of salt had been found a couple of years prior. It is estimated to hold 176 billion barrels of crude oil, and its production has tripled in the last four years, reaching 1,500,000 barrels of oil per day in 2018.

The Workers' Party government passed a law that made Brazil's state oil corporation, Petrobras, the leader of all operations in the pre-salt region, with a minimum 30 percent stake. As a result, all foreign companies who wanted to drill the pre-salt would need to join a consortium with Petrobras. The government ensured that most of the subsequent royalties would be reallocated to education.

The cables showed that big oil companies were repeatedly complaining to US diplomats about what they saw as the "political use" of the oil industry. The head of government relations for Chevron, Patricia Pradal, described how the industry had been "fighting a hard battle" to change the legislation; her main issue was that the regulations would make China and

---

[242] "No bastidores, o lobby pelo pré-sal," *WikiLeaks*, December 13, 2010, https://wikileaks.org/Nos-bastidores-o-lobby-pelo-pre.html.

Russia better competitors for Brazilian oil. According to Pradal, it would come down to who gives the Brazilian government the most profit. "The Chinese can outbid everybody," she explained. "They can break-even and it will still be attractive to them. They just want the oil."

The Chevron representative also revealed that a former Brazilian presidential candidate and opposition leader, José Serra, had promised US oil companies that he would change the law if he was elected. But he wasn't. Back then, the Lula government was very popular, and Congress wouldn't even discuss changes, complained the representative of Chevron. The focus of big oil, then, she explained, would be on the Senate, "which has a greater number of opposition legislators than the House of Deputies." She would enlist new partners to focus efforts "in order to win Senate amendments concerning the Petrobras chief operator role and Petrosal terms."

"Exxon Lacerda also stated industry planned to make a 'full court press' in the Senate, but, not leaving anything to chance, Exxon would now also branch out on its own to conduct lobbying efforts," read the cable. The companies also begged for the US ambassador to interfere.

The story, of course, developed. Six years later, on August 31, 2016, the government of Dilma Rousseff, who was Lula's designated successor—and a keen defender of his developmentalist agenda—was confronted with a highly questionable impeachment process, with widespread support in the Congress. Only two months later, a new law approved by the Senate ended Petrobras' share requirement of pre-salt blocks. José Serra, a vocal supporter of Rousseff's impeachment, and the very senator that had promised US oil companies in closed meetings that he would change the law, authored the legislation. Since then, giants like BP, ExxonMobil, Chevron, and Shell have all received their shares.

This is a remarkable collection of revelations that would make any journalist proud, and which has made many powerful people very angry.

But WikiLeaks and Assange's achievements go far beyond the documents. For me, it is crystal clear that WikiLeaks has inaugurated a new era in journalism, in which news outlets collaborate instead of compete.

By example, WikiLeaks opened the way for subsequent releases of insider information like the Snowden leaks. One of the most prominent investigative organizations today, the International Consortium of Investigative Journalists (ICIJ), has embraced leaks by whistleblowers, revealing a great deal of information about secretive offshore business in the Panama Papers[243] and Offshore Leaks.[244] They are doing exactly what WikiLeaks was doing ten years ago: collaborating across borders. Independent news outlets, such as Agencia Publica in Brazil, of which I am cofounder and codirector, blossomed thanks to WikiLeaks.

Is the world now a better place after Julian Assange and WikiLeaks— and that "jolly group of hackers and activists" sitting a living room— unveiled the fragility and cynicism of establishment political powers? It is hard to say. But it is certainly an entirely different world that is far more open than it otherwise would have been.

---

[243] "The Panama Papers: Exposing the Rogue Offshore Finance Industry," *International Consortium of Investigative Journalists,* https://www.icij.org/investigations/panama-papers/.

[244] "Offshore Leaks Database," *International Consortium of Investigative Journalists,* https://offshoreleaks.icij.org/.

RESPONDING TO ASSANGE'S CRITICS 23–29

Caitlin Johnstone, April 2019

Smear 23: "He endangered the lives of gay Saudis."

No he didn't. The Saudi Cables[245] were KSA government documents, i.e., information the government already had, so there was no danger of legal retaliation based on Saudi Arabia's laws against homosexuality. There is no evidence that anyone was ever endangered by the Saudi Cables.

This smear was sparked by the aforementioned Raphael Satter at AP, whose executives WikiLeaks sent a formal complaint[246] breaking down Satter's journalistic misconduct and requesting the publication of its response.

---

[245] "The Saudi Cables, Cables and other documents from the Kingdom of Saudi Arabia Ministry of Foreign Affairs," *WikiLeaks*, https://wikileaks.org/saudi-cables/.

[246] Melinda Taylor, "Letter to AP," August 24, 2016, https://www.docdroid.net/Gi3unfx/letter-to-ap-fv.pdf.

The WikiLeaks website explains:

The material in the Saudi Cables was released in June 2015 and comprises leaked government information—that is data the Saudi government already had, including evidence of Saudi government persecution. The release revealed extensive Saudi bribing of the media, weapons amassed by the Saudi government, its brutal attacks on citizens and on Yemen, and the deals cut with the US and UK to get Saudi Arabia into a key position of the UN Human Rights Council. After WikiLeaks' publication of DNC leaks in 2016, over a year after the material was published, an AP journalist made claims about the 2015 publication but refused to provide evidence when asked to do so. WikiLeaks has still not found evidence for the claims.

"Mr. Satter's article has itself highlighted specific private information which can be searched for on the Internet, and which is available independently of the WikiLeaks site (as Mr. Satter should know, the content of the Saudi Cables was published online before WikiLeaks collated it as the 'Saudi Cables')," the WikiLeaks complaint to AP noted.

Smear 24: "He's a CIA agent/limited hangout."

I'm probably going to have to revisit this one because it's so all over the place that it's hard for me to even say exactly what it is. It only exists in fringey conspiracy circles, so there's no organized thought around it and when I ask people why they're so sure Assange is a CIA/Mossad agent/asset I get a bunch of different answers, many of them contradictory and none of them comprised of linear, complete thoughts. Mostly I just get an answer that goes something like, "Well, he spent some time in Egypt and he criticized

9/11 truthers, and he's a few degrees of separation from this one shady person, so, you know, you connect the dots."

No, *you* connect the dots. You're the one making the claim.

None of them ever do.

You'd think this smear would have subsided since Assange was imprisoned at the behest of the US government, but I'm actually encountering it way more often now. Every day I'm getting conspiracy types telling me Assange isn't what I think he is, right at the time when the MSM has converged to smear him with more aggression than ever before and right when he needs support more than ever.

I've never encountered anyone who can present a convincing (or even coherent) argument that Assange is working for any intelligence agency, so I generally just declare the burden of proof unmet and move on. If there's anyone out there who believes this and would like to take a stab at proving their claim, I have a few questions for you:

Why is a CIA/Mossad agent/asset/limited hangout/whatever being rewarded for his loyal service with a stay in Belmarsh Prison awaiting US extradition? How does that work, specifically? Are you claiming that he was an asset that got "burned"? If so, when did this happen? Was he still an asset while he was languishing in the embassy in failing health and chronic pain? Or was it before then? His persecution began in 2010 and the US government was working on sabotaging him back in 2008,[247] so are you claiming he hasn't been on their side since then? And if you're claiming that he used to be an asset but got burned, why are you spending your energy running around telling people on the Internet he's an asset when he isn't one anymore, and now his prosecution threatens press freedoms everywhere? If you oppose his extradition, why are you engaged in this behavior? Are

---

247 Julian Assange, "U.S. Intelligence planned to destroy WikiLeaks," *wired*, March 15, 2010 https://www.wired.com/images_blogs/threatlevel/2010/03/wikithreat.pdf.

you just interrupting an adult conversation that grownups are trying to have about an urgent matter, or is it something else? Did you run around telling everyone that Saddam used to be a CIA asset instead of protesting the Iraq invasion? Or do you believe this whole US prosecution is fake? If so, what is Assange getting out of it? What's incentivizing him to comply at this point? What specifically is your claim about what's happening?

My past experiences when engaging these types tells me not to expect any solid and thorough answers to my questions.

I've been at this commentary gig for about two and a half years, and during that time I've had people show up in my inbox and social media notifications warning me that everyone in anti-establishment circles is a CIA limited hangout. Literally everyone; you name a high-profile anti-establishment figure, and at one time or another I've received warnings from people that they are actually controlled opposition for a government agency.

This happens because for some people, paranoia is their only compass. They wind up in the same circles as WikiLeaks supporters because the lens of paranoia through which they perceive the world causes them to distrust the same power establishment and mass media that WikiLeaks supporters distrust, but beyond that the two groups are actually quite different. That same paranoia which causes them to view all the wrongdoers with suspicion causes them to view everyone else with suspicion as well.

Paranoia happens for a number of reasons, one of them being that people who aren't clear on the reasons our society acts so crazy will start making up reasons, like the belief that everyone with a high profile is a covert CIA agent. If you can't see clearly what's going on you start making things up, which can cause paranoia to become your only guidance system.

Smear 25: "He mistreated his cat."

There's just no limit to the garbage these smear merchants will cook up. Concern for the embassy cat picked up when the Moreno government began cooking up excuses to oust Assange from the embassy, the most highly publicized of them being a demand that he clean up after his cat. From that point on the narrative became that not only is Assange a stinky Nazi rapist Russian spy who smears poo on the walls . . . he also mistreats his cat. Ridiculous.

A bunch of "Where is Assange's cat??" news stories emerged after his arrest, because that's where people's minds go when a civilization-threatening lawfare agenda is being carried out. The *Guardian*'s James Ball, who last year authored an article[248] humiliatingly arguing that the US will never try to extradite Assange titled "The only barrier to Julian Assange leaving Ecuador's embassy is pride," told his Twitter followers, "For the record: Julian Assange's cat was reportedly given to a shelter by the Ecuadorian embassy ages ago, so don't expect a feline extradition in the next few hours. (I genuinely offered to adopt it)."[249]

Assange's cat is fine. It wasn't given to a "shelter"; the WikiLeaks Twitter account posted a video of the cat watching Assange's arrest on TV with the caption, "We can confirm that Assange's cat is safe. Assange asked his lawyers to rescue him from embassy threats in mid-October. They will be reunited in freedom."[250]

---

[248] James Ball, "The only barrier to Julian Assange leaving Ecuador's embassy is pride," *The Guardian*, Janurary 10, 2018, https://www.theguardian.com/commentisfree/2018/jan/10/julian-assange-ecuador-embassy-wikileaks-us-sweden.

[249] James Ball, Twitter Post, April 11, 2019, 6:23 AM, https://twitter.com/jamesrbuk/status/1116285679728832518.

[250] WikiLeaks, Twitter Post, April 13, 2019, 3:18 PM, https://twitter.com/wikileaks/status/1117144943666106368.

Smear 26: "He's a pedophile."

Yes, of course they tried this one too, and I still run into people online from time to time who regurgitate it. CNN has had on guests who asserted that Assange is a pedophile, not once but twice. In January 2017 former CIA official Phil Mudd said live on air that Assange is "a pedophile who lives in the Ecuadorian embassy in London," and instead of correcting him on the spot CNN did nothing and shared the video on Twitter, leaving the tweet up until WikiLeaks threatened to sue. On what appears to have been right around the same day, Congressman Mike Rogers claimed on CNN that Assange "is wanted for rape of a minor."

These claims are of course false, designed to paint Assange as literally the worst person in the world with all the very worst qualities you can imagine in a human being.

These claims came months after an alarming narrative control operation[251] working behind the bogus dating website toddandclare.com persuaded a UN body called the Global Compact to grant it status as a participant, then used its platform to publicly accuse Assange, with whom it was communicating, of "pedophile crimes." McClatchy reports the following:

> *Whoever is behind the dating site has marshaled significant resources to target Assange, enough to gain entry into a United Nations body, operate in countries in Europe, North America, and the Caribbean, conduct surveillance on Assange's lawyer in*

---

[251] "Timeline 2016," *WikiLeaks*, October 16, 2016, https://wikileaks.org/Background-and-Documents-on-Attempts-to-Frame-Assange-as-a-Pedophile-and.html?update2.

> *London, obtain the fax number of Canada's prime minister and*
> *seek to prod a police inquiry in the Bahamas.*[252]

So that's a thing.

Smear 27: "He lied about Seth Rich."

I'm just going to toss this one here at the end[253] because I'm seeing it go around a lot in the wake of the Mueller Report.

Robert Mueller, who helped the Bush administration deceive the world about WMD in Iraq,[254] has claimed that the GRU was the source of WikiLeaks' 2016 drops, and claimed in his report that WikiLeaks deceived its audience by implying that its source was the murdered DNC staffer Seth Rich. This claim is unsubstantiated because, as we discussed in Smear 4, the public has not seen a shred of evidence proving who was or was not WikiLeaks' source, so there's no way to know there was any deception happening there. We've never seen any hard proof, nor indeed anything besides official narrative, connecting the Russian government to Guccifer 2.0 and Guccifer 2.0 to WikiLeaks, and Daniel Lazare for Consortium News documents that there are in fact some major plot holes in Mueller's timeline.[255] Longtime Assange friend and WikiLeaks ally Craig Murray maintains that he knows the source of the DNC leaks and Podesta emails were two different Americans, not Russians, and hints that one of them was a DNC insider.

---

[252] Tim Johnson, "The strange tale of a dating site's attacks on WikiLeaks founder Assange," *McClatchy DC Bureau*, October 27, 2016, https://www.mcclatchydc.com/news/politics-government/election/article110904727.html

[253] Other sections were added after Smear 27 on April 15, 2019.

[254] IPA Media, "Robert Mueller on Iraq War and WMD's," *Youtube*, August 8, 2017, https://www.youtube.com/watch?reload=9&v=uTDO-kuOGTQ.

[255] See https://consortiumnews.com/2019/04/18/the-guccifer-2-0-gaps-in-muellers-full-report/.

There is exactly as much publicly available evidence for Murray's claim as there is for Mueller's.

Mainstream media has been blaring day after day for years that it is an absolute known fact that the Russian government was WikiLeaks' source, and the only reason people scoff and roll their eyes at anyone who makes the indisputably factual claim that we've seen no evidence for this is because the illusory truth effect causes the human brain to mistake repetition for fact.

The smear is that Assange knew his source was actually the Russian government, and he implied it was Seth Rich to throw people off the scent. Mueller asserted that something happened, and it's interpreted as hard fact instead of assertion. There's no evidence for any of this, and there's no reason to go believing the WMD guy on faith about a narrative which incriminates yet another government which refuses to obey the dictates of the American Empire.

Smear 28: "He's never leaked anything on Trump." (Added 4/25/19)

I'm surprised I forgot this one since it comes up constantly, not so much from the more finessed professional propagandists, but from the propagandized rank-and-file who just repeat bits and pieces of things they think they remember reading somewhere.

First of all, Assange is not a leaker, he's a publisher, meaning all that he and WikiLeaks have ever done is publish leaks that are brought to them by other people. They're not out there prowling around, hacking into government databases and publishing the results; they're just an outlet which came up with a secure anonymous drop box and invited leakers to use it so that their leaks can be published safely. If nobody brings them any leaks on a given subject, they've got nothing to publish on it. In the run-up to the

2016 election there were leaks on Trump, but their leakers went to other outlets; Trump's tax information was leaked to the *New York Times*, and the infamous "grab her by the pussy" audio was leaked to the *Washington Post.* There was no need for them to leak to WikiLeaks when they could safely leak to a mainstream outlet, and WikiLeaks couldn't force them to.

Secondly, WikiLeaks has publicly solicited leaks on Trump, both before[256] and after[257] the election. WikiLeaks' controversial exchanges with Donald Trump Jr. (see Smear 14) were largely just a leak publisher soliciting a potential source for leaks in language that that source would listen to, and the leaks they were asking for were from Trump. It's apparent that they've always wanted to publish leaks on Trump, and would if given the material.

Thirdly, the 2017 Vault-7 CIA leaks *were a Trump administration publication.* It enraged the Trump administration so much that the next month Mike Pompeo gave a speech declaring WikiLeaks a "hostile non-state intelligence service" and vowing to take the outlet down, and a few months later Trump's DOJ issued a warrant for Assange's arrest on a made-up, bogus charge.[258] Assange smearers don't like to count the CIA leaks because they don't contain any videos of Trump with well-hydrated Russian prostitutes, but they were indisputably a blow to this administration and it's stupid to pretend otherwise.

---

[256] WikiLeaks, Twitter Post, September 26, 2016, 9:37 PM, https://twitter.com/wikileaks/status/780582100990828544.

[257] WikiLeaks, Twitter Post, January 22, 2017, 11:53 AM, https://twitter.com/wikileaks/status/823212055322853382.

[258] Caitlin Johnstone, "How You Can Be Certain That The US Charge Against Assange Is Fraudulent," *Medium*, April 11, https://medium.com/@caityjohnstone/how-you-can-be-certain-that-the-us-charge-against-assange-is-fraudulent-8eb0caa1c4f6.

Fourthly, typing the words "Donald Trump" into WikiLeaks' search engine comes up with 14,531 results[259] as of this writing from the DNC Leaks, the Podesta emails, the Global Intelligence Files, and other publications throughout WikiLeaks' history.

Smear 29: "He conspired with Nigel Farage." (Added 4/25/2019)

This is yet another smear geared toward painting Assange as a right-winger so as to kill his support on the left, this one marketed more to a UK audience.

Assange is known to have met with Brexit leader Nigel Farage one time, and one time only, in March 2017. Both WikiLeaks and Farage have said that Farage tried to secure an interview with Assange on his show with LBC Radio, and that the request was politely declined. That was the meeting.

There is exactly zero evidence anywhere contradicting this. There have been attempts to circulate a narrative that Assange met with Farage multiple times, which Farage dismissed as "conspiratorial nonsense" and WikiLeaks calls "fabricated intelligence reports" and "information fed from Ecuadorian intelligence agency SENAIN."

WikiLeaks' claim is obviously credible for a number of reasons, the first being that one of the times Assange is alleged to have been visited by Farage was April 28, 2018,[260] by which time Assange had long been forbidden by the Ecuadorian government from receiving any visitors apart from his lawyers. This would have made such a visit impossible. Secondly,

---

[259] "Advanced Search: donald trump," *WikiLeaks*, https://search.wikileaks. org/?q=donald+trump.

[260] Fernando Villavicencio and Cristina Solórzano, "Assange at the center of a global conspiracy," *Plan V* on *archive.today*, May 16, 2018, https://archive.fo/ JTOuJ#selection-615.245-615.264.

SENAIN was a source for the ridiculous *Guardian* story[261] alleging that Assange had met repeatedly with Paul Manafort, now known beyond a shadow of a doubt to have been false. Thirdly, Glenn Greenwald has described the Ecuadorian embassy in London as "one of the most scrutinized, surveilled, monitored, and filmed locations on the planet." It wouldn't be difficult for Ecuador or the UK to prove that Farage visited Assange apart from the March 2017 meeting, as determined as they've been to share information which smears him, but none of them ever have.

"Since the UK state engages in an illicit multi-million pound surveillance operation against my visitors, who are recorded using the hi-tech surveillance cameras it has emplaced on opposing buildings, I am sure it will be delighted to answer whether Mr. Farage visited me in 2016," Assange tweeted in January 2018.[262]

This was in response to congressional testimony made by former *Wall Street Journal* reporter Glenn Simpson, whose company Fusion GPS was responsible for the discredited Steele dossier. Here are Simpson's actual words to the House Intelligence Committee:

"I've been told and have not confirmed that Nigel Farage had additional trips to the Ecuadorian embassy than the one that's been in the papers and that he provided data to Julian Assange."

"I've been told and have not confirmed." By the Fusion GPS guy. In the midst of a disinformation campaign from Ecuadorian intelligence. That's not a thing.

This complete absence of anything tangible didn't stop Russiagate kooks like Seth Abramson, Marcy Wheeler, and the usual lineup of MSM

---

[261] Caitlin Johnstone, "Never, Ever Forget The Guardian/Politico Psyop Against WikiLeaks," *Medium*, November 30, 2018, https://medium.com/@caityjohnstone/never-ever-forget-the-guardian-politico-psyop-against-wikileaks-a7b9c99b9c9.

[262] Julian Assange, *Twitter* on *archive.today*, January 19, 2018, https://archive.fo/KAMC0#selection-3555.0-3613.279.

conspiracy mongers from running around treating this as an actual fact, and not unconfirmed hearsay from a guy whose major claim to fame is association with a notorious dossier that has been completely debunked by the Mueller Report.

The *Guardian's* answer to Rachel Maddow, Carole Cadwalladr, took these entirely imaginary associations between Assange and Farage and shoved it into mainstream British consciousness with article[263] after article[264] after article[265] filled with nothing but unsubstantiated conspiratorial innuendo and spin, and the smear was in the bloodstream. Cadwalladr has an established record of using dishonest and unprofessional tactics to deliberately smear WikiLeaks.[266]

And so you can see that this is yet another example of a cluster of half-truths and outright fabrications being spun in a way to make Assange look awful and untrustworthy, then circulated and repeated as fact over and over until the illusory truth effect takes over.

---

[263] Carole Cadwalladr, "When Nigel Farage met Julian Assange," *The Guardian* on *archive.today*, April 23, 2017, https://archive.fo/nMxaa.

[264] Carole Cadwalladr, "Who is the real Nigel Farage... and why won't he answer my questions?," *The Guardian*, November 25, 2018, https://www.theguardian.com/politics/2018/nov/25/why-wont-nigel-farage-answer-my-brexit-questions.

[265] Carole Cadwalladr, "Trump, Assange, Bannon, Farage... bound together in an unholy alliance," *The Guardian*, Octboer 29, 2017, https://www.theguardian.com/commentisfree/2017/oct/28/trump-assange-bannon-farage-bound-together-in-unholy-alliance?CMP=share_btn_tw.

[266] Caitlin Johnstone, "Don't Laugh—It's Giving Putin What He Wants," *Medium*, December 15, 2018, https://medium.com/@caityjohnstone/dont-laugh-it-s-giving-putin-what-he-wants-a962c63a5ed4.

EPILOGUE

Michael Ratner

From his forthcoming memoir *Representing the Many* (OR Books)

I have asked myself, "Why are truth tellers like Assange, Manning, Snowden, and Hammond so important to me?" The answer is that they have succeeded in doing what CCR[267] and I have been trying to do ever since the so-called War on Terror began in the wake of September 11, 2001. For more than a decade, we lawyers at CCR brought at least a dozen lawsuits seeking to expose and end rendition, illegal drone strikes, the wars in Afghanistan and Iraq, and the torture at Guantánamo and other US secret prisons. We tried to hold accountable those responsible for war crimes. But each time the government would go into court and say, "You can't litigate this. National security." Every lawsuit was dismissed. Even in the open-and-shut case of Maher Arar, a Canadian citizen who was taken off a plane at Kennedy Airport, sent to Syria, and tortured, we couldn't get past the

---

[267] The Center for Constitutional Rights is a non-profit legal and educational organization, where Ratner was president.

Circuit Court. And the one time we did win at the Supreme Court with *Rasul*, it was impossible to enforce the ruling.

We had reached a dead end. Then, all of a sudden, people like Chelsea Manning, Julian Assange, Edward Snowden, Sarah Harrison, Aaron Swartz, and Jeremy Hammond came out of nowhere. With acts of great courage, they revealed to the world what this country is actually doing. They sparked a much-needed public discussion of the US government's secret, illegal, and inhumane policies. And they brought people into the streets. As a result, we're seeing the unraveling of governments and corporations all over the world.

My experience has taught me that the truth has a way of coming out, even when the most powerful government on earth tries to crush it. Each time a whistleblower, a publisher, or a hacker has been jailed, tortured, or driven to suicide, other truth tellers have come forward. And there will be many more.

It's truly a remarkable time we are living in. What we must remember is that we are in this together. It's up to all of us to protect the truth tellers. If we do, we will have true democracy someday, in this country and in the world.

"The UK must resist, you can resist!"

—Julian Assange as he was dragged by UK authorities out of the Ecuadorian embassy in London, April 11, 2019

APPENDIX

SUPERSEDING INDICTMENT

IN THE UNITED STATES DISTRICT COURT FOR THE

EASTERN DISTRICT OF VIRGINIA

Alexandria Division

FILED
IN OPEN COURT

MAY 23

CLERK, U.S. DISTRICT COURT
ALEXANDRIA, VIRGINIA

UNITED STATES OF AMERICA	Criminal No. 1:18-cr-111 (CMH)
v.	Count 1: 18 U.S.C. § 793(g) Conspiracy To Receive National Defense
JULIAN PAUL ASSANGE,	Information
Defendant.	Counts 2-4: 18 U.S.C. § 793(b) and 2 Obtaining National Defense Information
	Counts 5-8: 18 U.S.C. § 793(c) and 2 Obtaining National Defense Information
	Counts 9-11: 18 U.S.C. § 793(d) and 2 Disclosure of National Defense Information
	Counts 12-14: 18 U.S.C. § 793(e) and 2 Disclosure of National Defense Information
	Counts 15-17: 18 U.S.C. § 793(e) Disclosure of National Defense Information
	Count 18: 18 U.S.C. §§ 371 and 1030 Conspiracy To Commit Computer Intrusion

SUPERSEDING INDICTMENT

May 2019 Term – at Alexandria, Virginia

THE GRAND JURY CHARGES THAT:

GENERAL ALLEGATIONS

At times material to this Superseding Indictment:

APPENDIX

A. ASSANGE and WikiLeaks Repeatedly Encouraged Sources with Access to Classified Information to Steal and Provide It to WikiLeaks to Disclose.

1.   JULIAN PAUL ASSANGE ("ASSANGE") is the public face of "WikiLeaks," a website he founded with others as an "intelligence agency of the people." To obtain information to release on the WikiLeaks website, ASSANGE encouraged sources to (i) circumvent legal safeguards on information; (ii) provide that protected information to WikiLeaks for public dissemination; and (iii) continue the pattern of illegally procuring and providing protected information to WikiLeaks for distribution to the public.

2.   ASSANGE and WikiLeaks have repeatedly sought, obtained, and disseminated information that the United States classified due to the serious risk that unauthorized disclosure could harm the national security of the United States. WikiLeaks's website explicitly solicited censored, otherwise restricted, and until September 2010,[1] "classified" materials. As the website then-stated, "WikiLeaks accepts *classified, censored,* or otherwise *restricted* material of *political, diplomatic, or ethical significance.*"[2]

3.   ASSANGE personally and publicly promoted WikiLeaks to encourage those with access to protected information, including classified information, to provide it to WikiLeaks for public disclosure. For example, in December 2009, ASSANGE and a WikiLeaks affiliate gave a presentation at the 26th Chaos Communication Congress (26C3), described by the website as an annual conference attended by the hacker community and others that is hosted by the Chaos

---

[1]   When the Grand Jury alleges in this Superseding Indictment that an event occurred on a particular date, the Grand Jury means to convey that the event was alleged to occur "on or about" that date.

[2]   One month later, the WikiLeaks website not only deleted the term "classified" from the list of materials it would accept, but also included the following disclaimer: "WikiLeaks accepts a range of material, but we do not solicit it."

Computer Club (CCC), which its website purports is "Europe's largest association of hackers." During that presentation, WikiLeaks described itself as the "leading disclosure portal for classified, restricted or legally threatened publications."

4.   To further encourage the disclosure of protected information, including classified information, the WikiLeaks website posted a detailed list of "The Most Wanted Leaks of 2009," organized by country, and stated that documents or materials nominated to the list must "[b]e likely to have political, diplomatic, ethical or historical impact on release . . . and be plausibly obtainable to a well-motivated insider or outsider."

5.   As of November 2009, WikiLeaks's "Most Wanted Leaks" for the United States included the following:

a.   "Bulk Databases," including an encyclopedia used by the United States intelligence community, called "Intellipedia;" the unclassified, but non-public, CIA Open Source Center database; and

b.   "Military and Intelligence" documents, including documents that the list described as classified up to the **SECRET** level, for example, "Iraq and Afghanistan Rules of Engagement 2007-2009 (SECRET);" operating and interrogation procedures at Guantanamo Bay, Cuba; documents relating to Guantanamo detainees; CIA detainee interrogation videos; and information about certain weapons systems.

6.   ASSANGE intended the "Most Wanted Leaks" list to encourage and cause individuals to illegally obtain and disclose protected information, including classified information, to WikiLeaks contrary to law. For example, in 2009, ASSANGE spoke at the "Hack in the Box Security Conference" in Malaysia. ASSANGE referenced the conference's "capture the flag" hacking contest and noted that WikiLeaks had its own list of "flags" that it wanted captured—

namely, the list of "Most Wanted Leaks" posted on the WikiLeaks website. He encouraged people to search for the list and for those with access to obtain and give to WikiLeaks information responsive to that list.

7.   ASSANGE designed WikiLeaks to focus on information, restricted from public disclosure by law, precisely because of the value of that information. Therefore, he predicated his and WikiLeaks's success in part upon encouraging sources with access to such information to violate legal obligations and provide that information for WikiLeaks to disclose.

B. Chelsea Manning Responded to ASSANGE'S Solicitation and Stole Classified Documents from the United States.

8.   Chelsea Manning, formerly known as Bradley Manning, was an intelligence analyst in the United States Army who was deployed to Forward Operating Base Hammer in Iraq.

9.   Manning held a "Top Secret" security clearance, and signed a classified information nondisclosure agreement, acknowledging that the unauthorized disclosure or retention or negligent handling of classified information could cause irreparable injury to the United States or be used to the advantage of a foreign nation.

10.   Beginning by at least November 2009, Manning responded to ASSANGE's solicitation of classified information made through the WikiLeaks website. For example, WikiLeaks's "Military and Intelligence" "Most Wanted Leaks" category, as described in paragraphs 4-5, solicited CIA detainee interrogation videos. On November 28, 2009, Manning in turn searched the classified network search engine, "Intelink," for "retention+of+interrogation+videos." The next day, Manning searched the classified network for "detainee+abuse," which was consistent with the "Most Wanted Leaks" request for "Detainee abuse photos withheld by the Obama administration" under WikiLeaks's "Military and Intelligence" category.

11.   On November 30, 2009, Manning saved a text file entitled "wl-press.txt" to her external hard drive and to an encrypted container on her computer. The file stated, "You can currently contact our investigations editor directly in Iceland +354 862 3481; 24 hour service; ask for 'Julian Assange.'" Similarly, on December 8, 2009, Manning ran several searches on Intelink relating to Guantanamo Bay detainee operations, interrogations, and standard operating procedures or "SOPs." These search terms were yet again consistent with WikiLeaks's "Most Wanted Leaks," which sought Guantanamo Bay operating and interrogation SOPs under the "Military and Intelligence" category.

12.   Between in or around January 2010 and May 2010, consistent with WikiLeaks's "Most Wanted Leaks" solicitation of bulk databases and military and intelligence categories, Manning downloaded four nearly complete databases from departments and agencies of the United States. These databases contained approximately 90,000 Afghanistan war-related significant activity reports, 400,000 Iraq war-related significant activities reports, 800 Guantanamo Bay detainee assessment briefs, and 250,000 U.S. Department of State cables. The United States had classified many of these records up to the **SECRET** level pursuant to Executive Order No. 13526 or its predecessor orders. Manning nevertheless provided the documents to WikiLeaks, so that WikiLeaks could publicly disclose them on its website.

13.   Manning was arrested on or about May 27, 2010. The "Most Wanted Leaks" posted on the WikiLeaks website in May 2010 no longer contained the "Military and Intelligence" category.

C. ASSANGE Encouraged Manning to Continue Her Theft of Classified Documents and Agreed to Help Her Crack a Password Hash to a Military Computer.

14.   During large portions of the same time period (between November 2009, when Manning first became interested in WikiLeaks, through her arrest on or about May 27, 2010), Manning was in direct contact with ASSANGE, who encouraged Manning to steal classified documents from the United States and unlawfully disclose that information to WikiLeaks.

15.   In furtherance of this scheme, ASSANGE agreed to assist Manning in cracking a password hash stored on United States Department of Defense computers connected to the Secret Internet Protocol Network, a United States government network used for classified documents and communications, as designated according to Executive Order No. 13526 or its predecessor orders.

16.   Manning, who had access to the computers in connection with her duties as an intelligence analyst, was also using the computers to download classified records to transmit to WikiLeaks. Army regulations prohibited Manning from attempting to bypass or circumvent security mechanisms on Government-provided information systems and from sharing personal accounts and authenticators, such as passwords.

17.   The portion of the password hash Manning gave to ASSANGE to crack was stored as a "hash value" in a computer file that was accessible only by users with administrative-level privileges. Manning did not have administrative-level privileges, and used special software, namely a Linux operating system, to access the computer file and obtain the portion of the password provided to ASSANGE.

18.   Had Manning retrieved the full password hash and had ASSANGE and Manning successfully cracked it, Manning may have been able to log onto computers under a username that did not belong to her. Such a measure would have made it more difficult for investigators to identify Manning as the source of disclosures of classified information.

19. Prior to the formation of the password-cracking agreement, Manning had already provided WikiLeaks with hundreds of thousands of documents classified up to the **SECRET** level that she downloaded from departments and agencies of the United States, including the Afghanistan war-related significant activity reports and Iraq war-related significant activity reports.

20. At the time he entered into this agreement, ASSANGE knew, understood, and fully anticipated that Manning was taking and illegally providing WikiLeaks with classified records containing national defense information of the United States that she was obtaining from classified databases. ASSANGE was knowingly receiving such classified records from Manning for the purpose of publicly disclosing them on the WikiLeaks website.

21. For example, on March 7, 2010, Manning asked ASSANGE how valuable the Guantanamo Bay detainee assessment briefs would be. After confirming that ASSANGE thought they had value, on March 8, 2010, Manning told ASSANGE that she was "throwing everything [she had] on JTF GTMO [Joint Task Force, Guantanamo] at [Assange] now." ASSANGE responded, "ok, great!" When Manning brought up the "osc," meaning the CIA Open Source Center, ASSANGE replied, "that's something we want to mine entirely, btw," which was consistent with WikiLeaks's list of "Most Wanted Leaks," described in paragraphs 4-5, that solicited "the complete CIA Open Source Center analytical database," an unclassified (but non-public) database. Manning later told ASSANGE in reference to the Guantanamo Bay detainee assessment briefs that "after this upload, thats all i really have got left." In response to this statement, which indicated that Manning had no more classified documents to unlawfully disclose, ASSANGE replied, "curious eyes never run dry in my experience." ASSANGE intended his

statement to encourage Manning to continue her theft of classified documents from the United States and to continue the unlawful disclosure of those documents to ASSANGE and WikiLeaks.

22. Manning used a Secure File Transfer Protocol ("SFTP") connection to transmit the Detainee Assessment briefs to a cloud drop box operated by WikiLeaks, with an X directory that WikiLeaks had designated for her use.

23. Two days later, ASSANGE told Manning that there was "a username in the gitmo docs." Manning told ASSANGE, "any usernames should probably be filtered, period." Manning asked ASSANGE whether there was "anything useful in there." ASSANGE responded, in part, that "these sorts of things are always motivating to other sources too." ASSANGE stated, "gitmo=bad, leakers=enemy of gitmo, leakers=good . . . Hence the feeling is people can give us stuff for anything not as 'dangerous as gitmo' on the one hand, and on the other, for people who know more, there's a desire to eclipse." Manning replied, "true. ive crossed a lot of those 'danger' zones, so im comfortable."

D. At ASSANGE's Direction and Agreement, Manning Continued to Steal Classified Documents and Provide Them to ASSANGE.

24. Following ASSANGE's "curious eyes never run dry" comment, on or about March 22, 2010, consistent with WikiLeaks's "Most Wanted Leaks" solicitation of "Iraq and Afghanistan US Army Rules of Engagement 2007-2009 (**SECRET**)," as described in paragraphs 4-5, Manning downloaded multiple Iraq rules of engagement files from her Secret Internet Protocol Network computer and burned these files to a CD, and provided them to ASSANGE and WikiLeaks.

25. On April 5, 2010, WikiLeaks released on its website the rules of engagement files that Manning provided. It entitled four of the documents as follows: "US Rules of Engagement for Iraq; 2007 flowchart," "US Rules of Engagement for Iraq; Refcard 2007," "US Rules of Engagement for Iraq, March 2007," and "US Rules of Engagement for Iraq, Nov 2006." All of

these documents had been classified as **SECRET**, except for the "US Rules of Engagement for Iraq; Refcard 2007," which was unclassified but for official use only.

26.   The rules of engagement files delineated the circumstances and limitations under which United States forces would initiate or continue combat engagement upon encountering other forces. WikiLeaks's disclosure of this information would allow enemy forces in Iraq and elsewhere to anticipate certain actions or responses by U.S. armed forces and to carry out more effective attacks.

27.   Further, following ASSANGE's "curious eyes never run dry" comment, and consistent with WikiLeaks's solicitation of bulk databases and classified materials of diplomatic significance, as described in paragraphs 2, 4-5, between on or about March 28, 2010, and April 9, 2010, Manning used a United States Department of Defense computer to download over 250,000 U.S. Department of State cables, which were classified up to the **SECRET** level. Manning subsequently uploaded these cables to ASSANGE and WikiLeaks through an SFTP connection to a cloud drop box operated by WikiLeaks, with an X directory that WikiLeaks had designated for Manning's use. ASSANGE and WikiLeaks later disclosed them to the public.

28.   At the time ASSANGE agreed to receive and received from Manning the classified Guantanamo Bay detainee assessment briefs, the U.S. Department of State Cables, and the Iraq rules of engagement files, ASSANGE knew that Manning had unlawfully obtained and disclosed or would unlawfully disclose such documents. For example, not only had ASSANGE already received thousands of military-related documents classified up to the **SECRET** level from Manning, but Manning and ASSANGE also chatted about military jargon and references to current events in Iraq, which showed that Manning was a government or military source; the "releasability" of certain information by ASSANGE; measures to prevent the discovery of

Manning as ASSANGE's source, such as clearing logs and use of a "cryptophone;" and a code phrase to use if something went wrong.

E. ASSANGE, WikiLeaks Affiliates, and Manning Shared the Common Objective to Subvert Lawful Restrictions on Classified Information and to Publicly Disseminate it.

29.   ASSANGE, Manning, and others shared the objective to further the mission of WikiLeaks, as an "intelligence agency of the people," to subvert lawful measures imposed by the United States government to safeguard and secure classified information, in order to disclose that information to the public and inspire others with access to do the same.

30.   Manning and ASSANGE discussed this shared philosophy. For example, when Manning said, "i told you before, government/organizations cant control information ... the harder they try, the more violently the information wants to get out," ASSANGE replied, "restrict supply = value increases, yes." Further, when Manning said, "its like you're the first 'Intelligence Agency' for the general public," ASSANGE replied, that is how the original WikiLeaks had described itself.

31.   Even after Manning's arrest on or about May 27, 2010, ASSANGE and others endeavored to fulfill this mission of WikiLeaks to publish the classified documents that Manning had disclosed by threatening to disclose additional information that would be even more damaging to the United States and its allies if anything should happen to WikiLeaks or ASSANGE to prevent dissemination.

32.   On August 20, 2010, for instance, WikiLeaks tweeted that it had distributed an encrypted "'insurance' file" to over 100,000 people and referred to the file and the people who downloaded it as "our big guns in defeating prior restraint."

33.   ASSANGE spoke about the purpose of this "insurance file," stating that it contained information that WikiLeaks intended to publish in the future but without "harm minimization," that is to say, without redactions of things, like names of confidential informants, that could put lives at risk. When asked how these insurance files could be used to prevent "prior restraint and other legal threats," ASSANGE responded that WikiLeaks routinely "distributed encrypted backups of material we have yet to release. And that means all we have to do is release the password to that material and it's instantly available. Now of course, we don't like to do that, because there is various harm minimization procedures to go through." But, ASSANGE continued, the insurance file is a "precaution[] to make sure that sort of material [the data in WikiLeaks's possession] is not going to disappear from history, regardless of the sort of threats to this organization."

34.   Similarly, on August 17, 2013, WikiLeaks posted on its Facebook account: "WikiLeaks releases encrypted versions of upcoming publication data ('insurance') from time to time to nullify attempts at prior restraint." The post also provided links to previous insurance files and asked readers to "please mirror" the links, meaning to post the links on other websites to help increase the number of times the files are downloaded.

F. ASSANGE Revealed the Names of Human Sources and Created a Grave and Imminent Risk to Human Life.

35.   Also following Manning's arrest, during 2010 and 2011, ASSANGE published via the WikiLeaks website the documents classified up to the **SECRET** level that he had obtained from Manning, as described in paragraphs 12, 21, and 27, including approximately 75,000 Afghanistan war-related significant activity reports, 400,000 Iraq war-related significant activities reports, 800 Guantanamo Bay detainee assessment briefs, and 250,000 U.S. Department of State cables.

APPENDIX

36.   The significant activity reports from the Afghanistan and Iraq wars that ASSANGE published included names of local Afghans and Iraqis who had provided information to U.S. and coalition forces. The State Department cables that WikiLeaks published included names of persons throughout the world who provided information to the U.S. government in circumstances in which they could reasonably expect that their identities would be kept confidential. These sources included journalists, religious leaders, human rights advocates, and political dissidents who were living in repressive regimes and reported to the United States the abuses of their own government, and the political conditions within their countries, at great risk to their own safety. By publishing these documents without redacting the human sources' names or other identifying information, ASSANGE created a grave and imminent risk that the innocent people he named would suffer serious physical harm and/or arbitrary detention.

37.   On May 2, 2011, United States armed forces raided the compound of Osama bin Laden in Abbottabad, Pakistan. During the raid, they collected a number of items of digital media, which included the following: (1) a letter from bin Laden to another member of the terrorist organization al-Qaeda in which bin Laden requested that the member gather the DoD material posted to WikiLeaks, (2) a letter from that same member of al-Qaeda to Bin Laden with information from the Afghanistan War Documents provided by Manning to WikiLeaks and released by WikiLeaks, and (3) Department of State information provided by Manning to WikiLeaks and released by WikiLeaks.

38.   Paragraphs 39 and 40 contain examples of a few of the documents ASSANGE published that contained the unredacted names of human sources. These are not the only documents that WikiLeaks published containing the names of sources, nor the only documents that put innocent people in grave danger simply because they provided information to the United States.

39.   The following are examples of significant activity reports related to the Afghanistan and Iraq wars that ASSANGE published without redacting the names of human sources who were vulnerable to retribution by the Taliban in Afghanistan or the insurgency in Iraq:

a. Classified Document C1 was a 2007 threat report containing details of a planned anti-coalition attack at a specific location in Afghanistan. Classified Document C1 named the local human source who reported the planned attack. Classified Document C1 was classified at the **SECRET** level.

b. Classified Document C2 was a 2009 threat report identifying a person who supplied weapons at a specific location in Afghanistan. Classified Document C2 named the local human source who reported information. Classified Document C2 was classified at the **SECRET** level.

c. Classified Document D1 was a 2009 report discussing an improvised explosive device (IED) attack in Iraq. Classified Document D1 named local human sources who provided information on the attack. Classified Document D1 was classified at the **SECRET** level.

d. Classified Document D2 was a 2008 report that named a local person in Iraq who had turned in weapons to coalition forces and had been threatened afterward. Classified Document D2 was classified at the **SECRET** level.

40.   The following are examples of State Department cables that ASSANGE published without redacting the names of human sources who were vulnerable to retribution.

a. Classified Document A1 was a 2009 State Department cable discussing a political situation in Iran. Classified Document A1 named a human source of information located in Iran and indicated that the source's identity needed to be protected. Classified Document A1 was classified at the **SECRET** level.

b. Classified Document A2 was a 2009 State Department cable discussing political dynamics in Iran. Classified Document A2 named a human source of information who regularly traveled to Iran and indicated that the source's identity needed to be protected. Classified Document A2 was classified at the **SECRET** level.

c. Classified Document A3 was a 2009 State Department cable discussing issues related to ethnic conflict in China. Classified Document A3 named a human source of information located in China and indicated that the source's identity needed to be protected. Classified Document A3 was classified at the **SECRET** level.

d. Classified Document A4 was a 2009 State Department cable discussing relations between Iran and Syria. Classified Document A4 named human sources of information located in Syria and indicated that the sources' identities needed to be protected. Classified Document A4 was classified at the **SECRET** level.

e. Classified Document A5 was a 2010 State Department cable discussing human rights issues in Syria. Classified Document A5 named a human source of information located in Syria and indicated that the source's identity needed to be protected. Classified Document A5 was classified at the **SECRET** level.

G. ASSANGE Knew that the Dissemination of the Names of Individual Sources Endangered Those Individuals.

41. ASSANGE knew that his publication of Afghanistan and Iraq war-related significant activity reports endangered sources, whom he named as having provided information to U.S. and coalition forces.

42.   In an interview in August 2010, ASSANGE called it "regrettable" that sources disclosed by WikiLeaks "may face some threat as a result." But, in the same interview, ASSANGE insisted that "we are not obligated to protect other people's sources, military sources or spy organization sources, except from unjust retribution," adding that in general "there are numerous cases where people sell information . . . or frame others or are engaged in genuinely traitorous behavior and actually that is something for the public to know about."

43.   ASSANGE also knew that his publication of the State Department cables endangered sources whom he named as having provided information to the State Department. In a letter dated November 27, 2010 from the State Department's legal adviser to ASSANGE and his counsel, ASSANGE was informed, among other things, that publication of the State Department cables would "[p]lace at risk the lives of countless innocent individuals—from journalists to human rights activists and bloggers to soldiers to individuals providing information to further peace and security." Prior to his publication of the unredacted State Department cables, ASSANGE claimed that he intended "to gradually roll [the cables] out in a safe way" by partnering with mainstream media outlets and "reading through every single cable and redacting identities accordingly." Nonetheless, while ASSANGE and WikiLeaks published some of the cables in redacted form beginning in November 2010, they published over 250,000 cables in September 2011, in unredacted form, that is, without redacting the names of the human sources.

44.   On July 30, 2010, the New York Times published an article entitled "Taliban Study WikiLeaks to Hunt Informants." The article stated that, after the release of the Afghanistan war significant activity reports, a member of the Taliban contacted the New York Times and stated, "We are studying the report. We knew about the spies and people who collaborate with U.S. forces. We will investigate through our own secret service whether the people mentioned are really

spies working for the U.S. If they are U.S. spies, then we know how to punish them." When confronted about such reports, ASSANGE said, "The Taliban is not a coherent outfit, but we don't say that it is absolutely impossible that anything we ever publish will ever result in harm—we cannot say that."

H. United States Law to Protect Classified Information

45.　Executive Order No. 13526 and its predecessor orders define the classification levels assigned to classified information. Under the Executive Order, information may be classified as "Secret" if its unauthorized disclosure reasonably could be expected to cause serious damage to the national security, and information may be classified as "Confidential" if its unauthorized disclosure reasonably could be expected to cause damage to the national security. Further, under the Executive Order, classified information can generally only be disclosed to those persons who have been granted an appropriate level of United States government security clearance and possess a need to know the classified information in connection to their official duties.

46.　At no point was ASSANGE a citizen of the United States, nor did he hold a United States security clearance or otherwise have authorization to receive, possess, or communicate classified information.

COUNT 1

(Conspiracy to Obtain, Receive, and Disclose National Defense Information)

A. The general allegations of this Superseding Indictment are re-alleged and incorporated into this Count as though fully set forth herein.

B. Between in or about November 2009 and continuing until at least September 2011, in an offense begun and committed outside of the jurisdiction of any particular state or district of the United States, the defendant, JULIAN PAUL ASSANGE, who will be first brought to the Eastern District of Virginia, knowingly and unlawfully conspired with other co-conspirators, known and unknown to the Grand Jury, to commit the following offenses against the United States:

1. To obtain documents, writings, and notes connected with the national defense, for the purpose of obtaining information respecting the national defense—namely, detainee assessment briefs related to detainees who were held at Guantanamo Bay, U.S. State Department cables, and Iraq rules of engagement files classified up to the **SECRET** level—and with reason to believe that the information was to be used to the injury of the United States or the advantage of any foreign nation, in violation of Title 18, United States Code, Section 793(b);

2. To receive and obtain documents, writings, and notes connected with the national defense—namely, detainee assessment briefs related to detainees who were held at Guantanamo Bay, U.S. State Department cables, Iraq rules of engagement files, and information stored on the Secret Internet Protocol Network classified up to the **SECRET** level—for the purpose of obtaining information respecting the national defense, and knowing and with reason to believe at the time such materials are obtained, they had been and would be taken, obtained, and disposed of by a person contrary to the provisions of

Chapter 37 of Title 18 of the United States Code, in violation of Title 18, United States Code, Section 793(c);

3. To willfully communicate documents relating to the national defense—namely, detainee assessment briefs related to detainees who were held at Guantanamo Bay, U.S. State Department cables, Iraq rules of engagement files, and documents containing the names of individuals in Afghanistan, Iraq, and elsewhere around the world, who risked their safety and freedom by providing information to the United States and our allies, which were classified up to the **SECRET** level—from persons having lawful possession of or access to such documents, to persons not entitled to receive them, in violation of Title 18, United States Code, Section 793(d); and

4. To willfully communicate documents relating to the national defense—namely, (i) for Manning to communicate to ASSANGE the detainee assessment briefs related to detainees who were held at Guantanamo Bay, U.S. State Department cables, and Iraq rules of engagement files classified up to the **SECRET** level, and (ii) for ASSANGE to communicate documents classified up to the **SECRET** level containing the names of individuals in Afghanistan, Iraq, and elsewhere around the world, who risked their safety and freedom by providing information to the United States and our allies to the public— from persons in unauthorized possession of such documents to persons not entitled to receive them in violation of Title 18, United States Code, Section 793(e).

C.   In furtherance of the conspiracy, and to accomplish its objects, the defendant and his conspirators committed overt acts including, but not limited to, those described in the General Allegations Section of this Indictment.

(All in violation of Title 18, United States Code, Section 793(g))

COUNT 2

(Unauthorized Obtaining of National Defense Information)
(Detainee Assessment Briefs)

A. The general allegations of this Superseding Indictment are re-alleged and incorporated into this Count as though fully set forth herein.

B. Between in or about November 2009 and in or about May 2010, in an offense begun and committed outside of the jurisdiction of any particular state or district of the United States, the defendant, JULIAN PAUL ASSANGE, who will be first brought to the Eastern District of Virginia, and others unknown to the Grand Jury, knowingly and unlawfully obtained and aided, abetted, counseled, induced, procured and willfully caused Manning to obtain documents, writings, and notes connected with the national defense, for the purpose of obtaining information respecting the national defense—namely, detainee assessment briefs classified up to the **SECRET** level related to detainees who were held at Guantanamo Bay—and with reason to believe that the information was to be used to the injury of the United States or the advantage of any foreign nation.

(All in violation of Title 18, United States Code, Sections 793(b) and 2)

COUNT 3

(Unauthorized Obtaining of National Defense Information)
(State Department Cables)

A. The general allegations of this Superseding Indictment are re-alleged and incorporated into this Count as though fully set forth herein.

B. Between in or about November 2009 and in or about May 2010, in an offense begun and committed outside of the jurisdiction of any particular state or district of the United States, the defendant, JULIAN PAUL ASSANGE, who will be first brought to the Eastern District of Virginia, and others unknown to the Grand Jury, knowingly and unlawfully obtained and aided, abetted, counseled, induced, procured and willfully caused Manning to obtain documents, writings, and notes connected with the national defense, for the purpose of obtaining information respecting the national defense—namely, U.S. Department of State cables classified up to the **SECRET** level—and with reason to believe that the information was to be used to the injury of the United States or the advantage of any foreign nation.

(All in violation of Title 18, United States Code, Sections 793(b) and 2)

COUNT 4
(Unauthorized Obtaining of National Defense Information)
(Iraq Rules of Engagement Files)

. A. The general allegations of this Superseding Indictment are re-alleged and incorporated into this Count as though fully set forth herein.

B. Between in or about November 2009 and in or about May 2010, in an offense begun and committed outside of the jurisdiction of any particular state or district of the United States, the defendant, JULIAN PAUL ASSANGE, who will be first brought to the Eastern District of Virginia, and others unknown to the Grand Jury, knowingly and unlawfully obtained and aided, abetted, counseled, induced, procured and willfully caused Manning to obtain documents, writings, and notes connected with the national defense, for the purpose of obtaining information respecting the national defense—namely, Iraq rules of engagement files classified up to the SECRET level—and with reason to believe that the information was to be used to the injury of the United States or the advantage of any foreign nation.

(All in violation of Title 18, United States Code, Sections 793(b) and 2)

COUNT 5

(Attempted Unauthorized Obtaining and Receiving of National Defense Information)

A. The general allegations of this Superseding Indictment are re-alleged and incorporated into this Count as though fully set forth herein.

B. Between in or about November 2009 and in or about May 2010, in an offense begun and committed outside of the jurisdiction of any particular state or district of the United States, the defendant, JULIAN PAUL ASSANGE, who will be first brought to the Eastern District of Virginia, and others unknown to the Grand Jury, knowingly and unlawfully attempted to receive and obtain documents, writings, and notes connected with the national defense—namely, information stored on the Secret Internet Protocol Network classified up to the **SECRET** level— for the purpose of obtaining information respecting the national defense, knowing and having reason to believe, at the time that he attempted to receive and obtain them, that such materials would be obtained, taken, made, and disposed of by a person contrary to the provisions of Chapter 37 of Title 18 of the United States Code.

(All in violation of Title 18, United States Code, Sections 793(c) and 2)

COUNT 6

(Unauthorized Obtaining and Receiving of National Defense Information)
(Detainee Assessment Briefs)

A. The general allegations of this Superseding Indictment are re-alleged and incorporated into this Count as though fully set forth herein.

B. Between in or about November 2009 and in or about May 2010, in an offense begun and committed outside of the jurisdiction of any particular state or district of the United States, the defendant, JULIAN PAUL ASSANGE, who will be first brought to the Eastern District of Virginia, knowingly and unlawfully received and obtained documents, writings, and notes connected with the national defense—namely, detainee assessment briefs classified up to the **SECRET** level related to detainees who were held at Guantanamo Bay—for the purpose of obtaining information respecting the national defense, knowing and having reason to believe, at the time that he received and obtained them, that such materials had been and would be obtained, taken, made, and disposed of by a person contrary to the provisions of Chapter 37 of Title 18 of the United States Code.

(All in violation of Title 18, United States Code, Sections 793(c) and 2)

COUNT 7

(Unauthorized Obtaining and Receiving of National Defense Information)
(State Department Cables)

A. The general allegations of this Superseding Indictment are re-alleged and incorporated into this Count as though fully set forth herein.

B. Between in or about November 2009 and in or about May 2010, in an offense begun and committed outside of the jurisdiction of any particular state or district of the United States, the defendant, JULIAN PAUL ASSANGE, who will be first brought to the Eastern District of Virginia, knowingly and unlawfully received and obtained documents, writings, and notes connected with the national defense—namely, U.S. Department of State cables classified up to the **SECRET** level—for the purpose of obtaining information respecting the national defense, knowing and having reason to believe, at the time that he received and obtained them, that such materials had been and would be obtained, taken, made, and disposed of by a person contrary to the provisions of Chapter 37 of Title 18 of the United States Code.

(All in violation of Title 18, United States Code, Sections 793(c) and 2)

COUNT 8

(Unauthorized Obtaining and Receiving of National Defense Information)
(Iraq Rules of Engagement Files)

A. The general allegations of this Superseding Indictment are re-alleged and incorporated into this Count as though fully set forth herein.

B. Between in or about November 2009 and in or about May 2010, in an offense begun and committed outside of the jurisdiction of any particular state or district of the United States, the defendant, JULIAN PAUL ASSANGE, who will be first brought to the Eastern District of Virginia, knowingly and unlawfully received and obtained documents, writings, and notes connected with the national defense—namely, Iraq rules of engagement files classified up to the SECRET level—for the purpose of obtaining information respecting the national defense, knowing and having reason to believe, at the time that he received and obtained them, that such materials had been and would be obtained, taken, made, and disposed of by a person contrary to the provisions of Chapter 37 of Title 18 of the United States Code.

(All in violation of Title 18, United States Code, Sections 793(c) and 2)

COUNT 9

(Unauthorized Disclosure of National Defense Information)
(Detainee Assessment Briefs)

A. The general allegations of this Superseding Indictment are re-alleged and incorporated into this Count as though fully set forth herein.

B. Between in or about November 2009 and in or about May 2010, in an offense begun and committed outside of the jurisdiction of any particular state or district of the United States, the defendant, JULIAN PAUL ASSANGE, who will be first brought to the Eastern District of Virginia, and others unknown to the Grand Jury, aided, abetted, counseled, induced, procured and willfully caused Manning, who had lawful possession of, access to, and control over documents relating to the national defense—namely, detainee assessment briefs classified up to the **SECRET** level related to detainees who were held at Guantanamo Bay—to communicate, deliver, and transmit the documents to ASSANGE, a person not entitled to receive them.

(All in violation of Title 18, United States Code, Sections 793(d) and 2)

COUNT 10
(Unauthorized Disclosure of National Defense Information)
(State Department Cables)

A. The general allegations of this Superseding Indictment are re-alleged and incorporated into this Count as though fully set forth herein.

B. Between in or about November 2009 and in or about May 2010, in an offense begun and committed outside of the jurisdiction of any particular state or district of the United States, the defendant, JULIAN PAUL ASSANGE, who will be first brought to the Eastern District of Virginia, and others unknown to the Grand Jury, aided, abetted, counseled, induced, procured and willfully caused Manning, who had lawful possession of, access to, and control over documents relating to the national defense—namely, U.S. Department of State cables classified up to the SECRET level—to communicate, deliver, and transmit the documents to ASSANGE, a person not entitled to receive them.

(All in violation of Title 18, United States Code, Sections 793(d) and 2)

COUNT 11

(Unauthorized Disclosure of National Defense Information)
(Iraq Rules of Engagement Files)

A. The general allegations of this Superseding Indictment are re-alleged and incorporated into this Count as though fully set forth herein.

B. Between in or about November 2009 and in or about May 2010, in an offense begun and committed outside of the jurisdiction of any particular state or district of the United States, the defendant, JULIAN PAUL ASSANGE, who will be first brought to the Eastern District of Virginia, and others unknown to the Grand Jury, aided, abetted, counseled, induced, procured and willfully caused Manning, who had lawful possession of, access to, and control over documents relating to the national defense—namely, Iraq rules of engagement files classified up to the **SECRET** level—to communicate, deliver, and transmit the documents to ASSANGE, a person not entitled to receive them.

(All in violation of Title 18, United States Code, Sections 793(d) and 2)

COUNT 12

(Unauthorized Disclosure of National Defense Information)
(Detainee Assessment Briefs)

A. The general allegations of this Superseding Indictment are re-alleged and incorporated into this Count as though fully set forth herein.

B. Between in or about November 2009 and in or about May 2010, in an offense begun and committed outside of the jurisdiction of any particular state or district of the United States, the defendant, JULIAN PAUL ASSANGE, who will be first brought to the Eastern District of Virginia, and others unknown to the Grand Jury, aided, abetted, counseled, induced, procured and willfully caused Manning, who had unauthorized possession of, access to, and control over documents relating to the national defense—namely, detainee assessment briefs classified up to the **SECRET** level related to detainees who were held at Guantanamo Bay—to communicate, deliver, and transmit the documents to ASSANGE, a person not entitled to receive them.

(All in violation of Title 18, United States Code, Sections 793(e) and 2)

COUNT 13

(Unauthorized Disclosure of National Defense Information)
(State Department Cables)

A. The general allegations of this Superseding Indictment are re-alleged and incorporated into this Count as though fully set forth herein.

B. Between in or about November 2009 and in or about May 2010, in an offense begun and committed outside of the jurisdiction of any particular state or district of the United States, the defendant, JULIAN PAUL ASSANGE, who will be first brought to the Eastern District of Virginia, and others unknown to the Grand Jury, aided, abetted, counseled, induced, procured and willfully caused Manning, who had unauthorized possession of, access to, and control over documents relating to the national defense—namely, U.S. Department of State cables classified up to the **SECRET** level—to communicate, deliver, and transmit the documents to ASSANGE, a person not entitled to receive them.

(All in violation of Title 18, United States Code, Sections 793(e) and 2)

COUNT 14

(Unauthorized Disclosure of National Defense Information)
(Iraq Rules of Engagement Files)

A. The general allegations of this Superseding Indictment are re-alleged and incorporated into this Count as though fully set forth herein.

B. Between in or about November 2009 and in or about May 2010, in an offense begun and committed outside of the jurisdiction of any particular state or district of the United States, the defendant, JULIAN PAUL ASSANGE, who will be first brought to the Eastern District of Virginia, and others unknown to the Grand Jury, aided, abetted, counseled, induced, procured and willfully caused Manning, who had unauthorized possession of, access to, and control over documents relating to the national defense—namely, Iraq rules of engagement files classified up to the **SECRET** level—to communicate, deliver, and transmit the documents to ASSANGE, a person not entitled to receive them.

(All in violation of Title 18, United States Code, Sections 793(e) and 2)

COUNT 15

(Unauthorized Disclosure of National Defense Information)

A.   The general allegations of this Superseding Indictment are re-alleged and incorporated into this Count as though fully set forth herein.

B.   From in or about July 2010 and continuing until at least the time of this Superseding Indictment, in an offense begun and committed outside of the jurisdiction of any particular state or district of the United States, the defendant, JULIAN PAUL ASSANGE, who will be first brought to the Eastern District of Virginia, having unauthorized possession of, access to, and control over documents relating to the national defense, willfully and unlawfully caused and attempted to cause such materials to be communicated, delivered, and transmitted to persons not entitled to receive them.

C.   Specifically, as alleged above, ASSANGE, having unauthorized possession of significant activity reports, classified up to the **SECRET** level, from the Afghanistan war containing the names of individuals, who risked their safety and freedom by providing information to the United States and our allies, communicated the documents containing names of those sources to all the world by publishing them on the Internet.

(All in violation of Title 18, United States Code, Section 793(e))

COUNT 16

(Unauthorized Disclosure of National Defense Information)

A.   The general allegations of this Superseding Indictment are re-alleged and incorporated into this Count as though fully set forth herein.

B.   From in or about July 2010 and continuing until at least the time of this Superseding Indictment, in an offense begun and committed outside of the jurisdiction of any particular state or district of the United States, the defendant, JULIAN PAUL ASSANGE, who will be first brought to the Eastern District of Virginia, having unauthorized possession of, access to, and control over documents relating to the national defense, willfully and unlawfully caused and attempted to cause such materials to be communicated, delivered, and transmitted to persons not entitled to receive them.

C.   Specifically, as alleged above, ASSANGE, having unauthorized possession of significant activity reports, classified up to the SECRET level, from the Iraq war containing the names of individuals, who risked their safety and freedom by providing information to the United States and our allies, communicated the documents containing names of those sources to all the world by publishing them on the Internet.

(All in violation of Title 18, United States Code, Section 793(e))

COUNT 17

(Unauthorized Disclosure of National Defense Information)

A.   The general allegations of this Superseding Indictment are re-alleged and incorporated into this Count as though fully set forth herein.

B.   From in or about July 2010 and continuing until at least the time of this Superseding Indictment, in an offense begun and committed outside of the jurisdiction of any particular state or district of the United States, the defendant, JULIAN PAUL ASSANGE, who will be first brought to the Eastern District of Virginia, having unauthorized possession of, access to, and control over documents relating to the national defense, willfully and unlawfully caused and attempted to cause such materials to be communicated, delivered, and transmitted to persons not entitled to receive them.

C.   Specifically, as alleged above, ASSANGE, having unauthorized possession of State Department cables, classified up to the **SECRET** level, containing the names of individuals, who risked their safety and freedom by providing information to the United States and our allies, communicated the documents containing names of those sources to all the world by publishing them on the Internet.

(All in violation of Title 18, United States Code, Section 793(e))

COUNT 18

(Conspiracy to Commit Computer Intrusion)

1.   The general allegations of this Superseding Indictment are re-alleged and incorporated into this Count as though fully set forth herein.

2.   Beginning on or about March 2, 2010, and continuing thereafter until on or about March 10, 2010, the exact date being unknown to the Grand Jury, in an offense begun and committed outside of the jurisdiction of any particular State or district of the United States, the defendant, JULIAN PAUL ASSANGE, who will be first brought to the Eastern District of Virginia, did knowingly and unlawfully conspire with others known and unknown to the Grand Jury to commit offenses against the United States, to wit:

(A)   to knowingly access a computer, without authorization and exceeding authorized access, to obtain information that has been determined by the United States Government pursuant to an Executive order and statute to require protection against unauthorized disclosure for reasons of national defense and foreign relations, namely, documents relating to the national defense classified up to the **SECRET** level, with reason to believe that such information so obtained could be used to the injury of the United States and the advantage of any foreign nation, and to willfully communicate, deliver, transmit, and cause to be communicated, delivered, or transmitted the same, to any person not entitled to receive it, and willfully retain the same and fail to deliver it to the officer or employee entitled to receive it; and

(B)   to intentionally access a computer, without authorization and exceeding authorized access, to obtain information from a department and agency of the United States in furtherance of a criminal act in violation of the laws of the United States, that is, a violation of Title 18, United States Code, Sections 641, 793(c), and 793(e).

PURPOSE AND OBJECT OF THE CONSPIRACY

The primary purpose of the conspiracy was to facilitate Manning's acquisition and transmission of classified information related to the national defense of the United States so that WikiLeaks could publicly disseminate the information on its website.

MANNERS AND MEANS OF THE CONSPIRACY

ASSANGE and his conspirators used the following ways, manners and means, among others, to carry out this purpose:

1. It was part of the conspiracy that ASSANGE and Manning used the "Jabber" online chat service to collaborate on the acquisition and dissemination of the classified records, and to enter into the agreement to crack the password hash stored on United States Department of Defense computers connected to the Secret Internet Protocol Network.

2. It was part of the conspiracy that ASSANGE and Manning took measures to conceal Manning as the source of the disclosure of classified records to WikiLeaks, including by removing usernames from the disclosed information and deleting chat logs between ASSANGE and Manning.

3. It was part of the conspiracy that ASSANGE encouraged Manning to provide information and records from departments and agencies of the United States.

4. It was part of the conspiracy that ASSANGE and Manning used a special folder on a cloud drop box of WikiLeaks to transmit classified records containing information related to the national defense of the United States.

ACTS IN FURTHERANCE OF THE CONSPIRACY

·In order to further the goals and purposes of the conspiracy, ASSANGE and his conspirators committed overt acts, including, but not limited to, the following:

1. On or about March 2, 2010, Manning copied a Linux operating system to a CD, to allow Manning to access a United States Department of Defense computer file that was accessible only to users with administrative-level privileges. ..

2. On or about March 8, 2010, Manning provided ASSANGE with part of a password hash stored on United States Department of Defense computers connected to the Secret Internet Protocol Network.

3. On or about March 10, 2010, ASSANGE requested more information from Manning related to the password hash. ASSANGE indicated that he had been trying to crack the password hash by stating that he had "no luck so far."

(All in violation of Title 18, United States Code, Sections 371, 1030(a)(1), 1030(a)(2), 1030(c)(2)(B)(ii)).)

5/23/19

DATE

A TRUE

Pursuant to the E-Government Act,
the original of this page has been filed
under seal in the Clerk's Office.

FOREPERSON

G. Zachary Terwilliger ·
United States Attorney

By: _____
Tracy Doherty-McCormick
First Assistant United States Attorney
Kellen S. Dwyer
Thomas W. Traxler
Gordon Kromberg
Assistant United States Attorneys

Matthew Walczewski
Nicholas Hunter
Trial Attorneys, National Security Division

EDITORS AND CONTRIBUTORS

Editors

Tariq Ali is a writer, filmmaker, and a longstanding editor of *New Left Review*.

Margaret Kunstler is a civil rights attorney in private practice. She coauthored *Hell No: Your Right to Dissent in Twenty-First-Century America* (2011).

Contributors

Pamela Anderson is a renowned actor, model, and animal rights activist, as well as a friend and supporter of Julian Assange.

Julian Assange is the editor in chief of and visionary behind WikiLeaks, as well as the principal subject of this book. As of this writing, he is serving a 50-week sentence in Belmarsh Prison in London and facing extradition to the United States.

Renata Avila is a celebrated Guatemalan human rights lawyer and digital rights expert. In recent years she has played a central role in the international team of lawyers representing Julian Assange and his staff.

Katrin Axelsson is a former spokeswoman for Women Against Rape.

Franco "Bifo" Berardi is the founder of the Italian magazine *A/traverso* and a philosopher. His latest books are *Breathing, Chaos and Poetry*, and *The Second Coming*.

Sally Burch is a British–Ecuadorian journalist. She is executive director of the Agencia Latinamericana de Información (ALAI), based in Quito (www.alainet.org), and writes regularly on issues related to democratizing communication and digital technologies.

Noam Chomsky is widely regarded to be one of the foremost critics of US foreign policy. He is Institute Professor (emeritus) in the Department of Linguistics and Philosophy at the Massachusetts Institute of Technology. He has published numerous groundbreaking books, articles, and essays on global politics, history, and linguistics.

Patrick Cockburn is an award-winning Irish journalist who has been a Middle East correspondent for the *Financial Times* since 1979 and, from 1990, the *Independent*.

Naomi Colvin is a whistleblower advocate and a long-term supporter of WikiLeaks. She led the campaign which stopped British–Finnish computer scientist Lauri Love being extradited to the United States in 2018.

The Courage Foundation is an international organization supporting those who risk life or liberty to make significant contributions to the historical record. Courage campaigns for the protection of all journalistic sources and the public's right to know generally.

Mark Curtis is a historian and analyst of UK foreign policy and international development. He is the author of six books including *Secret Affairs: Britain's Collusion with Radical Islam* and *Web of Deceit: Britain's Real Role in the World*.

Daniel Ellsberg is a writer, activist, and the former US military analyst of the RAND Corporation who leaked the Pentagon Papers to the press, for which he was charged under the Espionage Act, yet the case was dismissed.

Teresa Forcades i Vila is a physician, theologian, and Benedictine nun (since 1997) in the mountain monastery of Sant Benet de Montserrat (Catalonia, Spain). Among other books, she is the author of *Faith and Freedom* (Polity Press, 2016).

Charles Glass is a journalist and author most recently of *They Fought Alone: The True Story of the Starr Brothers, British Secret Agents in Nazi-Occupied France.* He helped to organize the Committee in Defense of Julian Assange & His Publishers and the "Anything to Say" sculpture of Assange, Manning, and Snowden.

Kevin Gosztola is the managing editor for Shadowproof.com and cohost of the *Unauthorized Disclosure* weekly podcast. His work has appeared in the *Nation*, Salon, Common Dreams, and other outlets. He regularly traveled to Fort Meade to cover Chelsea Manning's court-martial and has covered all things WikiLeaks extensively since 2010, as well as the wider war on whistleblowers.

Serge Halimi is the editorial director at *Le Monde Diplomatique.* He is also the author of *Le Grand Bond en Arrière.*

Nozomi Hayase, PhD, is a columnist and essayist whose writing is dedicated to liberation of all people. She has been covering issues of free speech and transparency, including the vital role of whistleblowers in strengthening civil society.

Chris Hedges is a Pulitzer-prize winning journalist who spent 15 years with the *New York Times.*

Srećko Horvat is a philosopher, political activist, author most recently of *Poetry from the Future* (Penguin, 2019), and cofounder of DiEM25 (Democracy in Europe Movement 2015).

Caitlin Johnstone is a 100 percent crowdfunded rogue journalist, bogan socialist, anarcho-psychonaut, guerilla poet, and utopia prepper living in Australia with her American husband and two kids. She writes about politics, economics, media, feminism, and the nature of consciousness. She is the author of the illustrated poetry book *Woke: A Field Guide For Utopia Preppers*.

Margaret Kimberley is editor and senior columnist at Black Agenda Report. She participated in the #Unity4J Online Vigils in support of Julian Assange and is the author of *Prejudential: Black America and the Presidents*, which will be published by Steerforth Press in February 2020.

Geoffroy de Lagasnerie is a French philosopher and sociologist. He is the author of *The Art of Revolt: Snowden, Assange, Manning* (Stanford University Press, 2017) and *Judge and Punish* (Stanford University Press, 2018).

Lisa Longstaff has been with Women Against Rape for over 30 years, campaigning for justice for survivors of sexual and/or domestic violence, including asylum seekers. WAR has achieved the criminalization of rape in marriage, and legal precedents such as the first private prosecution for rape in England and Wales.

Alan MacLeod is an academic and a journalist based in Glasgow, UK. His latest book is *Propaganda in the Information Age: Still Manufacturing Consent* (Routledge, 2019). His research interests include propaganda and the propaganda model, media theory, and Latin American politics.

Stefania Maurizi works for the Italian daily *la Repubblica* as an investigative journalist. She has worked on all WikiLeaks releases of secret documents, and partnered with Glenn Greenwald to reveal the Snowden files.

Craig Murray is a human rights activist, writer, whistleblower, and former British diplomat.

Fidel Narváez is a human rights activist, based in the UK, who served as diplomat for Ecuador for eight years. Fidel was the consul of Ecuador in London when Julian Assange requested political asylum. Previously in Ecuador, he was technical secretary of the Inter-American Platform for Human Rights, Democracy and Development and leader at the Permanent Assembly of Human Rights. Fidel has a degree in international trade.

John C. O'Day is a student and teacher of philosophy originally from Atlanta, Georgia. He writes on media, technology, science, and anti-colonialism. He hopes this small contribution serves the cause of freedom for Julian Assange.

John Pilger, renowned war reporter, filmmaker, and author, is one of only two to win British journalism's highest award twice. For his documentary films, he has won an American TV Academy Award, an Emmy, and a British Academy Award. His 1979 epic, *Cambodia Year Zero*, is ranked by the British Film Institute as one of the ten most important documentaries of the twentieth century. He is a friend and ally of Julian Assange.

Jesselyn Radack is an award-winning human rights lawyer who heads the Whistleblower & Source Protection Program at ExposeFacts. She has been at the forefront of challenging the government's war on whistleblowers, journalists, and hacktivists.

Michael Ratner (1943–2016) was an attorney and president of the Center for Constitutional Rights. At the end of his life, he served as Julian Assange and WikiLeaks' active defense.

Angela Richter wrote and directed the interactive Transmedia Project „Supernerds" on the topic of digital mass surveillance, whistleblowing, and digital dissidents, in collaboration with national television and theater. In 2018 she coauthored *Women, Whistleblowing, WikiLeaks* along with Sarah Harrison and Renata Avila.

Geoffrey Robertson is a human rights lawyer, professor, and founder and joint head of Doughty Street Chambers, an international set of barristers. He defended Julian Assange in his extradition proceedings in 2010.

Jen Robinson is a human rights lawyer and barrister with Doughty Street Chambers. She is currently Julian Assange's attorney.

Matt Taibbi is an author, journalist, and contributor at *Rolling Stone.*

Natália Viana is an award-winning investigative journalist from Brazil. She is a cofounder and codirector of Agencia Publica, an investigative non-profit, and a member of the Board of the Gabriel Garcia Marquez Foundation for New Journalism in the Americas.

Ai Weiwei is an internationally acclaimed Chinese contemporary artist, activist, and dissident, who has expressed much support for Julian Assange.

Vivienne Westwood is a renowned fashion designer, businesswoman, and supporter of Julian Assange.

Slavoj Žižek is a Hegelian philosopher, theorist of ideology, and social analyst. He is a distinguished professor at Kyung Hee University, Seoul, and International director of the Birkbeck Institute for Humanities, London. His latest publication is *Sex and the Failed Absolute* (London: Bloomsbury Press).

SUPPORT THE COURAGE FOUNDATION

The Courage Foundation is an international organization that supports those who risk life or liberty to make significant contributions to the historical record. It fundraises for the legal and public defense of specific individuals who fit these criteria and are subject to serious prosecution or persecution. It also campaigns for the protection of truth tellers and the public's right to know generally.

Courage has been there for its beneficiaries when they needed it most. It helped the Azerbaijani journalist and human rights worker Emin Huseynov escape to asylum and safety in Switzerland amid a crackdown in Baku. It saved Lauri Love from a virtual death sentence in the United States, winning an important battle for UK encryption rights along the way. It has made sure that Edward Snowden's revelations have a permanent impact by making every document published easily accessible, searchable by category, country, and keyword. It has funded commissaries and legal costs for its beneficiaries who are enduring abusive retaliation in prison. And now it's defending WikiLeaks' Julian Assange as he faces extradition to the United States, where he would face aggressive prosecution for his journalistic activity.

Find out how you can take action with Courage on its website: https://www.couragefound.org/

Contact the organization at courage.contact@couragefound.org